MILLWALL
IN THE FA CUP
THE ROAD TO THE MILLENNIUM

MILLWALL
IN THE FA CUP
THE ROAD TO THE MILLENNIUM

David Sullivan

breedon **books**
PUBLISHING

First published in Great Britain in 2009 by
The Breedon Books Publishing Company Limited
Breedon House, 3 The Parker Centre, Derby, DE21 4SZ.

ISBN 978-1-85983-755-9
Printed and bound by Gutenberg Press Ltd, Malta.

Contents

Acknowledgements   **6**

Introduction   **7**

1. Early Days   **9**

2. Lions of the South   **26**

3. 'Rise like Lions after Slumber'   **41**

4. Nowhere Men   **52**

5. A New Dawn   **75**

6. Great Times   **83**

7. Charles Hewitt Esq.   **103**

8. Watcha Cock   **117**

9. A Familiar Face   **121**

10. Parting of the Ways   **142**

11. Shocks and Scares   **150**

12. Fulham and Spurs   **162**

13. Fenton's Failures   **176**

14. More Horrors   **187**

15. Some Dark, Some Bright Days   **205**

16. The Doc   **218**

17. Some Style   **224**

18. The New Den   **229**

19. Mr Wise   **242**

20. The Road to the Millennium   **245**

Epilogue   **261**

Millwall's FA Cup Record 1887 to 2009   **263**

Acknowledgements

The individual task in compiling such a book would not have come to fruition without the help and assistance of many people, and I would like to thank fellow fans and collectors like Andy Sullivan, Chris Bethell and Richard Lindsay for the odd match report. Also Norman Epps, the Corinthian Casuals historian, was another willing lender.

My gratitude must go to Brian Tonks, the official Millwall FC photographer, whose vast amount of material is second to none. I would also like to thank the staff at Breedon Books who accepted my cold calling with courtesy when I was seeking a publisher, and the fruits of their labour are here laid before you.

I have consulted many newspapers, periodicals and books in the search for the correct information, but the most indispensable asset during the three years of writing the book has to be Mike Collett's *The Complete Record of The FA Cup* (Sports Books 2003). Finally, any errors are purely down to me, and I apologise for any unaccredited photographic items.

Introduction

Sometime in 2002 I decided to collate all my Millwall FA Cup-related memorabilia into some sort of order, mainly to contribute a series on the competition in the official match programme once all my other subjects had been exhausted. So out came all the old programmes, match reports and tickets to be placed into a special folder marked 'FA Cup'. However, I soon realised that I was missing many match reports. So, in 2003 I embarked on addressing the problem by obtaining them at regular intervals to build up a decent archive, all ready to unravel Millwall's ups and downs over the course of some 116 years' involvement in the Cup.

So you could imagine my delight when the Lions reached their first FA Cup Final in 2004 when I and probably most fans of the club would have settled for a fourth semi-final to go with those of 1900, 1903 and 1937. When the dust had settled on that once-in-a-lifetime day in Cardiff, I shelved the idea of a programme series and decided to put it into book form, and after nearly three years this is the result.

I started as one would do, at the beginning, with Millwall Rovers' match against Old Westminsters in 1887, and the book follows a chronological path right through to the Millennium Stadium Final in 2004. Within the covers you find all the games covered, some at length and others not so longwinded. All the heroes and villains whose part may have been minimal or longstanding, such as goalkeeper Obed Caygill and the forward Eddie 'Taff' Jones, the fleet-footed Alf Geddes, the sturdy full-back Jack Graham and with true-blue amateur J.H. 'Joe' Gettins, have their contributions described.

Those players, along with the likes of Jack Calvey, one of Millwall's early goal kings, laid the foundation for the club to reach the semi-final in 1900 with an exceptionally assembled team in which Walter Cox (goalkeeper) Arthur Millar, Bert Banks (who scored nine goals in 10 Cup ties) and the tireless skipper Dave Smith all played their part. Three years later in 1903 a new team had been built by Bob Hunter, and they equalled their predecessors only to fall again, this time to Derby County. This came after defeating the Lancastrian giants Preston and Everton. Joe Gettins was still there, along with John Sutcliffe, Jimmy Riley and the Welsh pair Dick Jones and Ernie Watkins, who made valuable contributions along the way.

The exhilarating tie against Plymouth Argyle in 1907 and the last big derby against the Arsenal two years later were games to savour for the fans before Millwall's departure to Cold Blow Lane in 1910. A new ground saw a new epoch begin at The Den with excellent Cup matches to relish, which started probably with Wally Davis' 'wonder goal' against Bradford City in 1913. When Middlesbrough visited in 1927 to lose by the odd goal in five this encounter was flagged up as possibly the best game seen at The Den at the time.

However, later generations might disagree, for a decade later Millwall under Charlie Hewitt reached their third semi-final after disposing of Fulham, Chelsea, Derby County and Manchester City to become the first club from the Third Division to reach such a stage. Dave Mangnall, the skipper, Ted Smith, Tommy Brolly, Jim McCartney and J.R. Smith all became household names, but the loss to Sunderland saw the main prize evaporate with some contentious referee decisions.

The post-war period saw just one decent run in 1957, when after toppling Newcastle United the Lions went out in the fifth round to Birmingham City. In was in this austere period that Millwall were on the receiving end of some disastrous defeats from Headington United, Worcester City, Bath City and Kettering, who in 1963 became the first non-League club to inflict a defeat upon Millwall at The Den since Lincoln City had done likewise in 1921. Since then a variety of sides have faced the Lions in the FA Cup, with my generation taking the games against Fulham and Spurs in the mid-1960s and defeats of Nottingham Forest and Everton in the early 1970s as the highlights, but never with a sniff of a Final, as Millwall as far as we was concerned did not do Finals, and most of us were happy to just go along with participation.

It was Dennis Wise's appointment as manager in 2003 that proved to be the catalyst in Millwall reaching their first FA Cup Final. His FA Cup pedigree stood up to scrutiny with the best and his will to win was soon embellished in his team. With the luck of the draw and a few scares along the way the Lions finally secured their place in a Final. Many Lions fans have now seen their club in the old First Division, have witnessed their appearance in an FA Cup Final and a brief excursion into Europe, and some will die happy at these privileges because there are those who had not dreamt of this ever happening to a club of Millwall's statue.

I hope you enjoy the journey you will take in reading the book as much as I have in compiling it. COME ON YOU LIONS!

David Sullivan,
September 2009

1. Early Days

Millwall Rovers' initial involvement in the FA Cup barely made a ripple after the club's committee took the bold decision to expose the team to the national competition in 1887. The fledgling outfit, having generally mastered the local scene and in the throes of winning their second East End Cup, decided to spread their wings a little, but their early FA Cup participation would be painful as the first three seasons would see Rovers fall at the first hurdle against sides from academic backgrounds. Rovers' first appearance was put on hold temporarily when their opponents, Casuals, scratched due to an oversight in registering certain players in time. This allowed the Dockers to pass unhampered into the next round without kicking a ball.

For Rovers, then, the baptism of fire was delayed a matter of weeks, for lying in wait in the second qualifying round was the renowned Old Westminsters, a formidable opponent for any club, let alone one making its inaugural appearance in the FA Cup. The tie was scheduled for 5 November at the Essex County Cricket Ground, Leyton. Millwall's expectations of taking anything from the match must have been minimal, but at the end of 90 minutes Westminsters had unleashed their own firework display by inflicting a most humbling experience with an 8–1 win. To dwell upon such a mis-match is not very pleasant, but needless to say it was far too easy for old boys of Westminster School. Their club had been formed in 1880, and the previous season they had reached the quarter-finals before losing to Glasgow Rangers on what was the last occasion a Scottish club would participate in the English competition.

Experienced in Cup matters and football in general, the old boys, given their social standing and educational background, of school, university and the progression of many of their class to international standard, had the scales tipped heavily in their favour. They would also have had more free time in which to hone their individual skills, a luxury the artisans and labourers of Millwall Rovers could ill afford. As well as all this, Millwall faced a team that included Ralph Squire the captain, a current England player, plus two other internationals in Rupert Sandilands and goalkeeper Billy Winckworth, who would earn their first England caps against Wales in 1892.

Despite their overall domination, it took Old Westminsters until the 25th minute before they broke Rovers' dogged resistance when Phillimore opened the scoring. Millwall were 3–0 down at the break, having been overly reliant on goalkeeper Harry Gunn, who despite everything had given an admirable display. He did not, however, deserve the cruel piece of luck dealt to him when Janson's shot was deflected past him for the seventh. Rovers' resolve, if truth be told, had wilted long before as Westminsters' skill and wherewithal nullified the Dockers' vigorous approach. The visitors' token riposte created a small piece of Millwall history when the little-known George Oliver scored their first-ever FA Cup goal in the second half, though how much gratification this slice of fame gave him will probably never be known.

Following such a traumatic debut, Rovers then embarked upon the club's long association with FA Cup, which would go on to become the 'Blue Ribband' of knockout competitions. Further chastisements over the next couple of seasons would make entry into the Cup a tortuous learning curve. Undeterred, Millwall were back for more of the same when they were drawn away to another old boys XI, this time made up by former pupils of another of England's leading public schools, Lancing College. The game was held at Surbiton and attracted around 1,000 or so paying spectators who witnessed an exciting match, but sadly for Millwall they went down to a more respectable – if predictable – 4–0 defeat. More of a concern, however, was the injury sustained by Duncan Hean, the long-term ramifications of which was a forced retirement from football and an early death at the age of 30.

After winning the toss, Rovers started the game but were immediately put under the cosh by Lancing, who started the game with 10 men before Millwall, with their usual 'in-your-face' approach, got their own game going and were a tad unfortunate not to have taken a lead into half-time after bombarding the Lancing goal. The tale of a team failing to capitalise on their possession is as old as the game itself, and Millwall were to pay a heavy price for their lack of diligence. Lancing, now back to full strength, gained the initiative soon after the restart when their outside-left Rooke opened the scoring, a feat he repeated with another equally fine effort shortly afterwards to register his and Lancing's second. At this point Lancing really took the game by the scruff of the neck, and when they scored a third it was the dominant Rooke who provided the chance for Jackson to score. Rovers were now feeling the effects of Hean's absence and conceded a fourth when Miller got the final touch.

Having now dropped the 'Rovers' from their title, Millwall entered the 1889–90 competition with the new suffix of 'Athletic', hoping a change of name would bring a change of fortune in the ensuing season's FA Cup. Well, lady luck made it halfway when she at last bestowed upon them a home tie. It pitted Millwall against Kent-based Schorne College, a team made up of past and present pupils. For the third season running, the obstacle in front of them proved insurmountable as the assemblage at the Lord Nelson Ground saw Athletic taken apart in another 4–0 drubbing. One amazing fact to come from this encounter was that the Schorne team had no fewer than five players with the surname of James playing.

There were four of them in the forward line and another appearing goal. It was A.B. of that ilk who opened the scoring just before the interval, following a swift counter by the collegiate, before J.C. James helped himself to a couple, with Colley adding the fourth in the second half. If the result had not been to the liking of everyone, the officials and supporters would have been heartened by the displays of the Warner brothers George and Henry and those of the full-back pairing of Tom Jessup and Jimmy Fenton.

Home advantage counted for nothing again in 1890 when Essex rivals Ilford stole the honours in a 3–2 win. Ilford, formed in 1881, steadfastly clung to their amateur status during much of the 20th century, before amalgamating with Leytonstone in 1979. Then, following further name changes, they lost their identity altogether to finally emerge as the organisation we know today as Dagenham & Redbridge. The 500 or so patrons who attended the FA Cup game saw the visitors race to a three-goal lead, which they held until the break. The Dockers responded in the only way they knew when a certain Mr Edwards, another player about whom little is known, pulled a goal back just after the resumption, before Harry Butler added a second. But no matter how much pressure Millwall applied, an equaliser was not forthcoming.

Finally, at the fifth attempt Millwall obtained a first-ever win in the competition. In 1891 (the year goal nets were introduced) they defeated Rochester by 2–1 down at Chatham in the first qualifying round. This hard-fought victory was prolonged by a period of extra-time that was mostly down to the performance of Lake in the Rochester goal, whose stubborn resistance was the sole reason the first half remained goalless. However, he was finally beaten just after the interval when Peter Banks's cracking drive beat him all-ends-up. But Millwall's lead was short-lived as Rochester set up an immediate response when some fine passing opened up Millwall to give Broad the opportunity to strike the equaliser. A competitive match had been marred on occasions by some over zealous indulgence by both sides, but when sanity returned Millwall grabbed the winner when Frank McCullough was on hand to score with a header following a corner.

Millwall's interest in the Cup was halted in its tracks in the most unfortunate, if not incredulous, way. The demise was inflicted, not so much by the footballers of the Highland Light Infantry, but by a very odd decision from the match official. It had appeared to be going Millwall's way after Fred Withington and Eddie 'Taff' Jones put them two up as well as having another three efforts disallowed. The referee concerned was none other than Mr Frederick Wall, later to become Sir Frederick – long-standing secretary of the Football Association and later an Arsenal director. His blinkered, fastidious view over a pair of boots that Frank McCulloch had merely tried on at half-time was that they were illegal as they did not have the regulation studs. Wall's failure to instil a smidgen of common sense, which would surely have led to McCulloch wearing an acceptable pair of boots, instead led to him taking it upon himself to be judge, jury and executioner. He flatly refused to listen to any explanations and arrogantly barred the little Scot from having any further participation in the game.

Needless to say, the Light Infantry took full advantage of the referee's intransigence to square the game at 2–2 at the end of 90 minutes. They obtained a further two goals in extra-time before Banks hit a third as Millwall exited the Cup. The club were naturally miffed about Wall's stance over wee Frank's dismissal, which was down to a misunderstanding, and the fact that Wall gallingly admitted this after the game was of scant consolation.

The Dockers went a round further in the following season's tournament, in which another innovative measure was introduced when pitch markings appeared for the first time. The new initiative seemed much to Millwall's liking as they opened the campaign with a resounding 6–1 thumping of Folkestone. The hapless Kent club were unmercifully swept aside and would suffer similar indignations from the Dockers over the course of next few seasons. Although Folkestone managed an equaliser with Redman's fine solo goal to cancel out Jimmy Lindsay's opener. He nevertheless went on to claim a first-half hat-trick, opening his spree with a penalty awarded for handball. In the second 45 minutes Folkestone doubled their efforts, but Millwall were a notch above their opponents, as their confident passing enabled McCulloch, Ingram and Eddie Jones to complete the rout.

A fortnight later it was the turn of another army unit, the 2nd Royal West Kent Regiment, to make an appearance on the East Ferry Road, but unlike the Highland Light Infantry debacle the previous year it was Millwall Athletic who won this particular skirmish. After winning the toss, Millwall saw the soldiers get the ball rolling, but following some bright football from both teams it was Millwall who made the most of possession by taking the lead. Twenty minutes had passed when Peter Banks was on hand to touch home after the ball had run loose from a scramble in front of goal. The early stages of the second half belonged to the military as they sought an equaliser, but they were repelled by the outstanding Obed Caygill, who was turning a few heads with his consistent displays.

After weathering Kent's bombardment, Millwall hit them with a sudden break when all five forwards bore down upon the soldiers' goal and saw Jimmy Lindsay fire in a piledriver; however, the fantastically named Sgt Pepper somehow managed to fist the ball out, but he was a mere spectator when McCulloch drilled the rebound home. The victory over the soldiers set up a mouthwatering prospect against Royal (later Woolwich) Arsenal, a club who were to become Millwall's biggest rivals over the course of the next decade or so until both clubs decided to locate on different sides of the Thames.

The day arrived, and Millwall made the short journey over the water for the face-off against the Arsenal, who were able to field their strongest team. Millwall, on the other hand, were bolstered by the presence of two Scottish guests, right-back Willie Hay from London Caledonians and outside-left Tommy Hyslop, a soldier from the Scots Guards. The opening salvos of this third-qualifying-round tie were witnessed by around 12,000 spectators, who saw Millwall actually outplaying their hosts with some delightful football. It was during this early domination that Millwall forged ahead when Eddie Jones was in the right place to convert Tommy Hyslop's superb pass, as Millwall's approach blended nicely with the unusually fine weather and the excellent playing conditions.

Goalkeeper and skipper Obed Caygill was once again showing what an excellent prospect he was becoming when he denied Henderson's efforts to bring the Arsenal level. In the days before goalkeepers became a protected species, Caygill and his fellow 'keepers had no such luxuries, and in this 1892 fixture an incident occurred after 30 minutes which highlighted the situation. Having saved Booth's shot, Obed was immediately set upon by the entire Arsenal forward line, who pounced like a pack of wolves in an attempt to force him and the ball into the goal in a mêlée resembling a rugby scrum. Caygill, now on his knees and still clutching the ball, saw his frantic attempts to clear prove fruitless. Left to their own devices, the Arsenal forwards piled in en masse to take all in their path, and with Obed unable to release the ball he was manhandled over the line for the equaliser.

Unsettled by this unruly (but at the time totally legal) spectacle, Millwall conceded again moments later when Arsenal's Howat scored with a more conventional effort when his shot cannoned in off a post. Early Arsenal pressure at the start of the second half was minimised by Caygill's assured handling as the Dockers looked to regain the initiative. A Rankin mis-kick allowed Hyslop to let rip with a thunderbolt that Bee in the Gunners goal managed to beat away with some difficulty. Nevertheless, Millwall's verve and tenacity kept the Arsenal on the back foot, and they were finally rewarded for their endeavours when Tom Green put in 'Taff' Jones to score the equaliser. The shift Millwall had put in began to take its toll as play became scrappy, with the Dockers looking increasingly leg-weary and drained. Arsenal, sensing Millwall's fatigue, went for the kill but were denied by the brave and gallant Caygill, but he could do nothing to stop Arsenal's winner when a tidy finish from Henderson gave them a third and decisive goal.

By the time the Cup came around again Millwall were well and truly committed to the path of professionalism, and to this end the 1893–94 campaign would be last in which they would not be solely reliant on the FA Cup to provide competitive football. The newly formed Southern League was beckoning and was ready to be launched for the 1894–95 season. So, as their amateur status started to fade into the past, Millwall, after receiving a bye in the first round, were obliged to face Ilford for a game that was raising a fair amount of local interest. A crowd of 4,000 that contained many from Millwall filed into the Essex club's cosy little enclosure. Rain had made the surface very slippery, and Ilford took advantage of the gusty conditions to bring pressure on the Millwall goal. But despite the nightmare conditions, Caygill was performing to his usual and now totally expected high standards by dealing with everything that came his way.

Against the run of play Ilford fell behind when their 'keeper Davies, who had comfortably dealt with a string of Millwall corners, was at fault for the opening goal. He failed to gather a bread-and-butter effort from Eddie Jones, that saw the ball fall invitingly for Jimmy Lindsay to smash home via the underside of the bar to give Millwall a half-time lead. When the game restarted, an invigorated Millwall had the better of the game until Ilford tested Caygill's abilities twice. A shot on the run from Edgar Porter brought a splendid save which Obed bettered seconds later when tipping Markham's bullet effort away for a corner.

After being on the receiving end for a lengthy period of time Millwall finally broke free of their restraints with devastating effects. Eddie Jones and Lindsay fashioned a move down the left, which left the latter the formality of scoring Millwall's second. Within seconds, however, Ilford reduced the deficit, which their non-stop efforts deserved. A free-kick from the Ilford skipper Watts found Worrall, himself a former Millwall player, to score Ilford's only goal. Eventually Millwall put the match out of Ilford's reach when the home team momentarily lost concentration at a free-kick. Eddie Jones's quick thinking found the equally elusive Lindsay, who cheekily back-heeled the ball past Davies to complete a memorable hat-trick, his second trio for Millwall in the FA Cup.

The third qualifying round saw Millwall pitched up against the Arsenal for the second season running. The game was scheduled to be played at Plumstead, and the rivalry these two antagonists were creating brought a crowd of almost 20,000 to witness a duel which gave Millwall a splendid chance to avenge the previous season's defeat. Recent history had favoured the Gunners as Millwall's record against them in any sort of fixture was not encouraging, and true to form this meeting ran the normal course. Arsenal ran out comfortable 2–0 winners in a very disappointing game that failed to live up expectations, with the only Millwall players displaying any high level of consistency being the imperturbable Caygill and right-back Jack Graham.

Arsenal took the lead after 20 minutes with no little assistance from a strong wind. There appeared to be no danger from Booth's corner-kick until it reached Davies, the Arsenal right-half, whose long-range effort was deviated by a gust of wind past a startled Caygill to nestle in the back of the net. The contest was settled in the second half when the troublesome Booth sent a stunning drive beyond Caygill for the second, who had kept the score respectable when he denied Shaw and Elliott from putting the Gunners out of sight with two stunning saves.

Millwall's lacklustre performance was aptly summed up during the second half when they could only muster two efforts to test Jeffrey in the Arsenal goal. These saves were the only occasions he touched the ball in that period. As Millwall trooped away from another derby defeat, little did anyone realise that this would be the last FA Cup tie Obed Caygill would play for the club. For in the final game of the season, a home friendly versus Stoke, he suffered a broken leg that would not only end his future aspirations but would also bring about his premature retirement from first-class football. It was a sad blow for all concerned and especially for the player, who was being touted by some observers as a future England goalkeeper.

The ground-breaking 1894–95 season saw Millwall emerge as a fully fledged professional concern, who had taken up the torch that the Arsenal had originally toted, whose original aim was to form a competitive League in the South to match the success of the Football League, which at the time was predominantly the preserve of clubs from the North and Midlands. As expected, with their new found status the club hired the services of a number of first-class players, with Alf Geddes from West Bromwich their first prominent signing, with whom he had gained an FA Cup-winners' medal in 1888. Despite becoming full-time professionals, they were still required to compete with those clubs who had not followed their lead in taking up professionalism in the Cup's qualifying rounds. Those teams, who once opposed Millwall on an even playing field, would now be ruthlessly brushed aside.

In the first tie of the new season Folkestone were led like lambs to the slaughter and were thrashed 5–0. This game had been switched from the Kent resort at the request of the Folkestone players, who probably fancied a night in town after the match. On status only, let alone form, this game should have been a cake walk for Millwall, who for 40 minutes battered the goal of Folkestone who had their inspired 'keeper Meates and a stout defence to thank for delaying the inevitable. It took a goal from an unlikely source to open the floodgates when Harry Matthews's long-range strike eluded the outstanding Meates.

The second half began like the first, but Millwall had to wait until the 65th minute to breach to visitors' defence once more. It was the whippet-like Alf Geddes who provided it when he fired home the second. Following this strike, Folkestone's resolve evaporated,

Obed Caygill was the first in a line of many fine goalkeepers who served Millwall in their history and was denied further honours when a broken leg finished his career 1894. Obed appeared in eight FA Cup ties for the club, a distinction he shares with Eddie 'Taff' Jones in Millwall's pre-professional days. [Unknown]

succumbing as they did to three quick-fire goals. Hugh Robertson notched the third before Harry's brother Jim got into the act to add the fourth and Geddes cemented the win with number five. At the end of the match the Folkestone 'keeper was sportingly applauded from the field for his sterling display between the sticks. On the other hand, Millwall's custodian Saunders had to be reintroduced to the ball as he had hardly seen it during the entire 90 minutes.

Millwall's victory earned them a trip to down to the Medway to face the Training Battalion of the Royal Engineers. This game attracted fewer than 260 spectators, with the attendance perhaps affected in some way by New Brompton having a home tie with local rivals Chatham in the vicinity. The visitors fielded an unchanged team, who, despite having the elements and sloping pitch in their favour in the first half, really made hard work of the task in hand, which was not helped by a tight and restrictive pitch.

The Sappers had the advantage of such confines and Millwall's hesitant start, saw them have just as much of the early exchanges as their guests. It came as no surprise when the Battalion opened the scoring following a misunderstanding between Graham and goalkeeper Saunders that allowed Nolan to fire home after Ward's original shot had been blocked. Millwall finally put their first coherent move together when Willie Jones opened the way for McKenzie to equalise, which made up for his disallowed effort moments before the break. The first 20 minutes of the second half was very much nip and tuck, with both teams vying to gain the upper hand.

It was Alex McKenzie's quality throughout that swung the tie Millwall's way with another excellent effort to put his team ahead, before Hugh Robertson struck a third. This was followed by a fourth from Man-of-the-Match McKenzie to complete a fabulous hat-trick five minutes from time. Having seen off the Engineers, Millwall then had to trek down to the same neck of the woods three weeks later to face New Brompton (who had beaten Chatham 2–0) on a fine, sunny autumnal day. Losing the toss, Millwall had the wind at their backs but had to play facing the sun, and they made two changes from the last tie, with Abraham Law taking over in goal and George Aitken replacing King in the half-backs.

McKenzie began where he left off against the Sappers when testing Russell in the home goal with a stinging drive, who later saved another piledriver from Joe Wilson at the expense of a corner. But in the 11th minute Millwall's early superiority was turned into a goal when a Jones centre was met by Geddes, whose low shot found the net. Millwall were now peppering Russell's goal at will, but they had a let-off when in a rare Brompton attack Rule thumped his drive against a post. Millwall had much the better of the game but only had the one goal to show for it when reaching the interval. The second half was more evenly contested, but Brompton were finding it difficult to make any headway against a resilient defence. Even so, Millwall were desperately seeking the security of a second goal, which thankfully arrived when Geddes reciprocated Willie Jones's earlier assist to allow the young Welshman to happily plant the ball into the Brompton net for goal number two.

Millwall were now just one game away from joining the 'big boys' in the first round proper, but before they could start dreaming of things to come they had to negotiate another away tie when paired with the Greenwich-based Royal Ordnance Factory. The opening exchanges had been fairly even, with both teams having their moments, but play went through a scrappy phase when Millwall tried to force the issue. It was the in-form McKenzie who came nearest to scoring when heading just over from a corner, but it was the recalled George King who finally broke the deadlock with a stunning shot to settle the nerves before Geddes doubled the advantage as he finished off a scramble in front of the Ordnance goal. The first big incident of the second half saw an Ordnance attack break down, from which Millwall swiftly countered to register a third.

The all-action McKenzie gained possession to initiate and finish a move, when after putting Geddes away the indomitable Scot was in the right place to convert the return centre. A few moments later the tie should have been put beyond doubt when indecision in front of goal by Geddes allowed Connolly to put in a last-ditch tackle to avert the danger.

Now in uncharted waters for the first time in their history, Millwall were hoping to draw one of the big clubs in the first round proper at home. Alas it saw them having to travel up to Bramall Lane to lock horns with First Division Sheffield United. This gave many of Millwall's ever-increasing support the opportunity to take advantage of the special return train fare of 16s 5d (83p). Those fans who did make the pilgrimage up to Yorkshire could hardly believe their eyes when their favourites got off to a dream start after the skipper Alf Geddes put them ahead in the seventh minute with one of his trademark specials that gave the Blades' legendary goalkeeper William 'Fatty' Foulkes no chance. The rapturous applause of the Millwall fans was sportingly added to by many of the United fans who generously acknowledged a fine goal.

The joy of an early lead was dampened shortly afterwards with the loss of Harry Matthew (echoes here of Duncan Hean in 1888) who went off injured. This handed Sheffield the impetus to turn the screw, and after some resolute defending Millwall's resistance finally gave way when the industrious Watson found Joe Davies, who like Geddes scored a stunning goal to bring the teams level. United were now working up a head of steam, keeping Billy Gibson, the Millwall custodian, on his toes, and the heroic defence finally conceded a second when Bob Hill put the home side ahead after a penetrating run from Blades' tricky winger Yates. The shrill of the referee's whistle for half-time came as a welcome relief to Millwall, who could use the break to reorganise. Ironically, United's two goals had come from a pair of lads whose career paths would eventually lead them to ply their trade with Millwall in final stages the 19th century.

As United intensified the pressure at the start of the second half, Millwall dug in with great fortitude to restrict their hosts to just one more strike. It came when Rab Howell (the first Romany to play for England) sent in another screamer, which Gibson failed to hold, allowing the onrushing Hammond to bundle both ball and 'keeper over line. Although the result looked respectable, the bottom line was that Millwall had been outclassed but not disgraced by a much stronger side. This game was Millwall's first and only defeat of the season.

A little over four weeks before Millwall's participation during the 1895–96 competition, the trophy which Aston Villa won the previous April had gone missing. A local Birmingham businessman had persuaded Villa to allow him to display the original FA Cup in his shop window, but on the night of 11 September it was stolen and never seen again. Villa were later fined £25 before the Football Association commissioned a replacement, after being fortunate enough to find a small replica of the trophy which was in the possession of Wolverhampton Wanderers, who had it manufactured to celebrate their success in 1893. This was used as the template for the second FA Cup in order to recreate an exact replica of the first.

When Millwall Athletic set out in pursuit of the new pot they were still unbeaten in the Southern League, and they carried this impressive form into the Cup. But their path through to the first round proper began nervously with a squeaky 1–0 success at New Brompton, a team Millwall had imperiously whipped 8–0 the week before. This time around, however, they found their opponents steeled for a battle, while Millwall appeared to have left their shooting boots back on the island. This was confirmed with a fortuitous winner after 75 minutes, when Willie Jones's wayward shot was heading nowhere until it cannoned off Alf Geddes' slight frame to beat the despairing dive of Gascoigne for the only goal.

For the second season running Folkestone were the opponents in the next round for a tie which again was switched to the Isle of Dogs. As a result, the hapless visitors conceded another five goals in a pretty one-sided affair. Cruising to a 3–0 lead at the break, Millwall had the half-backs to thank for two of them; George King opened the scoring in the 15th minute, then Jimmy Matthew added number two before winger Mickey Whelan secured the third. Normal service resumed after the break when a Geddes shot ricochetted off a defender for the fourth in the 63rd minute, and with a quarter of an hour left the former Small Heath player Charlie Leatherbarrow wrapped it up with a thunderbolt which flew past Clare for the fifth.

In the next round it was Sheppey United's turn to flounder in the East Ferry mud as rain made the playing area very heavy, added to which was a strong gale that badly affected the opening stages. Progress was ponderous until Millwall got used to the conditions and once in their stride Sheppey were thankful to Jimmy Carter, their goalkeeper, in restricting Millwall to just the four goals. After much probing Millwall went in front when George King's shot found the corner of the net after 30 minutes.

Carter, who was to join Millwall the following season, was beaten again when Tommy Malloch opened his Cup account following good work by Mickey Whelan to put Millwall two up at the break. Millwall started to play cat and mouse with Sheppey in the second half, who, finding it difficult to get over the halfway line, finally threw the towel in when Malloch was on hand to poach the third after Carter slipped when attempting to save from Geddes. Number four arrived in ever-increasing gloominess when Leatherbarrow scored as the match ended in near darkness.

A stiffer test lay ahead for Athletic as they prepared to visit Maze Hill to face Royal Ordnance, whom Millwall had beaten a month earlier by the only goal at the same venue. Any thoughts of this meeting being any easier were soon dispelled when the teams arrived at the break level at 0–0 despite Millwall being the better team. They had come up against another goalkeeper who was having a blinder. Gilmer, who gave such a valiant display in the previous season's Cup game, was up to his old tricks once more as he repelled the visitors on two occasions early in the second half. But on the hour it was Millwall who fell behind to a classic sucker punch when Ordnance suddenly countered. It left McKnight to coolly outfox 'Wiggy' Davis before thumping his shot past Abe Law. The Ordnance supporters' celebrations had barely subsided before it was the turn of the Millwall fans to let off steam when they greeted Joe Gettins's instant equaliser. Straight from the kick-off Joe raced through a bewildered Ordnance defence to smack his drive beyond an equally nonplussed Gilmer.

The game that had simmered for so long now reached boiling point as play swung in Millwall's favour, with Gilmer becoming the busier of the two 'keepers. After denying the visitors in quick succession with some excellent stops he was eventually beaten following a dreadful lapse by his defence that allowed Geddes to convert Whelan's fine centre for the winner. So within three minutes, after taking the lead Royal Ordnance found themselves in arrears and heading out of the Cup.

Millwall's reward was another traipse up north for the second successive season when they visited Anfield for the first time to take on Liverpool in the first round. The game on Merseyside started tentatively from Millwall's point of view and only some wayward shooting from the Liverpool forwards kept the game goalless for the first 30 minutes. During this time Millwall had only threatened once, and if ever a game needed a goal it was this one. All of a sudden it burst into life with three goals in quick succession. Firstly, Ross of Liverpool scored with a low drive which sparked Millwall into their best spell of the half as they began to exert some pressure on Storer's goal without really looking likely to score. Millwall fell further behind just before half-time when Becton took Bradshaw's sublime pass in his stride to place the ball wide of Saunders for the second.

Then, right out of the blue and with seconds remaining of the half, Alf Geddes reduced the arrears with an easy tap-in to register his ninth Cup goal for Millwall. If this goal had stimulated Millwall to give it a go in the second half, any pretensions they had of pulling the tie out of the fire were finally extinguished early in the second half when Allan notched Liverpool's third in the 50th minute. The game was finally put to bed when Bradshaw got the faintest of touches to Fred Geary's goal-bound shot for the fourth. After that blow Millwall were rarely seen as an attacking force and went out rather disappointedly 4–1; not only had they lost the game, but their unbeaten run was also at an end.

Despite the club's ever-improving record, the preliminary rounds still had to be negotiated and for the ensuing campaign's assault for honours the squad was boosted by the return of Alex McKenzie following a year at Sunderland. Also, at the behest of Joe Gettins's recommendation, Jack Calvey had been brought in from South Bank at the end of the previous season, and these were the players Millwall would be pinning their hopes on to score the goals. While the former Ayr and Manchester City player Dave Robson was signed to replace 'Wiggy' Davies to form a new full-back partnership with the old warhorse Jack Graham.

It took Millwall three attempts to be rid of Sheppey United in the third qualifying round, with the first match ending in a close and exciting 3–3 draw. It was Millwall who kicked-off with the breeze at their backs against a Sheppey side containing three former Dockers – Robson's predecessor Bill 'Wiggy' Davis had linked up with the former East Ferry Road favourites Willie Jones and Jimmy Matthew down in Kent – while Millwall fielded the former Sheppey 'keeper Jimmy Carter. In United's first real attack Carter injured a foot when saving from Rule which led to him receiving some treatment. On resuming, Rule gained possession to feed Edwards, who from almost on the touchline gave his team the lead after five minutes when he took advantage of Carter's incapacitation to fire home.

Following the restart play went from end to end, with both goals coming under intense pressure, but it came as no surprise when Millwall grabbed an equaliser when ex-Docker 'Wiggy' handled in the area after 38 minutes. The resultant penalty was tucked way with an air of nonchalance by Joe Gettins; however, no sooner had they drawn level, Millwall went behind again when Edwards registered his and United's second goal with another fine shot to give the home team a half-time lead. The second half was barely underway when Sheppey virtually put one foot into the next round after Arthur Rule increased the lead further with a third. With just 10 minutes left and staring defeat in the face, Millwall, having been penned back for lengthy periods, made a sudden surge up field. Catching Sheppey with no adequate cover, Calvey in the blink of an eye reduced the arrears with one of his customary ground shots.

Throwing caution to the wind, Millwall went all out for the equaliser in a game that started in fine weather and was now ending in heavy rain. A frantic-looking Sheppey side were fighting tooth and nail to retain their slender lead, and having kept the Dockers at bay for so long they finally wilted after 88 minutes. United's Lissenden was penalised for handball, and when a quickly taken free-kick was lofted into the Sheppey area it caused a tremendous mêlée, from which the effervescent Gettins supplied the vital touch to send the tie to a replay. Overjoyed by their late Renaissance, Millwall now held all the aces; however, the replay set for the following Wednesday fell foul to a 'peasouper' fog that descended with Millwall two goals up was abandoned at half-time. So, for the third time in seven days the two teams assembled to resolve the issue of who would play Northfleet in the next round.

Following the dose of midweek fog Millwall now had to contend with ice that had set in overnight and left the outlook appearing very bleak, with another deferment looking certain. But miraculously Mother Nature played her part, when a thaw on the morning of the match occurred that left the playing surface very wet but playable come kick-off time. The indifferent climate kept the attendance down to around 3,000, but those hardy souls who stumped up their hard-earned cash were entertained by a fast and furious encounter. When the teams appeared a special welcome greeted the Sheppey United team which contained three ex-Millwall boys in their line up who faced a home team making three changes from the previous meeting. It saw Tommy Moore replace Carter in goal, while half-back Arthur Millar came in for Peter Robertson and up front Welshman Joe Davies took over from McKenzie.

Play had been underway for some 30 minutes when Millwall gained a corner from which Gettins put Sheppey behind for the first time in the tie. United continued to be dangerous on the break and the early saves made by Button were to prove crucial five minutes later. Cottrell, the visitors' inside-right, made an exceptional run deep into Millwall territory to set up the speedy Willie Jones. The former Docker needed no asking as he finished Cottrell's excellent work with a fine equaliser to remind the home fans what a rare talent he was. Back came Millwall with another bout of pressure, and just as the referee Mr Stark was preparing to bring the first half to a close Geddes slung over an inviting cross that found its way unhindered to the waiting Calvey to score a finely executed goal to give Millwall a vital 2–1 lead at the break.

The second half continued at the same frenetic pace, as Button continued to foil Millwall at every turn as they sought to extend their lead. Sheppey retaliated with three excellent opportunities, all of which were spurned. Rule and Cottrell missed before Lissenden's marvellous shot took a lick of paint off the Millwall crossbar. Edwards then got the better of Graham, but he too shot extravagantly wide as Sheppey strived for the equaliser. Anxiously, Millwall sought some breathing space, but Button for the umpteenth time saved Sheppey's bacon by frustrating Gettins. Such was the pressure on Sheppey's overworked defence that it finally snapped two minutes from time when Calvey applied the final touch to Geddes's free-kick to beat the gallant Button for the third. So after two strenuous and wonderful games Millwall were thankful to be in the next round, whereas a beaten Sheppey were left to rue the two-goal lead they squandered down in Kent.

The next obstacle facing Millwall came in the shape of Northfleet in a home fourth-qualifying-round tie, but this clash was also deferred for 48 hours after fog once again blighted the East Ferry Road. The cancellation enabled the Dockers to recall Alex McKenzie for the unavailable Joe Gettins to play alongside Joe Davies. Also returning was goalkeeper Jim Carter, and Peter Robertson came in at centre-half. These minor distractions were of no consequence to Millwall as they completely dominated their opponents, whose resistance after conceding an early goal became non-existent in a one-sided contest, in which Millwall hardly busted a gut to establish such a crushing victory.

In this stroll in the park Millwall were given carte-blanche to mesmerise Northfleet at will and were aided by Fleet's insistence to press the self-destruct button which was activated barely moments after the kick-off when King scored own-goal. Joe Davies then went through unopposed to give Millwall a two-goal lead, and by the time George King rattled home a third Millwall were in cruise control. Northfleet finally got their house in order for a brief moment just before the interval when Wright reduced the arrears, but this was merely a blip for the Dockers.

Millwall began to indulge in 'playing to the gallery' in the second half, which impressed no one with Alf 'Jasper' Geddes the main culprit. Once they decided to cut out the showboating they shifted up a gear, making Northfleet look ponderous and sluggish. Getting back to the job in hand, Millwall looked a class apart as they capitalised on more woeful daydreaming in the Northfleet defence that let in Joe Davies for the fourth. Alex McKenzie celebrated his return to the side with the fifth after being set-up by Whelan, and near to the end Calvey put the Kent side out of its misery when he slotted home number six from the penalty spot.

Lady luck shone favourably again when the fifth-qualifying-round draw gave them a home match against Woolwich Arsenal and another chance to avenge those previous Cup defeats at the hands of the Gunners in 1892 and 1893. The Arsenal tie attracted some 20,000 spectators, and those who envisaged a classic were not disappointed. The excitement this clash of the titans generated was overshadowed by the untimely death of the Millwall trainer Jimmy Lindsay during the team's preparation for the big game. Poor Jim had been engaged in some light-hearted sparring with George King in a friendly bout of pugilism, when he suddenly collapsed and died on the spot.

A sombre feel hovered around the ground in the lead up to the kick-off as Millwall strode onto the pitch in an all-white strip which poignantly highlighted the black armbands the team were sporting as a mark respect to their beloved trainer. Jim would have been as proud as a peacock as his lads responded in the best possible way by dominating the first half. The

Dockers took a deserved lead after 23 minutes when Alex McKenzie's opener was greeted with an almighty roar of delight from the home support. The lead doubled 15 minutes later when Geddes slotted home from close range, and unbelievably in the 43rd minute Millwall made it 3–0 when Geddes eased home a Mickey Whelan cross.

To use a boxing term, and one which Jim would have reminded them about, Millwall had to keep their guard up. Their failure to adhere to a basic fisticuff rule allowed the Arsenal, who had hardly had a look in, to bring them back down to earth with a resounding bump. Arsenal managed to haul themselves back into contention with two goals in as many minutes just before half-time when Jimmy Boyle and Pat O'Brien took advantage of some dilatory Millwall defending.

Any apprehensions the team may have had at the start of the game would have all but disappeared after scoring those three blinding goals, only for it to resurface during the interval following Arsenal's quick-fire double. With their tails firmly up the Gunners commenced the second half in the driving seat and started to impose themselves on Millwall's goal, searching for a dramatic equaliser. Millwall's priority was to steady the ship and not concede any more soft goals, while exploiting the gaps the visitors may leave in their quest to even things up. The match was finely balanced and a bit cagey as the team scoring the next goal were likely to be the winners. What was needed was a moment of inspiration. But who was going to supply it? Would it be Docker or Gunner? Thankfully, it was the former when Millwall's famous Corinthian, Joe Gettins, created for himself an extra bit of space before sending a superb shot beyond John Leather into the net for the fourth and clinching goal.

Despite the few moments of pre-interval madness this had been an exceptional team performance, but the victory had been built around two men who stood head and shoulders above the rest. One was the foraging and cool Joe Gettins who, along with his strike partner, the splendid Jack Calvey, would in present-day football justifiably claim the accolade of Man of the Match.

Having navigated the prelims, Millwall were to contest the first-round proper for a third consecutive season in the hope of pulling out a 'plum' home tie. This time their wish was granted when one of the founders of the Football League, Wolverhampton Wanderers, followed them out of the hat to become the first club of renown to visit the Isle of Dogs for a competitive match. Founded in 1879, Wolves had a proven track record in the Cup, having played in three Finals, with the last coming the previous year when they were defeated 2–1 by Sheffield Wednesday at Crystal Palace.

The visit of Wolves attracted around an estimated 14,000 crowd to East Ferry Road, who would unfortunately witness a clash utterly ruined by the weather. Drizzle on the Saturday morning followed an overnight thaw left the pitch in a terrible state, and although it was liberally sanded many of the players had trouble in keeping their footing. The game was also marred by the lack of skilful football as brute strength and ignorance seemed the order of the day. The litany of fouls, many of them yellow card offences in today's game, began to accrue, with Billy Owen, the visitors' centre-half, being the leading transgressor whose sole aim appeared to be to see how may Millwall players he could foul as he went ruthlessly about introducing himself to more than one opponent.

Following a cautious opening quarter of an hour, Wanderers made some headway in the Millwall half, and only the alertness of goalkeeper Jimmy Carter stopped them taking the lead. A Millwall riposte saw Geddes set up Calvey, but Jack's effort lacked any real zip. Wolves forced a corner through McMain, which led to Billy Malpas putting in an effort that Carter was equal to, but when play was switched the prominent Calvey combined with Mickey Whelan but was halted by Hill Griffiths's (later to join Millwall in 1905) interception. Turning defence into attack, Griffiths put Joe Tonks away, and his screamer forced Carter to conceded another corner. Wolves striker Billy Beats thought he had given his team the lead, but the effort was disallowed for offside. Two other efforts came close to Carter's goal, the one from McMain just clearing the bar with Wolves finishing the stronger as the first half came to a close. Just before the break Millwall suffered a scare when injury befell Joe Gettins, which saw him led from the field with blood pouring from a wound on one of his knees.

Wolves' erratic shooting and Millwall's inability to supply their potential match-winners were the main reasons a disappointing first half finished goalless. One of those threats was Alf Geddes, who must have thought he had flogged a dead horse following his one and only decent inroad of the half to threaten the Wolves goal. Having left friend and foe in his wake on a cloying surface, the advantage gained was lost due to the lack of any genuine support.

The second half got underway following what seemed an interminable interval break as the pattern of play continued in the same vein with the bully-boy tactics of Wolves still evident. It was obvious they were not going to be the victims in any giant-killing act as their softening-up tactics, no matter how unsavoury, seemed vindicated when Beats scored after 57 minutes. Millwall responded instantly by forcing a corner which led to a spell of strong pressure, culminating in a penalty award for Millwall; however, the chance to draw level was squandered when Tennant became the Wolves hero by saving the spot-kick. The identity of the Millwall miscreant is not known, suffice to say both Calvey and Gettins had been successful with spot-kicks during the run, and whoever it was remained discreetly anonymous. McKenzie then became a victim dreadful tackle from Griffiths that brought a foolish but an understandable reaction from the Scot, who hurled a handful mud at the Wanderer. McKenzie got himself cautioned by the referee.

Wolves' calculated efficiency had worked Millwall into a right old lather with their spoiling play, but they showed their better side by producing some flowing football and were moving quickly and confidently on the ball and proving very dangerous on the counter. Millwall, though not at their best, continued to chip away in the hope that something might happen, but they could only offer two long-range efforts from Joe Davies that went straight into the waiting hands of Tennant. The game appeared to be meandering to a Wolves victory when the referee Captain Simpson's patience finally snapped when Owen got his comeuppance – not before time – and was finally booked for persistent fouling. This begs the question why had Simpson not taken a firmer grip earlier in the match? If he had, perhaps players and spectators alike might have been involved in and seen a contest to savour. Owen's booking did bring the crowd to life, however, and lifted the team in a final throw of the dice in the minutes that remained.

When Millwall won a corner it looked as though the ball was heading directly into the Wolves net. But in a heart-stopping moment it grazed the bar, only for it to drop to

McKenzie who lashed home a well-deserved equaliser as the home crowd rose in unison to greet the goal. Unfortunately, the joy was short-lived when two minutes from time disaster struck. As Carter went to collect Griffiths' free-kick he was challenged by the onrushing Tonks, letting slip the greasy ball from his grasp as the mortified 'keeper could only watch it roll agonisingly over the line for what proved to be a fortuitous winner. It was Carter's only mistake of the whole 90 minutes.

So ended Millwall's interest in the competition for another year, but the appetite had been whetted, and the club were pinning their hopes on being elected into the Football League at their annual general meeting during the coming summer. By receiving just one vote, their dreams of facing the likes of Wolves on a regular basis were dashed. The club's support was condemned to watch a diet of Southern League fare for the next 23 years, with the FA Cup alone the main course on the menu.

Over the next couple of seasons Millwall's FA Cup exploits were very disappointing. Drawn at home to Sheppey United in 1897, they dished out a football lesson when they thrashed them 5–1 in the third qualifying round; although an oversight in the registration procedure found Millwall had fielded an ineligible player named John Fitzpatrick. The FA ordered the replay to be staged at Sheppey seven days later, a decree that visibly lifted the Kent club who had been outplayed for most of the original game, as they took full advantage of Millwall's negligence to register an emphatic 5–0 win. To compound a miserable afternoon, Mickey Whelan missed most of the second half due to injury, at which time Millwall were just a goal down. But the farce over Fitzpatrick's registration was endemic of the season overall when they finished a disappointing ninth and seventh in the Southern and Western Leagues respectively. A disjointed campaign was underlined by the incredible use of eight different players at centre-forward in just 22 Southern League fixtures.

An improvement in their Southern League form saw Millwall finish third in 1898–99, but the Cup was a huge disappointment once again. They beat long-forgotten Brighton United at the East Ferry Road 3–0 on a miserably wet November afternoon in which Millwall's play frustratingly matched the weather. They entered the break goalless, and had it not been for goalkeeper Willie Allan's sharp reaction to McLeod's hard drive they could have gone in a goal down. Millwall perked up considerably with a bright start to the second half that paid early dividends. It was Scotsman Peter Turnbull's perseverance that nearly caused Caldwell to put the ball into his own net, but from the resultant corner Jack Calvey's opener in the 47th minute lifted the gloom.

The goal provided some much-needed impetus as Calvey began to revel in the conditions with his swashbuckling style causing concern in the Brighton defence. Their sole intention was to foul him at every turn before Joe Gettins then became the victim of another nasty tackle. On resuming, Gettins made the transgressor pay in the best way possible. Setting off on one of his mazy runs, he shook off one opponent to fire past Bullimer to make it 2–0, much to the crowd's delight. After Allan had denied McLeod, Calvey was again involved at the other end, but he missed by inches before Turnbull tested Bullimer with a cracking drive. Charlie Burgess, Joe Turner and Gettins had further chances to increase Millwall's lead, but they had to wait until Calvey notched his second when he pounced upon Farrell's mis-kick to give Bullimer no chance for the third.

For the fourth-qualifying-round tie at Gravesend United, Millwall's day got off to the worst possible start when they conceded in the first minute to a Billy Regan strike. It was left to birthday boy Joe Gettins to get Millwall level when he hit a stunning equaliser after nine minutes. Prior to the game, the illustrious amateur had had a pleasant surprise waiting for him when he arrived at the dressing room. Joe was highly thought of by the professionals at the club, and they showed their appreciation for his exceptional service and for being an all-round good egg by presenting him with a handsome, gold-mounted umbrella. Alas, for Joe and his teammates this would be thing last thing to celebrate. They fell behind once more when Gravesend took the lead on the stroke of half-time, and from that point Millwall never fully recovered. They conceded a third five minutes from time, but most worrying was that two of the Gravesend goals had come from dead-ball situations.

2. Lions of the South

Millwall Athletic's rise to eminence as one of the leading clubs in the south took on further significance in their quest for more FA Cup glory by reaching the first of two semi-finals in three years. Having dominated the early years of the Southern League they began to set their sights a bit higher, and the FA Cup offered that opportunity in what was becoming a most popular tournament among the clubs and their fans. The turnover of players was as frequent as ever, with the likes of Alf Geddes, Alex McKenzie and the Matthew brothers all seeking pastures new. But one fellow who was still around was the indomitable Joe Gettins, who would deservedly go on to become the only man to play in two semi-finals for Millwall and whose last game for the club would come on his 30th birthday in November 1904.

The Dockers were about to embark upon a sensational 1899–1900 season, the highlight of which was their appearance in the club's first semi-final. The trail started in late October against Clapton, who were unceremoniously dumped out of the Cup, with former soldier Herbert Banks having a field day by scoring four goals in a 7–0 bonanza, two coming in each half. It was then the turn of another old acquaintance, Chatham, to be sent packing 3–0, with Banks notching another two. This victory was achieved despite the absence of the regular wingers Dave Nicoll and Willy Dryburgh. Millwall were then required to make the short trip to Canning Town to face the new kids on the block Thames Ironworks, the forerunners of the present-day West Ham United.

After winning the obligatory toss of the coin, Millwall pressed the Irons straight away, taking advantage of the wind at their backs to take an eighth-minute lead when Hugh Goldie struck a great shot past Tommy Moore, who moments earlier had denied Banks from adding to his impressive tally of Cup goals. Following a bout of extreme Millwall pressure, Thames finally picked up some momentum when Dockers goalkeeper Dave Clear (who had replaced Walter Cox) had to be at his best to save Ken McKay's effort. Thames's Bert Carnelly, another to wear the colours of both clubs during his career, managed to get away but with the goal in range lost his footing at the critical moment as the chance went begging. A rare lapse by Charlie Burgess nearly let in Carnelly, but the blushes were saved by fellow Scot Arthur Millar before 'Wiggy' Davis took on the mantle of saviour by clearing a Bradshaw effort after Clear had failed to live up to his name.

The intensity of the game was creating a fantastic atmosphere which reached fever pitch when Thames drew level with Harry Bradshaw's tempting free-kick causing consternation in the Millwall ranks. The ball sped into the area, catching Dave Clear unawares, and it bounced off the luckless 'keeper and into the net. Bradshaw was the same player who had scored Liverpool's fourth goal against Millwall at Anfield nearly five years earlier, but for poor old Harry this game would be his last, for 16 days later on Christmas Day he died at the age of just 26.

One promising move was gallingly halted when Dryburgh was thoughtlessly caught offside, but Millwall's attacks were growing with intensity, channelling their aggression through the focal point that was Willy Dryburgh. It was from one such move that the canny Scot exchanged passes with John Brearley to open the way for Banks to net the decider from close range for his seventh goal in the competition. In their previous FA Cup escapades up north to Sheffield and Liverpool, Millwall had entered the task very much the underdog but after being paired with the little-known Jarrow from the North East the boot was clearly on the other foot.

The northerners had been narrowly beaten 3–1 at Everton the previous season and had set up the Millwall tie when they caused more than a stir by winning 2–1 at Second Division Middlesbrough. So concerned were the Millwall officials that they offered the Tynesiders a financial inducement. The idea of travelling to one of the country's footballing outposts and finishing up with egg on their face was not very appealing, so they hoped Jarrow would take the cash and make the trip to London instead. Although the offer was very tempting, they respectfully turned it down, and rightly so. The reasoning was they had a better chance of an upset on their own ground. After failing to persuade Jarrow to bite the carrot, Millwall, after a week of light training, hotfooted their way to Tyneside on the Friday with stick in hand to beat the Jarrow donkey.

On a fine day and in front of a record crowd of 6,000 the teams, who were both at full strength, entered the field of play, and any apprehensions Millwall may have had were quickly dispelled on a superb playing surface that suited the visitors to a tee. They then proceeded to kill the game stone dead within the first six minutes. After losing the toss Jarrow were forced to play into a strong wind, and they were soon on the defensive as Davie Nichol forced an early corner which saw Millwall go one up as the ball fell kindly for John Brearley to fire past Callaghan in the Jarrow goal after just three minutes. The home team then gained a corner of their own shortly afterwards, but nothing came of it as Millwall built upon their early success to go two up. With barely six minutes on the clock Bertie Banks continued his impressive run with Millwall's second as dominance and confidence began to grow; however, the game should have been a lot further from Jarrow's reach had efforts from Banks and Gettins hit the target. Gettins, unusually for him, failed to hit the target when well placed, before Banks with the goal at his mercy blazed wantonly over the bar from four yards.

Jarrow's stuttering attack finally stirred but rarely troubled Walter Cox in the Dockers goal, although it took the canny veteran Bill 'Wiggy' Davis (who rejoined Millwall in 1897 after a season at Sheppey) to block Goodchild's attempt. All the pre-match concern of an upset seemed frivolous as Millwall comfortably saw out the game to a conclusion, which was mainly due to the outstanding presence of the half-backs. This was the rock upon which Jarrow's ambition foundered and finally sank. Any despair Jarrow felt in defeat was tempered by the day's takings, which amounted to £130.

The club and the fans now awaited the draw for the second round with anticipation after surmounting what at first had appeared to be a difficult hurdle in the North East. When it arrived Millwall were given another strenuous task, albeit a lot closer to home, when they were drawn away to Queen's Park Rangers. The day arrived, and hundreds of Dockers fans deserted the island in their droves, carried by the many 'specials' from Poplar, and descended upon Kensal Rise in a cacophony of noise and excitement in an unprecedented level of Cup fever.

The foul weather in the preceding week had raised doubts of the game going ahead, but following a morning inspection by Mr King, the referee, it was decided that the game could go ahead. Millwall were forced to make one change from the previous round, with Eddie Allan replacing 'Wiggy' Davies, sidelined with a sprained ankle. 'Wiggy' was probably not that unhappy to miss what turned out to be a rough-and-tumble affair in very heavy conditions in which Millwall conceded more free-kicks than Rangers but clinched the win nonetheless.

Millwall were forced back as Rangers took up the initiative, with Smith leading their bombardment of the Millwall goal. Full-back Charlie Burgess began to revel as the battle raged with Rangers searching for an early breakthrough. It was made clear early on that Rangers' Smith was the main threat, causing all sorts of problems on the left. He forced Allan into a hurried clearance before he was denied an opportunity when Cox came careering out of his goal to save the day. Millwall struggled as a unit to find any sort rhythm, which was giving their supporters a fair amount of anxiety. But the trio of Gettins, Nichol and Willie Dryburgh gave them something to cheer about following one sweeping move, but this support petered out as the play deteriorated due to the clinging mud as the pitch started to cut up.

The more Rangers pressed the more Millwall dug in, with the Scottish triumvirate of Hugh Goldie, Dave Smith and Arthur Millar rising to the occasion as if their lives depended

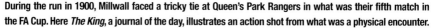

During the run in 1900, Millwall faced a tricky tie at Queen's Park Rangers in what was their fifth match in the FA Cup. Here *The King*, a journal of the day, illustrates an action shot from what was a physical encounter.

upon it. But they were all left helpless when Hitch found some space and, with only Cox to beat, powered his drive that had 'Goal' written all over it. But fans and players alike looked on in disbelieving wonderment as Walter deflected the effort for a corner with a miraculous save to keep the scores level. But with Rangers turning the screw, further heroics were needed from the Millwall custodian who displayed agility and bravery with an array of breathtaking saves that were later to prove vital.

Some respite came with one fanciful move conjured up by Brearley and Dryburgh, which ended with Banks being fouled. It nearly resulted in Millwall taking the lead when the free-kick cannoned off the crossbar for Gettins, whose spontaneous reaction was to crack the rebound past Clutterbuck. A dispute then arose about the goal's validity, which saw the referee consult one of his linesmen. The outcome was laughable when the official awarded Rangers a goal-kick, leading to the Millwall players venting their anger at his decision. As half-time approached former Docker Gavin Crawford rescued Rangers when he stooped to clear a goal-bound effort, while at the other end Bedingfield's unsuccessful shot brought the first half to a conclusion.

Rangers were the first to flex their muscles at the start of the second half when Millwall were penalised yet again as the home team laid siege to Cox's goal, but the die was cast as it appeared all of Rangers' attempts to break the deadlock were doomed to fail. Utterly unconvincing at the back, after being penalised following a rare Millwall break, anxiety began to creep into their play. Millwall gained a corner, which was cleared, but their approach play was beginning to exude a lot more confidence as they pegged Rangers back on the defensive. The away support sensed the tide was turning after seeing their team rebuff Rangers at every turn, and they began to encourage the team with roars of support as a horrible mist started to settle.

The catalogue of niggling fouls that had crept into the game saw the nastier of these perpetrated by Bedingfield, whose kick was aimed at Cox as he came out to clear. The status quo was confirmed moments later when Allan gave the dangerous Smith a retaliatory dig. Nicol and Dryburgh had shots blocked as Millwall stepped up the pace, before Hannah of Rangers made a fine solo run that was ended when he tested the magnificent Cox with a thunderbolt, which the 'keeper was equal to. With both teams going for broke, Millwall's Brearley and White of Rangers both went close before Joe Gettins's incisive break gained him possession until he was duly upended by Hitch just outside the area. Hitch's popularity among his teammates went down a couple of notches when Joe's thumping drive brought swift retribution to put Millwall ahead after an hour's play.

The biggest threat to Millwall's ambitions came not from Rangers but from the elements, with the mist getting thicker. Millwall began to tighten their grip in ever-increasing gloom when Gettins brought Clutterbuck to his knees with another stinging drive, which only delayed the inevitable by a minute or so. Gettins, not to be denied, characteristically crashed home his and Millwall's second goal with about 15 minutes to go, at which point many of the home fans departed, believing this particular contest was over. A fine drizzle added to the conditions, making the last few moments very miserable. But the weather was not going to stop the rejoicing Millwall supporters, who stayed to the bitter end and following the final whistle gave the team a splendid reception as they made their way back to the dressing rooms after a hard-fought but deserved victory.

The local press were, of course, ecstatic about the club reaching the point where they were just one game from their first semi-final, the *East End News* praising the feat with the following: 'Never in the history of the Millwall club has it ever reached so high in the English Cup competition, and never has enthusiasm risen to such a pitch as is now prevalent with the East Ferry Road club'.

So who would the Blues draw in the quarter-final? Heady days, indeed, for the club and their followers were heightened further after being paired with the mighty Aston Villa, the current Football League champions, who to many were favourites to lift the trophy later that season. Villa were proud and doughty Cup performers, having won three of their four finals in 1887, 1895 and 1897, the latter the year in which they accomplished the coveted double. Their only loss had occurred at the hands of Alf Geddes's West Bromwich side in 1892. In theory Millwall were just one game away from the semi-final, but the reality was it took them three games to be rid of Villa's challenge after they came within two minutes of ending the Dockers' interest before Millwall grabbed a dramatic equaliser.

The eagerly awaited clash drew around 20,000 spectators to the Island, who were not disappointed in what they saw. Villa themselves were well supported, as they had six specials bringing some 5,000 fans down from Birmingham. Extra seating had been brought in from the headquarters of the Essex County Cricket Club ground at Leyton to accommodate a larger, if not unexpected, crowd. For many of the fans this was an opportunity to set their eyes upon the Midland aristocrats Aston Villa and their array of English internationals. Eddie Allan was a last-minute replacement for 'Wiggy' Davis, who was not quite fit, as Millwall Athletic prepared to face their day of destiny. The Dockers, having lost the toss on an overcast afternoon, saw Gettins get the game underway, but first to show his class was Villa's speedy Steve Smith who, following one pacey run, looked likely to give his side an early lead until his indecision allowed both Burgess and Cox to deny him at the expense of a corner, which was cleared. On three occasions in the opening minutes Charlie Burgess had cleared his lines with his usual efficiency but could do nothing when Villa's early pressure came to fruition in the fifth minute. A magnificent cross from Charlie Athersmith was met by England's Fred Wheldon, whose stunning volley left Walter Cox a mere spectator.

Millwall were clearly finding the early going hard, with Villa's full-backs Spencer and Evans showing that their well-won reputations had not been exaggerated, with a passing game that was a real eye-opener to the home fans. Villa started to purr like a well-oiled machine, as shifting through gears with ease they threatened to steamroll Millwall's hopes. Their half-backs repelled all

On reaching their first semi-final in 1900, Millwall disposed of the then Football League champions Aston Villa, albeit after three games. *The King* published a set of action photographs, and the one here shows Millwall 'keeper Wally Cox saving a Villa effort under the bar.

that the Dockers could throw at them and in attack they swarmed around the Millwall goal like bees around a honey jar. From another corner Millwall nearly went further behind, but the excellent Burgess intervened once more when he stopped John Devey's effort from crossing the line.

Millwall in some ways were lucky to still be in the game, and when Villa eased off slightly Millwall launched an enterprising attack on Villa's goal when Willy Dryburgh, who had hardly had a kick all afternoon, put in a fine drive which brought Villa 'keeper Billy George into action for the first time. Back came Villa, however, with a quick-fire response that saw Wheldon crack in a thunderous drive only for Cox's splendid save to bring much merited applause. After Villa's early dominance Millwall were now having a better share of the game as Banks and Gettins combined to see the former fire in a powerful shot that appeared to be heading just below the bar until George pulled off a miraculous save to keep Villa ahead. Smith was still causing problems to the Millwall defence and had the chance to prod home Villa's second, only for John Brearley to coolly dispossess the Villa danger man at the expense of a corner.

After gaining possession, Gettins sped away on one of his mazy runs and fed Banks who was promptly robbed by Spencer, before Banks and the magnificent Gettins rallied again to set-up Dave Nichol whose cracking drive rebounded from an upright. Millwall were now getting the feel for the game, with play switching from end to end. Willy Dryburgh was warming to the occasion as his footwork and pace were causing some unusual panic in the Villa area, and they were mightily relieved to hack one of his dangerous crosses to safety. Cox was called into action at the other end to save Devey's strike, before Gettins showed some fine trickery to set Millwall off down the right, but after their shaky spell Villa regained their composure. The bubbly Dryburgh was beginning to ask Evans a few more questions of his ability. Cox was continuing to do his bit by saving three Villa efforts with distained arrogance to deny the visitors an extension to their lead before the interval.

The second half was seconds old when both Banks and Nicol clattered Bowman, and the ensuing free-kick forced Cox to save once more. Turning their attention back to the football, the Millwall duo made a quick break that enabled Banks to hassle Spencer for the ball, which resulted in Villa conceding a throw-in. Their frustration in their failure to score a second goal began to mount when a small piece of nonsense took place. Athersmith and Millar tussled for a loose ball, and after losing out the Villa man slyly kicked Millar on the leg as the ball was cleared up field. The game continued at a breakneck pace, but Villa were not having it all their own way, and Spencer thwarted Banks who was about to pounce, while at the other end Goldie cleared Smith's and Wheldon's threats for Villa to win yet another corner. A tidy spell of pressure from the visitors achieved very little in the way of chances, although Athersmith's rasping drive brought another impressive stop from Cox.

Millwall now began to force the issue when Brearley caused Evans to handle, which drew an excellent stop from George to deny Dryburgh's powerful shot. Encouraged by the crowd's roar, Millwall now sensed that they were good enough to a draw at least. The home support was soon reminded of Villa's potency as Garraty and Devey bored down on the Millwall goal, only for the presence of Goldie and Millar to avert the danger. The unrelenting pace continued as Gettins Banks and Nicol attacked, only for Spencer and Evans to repel them. Crabtree was then penalised for a foul, which led to Dryburgh's deep cross being missed by Banks, but the ball fell to Gettins who was eased out of the way as he was about to pull the trigger. Millwall saw another promising attack halted in its tracks when Nicol was pulled-up for offside. Another anxious moment for Walter Cox in the Millwall goal was alleviated when Burgess was on hand to clear before a Blues attack was broken up by Evans, whose fine play set his own team on the offensive.

We all know games can turn on an incident, and one that would linger long in the memory of those fans who saw it would confirm the defining moment of the tie had been reached. Following some strong Millwall pressure, a sudden break saw Villa's Billy Garraty in splendid isolation and with just Walter Cox to beat, he fluffed it big time. Cox's save brought the house down and could be likened to the one another former Millwall goalkeeper performed 68 years later when Alex Stepney, then of Manchester United, miraculously denied Eusebio of Benfica the chance to steal the glory in 1968 European Cup Final at Wembley Stadium and so paved the way for United to become the first English club to win the European Cup. One man's dream is another's nightmare, especially in the sporting context, and this miss must have haunted Garraty for the rest of his career and left Villa rueing the day their striker did not put that one away.

Garraty's misfortune was the boost Millwall needed as they went on to control what was left of the game. But with time running out could Villa hold onto their one-goal advantage? Villa 'keeper Billy George was trying his hardest to make up for Garraty's lapse by foiling the rampaging Banks and Nicol. It was all hands to the pump now, with Villa penned back in their own half and George, Spencer and Evans and company striving manfully to retain their lead. Millwall's salvation arrived at last when Arthur Millar cottoned on to a loose ball, and the brawny Scot made a surging run that carried him on until he found his fellow Scot, the well-placed Davie Nicol. With the crowd begging him to shoot, he did as they asked by powerfully driving home past Billy George as the ball took a slight deflection off Crabtree for a very well-deserved equaliser.

The din that welcomed the strike was likened to a heavy roll of thunder as umbrellas were waved and hats thrown into the air in an expression of frenzied delight. Three minutes later the final whistle went, and the East Ferry Road erupted once more with more raucous cheering as spectators, young and old, jumped the fences to congratulate and pat the backs of their heroes at the climax of probably the most exciting game seen on the ground. Following the final whistle came a scene straight out the playground. When a petulant Charlie Athersmith reached the gate to the pavilion he tried to purloin the match ball as a souvenir; however, Millwall's trainer Bob Hunter was having none of that and, with the assistance of three of his players, he finally grappled the ball back from Charlie's grasp, averting what could have been an ugly situation.

The replay was set for the following Wednesday, with the Dockers knowing full well that they would be in for another physical encounter that would test their resolve and mettle, as Villa would be attempting to put their non-League opponents well and truly in their place. Difficult as it was, Villa Park had probably never seen such a battle fought within its confines. Villa played the same side from the first game, with Millwall selecting Hughie Roberson for unavailable Joe Gettins, thus the Blues were fielding a team comprising three Englishmen and eight Scots. Among the 11,000 spectators was a fair smattering of Londoners who saw their team make the first inroads before Villa took up the gauntlet to pin the visitors back. The resilience shown by Cox, Burgess and Allan was of steadfast continuity and was effective in keeping Villa at arms length.

To a degree Millwall held their own for much of the first half, but with Villa calling the tune it was their awful shooting that let them down and was the main reason the first half ended goalless. Villa also had the lion's share of the second 45 minutes, but again indifferent finishing in front of goal was their Achilles heel; although to be fair both teams had managed between them to put the ball in the net four times (twice each). But on each occasion the referee Mr Lewis had disallowed them for offside. The extra 30 minutes saw Villa straining to get the vital breakthrough but Millwall held firm to withstand these exertions to force a second replay.

So, on a momentous Monday 5 March 1900, Millwall stood on the threshold of greatness, and after matching their illustrious opponents in three and a half hours of football they must have been confident of causing an upset. The third game was set for the neutral venue of Elm Park, Reading, a location more readily known to Millwall than Villa, with the Dockers having met the Royals on numerous occasions in the Southern League. Another omen was the unexpected stroke of luck of having Millwall talisman Joe Gettins back in the side, who was given permission to play from the head of the school that he taught at in the town. Forty-eight hours earlier Millwall had rested all of the regulars bar the surprising exception of goalkeeper Walter Cox in the defeat by Queen's Park Rangers. Villa, however, made four changes in an effort to halt their goal drought, and a third piece of good news awaited Millwall on their arrival at Elm Park with the absence of the fleet-footed Steve Smith, who was ruled out through injury.

Such was the enthusiasm for the game that some local factories had applied for a half-day's holiday for what was probably the town's biggest-ever game. Although an official gate of 9,164 was recorded, the general feeling was the attendance swelled to well over a five-figure total as spectators wedged themselves in to the tiny Berkshire ground. Millwall were led out by their indefatigable captain Dave Smith who, on a very cold day, personified Millwall's assured calmness. Play got underway, and during an early phase Villa's only real chance of a goal came when the ball inadvertently struck the head of referee Lewis and fell conveniently into the path of a Villa man, who failed to take any meaningful advantage to spurn another golden opportunity they were later to regret. The Dockers were encouraged by three train loads of fans, whose justification of losing a day's pay was rewarded in the 15th minute when Millwall took the lead for the first time in the tie. A well-flighted corner was headed on by Hugh Goldie to present Bertie Banks with the chance to gleefully lash home the loose ball.

Still savouring the early strike, the Millwall fans went berserk when, within the space of five minutes, their favourites doubled the lead as Gettins's late inclusion paid off handsomely. Joe went on one of his customary solo runs, leaving his opponent Evans floundering before unleashing a stunning drive that Billy George could do nothing about. Millwall were firmly in control and had the fans pinching themselves disbelievingly by sitting on a two-goal cushion. Millwall would continue to dominate the first half without adding to their score. If Villa had originally figured Millwall as Cockney upstarts, then the two goals they conceded may have changed their opinions. Severely jolted, they had to address the situation fairly quickly if they were to survive an embarrassing exit. Whatever was said in the Villa dressing-room had the desired effect, however, as they flew out of the traps and began to play like the champions they were in the second half.

As Villa went into overdrive, Joe Gettins picked up an injury that forced him to play the remainder of the game out on the right wing, and this only added to the tension and nervous nail biting on the terraces from Millwall's followers. But resolution had been the byword in Millwall's defending during the run, and despite all that Villa could offer they found themselves continuously ushered up blind alleys while desperately seeking that one opportunity that would bring them back into the game. Then it happened, with 10 minutes remaining, when for probably the second time during the course of this three-match saga Millwall were caught out of position. This allowed George Johnson, the Villa centre-forward, a clear run in on goal to beat Cox, thus giving the Villa fans something to cheer about at last.

The tension was at fever pitch in those dramatic closing minutes when the defining line between success and failure was reached as Villa sought the goal that would take the tie into another period of extra-time. A glimmer of hope appeared in the shape of Billy Garraty who, hoping to erase the memory of his miss at the East Ferry Road, was again denied when looking certain to score. Millwall's saviour on this occasion was Dave Smith, the ice-cool skipper appearing from nowhere to rob Garraty of the ball and his chance of redemption. This action highlighted the differing emotions of the fans. For Villa it signalled the end of their hopes of harnessing the much-prized double, whereas it was celebration time for the Lions. Millwall still had not finished, however, as the gallant and brave Joe Gettins managed to lift the Londoners' spirits with one last sortie but blazed his effort just wide. After denying Villa any further chances, it was left for Mr Lewis to call time and so set in motion a gala of festivities that not only east London could go crazy about but also the rest of the footballing fraternity in the South of England.

The press were naturally generous in their praise of Millwall: *The Daily Mail* eulogised 'It hardly seems possible…yet the London side thoroughly deserved their victory, as on the day's play they were undoubtedly the better side', while *The Sportsman* piped up with 'Millwall's achievement at Elm Park yesterday was no ordinary performance and the result was hailed with enthusiasm such has seldom been witnessed in the earlier rounds of the Cup'.

Indeed, this result would have to go down as the finest Millwall had gained in their short existence, and not only that but they also scuppered Aston Villa's chances of accomplishing the League and Cup double to truly become the 'Lions of the South'. Villa's consolation at the end of the season was to retain the Championship, but the Millwall defeat would surely rankle with them for weeks to come, especially when recalling Garraty's miss that would have put them two-up in the first game. Once the dust had settled following this epic, stamina-sapping trilogy, the draw was made for the semi-final, and out of the hat came fellow Southern Leaguers Southampton, whom Millwall would face at the Crystal Palace on 24 March. This gave Millwall a splendid chance to reach their first English Cup Final, and whichever club came out on top it would ensure a southern participation in the Final for the first time since 1883. Having lost at home to the Saints back in September, Millwall, or 'the Lions' as they were now being called, would be looking to reverse that defeat.

An extremely rare and no doubt a much sought-after item is the match card from Millwall's first semi-final appearance in 1900. The game failed to live up to its expectations, and with it went Millwall's chance of reaching the Final, for they lost the replay 3–0 to the Saints. [Richard Smart]

Like many semi-finals before and since, however, this one never really took off as spectacle and certainly did not live up to the expectations of many in the crowd of 34,760. Perhaps Millwall were the better side on the day, but many of the players who were experiencing this stage of the Cup for the first time simply did not perform to their usual standards. The game itself was a very boisterous affair, and although Millwall did manage to find the net from the unlikely source of left-back Eddie Allan in the first half, the strike was disallowed. Millwall continued to hold the balance of play up to the interval but rarely looked like getting the breakthrough. Had Bertie Banks showed some composure, Millwall may have been looking forward to another date at the Crystal Palace. His first effort forced Saints 'keeper Jack Robinson to make a splendid save before the debonair striker looked odds-on to score, but perhaps gripped by fear he blazed wildly over the bar after excellent approach work from Joe Gettins and Willy Dryburgh.

A cartoon from the *Athletic and Sporting Chat* in 1900 shows a wise tutor advising the two combatants not to repeat the team's boisterous play of the first game in the replay.

"Well boys, you had a good, stiff, stand-up fight on Saturday, but on Wednesday I must insist on a little closer attention to the ball, and less attention to the man."

Southampton commenced the second half with the wind in their favour and asserted more urgency into their game, especially after Banks had departed with a nasty gash over one of his eyes. They came close on two occasions when Arthur Turner was denied by Art Millar, and then a minute later Charlie Burgess's goalline intervention stopped Millwall falling behind. Banks's re-

Millwall's first FA Cup semi-final in 1900 is graphically shown in a revamped montage of the game against Southampton. [Chris Bethell]

F.A CUP Semi-final MILLWALL V. SOUTHAMPTON at the Crystal Palace, Saturday March 24th 1900

Clever Southampton forwards

Millwall's Burgess indulges in some mighty overhead kicks

Pretty head flay by Allan

Cox fisting out

A collision of heads 'Ouch'

Gettins gone away

Referee Kingscott besieged

emergence was greeted by a loud cheer, which dovetailed nicely as Millwall continued to press the Saints back as both Dryburgh and Gettins attempted to prise open the Southampton defence.

The number of bumps and bruises were accumulating as players of both sides needed treatment in a hard and uncompromising encounter. Southampton diligence saw them force three successive corners which came to nothing, and as full-time loomed Eddie Allan took a knock when foiling a Southampton raid. Millwall had given their all, and in the later stages of the game Southampton appeared the more likely team to score. The twin virtues of fortitude and stoicism that had seen the Lions reach this far were again evident against the Saints, but in a game they really should have won it finished 0–0. Given this reprieve, surely Southampton would hardly perform as badly in the replay? It was left to Millwallian, writing in the *Athletic and Sporting Chat,* to say 'Mr Kingscott was a capable referee but wasn't strict enough over the rough play, and I also noted that on the day the Lions forwards were a tad disappointing with John Brearley's confident showing alone being Millwall's main hope of a goal'.

The replay was earmarked for Elm Park, which gave the Reading officials the excuse to increase the cost of admission. Millwall went in as favourites, but to the disappointment of everyone favouring the Lions they did not seem to settle into their usual fluid passing game, which became erratic to say the least. Tension gripped the entire team, who, standing on threshold of greatness, failed to attain the level of consistency their fans, who had travelled down in four special trains, had become accustomed to. Southampton, however, rose to the occasion as a team. This became the deciding feature and the one that gave Southampton victory. Missing from the replay was the over-exuberant tackling of the first meeting, and this may have attributed to Millwall's demise; however, it was the Saints who were pulled up for the first foul of the afternoon, and one incident involving Dave Nicol confirmed to many that this was not going to be Millwall's day. The Scot was in an excellent position when he was pulled up for a foul by the referee Mr Kingscott. Many observers thought it purely accidental, but this was one of many odd decisions Kingscott made during the course of the game that clearly unsettled an already nervous-looking Millwall.

An uncharacteristic lapse by Burgess let in the Saints, but the powerful Scot was bailed out by the watchful Walter Cox, who saved at the expense of a corner. Ominously, Southampton's fluid approach was making inroads that rattled Millwall into conceding a countless number of niggling free-kicks. A sudden Millwall break saw Gettins get away, but he was stopped in his tracks by Meehan's clearance. Southampton returned to the attack through their outside-left Turner, who had been a constant worry to Millwall in the first match, but as the ball was swung out to his position he was mysteriously laid-out. It appeared to have been the result of an off-the-ball incident, and the blow, whether administered by accident or design, certainly affected him for the remainder of the game.

Millwall's defence, so often the mainstay, started to get very ragged, and this was emphasised when Southampton took the lead on 23 minutes when Alf Milward managed to out-muscle the Titan Burgess off the ball to smash home a cracking shot past Cox's despairing dive. The Lions 'keeper was nearly beaten again moments later when Harry Wood fired in an effort, which Eddie Allan thumped clear. Millwall's riposte was a well-placed Joe Gettins shot that went just over before Saints 'keeper Jack Robinson was brought into action twice in quick succession and Dryburgh sent in another screamer which flew just wide. Having settled a little, Millwall started to show some mettle as the game opened up, and an equaliser looked likely until Gettins was caught in possession before he could get his shot away. Southampton's response saw efforts from Milward and Wood, the latter forcing Cox to punch over the bar, and this brought the first half to an end.

A buoyant Southampton came at Millwall at the start of the second half when a Wood shot caused some panic in the Millwall goalmouth before the ball was finally hacked clear. Failure to capitalise on a couple of decent openings from Gettins and then Nicol were punished when Southampton claimed their second goal on the hour, helped in no small way by another erroneous decision by the referee. The luckless Joe Gettins appeared to have been fouled by Southampton's Peter Meehan, but incredibly the free-kick was awarded against him, and to rub salt into the wound it was Meehan's kick that led to the goal. Meehan put Chadwick in possession, who stood back to admire the result of his ill-gotten gain after supplying Milward to thunder home another brilliant strike, which flattened a tired-looking and leg-weary Millwall.

At this juncture both the Millwall players and supporters must have realised the game was up; although Banks forced Robinson to bring off a wonderful save with a fierce free-kick. But it was Saints who confirmed their overall superiority to register a third. In the last minute the ubiquitous Milward was involved in setting-up Jimmy Yates, whose shot nestled in the back of Cox's net. So the gallant run of east London's finest was over, but a promising future beckoned, not only for the following season but beyond.

Within weeks of their finest hour the euphoric air surrounding Millwall's feat subsided, when another crisis loomed. A plan to increase the size of the Millwall Dock was announced, which put the very existence of Millwall Football Club in jeopardy. Following the notice to quit the East Ferry Road ground, their blossoming advance as a power in football was about to be nipped in the bud. All the accolades that had come with their splendid achievements during a momentous campaign would be meaningless. The fast approaching season of 1900–01 appeared as though it would be Millwall's last in their very short and chequered history.

With no amenities and virtually no players, it was a distressing time for all concerned, but with an iron will and help from their friends they began a race against time to find a new site at which to base the club. Fortunately, one was found further down the East Ferry Road close to the site of the old Lord Nelson Enclosure. Against all the odds, the Herculean efforts of Elijah Moor and his trusty band of volunteers had paid off, and the construction of the new ground and the laying a new pitch was completed just in time for the start of the 1901–02 campaign. The new ground would be simply known as North Greenwich and would be Millwall's home for the next nine years, where they played out their remaining days on the Isle of Dogs until their relocation to the south side of the Thames at Cold Blow Lane in 1910.

But we are getting ahead of ourselves here a little, and despite the bad news Millwall did manage to retain the likes of Herbert Banks, Arthur Millar, Willy Dryburgh and the evergreen Joe Gettins, but due to the prevailing uncertainty they lost the services of the excellent Walter Cox and the full-backs Charlie Burgess and Eddie Allan, who both went to Newcastle United, while skipper Dave Smith signed for Notts County. Others like Hugh Goldie, John Brearley, Dave Nicol and Hugh Robertson also departed for pastures new. The unsettling events off the pitch did not seem to affect the team, however, as they prospered in both the Leagues the club competed in during the initial North Greenwich season (they finished fourth in the Southern League and took the runners'-up spot in the Western League), which encouraged a general feeling that another distinguished Cup run could be on the cards.

Millwall's previous exploits in the competition saw them exempt until the first round proper, and when the draw was made it paired them, and you could not script it, with an away tie at Aston Villa. With the Football Championship flag fluttering over Villa Park, Millwall were probably the only club Villa wanted, but Villa would certainly not have been Millwall's first choice.

Following such an upheaval, the turnover of playing personnel during a traumatic close-season saw Millwall have eight players making their FA Cup debuts for the club, including left-back Tommy Davidson, a Cup winner with Bury when they thrashed Millwall's conquerors Southampton 4–0 in the previous year's Final. Unfortunately for poor old Tom and his colleagues, they found themselves on the wrong end of a 5–0 thumping from a rampant and vengeful Villa side. A 5–2 scoreline would have shown a fairer reflection of the tie. The game was played at fast and furious pace despite the sodden state of the field of play, with Millwall starting the brighter and only being denied the opening goal by Crabtree's fine play. Surviving this scare Villa switched the play, which culminated in Millwall's new custodian, Fred Griffiths, having to come haring out to clear the danger. It was another newcomer to the ranks, right-back Hartley Shutt, one of four former Swindon Town players in the Lions line up, who appeared from nowhere to clear what appeared a certain goal with a massive clearance after Athersmith and John Devey had carved open the Millwall defence.

Just before Villa scored, Bertie Banks, a month away from gaining his one and only England cap, saw George miraculously save his goal-bound strike as both sets of forwards showed plenty of pace and skill on a surface that was fast turning into a morass. The home team's shooting, which had been their Achilles heel in the three matches the previous season, was much improved, with their aim and direction devastating this time around. Firstly, Devey scored via the underside of the bar, before Johnson's determined drive gave Griffiths no chance for Villa's second. Sandwiched in-between was Banks's effort that came within a whisker of an equaliser before Millwall fell further behind. A swift and telling move down Villa's left gave Johnson in the chance to fire home with Griffiths rooted to the spot.

The Lions opened sprightly enough at the start of the second half but could find no way through a well-organised Villa defence, as the run of the ball was certainly going Villa's way. This was highlighted when Steve Smith's hit-and-hope shot squeezed through a forest of legs and past an unsighted Griffiths for number four. The unplayable Johnson hit Villa's fifth to complete a well earned hat-trick. A well-contested game was the overall verdict, the result being a little unkind to Millwall's endeavours in which Dryburgh and Banks were the pick of the forwards, while centre-half George Henderson also showed up well, as did the backs Shutt and Davidson. Welsh international 'keeper Griffiths was in great form despite the five goals. It came as a blow that the envisaged Cup run ended as early as it did, and as a result the club coffers suffered.

As mentioned previously, Millwall's threat of closure came as a nasty surprise, but after many debates and public meetings a vibrant current of enthusiasm ensued for which there was only one decision possible, to carry on. The result of all this was to give the club's long-standing servant Elijah Moor one almighty headache. His first task was to convert a piece of wasteland into something resembling a football pitch and with barely six weeks in which to do it. Well, Elijah did manage it, and, as they say, the rest is history. It was Aston Villa who magnanimously agreed to officially open the new ground with a match on 18 September 1901, and their team included the former Lions Hartley Shutt, Tommy Wilson and the legendary pair of Arthur Millar and Bertie Banks.

The honour of becoming the first opponents to play at North Greenwich in an FA Cup game fell to Bristol Rovers for an immediate-round tie in December 1901. As usual, the playing staff had been overhauled during the summer, and the team opposing Rovers contained not one player from the side that had faced Villa earlier in the year. There had been some doubt about the match going ahead due to the inclement weather, as the rain had left the pitch in a wretched state. Surprisingly, the referee deemed the pitch playable following his inspection. Terrible surface or not, it was the visitors who adapted better and over the 90 minutes looked the more accomplished team. The Lions, now under the captaincy of centre-forward Ben Hulse, made heavy weather (no pun intended) of the horrendous conditions, with chances few and far between. It came as no surprise, therefore, when half-time arrived with the score sheet blank, with Welsh international Ernie Watkins being the pick of Millwall's new men.

Some much-needed excitement at the start of the second half saw an early Lions icon in the making, when goalkeeper John 'Tiny' Joyce denied Rovers on two occasions with worthy saves from Jones and Lamb. The game was then held up for a short period when Joe Gettins was in the wars after being injured. Another Millwall move was ended in great fashion when Dunn executed a clearance that saw the ball disappear over the horizon towards the River Thames. Joyce was then called upon to make a couple of saves as Rovers began to take control, and when Lions right-back Bill Halley miskicked Becton was on hand to put Rovers ahead. The only surprise was how long it took the visitors to score. However, the lead was short-lived as it kick-started Millwall into action for the first time in the match. Cartledge, the Rovers goalkeeper who had just one previous save to make, went missing when needed as Watkins, from almost on the goalline, prodded home a cross that had evaded everyone else in the vicinity. The Lions then nearly claimed an undeserved winner when John Hamilton's goal-bound strike was hoofed clear by Griffiths. But with the match heading for a 1–1 draw, Millwall breathed a sigh of relief in the dying embers when Rovers were caught offside twice when excellently placed.

For the replay Millwall made one change by bringing in local boy Dave Maher for the indisposed Gettins in what turned out to be a poor advert for a football match. A long-standing feature in some of the Millwall versus Rovers matches down the years is that many have been rather bland and uneventful, and this match was no exception. For one reason or another it has been difficult to explain why, so it is all the more remarkable that this instantly forgettable game was settled by the afternoon's only bright spot. A cracking goal from Jones that was totally out of character from what had gone on before and what was to follow as the Millwall roar became a muted meow as they bowed out without much of a fight.

3. 'Rise like Lions after Slumber'

The title of this chapter is a line from a poem by Percy Bysshe Shelley (1792–1822) and succinctly sums up Millwall's situation exactly, especially following the heady days of 1900 and the dark ones that ensued 12 months later when the Lions' very existence was severely threatened. With their future secured for the time being, Millwall began to build upon their reprieve with a renewed vigour to seek further glories in all competitions, including the FA Cup, for the eagerly anticipated 1902–03 season. In the ensuing days and months they were to roar like the Lions of the South of old, on more than one occasion. They were boosted by some very significant signings during the summer when Bob Hunter managed to cajole the England goalkeeper John Sutcliffe from Bolton, who was accompanied south by another ex-Trotter Harry Astley, and in keeping with the club's Caledonian tradition they were joined by two former Celts: outside-right Martin 'Mickey' Moran and the Scottish international full-back Dave Storrier, who had been persuaded to throw in his lot with Millwall after he had agreed to join a Football League club. Ben Hulse continued as captain.

Other than the 8–0 dismantlement of Watford, the League form leading up to the FA Cup had been patchy, but different competitions can lead to a change of fortunes, and this duly happened in Millwall's case when fate gave them an immediate opportunity to exact revenge over the team that had abruptly ended their involvement the year previous, Bristol Rovers. The two were drawn to face one another at Stapleton Road for an intermediate-round match just prior to Christmas. It would take Millwall three attempts to dispose of a stubborn opponent, and unlike the former season's matches these were something to remember.

It was Millwall who commenced the game, with Dick Jones replacing the effervescent Joe Gettins at inside-left, but it was the home team who attacked first, and only Andy

Easton's swift intervention stopped Rovers taking the lead. After gaining a foothold, Millwall were hit by a sucker-punch when Corbett's break found Wilcox, whose rasping shot beat Sutcliffe and gave Rovers the lead and put the visitors back to square one. Following the goal the game settled down into a phase of glorious end-to-end football, which was so unlike the tie when the teams last met in the Cup. The nearest Millwall came to scoring was when Rovers' Johnny McLean erred before the danger was cleared, and Rovers, now in the ascendancy, were themselves stunned in the 20th minute. As a Bristol move faltered, a quick-fire response saw Harry Astley fire home the equaliser before anyone in the Bristol defence could react.

Rovers then had two attacks nullified, with Marriot caught offside in the first and in the other Corbett was penalised for handball. Weathering further Rovers aggression, Millwall seized the initiative from Bristol's grasp to gain the lead through Harry Astley. The ex-Bolton man was on fire as he registered his second goal with a long-range effort that gave Cartlidge no chance. Millwall were flying and reached the break 2–1 up. As expected, Rovers intensified their efforts in the second half by forcing an early corner which came to nothing, but they nearly scored twice in as many minutes as Millwall's goal came under heavy pressure. The intensity was so much that even skipper and centre-forward Ben Hulse had to show his defensive qualities when robbing the dangerous Marriott at the expense of yet another corner. But Marriott was not to be denied his one moment of glory, and he set up John Graham, who, in keeping with game, scored another well-struck goal to make it 2–2. An injury to Mickey Moran meant the Lions had to play the last 10 minutes a man short as the hard-pressed Sutcliffe showed all his experience as Millwall clung on for the draw.

For the replay Millwall were unchanged, with Moran being declared fit after picking up a knock in the first match. On a bright but windy day a cat-and-mouse game ensued, but after nearly two hours of football the tie was still undecided at 0–0. The last 10 minutes of extra-time were forfeited due the encroaching darkness, which must have come as a welcome relief to the spectators – most of whom were chilled to the bone.

A third match was therefore needed to settle the tie, with Millwall toying with the idea of using Reading again, while Rovers for some reason favoured Birmingham. The conclusion of this mini-saga was to take place three days before Christmas when Rovers' wish for a Midlands venue was granted when both sides faced each other at Villa Park for the right to entertain Luton Town in the first round proper. Making a welcome return was Joe Gettins, who came in at the expense of the unfortunate Harry Astley. It was Joe who forced Cartlidge into making the first notable save of the game when he fired from a difficult angle in a brisk opening session that saw both teams looking for an early advantage. The prominent Gettins was Millwall's main threat in the early stages with his customary Corinthian style of courage and no small amount of skill as Millwall began to dominate. The pace slackened a tad following a flurry of attacks as both teams attempted a more subtle approach, but despite having the better of the game the Lions found themselves still deadlocked at 0–0 when half-time arrived.

It was Rovers who began the second half the brighter of the two teams as Sutcliffe denied Wilcox from long range, before Millwall's Mickey Moran showed a clean pair of heels to his unfortunate marker Griffiths but let himself down by placing his centre into the grateful hands of Cartlidge. At the other end Dave Storrier put in a hefty clearance as Rovers tried to prise an opening before further Bristol probing was halted by Ernie Watkins's fine run and dribble that took him clear to supply Hulse, who failed by a whisker to get his head onto the Welshman's sublime cross. A desperate tussle appeared to be heading for a further stint of extra-time with little likelihood of a goal arriving within the scheduled 90 minutes. Then, all of a sudden, just like London buses two turned up at once. With barely four minutes left, the first goal came when Millwall skipper Ben Hulse managed to rid himself of his marker to thump home a splendid goal. That sent the Millwall fans and players crazy in celebration for what surely must have been the winner. But just like the conductor of a packed bus's refrain of 'there's another behind', right on cue another goal came trolling along. With virtually the last word Mickey Moran capped a fine display by firing home the second, to leave Rovers crestfallen with no time to respond.

The attraction of two other Cup ties in close proximity to North Greenwich had an adverse effect on Millwall's gate which numbered just under 10,000, who were there to witness the game against old rivals Luton Town in the first round proper. The visitors, who were about to play their fifth FA Cup tie of the season, had already disposed of Queen's Park Rangers 3–0 and had then thumped Lowestoft and Fulham 5–1 and 6–1 respectively, before adding the scalp of Kidderminster with another 3–0 victory. Millwall's form of late had been electrifying, with five straight victories in the Southern League, which included the 7–1 trouncing of the perennial whipping boys Watford.

By virtue of scoring twice in the opening 10 minutes of each half, Millwall put paid to Luton's interest for another year; however, the Hatters did not just roll over and take defeat, as Lions 'keeper John Sutcliffe would testify, as he was called into action on many occasions when Luton were calling the shots. Their supremacy came following Dick Jones's departure through a clash of heads that gave Luton the advantage of an extra man. Millwall started the match playing into the wind after Luton had won the toss. Whatever benefit Luton had, however, was undermined within minutes of the kick-off when they fell behind after just eight minutes. It was Welshman Ernie Watkins who gave the Lions the early breakthrough when he evaded the attentions of both Lindsay and Fred Hawkes to thump home a spectacular opener past a statuesque Frail to give the home team just the start they needed.

Luton's riposte was instant, although the prominent Allsopp was pulled up for offside, but it was his teammate Gall who was next to cause the Lions some concern when he cashed in on Dave Storrier's lapse only to be denied by Sutcliffe's intervention. It was around this time that Jones sustained his injury, and this allowed Luton to gain control as they created an opening through Jimmy Riley's error that let in Allsopp, but his poor cross went behind for a goal-kick. Luton's Bert Moody, who later played for Millwall before and after World War One, was then presented with a chance but shot straight at Sutcliffe, whose form in goal brought him an England recall the following month.

Still Luton poured forward, using the extra man to telling effect when they won a corner that caused panic in the Millwall rearguard, which seemed to take an eternity to clear before Durrant relieved the anxiety by putting his shot over the bar. A couple of chances presented themselves to Millwall when Astley and Moran were denied, the latter just as he was about to pull the trigger. Luton's White then forced Sutcliffe into a spectacular save, and moments later he was relieved to see Gall screw the ball wide when it seemed easier to score. The Hatters were left to agonise once again when the inspired Sutcliffe proved unbeatable after foiling further efforts from Luton's pair of marauding strikers Gall and White.

Sutcliffe's day got even better at the start of the second half with another fine piece of goalkeeping following Storrier's failure to clear his lines. At the other end it was Frail's turn to earn some plaudits when both Hulse and Watkins had the opportunity to extend Millwall's lead. Luton's Blessington then profited on Easton's mistake but in doing so was penalised for fouling Sutcliffe, and from the resultant free-kick Millwall increased their lead in the 55th minute. Millwall, now back to full complement, saw the redoubtable Dick Jones pick his spot at the Cubitt Town End to finish off a splendid move that had involved the entire Millwall forward line.

With heavy rain falling, control of the ball was becoming extremely difficult, but it did not seem to affect the imperious Sutcliffe, who accomplished another fine save from the persistent Durrant. When Luton conceded a needless corner it invited a sustained spell of Millwall pressure in which Frail produced a couple decent saves including one from Astley's header; however, the noose around Luton's neck was pulled to its extremities when Williams was penalised for handball. The Hatters left-back could only stand and watch as Easton's superb free-kick found Hulse to bury his flashing header past a despairing Frail into the net for number three, with around 30 minutes left. Luton's frustration now manifested itself, with Bob Hawkes fouling Jones before Durrant was cautioned for a swipe at Easton, which was followed by another foul on his full-back partner Dave Storrier. This assault went unpunished and left the Scottish international limping for the remainder of the game, but despite conceding a few free-kicks for retaliatory fouls Millwall ran out deserved winners for a place in round two.

Since the draw was made (Millwall were the first out of the hat) the main topic of conversation in and around Millwall had been all about the visit of the once-mighty Preston North End to the island. The Lancashire club had been FA Cup winners in 1889, the year in which they had also achieved the elusive double by capturing the Football League Championship. Now languishing in the Second Division, they had beaten Manchester City in the previous round by three goals to one and were making their first visit back to the East Ferry Road since they were amazingly beaten 9–1 in a friendly match in November 1895.

Millwall made one change from their earlier success with Astley stepping down yet again for the available Joe Gettins. A raw winter's day brought the usual gusty winds and rain, and winning the toss would be vital. As the captains, Ben Hulse and Peter McBride, waited for the referee Mr Adams to do the honours, it became apparent when a hearty cheer went up that indicated Ben had called correctly and had, not surprisingly, decided to play with the elements in his favour. After North End started the game Millwall set about them by winning possession almost at once, with Preston's only effort in the opening period coming from Dicky Bond, who fired narrowly wide. Mickey Moran was the first Lion to test the visitors' resolve, but the move was terminated for offside. The pacey Scot then forced Preston 'keeper McBride to kick clear as he raced onto Gettins's through ball, and further attacks from the same pairing were causing Preston some problems before another promising move came to nothing when Johnny Bell fluffed his shot.

Ernie Watkins became the beneficiary of Moran's next piece of trickery but was denied by Derbyshire's last-ditch tackle before Gettins hoisted another effort just over the bar. Finally, the pressure paid off when excellent Millwall's ball retention paid dividends in the 20th minute. The masterful Gettins took a left-wing pass in his stride to feed Moran, whose stunning drive from 15 yards beat McBride for the opener. Not a team to rest on their laurels, the Lions went in search another goal and nearly got it when a corner from Jones was just missed by the foraging Hulse, who for his troubles found himself entangled in the Preston net. The game resumed after some running repairs, which led North End to test Sutcliffe, who up until then had been a virtual spectator. Even so, it needed Dick Jones to complete the clearance that laid the foundations for Millwall to take a two-goal lead in the 25th minute. Moran was at it his mesmerising best and latched on to Dick's pass to force a corner, from which North End's full-back Derbyshire's clearance was intercepted by the energetic Jones, who immediately set-up Gettins to notch the second. Gaining some respite, Preston, in a rare foray into the Millwall half, earned a free-kick when Easton was pulled up for a foul, for which he was given a dressing down by the official.

Excellent covering from Dick Jones following another Preston attack at the other end of the pitch led to Millwall winning a corner-kick that lead to their third goal. Moran took advantage of McBride's partial clearance to accurately lob the stranded 'keeper. Millwall could now enjoy their half-time cuppa by sitting on a three-goal lead. Despite having the weather in their favour at the start of the second half, North End were soon back-peddling under Millwall's onslaught, which saw the industrious Jones bring the best out of McBride, who made a stunning save. Sutcliffe, not to be outdone, emulated this feat with an equally magnificent stop to deny Pearson. The visitors now began to find some much-needed momentum. But their lack of control and loss of hard-won possession was costing them dearly, and Sutcliffe was taking an inordinate amount of goal-kicks to confirm Preston's wayward shooting.

Millwall continued to outplay their guests as Gettins and Moran carved out further openings before Moran and skipper Ben Hulse built up an attack that ended when Hulse's pass found the irrepressible Dick Jones. The indefatigable Welshman capped a memorable display with the fourth and best goal of the afternoon to underline Millwall's total dominance. With their fate finally sealed, North End found no solace in what was left of the match. Their token consolation was reward for their persistence, which eventually paid-off when Pearson's splendid cross-shot flashed past a surprised Sutcliffe to bring the scoring to an end.

A near everyday feature of the island, especially in winter, is the habitual presence of wind, sleet, snow and rain that always had a bearing in the outcome of many matches, and the one against Everton, which the Lions would now welcome for the right to contest a semi-final place, was no different. The Toffees, as Everton were nicknamed, were, like the previous visitors Preston, founder members of the Football League but surprisingly had never won the FA Cup – an honour they would have to wait another three years to achieve. On the day of the game Millwall took to the field in an all-white strip, because as was customary in those far-off days it was the home team who had to change if there was a colour clash. Everton appeared in their usual blue shirts and white shorts. Prior to the game Millwall had lost the services of the exceptional George Morris with injury, which would ultimately cost him a place in the semi-final. Ernie Watkins filled in for George at left-half, with Gettins moving to inside-left, and Watkins's place on the left flank went to the versatile Dick Jones. Morris's unavailability meant a recall for the patient Harry Astley. Everton's League form in Division One had been a bit indifferent, but in the Cup they had beaten both Portsmouth (5–0) and Manchester United (3–1) at Goodison Park.

The playing surface was again the victim of some terrible weather, making the game a lottery. Hulse correctly called with the spin of the coin again, and his decision to play with wind at their backs was no surprise. The pre-match colour clash appeared to be negligible, with Millwall's white turning brown and Everton's blue faring no better with only 15 minutes played. A crowd of around 14,000 saw both sides attacking in the early stages, with the tiny Moran making light of the conditions to be Millwall's best performer in this period. The latest addition to the Lions' ranks of internationals, John Sutcliffe, showed why he had been recalled to the England team when effortlessly fielding shots from Young and Taylor, before a promising Millwall raid was prematurely ended when Jimmy Riley's eagerness caused him to handle. Dick Jones then put in a lovely cross which Astley thumped over the bar as the Lions began to find their feet on a treacherous pitch, while the Toffees' finesse approach play was not as effective in the conditions. Jones was then at it again, powering in another centre which Moran put wide when he should done better. The excitement began to mount with plenty of thrills and spills, with both custodians making confident saves as Millwall started to edge their famous opponents back on the defensive.

Approaching the half-hour mark, the tie was turning into an excellent advert for Cup football, and Millwall conjured up a goal their early play merited. A fabulous build up on the right saw the ball laid back to Ernie Watkins, who without breaking stride hammered his drive from fully 35 yards. From his initial reaction Whitely in the Everton goal seemed to have the shot covered just above his head, but a momentary lapse saw the greasy ball slip from his grasp and into the net after 28 minutes as pandemonium broke out all around North Greenwich. Everton refused to be unruffled by this reverse as they continued to play with discipline that nearly gained them an instant reward when Sutcliffe slipped making a save, giving Taylor an opportunity, but the England 'keeper's timely recovery brought more wild cheering from the crowd. Taylor threatened again as Riley was forced to concede a corner, but it was Millwall who were asking most of the questions, with the busy Jones keeping the Everton right flank at full stretch as the Lions gained a succession of corners, all of which were unproductive. Jack Sharp (later a double international at cricket and football) then missed a good chance for Everton before Astley responded in kind with two of his own, which saw Whitley redeem himself somewhat before Mr Kirkham of Stoke brought a fascinating half to an end.

Everton's renewed vigour at the start of the second half saw them dominate for a solid spell as they battered Millwall's goal and looked very likely to score, but the commanding presence of Sutcliffe, who was producing another master class, saw off the all the efforts they could throw at him. As the wind picked up, the rain became remorseless, and anything Everton came up with was repelled. A further period of Everton pressure was then brought to an end when Walter Abbott shot wide following a gutsy run. The pitch then took the full force of a pitiless hailstorm that added to the unpleasantness, which saw the official speedily take the teams off for five minutes to see if the rain would abate.

The 1903 encounter with Everton was an intense affair which Millwall (in white) won 1–0, and here Everton are denied by the combined efforts Dave Storrier (left), goalkeeper John Sutcliffe and Andy Easton. [Bowden Bros]

On the resumption, the pitch resembled a quagmire and looked unplayable, but credit must be given to the teams as the frenetic pace never slackened for the remainder of the match. Having weathered the Everton offensive, Millwall went chasing a second goal, and they were given a splendid opportunity to put the game beyond doubt when they were awarded a penalty. Up stepped Dave Storrier to seal the victory over his old club, only to see his drive cannon off the crossbar. Reacting quickly, the Scot reached the ball first, only to see his header fall into the grateful arms of Whitley. Frustration began to creep in and the

A scene from the Millwall versus Everton tie of 1903 that saw the Lions progress to their second semi-final in three years. The match was played in terrible conditions and was won by an incredible goal from Ernie Watkins. [Unknown]

Millwall reached their second semi-final in 1903, and of the 11 players shown in this team group eight would appear in all seven FA Cup ties that season; they are: Easton, Riley, Sutcliffe, Bell, Watkins, Moran, Hulse and Jones. [*Sunday Pictorial*]

Everton 'keeper was lying prone on the ground when Gettins and a couple other Millwall forwards tried to prise the ball from his hands, but peace was restored after the intervention of his Toffee teammates.

In desperation, Everton threw everything into attack, but the imperturbable trio of Sutcliffe, Easton and Storrier were unyielding in their defence. But Sharp and Settle did get clean through for what was their last meaningful attack but were denied by Sutcliffe's brave save at Settle's feet which momentarily laid out the giant 'keeper. The Yorkshireman rose back on his feet and was ready to carry on as Everton's Jimmy Settle became the target of the boo-boys for what they perceived as an intentional foul on the Lions 'keeper. Sufficiently wound-up, Settle clashed with Sutcliffe again moments later, but before the pair came to blows, Lions skipper Ben Hulse stepped in to calm down the two England internationals. That incident was virtually the last of the action, and it was a shame that an exciting encounter had finished on such a sour note. Shortly afterwards, the final whistle sounded, which saw the hero of the hour Ernie Watkins carried shoulder high back to the dressing rooms, where the directors congratulated the players on a splendid performance before they retired to take a substantial tea at the Lord Nelson. So Millwall had done it again, claiming a second coveted semi-final spot in three years as Bob Hunter the trainer, accompanied by the players, retreated back to the Essex training quarters to prepare for a meeting with Derby County at Villa Park.

There appeared to be no new injury worries before the Derby game; although, in the last match before big day the players' thoughts were obviously elsewhere as they went down unexpectedly 3–0 to Wellingborough. There was concern over John Sutcliffe's wellbeing, however, as he had stated that he had been feeling unwell in the days leading up to the Villa

Park clash. In his bid to get fully focused, he spent some time recuperating in the Midlands and met up with his teammates on the Friday before the game. Another player missing was Joe Gettins, whose job as a Reading schoolmaster meant he, like Sutcliffe, would have to rendezvous later. The Millwall party, including players and officials, would travel up from Euston on the Friday afternoon, and they would, in turn, be followed by thousands of their supporters on the Saturday morning. Among the excitement and banter on the trip up, the questions on the fans' lips would have been over Sutcliffe's fitness, but more importantly could Millwall reach their first-ever FA Cup Final? So, a fortnight after dispatching Everton, the Lions faced First Division Derby County, who were missing the legendary Steve Bloomer, while Millwall, Sutcliffe included, were unchanged.

Within 12 disastrous minutes of the 3.30pm kick-off the supporters' main question was brutally answered as Millwall's dreams lay in tatters, two goals down and a Final looking as remote as the Moon. The pre-match declaration of John Sutcliffe being fully recovered appeared not to be the case. His authority was undermined when County's Warren, on receiving the ball from a throw-in, from fully 50 yards hit the ball so high it would not have surprised anyone if it had come down encrusted with snow. The elements and human frailty took over as the ball caught in the wind, as Sutcliffe advanced from his goal in an attempt to catch the ball at its highest point but was temporarily blinded by the bright sunshine. Turning in horror, he saw the ball bounce once before entering the net. If John had stayed in his original place, he would have been on hand for a bread-and-butter save.

The Lions of the South, as Millwall became known; luck finally ran out against Derby County at Villa Park in the 1903 semi-final at Villa Park, and this photo shows a very crowded County goalmouth as Millwall attempt a breakthrough. [Bowden Bros London]

Joe Gettins, the famous amateur, is the only Millwall player to appear in two semi-finals (1900 and 1903), who also holds the record of making the most FA Cup appearances, 23 for the club during their Southern League days. [Unknown]

Jumping for joy, the County players could not believe their luck while the equally bemused Millwall lads stood there motionless, hands on hips. Five minutes later another catastrophe followed when the distraught 'keeper was again at fault. A shot from Derby's Boag was so soft that Sutcliffe could have thrown his cap on the ball as it sneaked over the line after it had rebounded off Storrier. It seemed that lady luck had deserted Millwall on the second-biggest day in their history. Even when County's Davis was carried off injured in the first half they could not raise their game enough to take the advantage of the extra man, as Morris organised the shortfall to great effect. Overcoming these unfortunate setbacks and a bout of self pity, Millwall rallied admirably to give an excellent account, but the contest was finally killed stone dead when Richards hit home the best goal of the game 11 minutes into the second half.

Millwall's day of woe continued unabated when a Jack Bell header look destined for net, but even that consolation was denied as County managed to scramble the ball to safety. Millwall bemoaned the lack of good fortune and, despite having a fair proportion of the match, the club and its supporters returned home disappointed once more. Both had to wait another 34 years before they reached the dizzy heights of the semi-finals again. But no one could probably feel the despair more than one of England's finest goalkeepers, John Sutcliffe, who during the close-season bade farewell to the island to join Manchester United.

4. Nowhere Men

The period leading up to World War One saw Millwall's well-earned Cup pedigree take a severe knock, with only the occasional high-profile game to reconcile the fans, who by this time had become used to the club being involved in decent runs. By now the competition was changing, and so was the game itself. Millwall's exploits over the previous three years had been recognised, and for the 1903–04 season they were exempt until the first round proper. An added bonus was the chance to meet clubs from the Football League, and this is exactly what they got when they drew First Division Middlesbrough. The reader by now should be in no doubt that choice of ends and the prevailing weather conditions at North Greenwich were the main factors to be taken into consideration come kick-off time. The playing surface, despite being liberally sanded, was often in a horrible mess with some parts underwater.

The new skipper was the summer arrival from Bristol Rovers, John McLean, and he carried on the great tradition of his predecessors by winning the toss at the Middlesbrough match and decided to take advantage of a stiff wind at their backs, so leaving the task of starting the match to Sandy Brown, the Boro centre-forward. Early Millwall pressure from Middlesbrough-born Joe Gettins and Ernie Watkins came to nothing as the surface began to cut up alarmingly. But overall both sets of players coped well in the muddy conditions, although it was the reason the visitors nearly took the lead when another newcomer, full-back General Stevenson, under hit a back pass to goalkeeper 'Tiny' Joyce, whose frantic interception from Atherton saved the day.

It was the former Scottish international Willie Maxwell who was the next to vie for an opening in the cloying mud, before Harry Astley drew the crowd's appreciation with a fine overhead attempt that narrowly missed; thereafter Millwall generally held sway for long spells. Boro's 'keeper Tim Williamson was forced to concede corners following efforts from McLean Gettins and Maxwell, before Blackett became Middlesbrough's saviour when clearing after his 'keeper's partial save from Astley's stinging drive.

The mud then denied Maxwell's effort, as it did Dick Jones's attempt that deserved better, and then Brown got the visitors on the move before being overwhelmed by the presence of Easton and Millar. Millwall's domination continued when Blackett's miskick let in Astley, but to the crowd's consternation Gettins was unable to free himself from the mire and failed to reach Astley's fine cross. Despite having wind assistance, Millwall had not made enough of their possession and were made to pay in the 41st minute when a Boro attack down the left caught the Lions by surprise and Goodson's cross found Brown, whose hard shot beat Joyce to take the wind out of Millwall's sails.

An uphill task was presented to Millwall at the start of the second half when, facing the wind, they began the brighter of the two teams when both Gettins and Jones were denied an equaliser by the surface, which enabled Boro to clear their lines and put Millwall under the cosh for the first time in the match. It was another close-season import, Willie Maxwell, who then caused the home fans to groan when he too was foiled by the pitch. This farcical scene was fast becoming the feature in the Lions' inability to overcome the conditions, as Boro's economical approach to the elements finally sealed Millwall's fate after 70 minutes. The live-wire Brown, hero of non-League Tottenham's Cup Final success in 1901, outfoxed Andy Easton in front of the goal to calmly take the ball around Joyce to notch his and his team's second goal, much to the delight of the travelling support. Millwall claimed Brown was offside, with 'keeper 'Tiny' Joyce protesting the loudest, but after consulting with his linesman Mr Hines the referee allowed the goal to stand.

Annoyingly, Millwall were still creating chances and missing them, with the most clear-cut arriving in the last 10 minutes or so when Williamson held a shot and was immediately besieged by four Millwall forwards in an attempt to force him over the line, but he was resolute enough to clear the ball for a corner. Following this escapade, most of the crowd began streaming for the exits, when Boro's Cassidy found himself in the clear only to be felled by Easton's tackle in the area for which Mr Hines awarded a penalty. It was 'Tiny' Joyce's turn to take centre stage as he produced a magnificent save, managing to paw the ball away for a corner to give the home support something to cheer about. With the game heading to its inevitable conclusion Millwall contrived to miss another couple of excellent chances before the final whistle blew as Millwall's hopes of producing another protracted run were swallowed-up in the mire of North Greenwich.

In the following season of 1904–05 the Lions were drawn away for the first time in over two years when they were faced with having to head up to Yorkshire to face the newly formed Bradford City. They had converted from rugby football in 1903 and were fast-tracked with undue haste into the Second Division of the Football League later that year. With home advantage and confidence soaring following a team-bonding exercise at Harrogate, City, after despatching a non-entity from the North East by the tune of nine goals to nil, looked a formidable opponent on paper who were eagerly awaiting the arrival of the 'Southern softies' to cause an upset by defeating a team with an excellent Cup record. City were further encouraged by Millwall's lowly position in the Southern League.

Scottish international Willie Maxwell was an exceptional goal taker, with 34 from 54 games in his two seasons with Millwall, whose three goals in the FA Cup was the result of his hat-trick at Bradford City in January 1905. [Unknown]

This intermediate-round tie would be the last Millwall would have to encounter as further expansion of the competition meant that in future the Lions would have to enter the competition at either the first or third-round stage. Having won their previous two fixtures, Millwall went into the tie with a fairly settled line up, which included the usual bevy of Scots including the pacey Billy Hunter, the two Bobby's, McLaren and McLean, and another signing, wing-half John Blythe from West Ham, plus the return of old favourite Jack Calvey from Nottingham Forest. But it was the vastly experienced striker Willie Maxwell who gave City cause to remember him (23 goals in 29 League matches in the previous season), as he led the Lions to an emphatic 4–1 victory with a finely executed hat-trick. The Millwall captain's prowess in winning the toss was again in evidence when John McLean called correctly to let City have the kick-off.

McLean must have been patting himself on the back as his team raced into a two-goal lead, which they held comfortably until the interval. Following a near miss from Calvey, it was Maxwell who fired the visitors ahead within 15 minutes, his shot passing through the legs of a nervous looking Bradford 'keeper Mearns – a lapse that did not go down too well with the locals. But if the small band of travelling fans were ecstatic now, then 10 minutes later they were really over the moon when old stager Dick Jones put the Lions two up after heading home a 25th-minute corner-kick. The City team were looking very tense and nearly conceded a third when Maxwell came within a whisker of heading in Hunter's superb cross. Any inroads City attempted to make into the Millwall half during this time were usually nipped in the bud by the defence, which was ably marshalled by the formidable General Stevenson.

City must have got the 'hair-dryer treatment' from manager Bob Campbell at half-time as Millwall were forced back on the defensive for long spells for the first time in the game just after the interval. Inevitably a City goal arrived when Conlin's fine shot reduced the arrears in around the 66th minute, and then they nearly drew level when McGrachen thumped his effort against an upright. The contest was evening itself out as Millwall, with Joyce and McLean excelling, survived a further spate of strong City attacks. Having failed to breach Millwall's defence again, it was left to Maxwell to burst Bradford's bubble when he notched a third, and close to the end of the match City's fire was finally extinguished when the Scot completed his hat-trick with Millwall's fourth.

Bogey team Southampton awaited Millwall in the next round, nearly five years after they had ended the Lions' ambitions in the semi-final. This first-round tie at The Dell resulted in a similar annoying loss to that 1900 encounter. Millwall did manage to score this occasion, but as far as Cup football goes the Saints had proved to be Millwall's nemesis, and to this day the south-coast club have yet to taste defeat at the hands of the Lions in any Cup competition.

The all-round superiority of the Saints' forwards' ability was the difference between the teams, and it came as no surprise to anyone that 'Tiny' Joyce's took the accolades for his heroics between the sticks. He became the Lions' saviour on more than occasion in a game of relentless pace and untiring effort. Skipper John McLean's habitual success with the coin toss counted for nothing following a whirlwind start. Southampton broke away through John Fraser, whose shot-cum-cross was going nowhere until Charlie Webb retrieved it. He promptly returned it for Fred Harrison to head home before a Millwall player had touched the ball. Even at this early stage Saints' left flank was causing Millwall endless problems. Joyce, with a nonchalant tip over the bar, then foiled Webb as more sustained pressure saw Millwall at sixes and sevens under the onslaught.

It was no surprise, therefore, when the Southampton netted again when Bluff sneaked his way through for number two with less than 10 minutes played. Billy Hunter and John Blythe finally responded with Millwall's first promising move, but it floundered on a resolute defence before Millwall dragged themselves back into contention when Hunter fired in a shot that glanced off Benson into the net. But the self-congratulatory mood abruptly altered when Southampton restored the two-goal cushion when Edgar Bluff scored his second within a minute. Disappointingly for the two trainloads of Lions fans who ventured down to the game, Millwall's aspirations of lifting the 'pot' vanished in a game that produced four goals in the first 13 minutes.

Two goals awry, Millwall began to find their feet and some rhythm by laying siege to the Saints goal, with Jack Bradbury's stinging drive the closest the Lions came to scoring. But with the ever-dangerous Bluff on the prowl for his hat-trick, it was left to Joyce to deny him that honour with another splendid save. It left the Saints man shaking his head agonisingly, but he only had himself to blame for not claiming the match ball, as another two chances presented themselves later on; however, he blasted both of them wildly over the bar with only 'Tiny' to beat. In a Millwall raid Bradbury was clattered in the box, but the referee turned down the appeal for a penalty, probably assuming that there had already been too much excitement, before Bluff again and then Harrison were denied goals by hitting an upright and crossbar respectively, after which the official called time on a pulsating affair. In the course of the season Millwall bade farewell to sportsman supreme Joe Gettins, who played his last game for the club against Luton Town at home the previous November on his 30th birthday.

Millwall's form in both the Southern and Western Leagues in season 1905–06 had been patchy to say the least, and going into the home tie against 'Tiny' Joyce's home-town team of Burton United the Lions had lost the previous week's 'East End' derby at West Ham by the only goal. So a decent run in the Cup was essential, and Millwall were given the added fillip of an early goal in a game affected by typical Isle of Dogs weather – wet and windy. Due to the insufficient drainage, the pitch was a travesty, with pools of water still discernable when the game got underway. Making light of the conditions, Millwall went on to control much of this tie but had to rely on a strike from Sid Heaton for the game's only goal. It came within four minutes from the start when the former Accrington man converted Billy Hunter's cross to put his new club one up. If the supporters were expecting a goal glut then they were out of luck.

The reasons why Millwall did not add to their tally are twofold: one was their failure to take the chance when offered – culpable here was the normally reliable Dick Jones and summer arrival Percy Milsom, who ballooned one chance wastefully over bar – and the other was the outstanding performance of Clutterbuck in the Burton goal, who after a shaky start showed excellent manipulation of a greasy ball with added assurance. Despite Millwall's dominance, Burton's best efforts came initially from Davis, whose effort skimmed the Lions' crossbar, and just before the interval they fired another warning shot across

Millwall's bows with a fine effort, indicating the game was far from won. A bit more aggression entered Millwall's play at the start the second half, forcing Burton back on the ropes with Jack Bradbury leading the way. The visitors gained some initiative without really threatening the Lions goal, and when they did the accomplished Stevenson, who had came very close to gaining international honours the year before, went coolly about denying Burton the space they hoped to exploit with some exceptional tackling and positional play; however, it was Burton who had the final say when forcing an unfruitful corner as the game petered out into a fairly comfortable, if not convincing, 1–0 victory.

A difficult game awaited Millwall for first visit to Owlerton, later to be renamed Hillsborough in 1912, for a second-round encounter versus a Sheffield Wednesday side who had been Football League Champions in 1903 and 1904. They had been denied a shot at the Cup and League double twice after losing both FA Cup semi-finals in both of those years. The Lions spent a fortnight in preparation for this game at their Cup headquarters out at High Beech near Epping, where they realised a formidable task awaited them against a team who had only lost twice at home all season and whose team contained four England players. Nevertheless, the Lions set out from their Essex idyll very confident of causing an upset.

Missing the services of Percy Milsom, the victim of an overnight virus, Millwall turned this negative into a positive to take the lead in front of a crowd approaching 22,000 when the combination of Johnny Blythe, Dick Jones and Billy Hunter saw the young Scot stride forward a few paces to unleash a 30-yard effort past a startled Lyall in the 36th minute. Only the superb interventions of Wednesday's Layton denied Heaton and then Jones from Millwall adding to their lead as the visitors looked anything but overawed. After an embarrassing first half, Wednesday rallied sufficiently after the break to snatch an equaliser when 'Tiny' Joyce, of all people, made a fatal error. Thinking Stewart's effort was clearing the crossbar, he misjudged the flight, only to see the ball sail over his head and ricochet down from the underside of the bar and down onto the goalline. But the well positioned referee Mr Brodie immediately signalled that the ball had crossed the line and gave the goal. Wednesday, galvanised by Stewart's piece of good fortune, looked the more likely to achieve the win as both sides made strident attempts to secure the victory.

Following a splendid team performance at Sheffield, Millwall returned to their Essex base in readiness for Thursday's replay, the incentive being a home tie against First Division Nottingham Forest, a mouth-watering prospect which meant more money finding its way into club's kitty should they beat Wednesday first. Predictably, the North Greenwich weather was, as usual, inhospitable, with a gale-force wind that Millwall had to play into accompanied by a sudden hail storm, which delayed the start. When it relented somewhat, both teams got stuck into one another, but it was Wednesday who took an early lead when Davis sent in a swerving shot that caused Joyce some anxiety. In rushing out to attempt the clearance 'Tiny' dropped the ball at the feet of Simpson, the visiting outside-left, for an easy tap-in. Billy Hunter thought he had drawn the sides level, and so did the crowd, but their celebrations were cut short by a linesman's flag before Watkins narrowly failed to reach Jack Bradbury's inviting cross.

Hunter then saw Lyall save another of his efforts as the Lions went in search of parity, and then George Marshall fired in a tremendous shot which skimmed the crossbar. There

Millwall Football Club   *Feb 2nd 1906*

The following Players Trained here for their 'Cuptie' against Sheffield Wedensday under the able management of Mr. G. et. Saunders. Trainer. Bob Hunter: and we were highly satisfied with the accomadation

R. Hunter

G. Stevenson
J. Bradbury
J Blythe
A. E. Watkins
J. McLean
J. Heaton
R Campbell
H Murrall
P. Milton
J Wo Joyce
W B Hunter
R Jones

G. A. Saunders Manager

Before World War One Millwall normally went to their favoured retreat near Epping Forest for their important Cup ties and here are the players' and management's signatures approving their satisfaction of the accommodation before the meeting with Sheffield Wednesday in 1906. [Richard Lindsay]

then occurred the incident that turned the game on its head and which gave Wednesday an unassailable lead. The Owls' centre-forward Wilson appeared to have fouled Joyce when challenging for the ball; however, the giant Millwall custodian's temper got the better of him, and he foolishly exacted his retribution on his assailant, only for the referee, Mr Hines of Nottingham, to award a penalty-kick to Wednesday. The task of converting the spot-kick was given to Harry Davis, all 5ft 4in of him and one of Wednesday's England representatives. The pocket-sized Davis punished Joyce's momentary lapse of self-control with a successful attempt to give his side a two-goal lead at the interval.

The mutterings of the disconsolate Millwall fans at half-time centred on how their team would respond, with many concurring that Millwall's best chance of winning the tie had been up at Sheffield; however, Dick Jones raised the hopes of the fans at the beginning of the second half but he shot too high. Play switched from end to end, but neither 'keeper was severely tested; although Milsom's snap-shot did cause Lyall to concede a corner. By now the Lions must have realised that they were banging their heads against a brick wall, a fact underlined when the busy Simpson sent in a long-range strike which surprised Joyce who could only parry the shot to the loitering Chapman, who prodded home Sheffield's third and final goal.

After their experiences against teams from the Football League over last couple seasons, Millwall's 1906–07 Cup saga featured meetings against more familiar adversaries in Plymouth Argyle and Bristol Rovers. The Lions' form going into the Argyle match had been poor, having lost every match played in December, a run of seven straight defeats. By the turn of the year Millwall had halted the slump by warming up for the home tie against the Devon club when they obliterated Watford 10–1. The free-scoring Alf Twigg obtained a personal landmark when he grabbed five of the deluge. Comparisons between run-of-the-mill League football and the Cup should really be discounted out of hand, but psychologically Millwall had one small advantage over Plymouth, having already beaten them twice that season. A healthy-looking crowd of 14,230 packed into the North Greenwich ground as Millwall included one of their summer signings Fred Shreeves at right-back, who had been member of the Burton side beaten in the home tie 12 months earlier. Keeping goal for Argyle was none other than one of the Millwall heroes from 1903, John Sutcliffe.

The opening threats, as one would expect, came from Millwall, who netted very early on when Twigg converted Hunter's free-kick after he had been fouled, although the former Gainsborough Trinity man's effort was ruled out for offside. Sutcliffe then foiled Milsom by scooping a goal-bound effort away with great effect before Alf Dean had the misfortune of seeing his shot deflected to safety after hitting Argyle's defender Noon. As half-time loomed, the dangerous Billy Hunter was once again singled out for some extremely rough treatment from Argyle's rugged defenders, before skipper Stevenson became another casualty when he was led from the field with blood oozing from a knee injury.

Millwall were without Stevenson at the start of the second half, though he was hardly missed as the Lions dominated the period of play which saw Milsom clatter a post as an already pulsating Cup tie began to get quicker and more intense. The return of the Lions skipper back into the fray brought some rousing and hearty cheers. Argyle, as they had for a spell in the first half, began to get back into their stride when Swann went very close with an effort. The undercurrent of ill-feeling from the first half surfaced again, with both teams guilty of some malpractice before Millwall deservedly broke the deadlock. Goalkeeper 'Tiny' Joyce launched one of his mighty clearances, which Twigg deftly controlled in one swift movement to rattle Sutcliffe's crossbar with a cracking drive. Before the groans from the crowd could fill the air, however, the quick-witted Milsom buried his header beyond

Sutcliffe's reach, causing pandemonium to brake out all around the arena. The lead was no more than the Lions deserved, as they had kept up unrelenting pace with breathtaking athleticism. Tactically, the injury to Stevenson was beginning to be a worry to the defence, but the admirable Shreeves covered his skipper's misfortune with a magnificent performance which meant that Millwall crossed the winning line without too much trouble.

Beleaguered Plymouth were flagging, their strength sapped due to Millwall's persistent pressure, and as a result they lost their shape and became very ragged, as did some of their tackles with George Comrie becoming the latest crock. It seemed that the Lions possessed unlimited stocks of willpower and adrenalin as they went in search of the goal that would finally kill off Argyle's challenge. Two minutes remained when winger Alf Dean added the second to put the gloss on an unforgettable match. It had been an exhilarating display from both teams, a bit tetchy at times, but full of commitment and passion. This amazing game had left the older Millwall fans scratching their heads in wonderment, trying to recall if there had ever been a game played previously on the Isle of Dogs that had contained such unremitting pace as this one.

In the lead-up to the second-round tie at Bristol Rovers, the Lions nearly replicated the Watford result when they creamed Queen's Park Rangers 7–0 with Alf Twigg plundering another hat-trick. The recent triumphs that Millwall had achieved with their highly powered football would come at a price, however, and something had to give. Unfortunately the breaking point cropped up in the Rovers game, but even so the final result was a wee bit surprising. Since the Argyle match Millwall had welcomed two new additions to the squad, one being the returning, tireless, Sammy 'Snowball' Frost, who had left the club after the threatened closure in 1901 and who in meantime had, in 1904, become the first man from the Isle of Dogs to win a FA Cup-winners' medal, when Manchester City beat Bolton 1–0.

Joining Sam was his former City colleague and ex-England custodian, the controversial Jack Hillman. Hillman had already missed one complete season after the authorities had found him guilty of attempted bribery before and during a Burnley versus Nottingham Forest match in 1900. It was only his previous good conduct that had saved from being banned permanently. He had joined City a year after Frost, where later they became embroiled in another scandal after which Jack, Sam and many others of the City team, including the legendary Welshman Billy Meredith, were required to find alternate employment elsewhere, which many did with neighbouring Manchester United.

A week after making his first and winning start against Rangers, Jack Hillman took the place of 'Tiny' Joyce in the team. After winning the toss Millwall started in what was becoming their customary exuberant style. Dick Jones (who had also spent a season with Manchester City) and Percy Milsom combined to give Twigg the opening to add to his recent tally, but this time the lethal marksman mistimed his effort.

More than once Millwall had the opportunity to open the scoring, and they were made to rue their early extravagance when they fell behind following a decisive Rovers move, who then went two up in the blink of an eye. If this was not bad enough for the visitors, it got immeasurably worse when Hillman, in attempting to save the second, damaged his shoulder, which necessitated General Stevenson donning the goalkeeper's jersey. The skipper made a decent fist of his new role but could not stop Rovers adding a third in the second half. So bad was Hillman's injury that he was forced to retire from the game and so terminate one of the shortest playing careers in Millwall's history, with just two starts. To rub salt into the wound, this defeat meant the club were deprived not only of an experienced 'keeper but also a lucrative home tie against Woolwich Arsenal in the next round. For the record, the Rovers goals came from Jarvie, Clark and Hutchinson.

In January 1908 Millwall faced their first trip up to Lancashire for 12 years when they were drawn away to First Division Bury at Gigg Lane. The Shakers' halcyon days as prodigious Cup-fighters were fast disappearing into the mists of football history. Having won the Cup in 1900 and 1903, Bury still hold the record of the biggest winning margin in a Final from when they defeated Derby County 6–0 in 1903. Ironically, the two years they were victorious coincided with Millwall's two semi-final appearances. This encounter, like many of the Lions' Cup games, proved to be a tad tetchy against full-strength Bury, who had spent the previous week in special training at Lytham. Millwall had left their hideaway at Southend on the Friday for an overnight stay in Manchester before making the short trip to Bury on the morning of the game. The Lions started the match in what was their now accustomed trait of fast, exciting and tenacious football played with an edge, and they gave Bury an early fright when Billy Hunter, who within a year would find himself playing in the North after his transfer to Bolton Wanderers, had only Raeside to beat but contrived to fluff his shot. If Bill's effort was poor, so too was the double attempt by the Bury 'keeper to clear his lines. Twice the ball fell to the eager visiting attack, and Millwall's new boy, the Lancashire-born Dan Cunliffe, whose ping at goal was fisted out by Raeside, slipped the rebound to the lurking Dick Jones, who promptly dispatched his drive into the Bury net after just five minutes.

Millwall's early initiative put their star in the ascendancy as the tricky Hector Shand began dictating play on the right, with his uncanny knack of dropping his crosses in the right areas, which on two occasions necessitated the timely interceptions of Bury's full-back Lindsay, thus depriving Twigg the chance of extending Millwall's lead. After weathering the Millwall storm, Bury finally got into contention when Billy Hibbert broke into the Lions area to shot past the onrushing Joyce as both players collided into a heap. Fortunately, both resumed their places after some treatment, but this was a warning for the visitors. The same pair was at it again moments later but in a more conventional style when Hibbert's strike forced 'Tiny' to make a brilliant stop as the tempo began to quicken. MacMahon, Bury's other full-back, was being given a torrid time by Shand, but his colleague Lindsay again proved the saviour when he foiled the bubbly Dick Jones. Moments later, Dewhurst skimmed the Millwall crossbar with a powerful shot, while both Shreeve and Stephenson were working overtime to stem a string of Bury assaults.

Early in the second half Millwall had a let-off when the dangerous Hibbert and the former Manchester City player Booth set-up Currie, who missed his kick completely from a yard out. The persistent Hibbert was pulling the strings in midfield, and his prompting and probing allowed his teammates to find some alarming gaps in the Millwall defence. Finally the pressure told as the Lions buckled when Hibbert drew Bury level following a solo run that left Stevenson and Shreeve trailing in his wake before he placed his shot wide of the advancing Joyce. The goal unnerved Joyce who caused further flutters when he fumbled a strike from Kay, before the game turned with a sending off. Involved was Bury's England prospect and Man of the Match to that point Billy Hibbert, who took exception to the treatment he had been subjected to from George Comrie and Johnny Blythe. Hibbert, on impulse, suddenly aimed a flying kick at Comrie, hoping to land one if not both feet on some part of the defender's anatomy. This bit of kung-fu was seen by the referee Mr Barker of Hanley, whose only available action was to despatch the errant Hibbert from the playing area. The Bury man's lack of self-control marred a splendid personal and skilful performance, and for this act of folly he was later suspended for a month without pay.

The dismissal of the petulant Hibbert appeared to galvanise his colleagues as they pressurised Millwall's resolute rearguard that appeared to be holding out comfortably for a replay. Bury, on the other hand, not relishing a trip to London, conjured up a sting in the tail. They corralled the last remnants of energy to score the winning goal in the 88th minute. It was Rae, their forceful wing-half, who pounded down the wing to drive in a vicious, hard, low cross for the onrushing Currie to make amends for his horrendous miss earlier, and he lashed the ball past a bewildered Joyce to dent Millwall's ambitions once again.

Their early exits from the Cup during the previous few seasons had deprived Millwall of meeting two of the country's bigger clubs, namely Nottingham Forest in 1906 and local neighbours Woolwich Arsenal a year later. But the chance of meeting these two teams came around a lot sooner than most fans could have anticipated. Following a gritty and plucky performance at Luton Town in the first round, the Lions had the opportunity to face both of these clubs during the course of the 1908–09 campaign. The game at Luton was interesting in that it produced some characteristics that would become synonymous with Millwall Football Club over the years and which would be added to the list that already included such traits as spirit and ruggedness. These, and other descriptions, could now be condensed in the sobriquet 'The Lions of the South', which they were given after their daring-do exploits at the dawn of the 20th century. All of the Lions' features were abundantly visible at Kenilworth Road.

The large Millwall contingent among the crowd met Stevenson's correct call with the coin with a chorus of cheers and a cacophony of ringing of hand-held bells. It was those fans who nearly saw their favourites take the lead in the opening moments when Jones fired narrowly wide. The Lions' sprightly Alf Dean and Twigg kept the Luton defence on their toes, the latter narrowly failing with a splendid chance to open the scoring. Up until then the home team had not had a kick, but they suddenly broke away on the right through Brown in the 10th minute to provide Menzies with the opportunity to put the Hatters one up against the run of play. Holding their nerve at this reverse, Millwall continued to play a high-tempo game, and following the breakdown of a vigorous Luton attack Stansfield, their outside-left, exchanged some pleasantries with 'Tiny' Joyce after the burly 'keeper had denied him. Millwall's endeavours could not buy a goal at this stage, despite Dean's endless flow of crosses and centres, most of which were cleared. Luton still held the upper-hand when the half-time whistle sounded.

The second half saw Millwall come out with all guns blazing to push Luton back deep in their own half. It got to the stage where it seemed inevitable that Millwall would score. That moment nearly arrived when Hector Shand thought he had struck the equaliser with a tremendous shot, but the Scot watched in disbelief as Platt brought off a wonderful save. The prompting and probing of Dick Jones and Alf Dean started to weave some magic which was finally rewarded on the hour when Dean's superb cross-shot found the net after the excellent Shand had drawn the Luton defence. The battle intensified, with both sides guilty of many biting and reckless tackles, and in one incident Alf Twigg was led from the field with an injury, before Menzies was dumped to the ground by another hefty challenge, but the penalty he and Luton craved was not forthcoming. The indomitable Millwall half-backs, Riley, Comrie and Blythe, continued with their resolute 'they shall not pass' attitude and were boosted with the return Alf Twigg to play at outside-left, with Joe Tellum moving inside to fill Alf's role.

The more Luton forced the issue the more they were repelled as the game reached the final 15 minutes. The troublesome Stansfield got away again, but his effort was poor. Millwall retaliated with a few speedy raids themselves, and from one such incursion they confirmed their entry into the next round. Joe Tellum's last-gasp effort was not without controversy when he beat Platt amid appeals for offside, which were thankfully and rightly turned down. From the very moment that Millwall followed Woolwich Arsenal out of the hat an air of confidence pervaded the club, with officials, players and supporters confident that Millwall could match their Football League rivals from across the river, home or away.

Prior to the match the many Arsenal fans, sporting their red-and-white favours, were matched in equal numbers by the Millwall supporters displaying their blue, all milling around weighing up the chances of their teams and waiting for kick-off. The Millwall fans had made their way over the water to Plumstead by various modes of transport: using buses, brakes (horse-drawn carriages) and some of the more enterprising taking turns to push one another on borrowed market barrows. Two of Millwall's most celebrated followers at the time were the thespian brothers Huntley and Fred Wright, who days before the game had been pestering the life out of the Lions chairman John Skeggs, insisting that he should somehow obtain them seats, with Fred hoping to attend the game after travelling the vast distance from Monte Carlo. Whether the brothers obtained their precious seats is not known, but those Millwall fans among the record 32,000 crowd witnessed a cracking game.

From first to the last, every minute the match was full of incidents, and probably for the first time Millwall employed a system where every member of the team had his own particular task. Alf Twigg played as the lone striker (as we would call it today), with the two wingers, Dean and Tellum, instructed to hug the touchlines, with Shand and Jones both deployed as deep-lying inside-forwards who in turn would support the solitary spearhead, Twigg. The tactic seemed vindicated when it bore fruit in the 20th minute as Twigg seized an inch-perfect cross to hammer the ball past McDonald. At this point the Gunners were all over the place, but to their credit they regained their composure to quickly equalise 10 minutes later when Lewis scored an equally stunning goal from Greenaway's centre. Having slightly the better of the things up until the interval, Arsenal were denied any further opportunities thanks mainly to the sterling work of Joyce and the new full-back pairing of Stevenson and Jim Jeffrey. During the course of the second 45 minutes Millwall should have been home and dry, and the reason they were not was the excellent display of the Arsenal 'keeper McDonald, who held the Lions at bay with a string of superlative saves to earn a replay. His relief and that of his teammates at the conclusion of play had to be seen to be believed, and there was no guessing which side was more than happy to hear the final whistle.

The incentive for both was a visit to First Division Nottingham Forest in the third round, with Millwall looking to boost the coffers with an expected large attendance; however, the highly exaggerated capacity figure of 20,000 for the North Greenwich ground after its completion was wide of the mark. As it was, the 16,285 who managed to gain entrance were packed in like sardines to watch what was to be the last-ever FA Cup match on the island. Millwall fielded an unchanged team, whereas Arsenal replaced Tom Fitchie with Charlie Satterthwaite. The replay game carried on in the same vein as the one over at Plumstead with both teams providing some very exciting football. However, in the early stages nothing tangible in the way of clear-cut chances occurred despite both teams' endeavours. It was the Arsenal who threatened initially when Greenaway thumped in the game's first telling attempt on goal, which went straight to the waiting Joyce.

From an Alf Dean centre Dick Jones sent his header just over the bar, before Twigg forced McDonald into a hurried clearance which fell invitingly to Jones, whose crisp shot was heading for the net until Shaw deflected the ball to safety. The combative nature of the game was the cause of many stoppages, with Twigg, McDonald, Gray and Shand all having to receive treatment. Millwall were now beginning to take a grip on the game, but this resulted in Jones and Jeffrey receiving some heavy knocks from an Arsenal side that was getting rattled. It was a mystery to all and sundry how the Gunners managed to reach the interval still level, considering the innumerable escapes their goal had had during a frantic opening half. On the resumption, Stevenson mopped up Arsenal's first real attack before Jimmy Riley wasted a free-kick on the edge of the Gunners area which initiated the visitors' best spell of the tie. They tested Joyce's ability by forcing him to tip away a stunning drive before foiling Satterthwaite, whose dithering in front of goal allowed the Millwall 'keeper to clear the danger.

Millwall survived the protracted spell of Arsenal pressure, and the game entered the final third of what had been an extremely competitive tie before the Lions at last got the all-important goal after 63 minutes. How apt it was when local boy Dick Jones beat the magnificent Hugh McDonald with an exceptional shot. With the tension finally relieved, the crowd began roaring the Lions on, willing them to score another. But Arsenal had other ideas, and they soon reminded everyone there was still enough time for an equaliser. This they nearly achieved, in fact, in the frantic remaining minutes. Firstly Joyce was forced to dive full length to divert Andy Ducat's piledriver to safety, and following the corner the giant Millwall 'keeper foiled two attempts from Sands as the desperate Gunners searched in vain for a goal.

Still the game went on, with the crowd urging the referee to call time, as more woe befell Arsenal, who had created more chances in the final 15 minutes than they had previously in the match. A penalty shout for handball against Comrie was turned down before Satterthwaite caused more nail biting three minutes from time when his drive thudded against the Millwall crossbar. The heroic Joyce then performed the last act of defiance by stopping Lewis's goal-bound shot before the official brought a memorable game to a close seconds later. How many, I wonder, of those celebrating Millwall fans on leaving the ground would have realised that the biggest game held at the venue since those halcyon days of 1903, or the goal scored, would be the last in the FA Cup at Millwall's spiritual home on the Isle of Dogs? How fitting was it that the scorer of that famous goal was Dick Jones, one of Millwall's home-produced players.

Having seen off the Arsenal, it was First Division rivals Nottingham Forest who now lay in wait for Millwall by the banks of the River Trent in the third-round tie. For Forest this was the third consecutive home Cup match of the season, having previously beaten Aston Villa 2–0 in the first round followed by a single success over Brentford in the second. Losing the toss for once, the Lions had to face into the bright winter sunshine and were again supported in great numbers by the fans who travelled up, displaying a huge blue-and-white banner just as Twigg got the match underway. A boisterous opening created a fantastic atmosphere as excitement mounted from an early stage. When Forest threatened, Millwall were saved by Jim Jeffrey's immaculate rescue act, while at the other end Alf Dean found himself in an excellent position after Maltby had fallen when attempting to clear, but Linacre in the Forest goal read the situation well to snuff out the danger. Forest were no doubt aware of Millwall's high-powered up-and-at-'em style and decided to take the bull by the horns to mount their own version of the Lions' aggressive play with some frequent and very belligerent attacks that took Millwall by surprise in the opening quarter of an hour.

Against all this, Millwall managed to get their noses in front when island-born Fred 'Buck' Vincent, a replacement for Jim Tellum, outfoxed Hughes to set up Twigg, whose first-time effort was blocked by Linacre, who could only watch as Hector Shand walked the ball into the unguarded net. It was the first Cup goal Forest had conceded in the campaign, and their response was instant. Their game was sufficiently raised when Enoch 'Knocker' West fired just over Joyce's bar before the Lions' custodian saved splendidly from Morris. He then foiled Morrison with an equally fine left-handed stop as the traffic became all one-way. Having withstood constant pressure, in which West was dominating, Millwall finally buckled six minutes before the break when the Forest man got the better of Jeffrey to equalise with a fine shot. Forest nearly added a second soon after when 'Tiny' could only parry a powerful drive, and it was left to Stevenson to complete the clearance.

After the restart the Lions seemed unprepared for the onslaught that followed, for barely six minutes into the half their composure vanished when Jeffrey tripped the persistent West in the box. Up stepped the Forest man to expertly dispatch the penalty beyond Joyce's reach. Soon afterwards, play was held up when George Comrie, who had been limping, suddenly collapsed after his knee gave way and had to be carried off. Following some penetrating runs from Hector Shand, play was mainly confined to the Millwall half as Joyce and his backs pulled out all the stops to keep their team in contention. An overworked Joyce could hardly be blamed for Forest's third when Hughes hit a speculative long-range shot that deceived 'Tiny' in flight to nestle in the back of the net for the third and clinching goal. Despite their FA Cup failure, however, Millwall's season was not without silverware, as they managed to lay their hands on one piece after defeating Leyton in the inaugural Final of the London FA Challenge Cup.

Millwall's participation in the FA Cup in the ensuing 1910 and 1911 campaigns faltered at the very start in both. With King Edward VII's reign nearing its end, the Lions' Cup involvement was also of a short duration. The trip up to their 1903 semi-final opponents Derby County, who were going well in Division Two, came with some familiar faces missing from the Lions ranks. Goalkeeper Tiny Joyce was replaced by Harvey Carmichael, while General Stevenson had reportedly returned to Lancashire to run a public house and Jim Riley had also left. Through the door came young right-back Atkinson from the Charlton area, as did Joe Wilson and Johnny Martin from Brighton & Hove, who were complemented by the token Scotsmen Billy Semple (from Celtic) and Archie Garrett (from Hamilton), but still in harness were the likes of Dick Jones, Alf Twigg and John Blythe.

From the off, Millwall were under the cosh as Carmichael was kept busy, fielding efforts from Hall, Bauchop and Bentley. The heavy Baseball Ground surface was a cause of concern, and in the 12th minute the Lions stopper's fears were realised when Hall's long-range shot found the net, aided in no small way by the inconsistencies of the pitch. This set-back was nearly compounded moments later when County nearly scored again. It was Atkinson's inexperience that let in Davis, who crossed for Thompson to blast from point-blank range straight into Carmichael's midriff, winding the 'keeper who doubled up in agony. While the luckless custodian was receiving attention behind the goal Derby scored again. Jim Jeffrey, having taken over in goal, saw Bentley take advantage of Millwall's disarray to register Derby's second before a fully recovered Carmichael resumed his place. He managed to maintain his form in brilliant style but was helpless when County obtained a third after 25 minutes when Hall capped a fine solo run to score his second goal of the game. Poor Millwall could not make any sort of impression, despite Derby losing the injured Barnes for the rest of the half, but the 10 men of County, with three goals in the bag, comfortably saw out time until the interval.

Both teams resumed the game with their full entitlement as Derby continued to have the lion's share of the match. Carmichael was again tested by efforts from Derby's three inside-forwards, and it was Davis who added a fourth in the 57th minute, following a corner, to finally dash any Millwall hopes. With only pride to play for, Millwall sought to limit any further damage, and they did come close to reducing the arrears on two occasions. Firstly Jones nearly forced Nicholas to concede an own-goal before Joe Wilson saw his shot tipped onto the bar by Scattergood, but these were the only worthwhile efforts from the Lions in the half. Impressive Derby pressed for more goals, and Morris hit the post before tamely putting the rebound over, but with time running out Barnes set the seal on a day Millwall would want to forget when he chipped in with County's fifth. As the Lions trudged off a quagmire of a pitch (a problem that continued to haunt the Derby club until their move to Pride Park in 1997), the statisticians among the Millwall support took no comfort in seeing their team equal their biggest Cup defeat as a professional club since Aston Villa beat them by the same margin in 1901.

It was the attendance for the Arsenal game in 1909 that had convinced the Millwall directors that a new ground was needed if the club was to progress, even if meant leaving the island. The wheels were set in motion to find a new location, and a little over 18 months later the Lions had acquired their new headquarters with a move south of the river to Cold Blow Lane in New Cross. The task for the design, layout and construction fell once more on the broad shoulders of Elijah Moor. Their new home was to be named 'The Den', tailor-made to coincide with the club's nickname. The envisaged accommodation figure of around 40,000 spectators appeared to be wishful thinking on somebody's part, but nevertheless Cold Blow would be far bigger than anything Millwall had appeared on over on the island. In the course of their 83-year residence at the new venue it would play host to some of the Lions' most stirring FA Cup ties.

What the club needed now to test the capacity of the new stadium was a home match against one of the leading clubs, preferably a London one. But Millwall had to patiently wait another two years before opportunity arose, for in 1911 they were asked to make the short journey back over the river to White Hart Lane for their first-ever FA Cup meeting against Tottenham Hotspur, who had won the trophy back in 1901.

The weather in north London was bright sunshine, though it was very cold and a tad foggy – most unlike the usual Isle of Dogs concoction of rain and wind at that time of year. It was an ideal day for watching football, but with other local attractions it kept the gate to just fewer than 21,500. Another added ingredient was the inclusion of former Spurs player Bob Walker in the Millwall line up, and also included was the ex-England player Bert Lipsham at outside-left. Bert, who was later to become Millwall's first-ever player-manager, had been signed from Fulham the previous May. Millwall put in an excellent shift that merited much more than a share of the match takings of £769 10s 6d, especially as the deciding score came through an own-goal. It was Spurs who opened the scoring in 13th minute when Billy Minter's initial shot spun off a defender into the air and caused a frantic mêlée yards from the Lions goal before Minter lashed home the loose ball. As the half was drawing to a close Millwall gained an equaliser following Jabez Darnell's foul. From the ensuing free-kick the disconsolate Spurs player could only watch as Johnny Martin's downward header hit a frozen part of the pitch which caused the ball to deviate, making Tommy Lunn's desperate dive all in vain, as Millwall celebrated their piece of good-fortune.

This set up a fascinating second half in which both teams went hammer and tongs to produce a typical Cup tie, with the Lions, it must be said, looking the more likely to take the honours. But Tottenham's rearguard was proving a hard nut to crack. If the gods had been smiling on Millwall for their goal then it was Spurs' turn to be favoured by the deities when they gained a corner in the 55th minute. Tottenham's John Curtis sent it over, and as Carmichael attempted to collect he was challenged by Spurs' recently signed centre-forward Ellis Crompton. This caused Harvey to lose his balance, and in doing so he could only punch the ball into his own net. So poor old Harvey, having let in five at Derby the year before, had now unwittingly provided Tottenham their passage into the next round.

A further 12 months elapsed before Millwall could 'christen' The Den with an FA Cup tie, for in 1912 the draw had been unkind yet again by pairing them with Bury for the second time in four years. Despite making financial overtures to the Lancashire club to switch the tie to Cold Blow Lane, they were rebuffed just has they had been by Jarrow in 1900, so the game went ahead at Gigg Lane. The attendance of just 8,027 reflected the fact that Millwall were no longer the drawing power they once were, and given their poor showing in the Cup over the previous few seasons this was hardly surprising. The game had barely started when Millwall nearly scored with their first attack when McDonald, the Shakers' goalkeeper, bailed his team out following Greaves's error. The 'keeper then sent the ball to Currie, who fed Duffy, whose mesmerising run along the goalline finished when he sent in a shot from a nigh on impossible angle which Lions 'keeper Harry Shaw allowed to slip through his hands and into the net to give Bury a sixth-minute lead. Millwall hit back in determined fashion, with Lipsham forcing McDonald into a fine save, but it was Charlie Carvosso who should have levelled but sent his effort high over the bar when it looked easier to score.

Wilting under continual Millwall pressure, Bury were fortunate to scramble clear a dangerous corner before their colours were lowered with Millwall's equaliser. In the game four years previously it was Welshman Dick Jones who claimed the Lions' goal that day. Who said lightening did not strike twice? Well in this game it did, twice in fact. The first instance came when Dick's compatriot Wally Davis duly obliged with a splendid effort to bring the teams level after 35 minutes. It was Bert Lipsham's fine cross and Sid Wayment's deft touch that enabled Davis to score, despite him being tackled by both the Bury backs. The Lions looked much the better side after the restart when Wayment forced McDonald into a fine save. But the Bury 'keeper was saved by a post to deny Lipsham's a goal. Bury's overworked defence were on the verge of caving in under Millwall's grilling, but then, with a replay looking odds-on, Bury claimed the winner. Lightning stuck twice for the second time when they managed to score a dramatic winning goal right at the death. Their right-half Cannon blasted in a hard drive which Shaw partially saved but could not hold, leaving the jubilant Shaker to run up to tap the loose ball over the line. Millwall came storming back in their usual way, with Vincent going close and Carvosso grazing the crossbar before finally running out of steam. Ever since John Sutcliffe's painful aberrations at Villa Park in 1903 the number of goalkeeper-related mistakes had cost Millwall dear in virtually every season since.

It was third time lucky when the Lions finally had their wish granted for New Cross to witness its first FA Cup tie, when Millwall were drawn against First Division Middlesbrough. Boro would be the first team to oppose Millwall in the Cup on both sides of the river. Despite Millwall being the better side and controlling much of the match, however, it finished all square. The strong wind did not help as it varied at regular intervals, even when the sides were playing with and against it. But the wind was not to blame when Millwall, through Davis, Vincent and Bert Moody, spurned three gilt-edged chances on offer that allowed the visitors to escape with a 0–0 draw, which in all honesty they had hardly deserved.

Millwall took some heart from their performance on the Saturday and set off in good spirits for the Wednesday replay, expecting to put up a decent display at Ayresome Park. This they achieved for the first half-hour, in which they held the advantage, albeit over a 10-man Boro team who had lost Joe Crosier in the very first minute after a collision with John Borthwick. The Lions set about the home team with some fine attacking football, and when Wally Davis broke through he was unceremoniously brought down by Joe Hisbent. Borthwick's free-kick was met by Joe Wilson's scorching volley that hit the back of the Boro net without touching the ground. But that was as good as it got for Millwall, as following Crozier's return the home side became a lot more vigorous in all aspects. They finally got back on terms when Borthwick was alleged, on the word of a linesman, to have stopped Jock Stirling's run illegally, and from the penalty spot Jackie Carr made no mistake. But the tie turned crucially on the stroke of half-time when George Elliott beat three Millwall defenders in a mazy run to set up Carr for the second.

The heart and determination Millwall usually carried into their games had all but disappeared after the interval. The forwards, if not demoralised, were hopelessly ineffectual, and the inconsistency that blighted their displays in the Southern League reared its ugly head in a woeful second half showing. Middlesbrough, on the other hand, could do no wrong, taking Millwall's hapless defence to the cleaners time after time. The ineptitude displayed in front of him would have had Lions 'keeper Martin Spendiff running to find the aspirins. Jackie Carr, the home team's leader who was later to win two England caps after World War One, claimed his hat-trick by heading home a corner before Elliott, another future international, scored the fourth with a well-placed shot. At least centre-forward Wally Davis had something to look forward to, for a week later he would join the ranks of Lions internationals when he won his first cap for Wales. In his absence Millwall went down 2–0 at Norwich in what had been depressing week.

In the two seasons leading up World War One Millwall had marginally better runs in the Cup, but their form in 1913–14 season was again cause for concern. They did not win their first Southern League fixture until the last Saturday of October and won just 11 matches in total to finish in 15th place. Hopefully the Cup could offer some respite from the mediocrity of what had gone on before, and the draw against London rivals Chelsea was a much-needed shot in the arm. Chelsea were virtually newcomers to the football scene in London, having been around for less than a decade, and in their short life they had gained a reputation as a yo-yo club. Their tenure as members of the Football League so far had seen them gain a couple of promotions and suffer relegation once. The match was typically boisterous, as one would expect from a 'derby', but had too many free-kicks for the fans' liking as they were stifling the flow of the game. The culprits came from both teams, but it was Chelsea who were condemned as the main protagonists as the players appeared pumped-up as much as the crowd, on an overcast day where the air was filled with unseasonable humidity. It was Millwall who came closest to scoring, but the scenario of missed chances replicated the Boro game from the previous game. To the fans' consternation Millwall failed to put away two straight-forward chances that would have put them on easy street.

Occasionally Chelsea, with the famous amateur Vivian Woodward in tow, played some neat and attractive football, and it was only Bill Woodley's timely intervention that stopped the iconic Woodward from scoring. Bob Dilley's reply was to send in a pile-driver, followed soon after by two of 'Banger' Voisey's specials, which were saved by goalkeeper Jim Molyneux. Woodley again mopped up another Chelsea raid before Bridgeman's fine shot tested Joe Orme in the Lions goal, who was relieved to see Freeman's low drive go narrowly wide. But with the defences generally on top, it came as no surprise when half-time was reached with no goals. After the restart Chelsea's Harry Ford's exhilarating run ended when he fizzed in a shot inches over Orme's crossbar, followed seconds later by a similar effort from 'Buck' Vincent at the other end. Bert Hall (a winner with Aston Villa in 1905) then set up the Lions' best chance of the game with a pin-point cross that both Davis and Vincent went for and missed.

Millwall's attacks were growing with intensity, and full-backs Joe Kirkwood and Bill Woodley were joining the forays into the Chelsea half but unfortunately found one of their opposite numbers, Chelsea full-back Owen Marshall, in outstanding form. Hall added to the litany of misses as the Lions continued to extend Chelsea to the limit. Viv Woodward, who had been kept fairly quiet by Joe Wilson's attentions, then sniffed out three chances in quick succession. The first occurred when Kirkwood mis-kicked, but fortunately Joe managed to regain his ground to block the Chelsea man's goal-bound shot. He then dummied Wilson to curl a second effort just wide, before forcing a splendid save from Joe Orme. Millwall's response was efforts from Bert Moody and Davis, but neither tested Molyneux unduly, and with nine minutes left Millwall should have gone ahead. One would put their house on Wally Davis to score when he was presented with a chance on a plate. Bert Hall had created it for the Welshman, but to everyone's astonishment the master craftsman missed with the goal at his mercy. 'Oh, Wal!' you could hear the Lions fans cry, along with some other fruity comments, as they stared in disbelief as The Den still awaited its first FA Cup goal. Chelsea were relieved and thankful to earn a goalless draw which, to their credit, had been achieved for the most part without the services Jack Harrow. He had been dismissed during a rumbustious opening 20-minute spell when kicking, biting and everything else seemed to be the norm.

For the Wednesday afternoon replay at Stamford Bridge an unchanged Millwall drew a crowd of 35,000, the biggest attendance to watch the Lions in a FA Cup tie since the 1903 semi-final. This contest was of a more sporting nature, with the teams concentrating solely on the football. Both Chelsea and Millwall had early chances to score, the best being when Norman Fairgray tested Orme. George Hunter of Chelsea was then penalised for a trip. Billy Voisey's free-kick caused Marshall's partial clearance to fall invitingly for the lurking Wally Davis, who inexplicably lofted the ball over the bar with just the goalkeeper to beat. Unfazed by Wally's howler, Millwall forced three successive corners in a fine passage of play that came to an end when Dilley fouled Molyneux. Chelsea replied with Freeman failing narrowly to connect with Ford's tantalising cross before the winning goal arrived in the 17th minute. After Millwall had defended a Chelsea corner, they broke with a devastating counter when Bob Dilley cashed in on George Hunter's mistake and took flight down the right to plant his exquisite centre into the path of the onrushing Davis. In an instant the Welshman's audacious shot rippled Molyneux's net before the 'keeper could move. Wal's atonement was complete, following his earlier failures.

Stunned momentarily, Chelsea then set about Millwall with a spell of frenzied attacks in which Lions goalkeeper Joe Orme twice came to the rescue. His expertise at narrowing the angle denied Harold Halse as he bore down on goal and then foiled Woodward with a splendid save, which he surpassed when dealing superbly with Hunter's free-kick just before half-time. After the interval Millwall nearly doubled their lead before the ex-Croydon Common full-back Jack Harrow foiled the dangerous Dilley. Huge amounts of energy had been expended by both sides, and so play slipped into a lull. This suited Millwall best, who were content in their ability to ride out the Chelsea storm. The Pensioners had created many chances, but their failure to take any of them bordered on the criminal. The tally and the frustration increased when Tommy Logan and Charlie Freeman failed as Chelsea's attacks took on manic proportions. On the rare occasions Millwall did venture to threaten Molyneux's goal they looked very likely to add to their score, and they would have done had Davis and Moody shown a bit more composure. The door on Chelsea's hopes was firmly shut when Halse volleyed narrowly wide from Fairgray's centre as the final phase became very scrappy. Millwall tenaciously held on to what they had, although they did have the last meaningful efforts on goal from Davis and Vincent, which Molyneux struggled to keep out. But Millwall's progress in the competition was confirmed by the blast of the referee's whistle moments later.

Awaiting the Lions in round two were Bradford City, who, having lost a Cup tie to Millwall back in 1905, had in the interim contested and won the FA Cup Final of 1911 by defeating Newcastle United 1–0 after a replay. Since that earlier meeting City had improved immensely, having won not only the Cup but also the Second Division Championship in 1908, and as members of the First Division they were a model of consistency. One Bradford player who was party to City's success was former Lion and right-back Bob Campbell, who had a solitary season on the island in 1905. Superstition ranks high within football and with certain players and clubs succumbing to its wiles. After their excellent win at Chelsea, the Lions decided play in their unaccustomed red shirts for this match, hoping the trick would work again as it had at Stamford Bridge.

City commenced the game at a fair rate of knots and had a potential match winner in outside-left Bookman, whose pace and guile could exploit the counter-attack to the full. For Millwall, Davis was at his most productive. However, it was City's trio of Bond, Bookman and Storer who initiated the best move of the game in what had been a dour and goalless first half with both defences looking solid. The Lions had come close on two occasions, with Fred Vincent striking the initial effort, only for City's Ewart to make an incredible save from point-blank range. What the game needed was a goal to inject some excitement, and when it finally arrived after 56 minutes the tie finally burst into life. From a throw-in Voisey gained possession, and he in turn found the deep-lying Davis. Taking Voisey's pass, Wally went on a unforgettable and mercurial run from the halfway line. Setting off with his subliminal ball control, the Welsh Wizard feinted past Robinson then outwitted former Lion Bob Campbell before the covering Boocock fared no better, which left him with just goalkeeper Ewart to beat. As the City man advanced to meet Wally, the Millwall striker kept his nerve in what seemed an eternity, then looked-up and assuredly slotted the ball just inside the far post to complete a breathtaking piece of individualism.

Millwall were on fire, and when Davis netted again he was pulled up for offside as City made attempts to rescue their predicament by putting in some desperate attacks. Following one such skirmish Lions 'keeper Joe Orme was injured but refused to leave the pitch, and after some hasty repairs he carried on to help Millwall to record a truly historical and momentous victory. In the after-match postmortem it was generally agreed that Bradford had been the more polished team throughout, but they could not overcome Millwall's perseverance and resolve they had displayed over the 90 minutes, during which they had proved to be the better side. The press reaction after the game was one of glowing enrapture, some bestowing upon Davis's wonder strike the title of 'The Goal of the Century'.

Millwall's reward for the success over City came in the form of a match with their Yorkshire neighbours Sheffield

PROMINENT FOOTBALLERS.

W. DAVIS.

MILLWALL.

Welsh international Wally Davis was the scorer of Millwall's first-ever FA Cup goal at The Den with a sensational effort in the 1–0 victory over Bradford City in 1914. [Author]

United, who were set to make their first visit to The Den for a third-round meeting, some 19 years after the clubs had first crossed swords in 1895. The day of 21 February 1914 was the day the gods conspired against the Lions from the very start. Following some heavy rain The Den's playing surface was reminiscent of the old days of North Greenwich, and this affected the attendance, which was less than 17,000 paying customers. Millwall, sporting their 'lucky' red shirts, never at any stage mastered the situation and relied too much on individual effort, whereas United adapted a lot better to the conditions and as such were the more coherent team. Millwall's approach made Wally Davis ineffectual by the lack of any decent service to the Welshman, but this was not all they had to contend with. United were slick and not really in need of a helping hand, but they got one all the same when the referee, Mr Baker of Nantwich, spotted a nothing offence in the Millwall area and awarded the Blades a penalty. Up stepped their man Kitchen to beat Orme, which gave the visitors the lead they never surrendered. The Lions' only visible effort of the half came just before the break when Fred Vincent's effort scraped United's cross-bar.

There seemed little doubt that there had been some harsh words spoken at half-time by the Millwall manager and ex-Blade Bert Lipsham, as the team set about trying to claw back the equaliser, with Bert Moody setting the tone by sending in a rasping drive that was followed by a similar effort from Hall. Joe Orme was then called upon to make his first save of the half before another contentious point occurred at the Sheffield end when, following a corner-kick, Vincent claimed his effort had been carried over the line by United's 'keeper Gough before clearing. Astonishingly, the official awarded Millwall another corner which came to nothing amid more frustration for the home team. With 11 minutes to go the Lions were still seeking the goal that would earn at least a replay, but they fell hook, line and sinker for a Sheffield smash-and-grab. When many of the fans were moving towards the exits United hastened their departure further by scoring three times in an eight-minute spell. First Utley unselfishly supplied Gillespie to score Sheffield's second, before Utley then bagged a brace to complete the rout. A small piece of ironic trivia to occur from the run was that the three teams the Lions had met would fill consecutive places in the First Division at the season's end, with Chelsea finishing eighth, Bradford City ninth and Sheffield finishing 10th.

Before a ball had even been kicked at the start of the 1914–15 season, the structure of Europe was threatened with the assassination of Archduke Ferdinand in Sarajevo by Serbian nationalists; this deed was the catalyst for the outbreak of World War One. After the declaration of war the calls for the cancellation of football in its entirety were loud and vocal from the non-footballing fraternity. Nevertheless, Millwall, like the rest of football, carried on; although this was to be last season of all competitive football for five years. Millwall's form leading up to the New Year and beyond bode well as they had only lost only three Southern League games all season, one of them at Croydon Common a week before the first-round tie against Clapton Orient at Cold Blow Lane. Manager Bert Lipsham had been pretty active in the transfer market during the close-season, securing the services of a fine full-back Jack Fort, his former Exeter City teammate Fred Whittaker and John Nuttall, a wing-half from Doncaster Rovers.

The Orient encounter ended in controversy following an 87th-minute bust-up between Lions goalkeeper Joe Orme and Clapton's inside-forward Billy Jonas. After saving at full-length, the stricken custodian was not best pleased with Jonas's enthusiastic follow-up and meted out some swift retribution on Jonas before players from both sides intervened to calm the situation down. Ironically, both Orme and Jonas would be off to Kingsway to enlist in the Footballers' Battalion on the following Monday. It appeared to many that they wanted to get some hand-to-hand combat in before they got to the front. Mr Pearson, the referee from Derby, was not impressed, and decided to send off the truculent pair. John Nuttall was given the task of defending Millwall's slender lead after taking Orme's place for the last three minutes.

Before the kick-off both teams were under strength, with Millwall missing Wally Davis and winger Sammy Lamb. Billy Voisey was now in uniform, serving with the Royal Field Artillery, but he nevertheless filled in for Davis, while the O's were without the talismanic Richard McFadden. It was his replacement, Billy Jonas, whose clash with Joe Orme had caused such a furore that the O's supporters had to be escorted out of the ground at the game's end. After a nervous opening quarter of an hour, the Lions settled down to have the rest of the game up until the break, in which Jimmy Hugall, the Os' 'keeper, was in outstanding form. He was beaten just once, in the 30th minute when Johnny 'Ginger' Williams, a Lions recruit from Crystal Palace a year earlier, thumped his shot against a post only to see Bert Moody thrash home the rebound.

The O's came on strong at the start of the second half but missed a great chance when Dalrymple failed to connect with the ball, which left him cursing his luck. He had more reason to groan moments later when Millwall went two up after 53 minutes after Williams initiated a great move with Nuttall, whose delightful pass put in Moody, who finished with great aplomb. Orient were given a lifeline 12 minutes later, however, when Joe Kirkwood handled in the box, giving Jonas the chance to convert the penalty. Orient, now in the ascendancy, sought an equaliser and should have got one after Bob Dalrymple and Arthur Layton penetrated a lax Millwall defence, but in their eagerness contrived to miss the target. 'Spider' Parker's astute pass then set up O's teammate Joe Dix who frittered away another certain goal. So it went on, as the east Londoners continued to create and then miss a string of chances that was to seal their departure from the Cup in what for them was a disappointing performance, especially in the first half.

For the second round the Lions were paired with another club from football's elite, Bolton Wanderers, at Burnden Park. Having held out for 90 minutes, Millwall had to endure an extra 30 minutes' play, but they still managed to come away with a creditable 0–0 draw. Due to travel restrictions the replay was set for the following Saturday, and it saw Millwall more than hold their own against such an illustrious team and take a 1–0 lead into the break courtesy of Bert Moody's searing drive from the edge of the area after 35 minutes. At half-time the crowd were entertained by the band of the newly formed Footballers' Battalion, who were holding a recruiting drive at the game. At the commencement of the second half both goalkeepers were called into action, with Wally Davis just failing to extend the home team's lead before Fred Wood brought off the save of the match from Jones, the Wanderers inside-left. Eventually the magnificent Wood was beaten by Smith's penalty-kick to send the tie into extra-time. Davis, with his fourth FA Cup goal, put Millwall ahead once again, but following a lapse in the Lions defence it was Wal Davis's Welsh international teammate Ted Vizard who scored five minutes from time to make the final result 2–2.

Millwall faced First Division Bolton Wanderers three times in 1915, and due to travel restrictions all the games were played on successive Saturdays, finally seeing the Lancashire side emerge victors 4–1 in the second replay at Burnden Park. [E. Hulton]

For the second time in a fortnight Millwall had to treck up to Bolton to see who would earn the right to face Burnley in the next round. But this third meeting was to prove one match too many for the Lions as Bolton made their undoubted class tell to record a resounding 4–1 success. Outplayed for most the game, Millwall strived manfully against the odds on an unhelpful pitch which one team mastered (Bolton) and the other (Millwall) could not. The Lions found themselves three goals adrift before the half-hour mark, and had it not been for Fred Wood's heroics between the sticks the margin of defeat would have been far greater. Bolton continued their bombardment of the Millwall goal, whose only respite came when Fred Whittaker created a chance for Davis to give the Lions a glimmer of hope when his accurate drive beat Edmondson. But it was that man Vizard again who administered the last rites with Bolton's fourth as Millwall's Cup aspirations were over, not just for the present but for five long years.

So as the nation prepared for the many sacrifices to come, for two of Millwall's finest players it would be their swansong in the competition. For Wally Davis, his goal at Bolton was be the last he would plunder for the Lions in Cup football. But more poignantly for John Williams it was his last-ever match in the FA Cup, for 'Ginger', as he was known, was to lose his life the following year while serving in France with the Footballers' Battalion.

5. A New Dawn

Following the indescribable carnage of the 'War to end all wars', the country was reconciled to getting back to some normality, with Millwall and their supporters included. Long-time trainer Bob Hunter had taken over the manager's job from Bert Lipsham as the Lions prepared to enter what would be their last season in the Southern League. The following May at the Football League Annual Meeting it was proposed to invite all members of the First Division of the Southern League to move en masse to form the League's new Third Division for the 1920–21 season.

Millwall's Cup run during their final days as a non-League outfit lasted just one match following a defeat at Notts County before a then record attendance of over 35,000. Millwall's team, as expected, had changed a great deal since 1915; as mentioned Jack Williams had been lost at the front, while Wally Davis and Jim Jeffrey had retired; however, evergreen Bert Moody was back and was joined in attack by another veritable net-buster named Jimmy Broad, who, along with Joe Wilson and the highly decorated combatant Billy Voisey, had all returned safely and were raring to go. But had First Division Notts County taken two early chances from McLeod and Hill, Millwall's participation could have been over before it started as County set the pace in what turned into an intriguing encounter. After weathering County's early dominance, Millwall took control when the hard-hitting Broad hammered in two stinging drives to warm the hands of Streets in the County goal. Having looked the more likely to score, Millwall let County off the hook, and right on cue they promptly went down to the other end to open the scoring after 37 minutes when Hill converted McLeod's thoughtful pass. This goal certainly boosted County's confidence, which at the start of the second half knew no bounds as their growing superiority was underlined

when McLeod made amends for his earlier miss by striking home a centre from Henshall for the second to sever Millwall's hopes of an upset.

Millwall's first season as a founder member of the new Third Division saw them enter the first-round tie against Lincoln City of the Midland League on the back of a formidable home record. They remained unbeaten at The Den, but more incredulously they had not conceded a goal in 11 fixtures at home. But all that was to change over the course of the next hour and a half when this extraordinary record came crashing down around their ears. Even so, the spectators attending the game would not have dreamed of what was to unfold before their disbelieving eyes once the game got underway.

Following such a one-sided game, the irony would not have been lost on those Lions fans once they had seen the results relating to the clubs in the new enterprise. Most of the new Third Division had a most invigorating time by winning their ties. Local rivals Crystal Palace, the champions elect, took the scalp of First Division Manchester City 2–0, but Millwall, God bless them, created a most unwelcome stat by becoming the Division's first noted victim of a giant-killing act.

In front of what was the Den's biggest gate of the season of 31,580, Lincoln gatecrashed the party to blow Millwall out of the water. Despite the neat and tidy play from the amateur pairing of Bobby Noble and Alf Moule that promised so much, their eager promptings went unfulfilled during a sprightly opening 10 minutes. To be brutally frank, Bob Bainbridge, Lincoln's goalkeeper, had nothing come his way that could be described as dangerous all afternoon, despite Millwall having Jimmy Broad (32 goals in the previous season) spearheading the home attack.

If City goalkeeper Bainbridge had been virtually redundant then his Lions opposite, Joe Lansdale, was kept on his toes throughout the whole 90 minutes. It was Lincoln who threw down the gauntlet early on when Rippon smacked his effort against the bar to give Millwall a sample of what to expect. Nevertheless, despite running the show from the start City had to wait until the 42nd minute to see Lansdale pick the ball out the net for the first time when

Bird's exquisite pass put Tom Rippon in to gain his overdue reward. It was one-way traffic on the resumption as Lincoln peppered Lansdale's goal at will without adding to the score. Exposed to the Imps' attacks time after time, Joe Lansdale must have wondered where and what his defence was doing about it. Belatedly the Lions began to resemble a football team, but their attempt to pressure the visitors' goal did not last long before Lincoln went further ahead. Millwall had no answer to the blistering pace of Rippon as he raced unhindered to put in a cross that was met by Bretnall to easily beat Lansdale after 63 minutes.

Having conceded their first home goals of the campaign Millwall were in danger of being completely swamped, such was City's dominance. Jack Fort, the only member of the Lions defence to display any sort of resistance, received little or no help from his out-of-sorts colleagues. A most miserable day was made complete 11 minutes from time when City hammered the final nail into Millwall's coffin when Bird and Bretnall combined to give Rippon the opportunity to show his opponents a clean pair of heels once again to claim the third. It left Millwall licking their wounds in total disarray and highly embarrassed.

Following this blip, however, Millwall would get to like their Football League surroundings during the 1920s as with Bob Hunter at the helm they had a manager who over the course of the next six seasons would bring in the quality to fuel the desire and expectancy of both club and supporters. Indeed, the future looked very rosy as the Lions were set to finish no lower than 12th during their initial stint in the Third Division. It was during this period of growth that Millwall would go some way to reclaiming their reputation as doughty Cup-fighters as the 1921–22 FA Cup campaign got underway with a first-round home tie against Ashington, who like Lincoln City had become founder members of the Football League's newly instituted Northern section of the Third Division. Hopefully a repeat of the Lincoln fiasco would be avoided.

Any very late arrival entering The Den during the half-time interval of the Ashington match would have been extremely unlucky to say the least. Had they done so, all the action and scoring of all six goals would have been missed; Millwall having obtained their four in the first 20 minutes. Getting off to the best possible start is always a boost, and for the Lions it arrived after just three minutes when left-back Billy Woodley got his wing moving, which ended with Billy Keen opening the scoring, before the former Brentford player George Taylor finished his mazy 30-yard dribble with a shot on the run to acquire the second.

Keen by name and keen by nature, and not to be overshadowed by Taylor's strike, Bill added the third when he sliced open the visitors' defence, and with Ashington on the ropes and reeling Moule then got his head to a Taylor cross for number four. The home fans were lapping it up, but following the goal blitz Millwall appeared to switch off, content to 'showboat' their passage into the next round. Ashington did not take too kindly to having the Mickey taken out of them and reminded Millwall that the game was not yet won, bringing them down a peg or two when visiting centre-forward Robertson reduced the deficit by netting two glorious headers before the interval. Approaching the second half in a more soberly and thoughtful fashion, Millwall cut out the fancy stuff to mirror the best of their first half performance, although there was no addition to the six first half goals.

It was 'derby' day when Second Division Crystal Palace drew the Lions in the second round, but following the short trip to Selhurst Park the game finished goalless. It was a

The Nest, Croydon Common's former ground, was the setting in 1922 for the second-round tie against Crystal Palace, which ended 0–0. Skipper Billy Voisey is seen with Palace counterpart, deciding the toss. [Chris Bethell]

match of very few chances, with the best two falling to Millwall, both involving Billy Keen. The first arrived just after play started when he deftly controlled Taylor's high cross that nearly caused Palace's Little to put through his own goal. His second chance came in the 85th minute when he got himself between two Palace defenders but just as he was about to pull the trigger on Joe Dorsett's inviting cross he was surprisingly given offside. In-between Keen's two chances, Alderson in the Palace goal had a relatively quite afternoon, with the game's only other decent effort coming Palace's way when Jack Conner failed to make the best of Dick Hill's error by tamely shooting into the waiting hands of Joe Lansdale.

If Palace had shaded the first match then it was the Lions who dominated the replay with an air of confidence by taking a firm control from the start in front of a splendid crowd of around 36,000, who nearly witnessed a goal after five minutes. The chance arose when Palace full-back Jack Little was guilty of handball, and Alf Moule blasted home the resulting penalty-kick; however, the Lion was ordered to retake the kick as the referee had not blown his whistle. Stepping up for the second time, Moule looked on in horror as Jack Alderson saved his shot and in doing so appeared to bring the ball back from over the line; however, seeing nothing untoward, the official waved play-on. Remaining unfazed, Millwall kept the pressure ticking over and were rewarded for their patience with a piece of good fortune. There appeared no danger when Dorsett floated over a cross from out on the touchline, but as Alderson went up to collect he fumbled the ball by allowing it to drop over the line for the opening score. In another Lions attack Charlie Hannaford thought he had secured a second, but his celebrations were stifled when his shot bounced off a post to safety. A Palace response saw Bert Menlove set to equalise, but he unbelievably volleyed clear of the crossbar from six yards, before Millwall settled the tie with their second 10 minutes from time. It followed a bout of nonchalant head tennis, after which Dorsett's centre was expertly cushioned back across goal by Taylor for the onrushing Moule to place his header wide of Alderson to round-off a fine team display and a home match against Swansea Town in round three.

By the time the Swans visited The Den in the middle of March they had already collected three League points off the Lions, who were in a desperate run of form, not having tasted victory since the 1–0 win over Gillingham three long months previously. But on this red letter day all the pent-up despair eroded as Millwall swept past the Welshman with a scintillating display by repeating Swansea's early-season reputation of pacey, powerful and exciting football. The Swans were taken to the cleaners as Millwall dished out a dose of unpalatable medicine upon a side that on the day could not live with the lively Lions. The game was a personal triumph for striker Billy Keen, who, having missed the majority of the season with injury, made up for lost time by claiming all four goals in a 4–0 rout. The instigator of all things good was Alf Moule, his succession of long-raking passes to the flanks keeping the Swansea backs at full stretch. When Keen opened the scoring in the 12th minute with a scrambled effort it was so unbecoming of what was to follow as it set Millwall on a path from which they never looked back. They went on to produce some excellent football before Joe Dorsett's pass provided Keen with the opportunity to notch his second just before the break to put Millwall firmly in control. The game, however, was played in very foggy conditions, with one supporter reminiscing many years later of seeing Billy Voisey emerging from the shrouded pitch to inform spectators that Keen had popped in another one.

Millwall sustained the unremitting pace during the second half as they set about to kill off Swansea's challenge, which finally dissolved when Keen added a further brace to complete his outstanding tally. Bill's four-goal haul has yet to be broken (although it has been equalled) as he became the first Millwall player to score four times in an FA Cup match since the club entered the Football League. Millwall were then faced with the daunting task of facing of a club that was to dominate English football for the best part of a decade, Huddersfield Town, who had turned their Leeds Road ground into a fortress. If successful, the Lions would be in their third semi-final – but it was a big 'if' to become the first club from the Third Division to reach the last eight.

Millwall's fate was sealed as early as the sixth minute against Huddersfield after they conceded the initial goal, and from thereon in they remained on the back foot. A history-making comeback would have been of Herculean proportions, and it was clear to all that it just was not going to happen. With Town's Clem Stephenson at his imperious best, one had to feel for poor Billy Stanton, who was given the onerous task of marking one of the country's finest players. Bill would have had more chance of catching pigeons. It was Stephenson who pounced on a rebound to claim Huddersfield's early lead when he scored via the underside of the bar. His second strike embarrassed Lions 'keeper Joe Lansdale, whose concentration was elsewhere when Stephenson's shot from 25 yards found the net when it should have been saved. No one was more surprised than the Huddersfield man to see the ball creep in. This strike really knocked the stuffing out of Millwall, and the only surprise was that Town added just one more goal when Islip netted Huddersfield's third. With all things considered, 3–0 was not a bad return given Millwall's performance in a game in which they were totally outclassed. 'Banger' Voisey was the only Lion who played to his own high standards. The Yorkshire outfit went on to lift the Cup that year and then achieved three consecutive Football League Championships, two coming under Herbert Chapman in what was surely Huddersfield's 'Golden Age'.

Too many draws, 12 in all, in the opening half of the 1922–23 season condemned Millwall to 'also ran' status in the promotion stakes, but the foundations were nevertheless in place on which to build an excellent team. A solid defence was already in place and was the rock on which Clapton Orient's hopes foundered during the FA Cup first-round encounter in east London that season. Clapton's Lea Bridge stadium hosted a record crowd of nearly 37,000 fans that included many unemployed, who were let in for free. The game was in doubt up until 45 minutes before the kick-off, however, due to a dense fog enveloping the stadium. Orient were confident they would see off their London rivals, and the key to victory, opined the know-alls in the press, was the Clapton forwards who would master the Lions' watertight defence. But the satisfaction the players had in proving wrong the smug media hacks must have been immense following a splendid 2–0 success. The steadfast reliability of the Millwall half-back line of Alf Amos, Jimmy Riddell and Arthur Pembleton was the main element that doomed the Orient attack to impotency, a charge that had been levelled at Millwall's misfiring forwards on more than one occasion over the proceeding months.

Stung by the barbed criticism, Millwall galvanised themselves into producing a display of bright, vibrant football, and had they taken the many chances that came their way the margin of victory would have been a lot greater. So precise was the passing from the start that an early Lions goal could not be discounted, and after seven minutes it materialised. A move instigated by Jimmy Riddell saw the former Tufnell Park amateur Charlie Hannaford take Jimmy Dillimore's pass to sneak through a hesitant O's defence to shoot past Arthur Wood from 12 yards. Some 16 minutes later the game was put out of Orient's reach when Pembleton's free-kick from the halfway line found Hannaford in a perfect spot to secure his second goal of the match and so stuff the words of their most vitriolic critics back down their throats.

Millwall could not believe their ears when the draw for the second round pitched them with a home game against the holders, Huddersfield Town – the very team who had sent them packing a year earlier. The tie would give Millwall a window of opportunity to avenge the defeat in front of a boisterous Den support, and Cold Blow Lane was bursting at the seams as a record crowd of 39,700 witnessed a game in which Huddersfield were denied at every turn. Millwall covered and tackled anything in a Town shirt, with the full-back pairing of Jack Fort and Dick Hill keeping a tight rein on the Huddersfield wingers. Although the Millwall forwards looked sharp, their endeavours proved futile as they were kept at bay by outstanding displays from Teddy Taylor in the Terriers' goal (he was the man who ultimately denied Lions' 'keeper Joe Lansdale a sniff of an England cap) and centre-half Tom Wilson. Before the game there had been some good humoured banter between both sets of fans, but following Millwall's exemplary show a significant amount of the Town support grew quieter and quieter as the game progressed.

The replay at Leeds Road was, from Millwall's point of view, a case of *déjà vu* as Huddersfield made no mistake by repeating previous season's score of 3–0. They had taken a two-goal lead into half-time, and it was only the astuteness of Fort and Hill that denied Town any further joy. Poor old Joe Lansdale would never regard the number 25 as lucky, having gifted Town a goal the year before from 25 yards and was again beaten from that distance on two occasions during the course of this match. The initial strike from Charlie Wilson, who scored his second goal of the afternoon, with the second coming from Richardson who, after skipping past Hill's challenge, rattled home Huddersfield's third.

Over the course of the next two seasons Millwall continued their progress in climbing the Third Division table by finishing third in 1924 and fifth the following year. There was no doubt where their priorities lay, as whatever scalps they gained in the Cup were always overshadowed by the club's ambition for a higher standing in the Football League hierarchy. During this period, the FA Cup came to be seen as something of a bonus to Millwall's season.

In 1924 the first round brought West Bromwich Albion to The Den in January for what was an instantly forgettable match. Given Millwall's recent form, the lacklustre display was a surprise, having won the four previous games in which Alf Moule registered five goals out of the 10 scored. The tawdry affair was appropriately settled by an equally sloppy goal in the second half when Lions 'keeper Sid Crawford collected Fitton's shot-cum-cross just under the crossbar. Sid's inability to release the ball quickly enough, however, made him a sitting target for the Baggies centre-forward Carter to bundle the ball out of his hands and into the net. What made it worse from a Millwall standpoint was that Albion were so poor that one correspondent penned that in all his years of reporting this was the worst Albion forward line he had seen in 25 years. That rejoinder was scant consolation to Millwall, who despite the scarcity of chances had the majority of them but were let down by some woeful finishing, which brought a post-match comment from one Albion director, who said 'Thank goodness they can't shoot' – and that summed it up in a nutshell.

Another home draw the following season came when Second Division Barnsley (winners in 1912) graced The Den with their presence, which saw the Lions extend their participation by earning a replay following a 0–0 draw. There was frustration all round in the somewhat disappointing first-round meeting, as Millwall had beaten better teams in their own division that year, and the Tykes seemed more than happy to contain the Lions without showing too much enterprise themselves. What was becoming a tedious trait was Millwall's misfiring attack, especially in front of goal. It was a weakness that cost had them dear against Albion 12 months previously, and this perplexing feature of Millwall's play was again evident during this encounter.

It seemed very likely that one goal would settle the tie, and most would have put their week's wages on the much-travelled Dick Parker to score it. But the usually dependable striker fluffed it with the goal at his mercy when he missed the ball completely. Jimmy Dillimore nearly got the deserved breakthrough following his fine run which opened up the Tykes defence, but as his effort was about to enter the net he could only watch in wonderment as Hodgkinson managed to clear from under the bar. Alf Moule, Parker and Dillimore combined to pile on the pressure on an overworked Barnsley rearguard, whose sole thought was to survive until half-time. Instead of sitting pretty with at least a two-goal lead at the break, Millwall went in level and at the commencement of the second half looked completely down in the dumps. They could even have suffered the injustice of a very late defeat if Barnsley's striker Curran had shown more composure, Sid Crawford would have been picking the ball out of the net.

The replay in South Yorkshire was set for the following Thursday and saw Millwall make four changes from the game at The Den. Joe Lansdale replaced Crawford in goal, Alf Amos took over from Archie Gomm in the half-backs, and into the forward line came Dave 'Abe' Morris and Andy Lincoln for Parker and Dillimore. It was one those replacements who set the Lions on their way when Lincoln netted after 14 minutes, with the quick-thinking Sid Gore creating the chance. Barnsley, however, were a different proposition on their Oakwell pitch and were back on level terms when Kelly equalised following a scramble in front of the Millwall goal. Most of the second 45 minutes went in Barnsley's favour as the Lions' strength began to ebb on a stamina-sapping pitch. The trainers were kept very busy as the teams struggled in trying conditions, before the Tykes finally prevailed. Tiredness was now a factor in Millwall's play, and whatever resolve they had finally evaporated when Fletcher cracked home a splendid drive for the winner.

6. Great Times

Manager Bob Hunter had been busy in his summer recruitment but also knew he would hardly have to tinker with the well-oiled machine that Millwall were fast becoming in order to bring success. Little did he know that great times lay ahead, and success was to come sooner rather than later. Additions to the squad included the amateur W.I. (Billy) Bryant, already a full England international; Fred Fox, the Gillingham goalkeeper who would play for England before making his Lions debut; and his Gills teammate George Chance. From the ranks of non-League Grays Athletic came a goalscoring inside-forward named John Landells. Now with the likes of Len Graham, Moule, Dillimore, Hill and Fort, Millwall had drastically shortened their odds of reaching the Second Division despite an extended Cup run. The competition had been reorganised for the 1925–26 season, and according to the records held at the FA the club would now be known as Millwall with the suffix Athletic being dropped from the title, and they would now enter from the third round until after World War Two.

The luck of the draw saw them first out of the hat to oppose the Lancastrians Oldham Athletic of Division Two, who would be making their first visit to Cold Blow Lane. It was one-way traffic from start to finish as Millwall bombarded the Oldham goal at will. As such, the Latics attack was rarely seen, and they could count themselves fortunate in not having been on the receiving end of a four-goal mauling. But Millwall's timidity in front of goal was annoying, as they were unable to capitalise on the many chances created in a totally one-sided affair. The Latics defence was stretched to breaking point, but miraculously they survived to earn a replay. On the one occasion their under-worked forwards got away they scored. Having been buffeted from pillar to post, they secured a lead after 37 minutes when

Pynegar gained possession to put Watson away, whose pin-point cross found Stepney-born George Douglas in splendid isolation to pick his spot to beat Lansdale.

Jimmy Dillimore was at his tantalising best but fell into the trap of overdoing his fancy footwork and losing possession on numerous occasions, which gave the crowd the right hump. It appeared that despite all of their excellent approach work and the obligatory huffing and puffing, Millwall were going to come away empty-handed. But then fate played its benevolent hand. After all the clear-cut chances Millwall had passed up, it was a fluke that got them back level in the 77th minute. Having seen all their better efforts fly wide or be saved by the excellent Gray, a harmless looking centre from George Chance became the saving grace. Hit more in hope (or was it frustration?), a number of players vied for the ball, and like everything else in the game (bar the Latics goal) it eluded them all to bounce into an unguarded net for a deserved if fortuitous equaliser.

The incentive for victory in the replay was all Oldham's, as if they were successful they would have earned a fourth-round tie against local rivals Bury at Gigg Lane. Millwall's Cup record against the Shakers was nothing to write home about and would not have instilled overconfidence among the Lions fans, especially with Bury hobnobbing it in the First Division. But the game at Oldham saw the boot firmly on the other foot, with the Latics showing, as expected, a lot more attacking intent. Vastly superior on this occasion, it was Oldham who fell for the sucker-punch as Millwall rode their luck. It took another late strike 10 minutes from time to secure the trip to Bury when Alf Moule collected the ball from a throw-in near the corner flag. In an instant he whipped in a wicked cross for the lurking Andy Lincoln. Andy's header inadvertently took the ball away from goal but luckily straight onto Dick Parker's head, and his instinctive and unerring header gave Oldham's replacement goalkeeper, the veteran Howard Matthews, no chance. In the remaining minutes Oldham nearly forced extra-time with the crowd shouting 'goal' prematurely as Dick Hill managed to head away Watson's dangerous cross from under bar, only for his clearance to fall to Oldham's full-back Sam Wynne whose half-volley went flying over the bar. But it was Millwall who had the final say when Parker nearly doubled the lead with a fearsome shot that was well saved by Oldham's 47-year-old veteran custodian.

A little over a fortnight later Millwall made the journey back up to the Lancashire for the fourth-round clash with Bury, and with the help of two penalties they managed to eke out a favourable 3–3 draw on the ground that had seen them lose on two previous trips there to last-minute goals in 1908 and 1912. In those earlier games Millwall probably deserved to get at least a draw, whereas in this match Bury were the more deserving. It may have appeared to be easy pickings for Bury, who were to finish in fourth place in the First Division that season, but Millwall stormed away in search of any early goal. This they nearly achieved when Parker brushed aside the challenge from the burly Bradshaw to race away and fire in a cracking goal. The referee, however, after awarding the goal was persuaded to consult a linesman following Bury's half-hearted appeals, and to Millwall's amazement he disallowed the effort for a foul by Parker.

Bury celebrated this reprieve by going straight down to the other end to win a penalty when the ball struck Gomm's hand, although it was more ball to hand than the other way round. It was left to Matthews to put away the spot-kick for the only goal of the first half. If the Lions felt hard done by, worse was to follow in the 48th minute when Bullock obtained Bury's second. Millwall seemed to be heading for exit door as the Gigg Lane 'jinx' struck again. A brief spell of Millwall attacks saw them reduce the arrears, however, when Alf Amos despatched the second penalty of the match before Ball restored Bury's two-goal cushion. Millwall still had some time to make a game of it, and when Amos then stepped up to slam home his second spot-kick, it meant the tie was all to play for. A now rejuvenated Millwall went in search of an equaliser, and when Parker was given the opportunity to let rip he sent another screamer into the Bury net to make the score 3–3. With the bit firmly between their teeth, Millwall nearly scored a sensational winner when Andy Lincoln found himself in great position but in his excitement looped the ball over the bar instead of under it.

The norm on a Thursday afternoon in parts of south-east London at that time was the early closing of retail shops, and this was part of the reason Millwall expected and got a marvellous attendance of 32,115 for the replay. There was also the chance of another big gate for the visit of Swansea Town in the next round if they could only dispose of Bury first. They achieved this in a game full of pace and precision that was an uncomfortable 90 minutes for the visitors. The goals, however, when they arrived, were out of keeping with Millwall's fine approach work. A minute before the break, George Chance's spectacular over-head kick hit the bar, only for the ball to brush Parker's body before going over the line. Then, immediately after the restart Millwall scored number two when Chance sent over a free-kick from near to the corner flag, and the Bury 'keeper Richardson managed to get his fingertips to the ball but was powerless to stop the deserving Moule from scoring off a post to run out worthy winners. Lions wingers Chance and Sid Gore put in exceptional performances up front, with Tilling, Hill and the ungainly Gomm the pick of the defenders.

Next it was time for old rivals Swansea Town, who were now playing a division above Millwall and were probably still nursing a grievance from the four-goal mauling they received in 1922. Against the high-riding Swans, Millwall put up a sterling performance in defence, only to go down to the only goal of the game two minutes from time when Fowler netted the winner, while Millwall's attack were very much second best with Dick Parker being well marshalled by Sykes. Swansea's short passing game was always a threat, but they were inclined to over elaborate, but the bottom line was that Millwall had come up against a very classy side. It was hardly a surprise, therefore, that Swansea went on to reach the semi-finals and finish fifth in their Division. As for the Lions, some saw this defeat as a blessing in disguise as they could concentrate on winning promotion, which seemed very likely and which would mean joining the Swans in Division Two the following season. That was until the last four fixtures saw Millwall get a case of stage fright, however. Obtaining just two out of eight points available, they not only lost out on the big prize but also the runners'-up spot to agonisingly fill third place yet again for the third time in four years.

At the culmination of the 1926–27 season the Lions were again destined to finish third, six points behind champions Bristol City and four behind the perennial runners-up Plymouth Argyle, who had finished in second place for the last six seasons. By the time the FA Cup came around in January, Millwall had had a mini-run of three straight victories after coming off a 6–0 hammering at Luton on Christmas Day. They repaid the Hatters in kind with a similar pasting at The Den two days later, even going one better by thumping seven goals without reply. Watford had then put four past them before Southend were beaten 2–0, a week before the third-round visit of Huddersfield Town, the current Football League champions who were on course for a fourth consecutive title. The clubs had now been drawn against each other three times in the last four years. The key ingredient in Millwall's form was the continued fitness of Dick Parker and Wilf 'Peanut' Phillips, who both came through the holiday period unscathed to the benefit of all concerned. Dick Parker would eventually finish up with 38 Cup and League goals that season – a record that was not equalled until Peter Burridge achieved it some 34 years later.

To the surprise of many, but not all, Millwall ran out convincing winners, and the final result of 3–1 did not get anywhere near to describing how decisive the victory was. All this was obtained despite Huddersfield taking the lead through one of their England players, George Brown, who side-footed home Smith's cross in the 30th minute. This came after what looked like a legitimate goal from Alf Gomm had been chalked off inside the first 10 minutes, which could have seen Millwall fold at this stroke of misfortune. It was a change of tactics from Millwall that changed the game, as they began to play the percentages in utilising the long ball to make the most of Archie Gomm's height and started to unsettle their visitors with a persistent aerial bombardment and very direct approach. This ploy was to pay handsome dividends when the ball dropped for the industrious Phillips to shoot the equaliser low into Turner's net in the 38th minute.

Following the goal, the game took on a different complexion and was won conclusively three minutes into the second half when Town's left-back Sam Wadsworth misjudged the flight of another high ball to allow the lanky Gomm to despatch his header beyond Turner for 2–1. It was a sorry-looking and dispirited Town side who conceded a third when George Chance took advantage of more disarray in the Terriers' rearguard to find his fellow winger Alf Black. Described in the press as 'the human greyhound', Alf was left to hammer the ball past Turner for number three. Now with breathing space, Millwall started to express themselves in what was fast turning into a vintage display. The majesty of Billy Bryant, Dick Parker and Wilf Phillips was closely followed by the wide-men Chance and Black, and in reality all were contenders for the Man of the Match award. Skipper Len Graham was moved to say in a post-match comment 'I was not greatly surprised at Millwall's success. I felt ever since the draw has been made that if Millwall played as well they could play, the League champions' interest in the Cup as far as this season was concerned would evaporate at the first hurdle.' And so it did.

Having laid one particular ghost to rest, the Lions had the chance to repeat it when they were drawn against another Division One outfit and old Cup foes Derby County at the Baseball Ground in the fourth round. Millwall definitely owed the Rams one, if not more, having been beaten in two previous encounters, including the 1903 semi-final and a first-round tie seven years later. The task facing Millwall would be hard to overcome as Derby had only lost twice at home that season, but the job was made a lot easier when County, for reasons best known to themselves, dropped their best forward and topscorer, Gill.

If Lions 'keeper Joe Lansdale had been a virtual spectator in the Huddersfield match, against the Rams he had plenty to do, not so much in the way of saving shots; although his exceptional display in handling anything that came within his domain was the reason Derby failed to breach his defence. He had an outstanding game and was ably assisted in the cause by the no-nonsense tackling of his fellow defenders. The half-backs, not for the first time in Millwall's Cup history, excelled in keeping the score sheet blank at the break. The very committed Derby side attacked at the start of the second half before Millwall's confidence soared when they opened the scoring, albeit with a slice of luck. When Dick Parker's effort rebounded off the bar it fell to Derby's left-half Plackett, whose miscue found its way past his 'keeper Olney and into the net. Looking the stronger and with their confidence soaring, Millwall went for the kill and 12 minutes later went two up through industrious workhorse Dick Parker. Looking more like a prized stallion than a footballer, he sprinted clear into the County area only to be felled by Derby's last covering defender, Crilly. Without hesitation the official pointed to the spot. Up came Wilf Phillips to extend the Lions' lead with great accuracy to secure a very sweet success with a well struck penalty.

With other southern clubs like Brentford, Swansea and Reading still left in the competition, Millwall were hoping to draw one of these – going on the premise that it is better the devil you know. As it turned out they were given a home match against Middlesbrough, who were on their way to winning the Second Division title, led by the free-scoring George Camsell, whose 59 goals in 37 games that season is still a Second Division record. So, having taken the scalps of Huddersfield and Derby, some of the older Millwall supporters would probably have realised that here was another opportunity to gain some overdue payback against a team who had halted the Lions' progress in 1904 and 1913. Those fans helped pack The Den to the rafters as 44,250 (another new ground record) squeezed into every nook and cranny, and those fans saw Millwall explode into action by going three goals up in the opening half an hour. The first goal arrived after just three minutes, when the rangy Archie Gomm, whose height had caused Huddersfield so many problems, converted George Chance's hanging cross.

Boro's 'keeper Billy Mathieson was picking the ball out of the net again 10 minutes later when Alf Black's fabulous cross-shot made it two; however, the whirlwind start was held in check immediately when the visitors were awarded a penalty in their first promising move. Alf Amos was pulled up for a foul on the prolific Camsell, and it was the goal-machine himself who took the kick but saw his blistering drive smack against the crossbar. Poor George suffered a further indignation moments later when another drive thumped an upright. With nearly 30 minutes played, Millwall strengthened their grip with a third goal. When George Chance received the ball he went on a mazy run (reminiscent of Wally Davis's versus Bradford City in 1914) that took him past four opponents and left him with just Mathieson to beat. Like Wal, 13 years previously, George slipped the ball past the advancing 'keeper as Millwall cashed in on Boro's embarrassing frailties in defence.

Middlesbrough's wretched luck continued when Camsell, and then Billy Birrell, both struck Joe Lansdale's timber frame, leaving them wondering what had they to do to score. The missing of gilt-edged chances continued when Harold Pease failed to score from a second Boro spot-kick, at which point they must have realised it was not going to be their day. Nevertheless, it remained a mystery to the head-scratching Boro players how Millwall reached half-time three goals to the good. It was no more than the Lions deserved, though, as they played skilful, attacking and lightening-paced football of the highest quality that left their opponents' defence mesmerised. Boro refused to roll over, however, and to their eternal credit continued to press forward, and their resolve was rewarded when their fortunes took a turn for the better after the break. The lively and pacey Pease redeemed himself to reduce the arrears following his penalty miss, and as the half progressed he became a constant threat to Millwall. He also had a hand in Boro's second goal when he sent in another meaty effort, which Millwall could only partially clear. The ball was quickly seized by the former Clapton Orient player Owen Williams, who hit a spectacular cross-shot which found the far corner of Millwall's net.

This set the nerves jangling for a while, but slowly and surely the kingly Billy Bryant took command by shackling the rampaging Camsell. Marshalling his defence, he bestrode The Den with an air of confidence, regularly supplying his forwards and cajoling his colleagues for the remainder of the game to see Millwall home. The final whistle brought to an end one of the greatest and exciting matches seen at Cold Blow Lane, and the crowd surged onto the pitch to hoist the heroic Joe Lansdale shoulder high and carry him from the field in celebration of a well-earned and deserved victory.

If the ball had been rolling Millwall's way, it was now to deviate in favour of their sixth-round opponents, who happened to be old adversaries Southampton. The Lions were given, for a fourth successive Cup tie, the opportunity to set the record straight with a long-awaited FA Cup victory over the Saints. But looking beyond the Saints game, Millwall really did have a wonderful chance of reaching not only the semis but also the Final itself, as there were only two First Division clubs left in the tournament.

At the end of an insipid 90 minutes, which ended in a goalless draw, it was clear that the Saints hoodoo was still hovering over the Lions. Millwall wasted their best chance to progress when Wilf Phillips drove his penalty-kick wide after Gomm's shot had been handled. The disbelieving fans who had been spoilt rotten following the treats served up against Huddersfield and Middlesbrough were left to rue Wilf's aberration. For this game, however, the other side of the coin was seen all too clearly as the home attack misfired for the first time during the run. The astute passing of late went completely to pot, whereas the Saints could not put a foot wrong. After Phillips's miss an air of pessimistic inevitably settled around The Den, a feeling carried on into the replay in which Millwall were not helped by the absence of Billy Bryant. With Mick Collins replacing the charismatic Bryant, Millwall fell to a brace

The ticket from the Millwall versus Southampton sixth-round meeting in 1927 when Lions once again failed to lay their Cup 'bogey' over Saints as this game petered out to a goalless draw. [Andy Sullivan]

of first-half goals by Bill Rawlings from which they never recovered. The first was a scrappy effort that came off his shoulder, and the goal that clinched their semi-final meeting with the Arsenal came when a hard, swerving shot gave Lansdale no chance. It was definitely a bad day at the office that again left Millwall so near yet so far away.

The 1927–28 season was the occasion Millwall finally delivered in the League, taking the title by 10 points from Northampton Town, who had inflicted upon the Lions an opening day reverse of 5–2. Millwall's extravagance in the merciless way they achieved their title had many of the opinion that a run in the Cup could become an encumbrance. As it turned out, the opponents for the season's only game in the competition were Derby County who themselves were challenging at the top of the First Division. The game attracted the biggest gate of the day, but for the Lions there was to be no further involvement this time around as County took the game by the odd goal in three, with Lions' recent signing, the former England international Jack Cock, scoring the goal. Jack would prove an inspirational capture who would register 25 goals in 27 games as the Lions took the Third Division (South) Championship in some style.

In such a momentous season, if a team are going to have an off-day then there is none better than choosing a match where points are not an issue – and the game against County was such a match. Millwall were again lacking the excellent Bryant, and this appeared to affect the whole team, with Alf Black especially out of touch. Then there was George Chance trying to dribble past everyone when a pass seemed more appropriate, and with County's Davison subduing the veteran Jack Cock for the most part Millwall's attack was pretty ineffective. It was County who secured the lead after quarter of an hour when Stephenson's low drive beat George Harford, but surprisingly Millwall were level before the half hour was up. John Landells' spade work set up a tap-in for Jack Cock before Derby's winner arrived in the early part of the second half. Goalkeeper George Harford went down to save Whitehouse's tame effort, but he only succeeded in pushing the ball into Bedford's path and he netted with ease.

Millwall's newly acquired Second Division status signalled a period of consistency in which they finished in 14th place in three consecutive seasons from 1928–29 to 1930–31. During those first two campaigns they played 10 Cup ties but did not proceed beyond the fifth round. For the third-round tie against Northampton Town in January 1929 they was fortunate enough to be drawn at home at this stage for the sixth time in a row and were, for once, indebted to a refereeing decision that gave them a another chance of progression with a replay.

Third Division Northampton had taken the lead after 15 minutes when Harford in the Millwall goal made an error – not an unusual thing for him to do in the Cup. He completely misjudged the pace of Weston's centre by taking his eye off the ball and not only let it pass through his arms but also his legs for a very poor goal. Halfway through the second half came the refereeing incident in which Millwall were given the benefit of the doubt. The match official interpreted Jack Cock's dramatic fall in the box as a foul when it appeared he received no more than a fair shoulder charge from the Cobblers' left-back Brett. This must have brought some mirth to the watching fans who thought Jack's dying swan act was more embarrassing than Harford's gaffe. Not one to ignore a gift horse, 'Peanut' Phillips duly slammed home the spot-kick. George Harford redeemed himself in the eyes of the fans late in the game with some excellent saves. Nevertheless, Northampton were getting a tad rattled with all their best efforts coming to nothing. A change of tactics may have been more beneficial, but they continued to play into Millwall's hands with their direct approach down the middle when it was blindingly obvious that the flanks would offer a better option.

For the replay Millwall made four changes: out went Harford, Bryant, Landells and Phillips, to be replaced by Lansdale, Collins, Readman and Harley. Despite the changes having the desired effect initially, the teams were still deadlocked after 90 minutes. It was Millwall who drew first blood when early pressure initiated a lapse in the Town defence, which enabled Jack Cock to open the scoring after 20 minutes, this time with no theatrics. The pitch resembled a skating rink, and as a result the game suffered as a spectacle, but the conditions did not stop Northampton, who were level within 60 seconds following some nifty passing between Smith and McNaughton which opened the way for Hoten to drive home from 20 yards. This was how it remained until the end of the game. The period of extra-time was the first Millwall had faced since the tie at Aston Villa back in 1900. When Town's Hoten scored his second goal to put them ahead in the 95th minute, his strike appeared to be the likely winner. But with time running out Millwall launched one last effort to rescue the game, and amazingly it brought the equaliser. The unfortunate Brett, as he had in the first game, again became the Lions' unwitting saviour by needlessly giving away a free-kick after fouling Fred Martin. There was barely time to take the kick but Joe Readman set his sights to thump home a face-saver.

In 1929 penalty shoot-outs were light years away, and so after having two bites of the cherry Millwall had the fruit of progression dangling in front of them for a third time. Surely now, with the second replay set for Highbury, they could make their class tell and finish off a brave Northampton team. Millwall, by utilising the strengths of wingers George Chance and the ex-Nottingham Forest and Leicester City raider Harry Wadsworth to maximum effect, finally reached the next round with a convincing 2–0 success. George was at his creative best by setting up both goals, and his first telling contribution came in the 42nd minute when he heaped more torment on the luckless Brett by showing him the ball then dummying inside, where he found Landells and Wadsworth totally unmarked. It was the better-placed Landells who took full advantage of the space to fire in the opener. There was a touch of comedy with the second when Phillips tried to pounce on another of Chance's centres, only to fluff his shot which inadvertently fell to a surprised Jack Cock, who rocketed home the loose ball to ensure a meeting with neighbours Crystal Palace.

With Northampton finally out of the way, the Lions would now face Palace, who would take the runners'-up spot behind champions and fellow south Londoners Charlton Athletic in the League. The fourth-round meeting with Palace drew a crowd of over 40,000 to The Den with the expectancy levels for a thrilling game high, and the fact that it was a local derby to boot only added further spice. But, as on many such occasions, the match never really lived up to the pre-match hype and finished in a drab, goalless stalemate. There was nothing to recommend or excite the spectators in the encounter, with most of them long gone before the final whistle was blown.

If the first match had been devoid of the usual ingredients of Cup football, the replay certainly made up for all that had been missing down at Cold Blow Lane. Mistakes, blunders, goals and controversy – this match had them all. Millwall had had some fortuitous moments against Northampton, but the rub of the green in this meeting was all Palace's. The first error manifested itself early on, when they took the lead in the 10th minute as Joe Lansdale could only push Harry Havelock's header to the waiting Hubert Butler, who drove home the loose ball. A contentious point, the first of many, then occurred when Palace scored their second. One of the linesmen was flagging furiously for offside against the Palace duo Clarke and Griffiths, but a myopic referee chose to ignore it, as he did Millwall's protestations, allowing Griffiths' effort to stand.

Hackles well and truly rose as Millwall set about righting the wrongs with a magical five-minute spell that unbelievably brought them level just before the interval. Jack Cock reduced the arrears with a glorious header from Chance's cross before Billy Callender's fine save denied Landells as they continued to pummel the Palace defence. Their persistence was rewarded when Callender failed to gather one of George Chance's numerous centres, and this allowed Alf Black sufficient time to make no mistake for the equaliser. Almost immediately after the break the second controversial point arose. A home defender had clearly handled the ball to stop it entering the net, but the referee appeared totally oblivious to the events happening around him turned down vociferous Millwall appeals for a penalty, and the Lions then committed the cardinal sin of not playing to the whistle. Palace careered up field with no Lion in pursuit – their remonstrations with the officials had left a hesitant and bewildered Lansdale high and dry (and a little red-faced), and his lack of anticipation to Harry's high centre gave Butler the easy task of netting Palace's third.

The catalogue of unmitigated disasters continued unabashed when Jimmy Pipe's clearance, which would have found safety 99 times out of a 100, dropped just right for Bert Harry to plunder Palace's fourth. There was even a hint of offside about Palace's fifth, which enabled Butler to complete his hat-trick after 77 minutes, but by then Millwall had given up the ghost of receiving any partiality; however, it was John Landells who had the final word when he defiantly lashed home Millwall's third eight minutes from time.

Millwall's opening foray into the 1929–30 FA Cup competition came in a third-round tie against the bastions of the amateur game – the famous Corinthians – at the Crystal Palace, the arena in which the Lions had appeared for the their first semi-final in 1900. The amateurs, having been founded 1882, had it not been for their own stringent rules which forbade them taking part in competitive fixtures would have surely won the FA Cup when they had a vast pool of players to call upon, including Millwall's very own Corinthian J.H. (Joe) Gettins. By the time they finally entered the competition in 1922 they may not have been the power they once were, but they still had the talent to give their professional counterparts a game – as Millwall found out in three very competitive encounters.

The first meeting was played on a raw day with icy conditions underfoot, not aided by a combination of sleet and rain. Claude Ashton earned Corinthians a replay with a last-minute strike to bring a glorious match to a dramatic conclusion. Millwall, who started the more promising, had forsaken the temptation of being overawed by their illustrious and skilful opponents. Their first effective move bore fruit after just 15 minutes when Corkindale's burst down the right saw him get free to place the ball into the path of Jimmy 'Chisel' Forsyth to do the honours. Following this reverse, the Corinthian attack took control as they

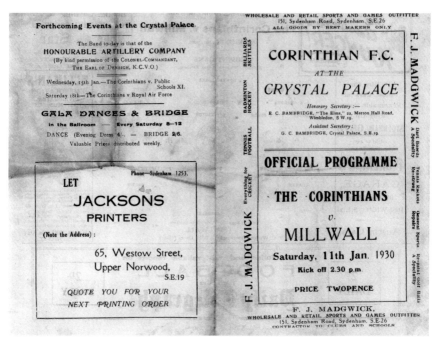

The cover of the Corinthian versus Millwall match programme, held at the old Cup Final ground of Crystal Palace. Goals from Jimmy Forsyth and Wilf Phillips earned the Lions a 2–2 draw. [Norman Epps]

pressed Millwall back onto the defensive, and as a result they started to concede corner-kicks with monotonous regularity. Lions defenders Sid Tyler, Jim Pipe, Alf Gomm and Len Graham had to be at their best in fighting a rugged rearguard action to see the side through to half-time with their lead still intact.

The situation changed five minutes into the second half, however, when Norman Creek sent Ken Hegan away, but his initial attempt was blocked and the ball ran to Robins, who blasted it past Lansdale for the equaliser. After 70 minutes Millwall regained the lead when Wilf Phillips, who had been receiving some pitch-side treatment, was back in the thick of the action to finish off a cross that had eluded both Cock and Corkindale to steer it past Howard-Baker in the Corinthian goal. This strike was to be Wilf's last vital contribution for the Lions as the injury he received worsened and eventually finished his career with club the following summer. This was how it stayed until the persistent Ashton at last managed to find the net in dramatic style with virtually the last kick of the match.

After such a thrilling first instalment, the fans were left wanting more of the same, and the excitment of the first game ensured another massive crowd would flock to The Den for the replay the following Wednesday in the hope of witnessing another enthralling and captivating game. Millwall made two changes for the game, with John Landells replacing the injured Phillips, while at right-back Sid Sweetman came in for Tyler. For Sweetman, the afternoon would be a test of his abilities that were stretched to breaking point as he was given a torrid time by the dashing Hegan. It was the former Army man who stood out as the Corinthians's main threat, as his outstanding ability was to take on and beat his man at break-neck speed.

Hegan's pace was shown to its extent when he went scampering in pursuit of Alf Bowers's clearance to create the opening goal for the visitors with a breathtaking smash-and-grab raid. Centring the ball from on the goalline, his intended recipient Ashton missed it but instead found the supporting Robins to lash in an unstoppable drive past Lansdale. The scenario at the break replicated the first game, but this time it was Millwall who were a goal down. The Lions did manage to force a succession of corners and crosses early in the second half from Jimmy Poxton, but they all came to nothing. Nevertheless, Millwall eventually drew level following a mêlée in front of the Corinthians goal, which saw the ball come the way of an unmarked Jimmy Poxton, who was on hand to easily beat Howard-Baker from close range. Millwall continued to push forward, but resolute defending by the amateurs kept the home team at bay to force extra-time. Having encountered rain and sleet at the Palace, it was fog that threatened to scupper the proceedings as Millwall started extra-time with vitality by forcing Howard-Baker into two excellent saves in as many minutes. But the game gradually fell away after this as tiredness crept in, although Hegan extracted some extra stamina from somewhere to rekindle his earlier threat. Claude Ashton fired wide after

The third-round meeting between Millwall and the Corinthians in January 1930 aroused great interest as two football cultures clashed. The Lions, seen as the working class, were pitted against the true-blue idealism of the amateurs, and it took Millwall three attempts to get past their illustrious contemporaries. Over 136,000 spectators watched the three games, and shown here is a crowded Cold Blow Lane prior to the first replay. [Unknown].

The equaliser from Jimmy Poxton beat Corinthians goalkeeper Howard Baker in the third-round replay at The Den in January 1930. Following extra-time the game finished 1–1, the outcome of which was a second replay. [Unknown]

Hegan set him up, as Ashton again, Creek and Doggart all had efforts on the Millwall goal before the match finally petered out to draw, with the amateurs, it must be said, finishing the stronger.

Having failed to settle their differences, the teams were required to meet at Stamford Bridge for a second replay. This game attracted a stunning 58,775 paying customers, which amassed a figure in access of £4,000 at the turnstiles and an accumulative attendance figure of over 135,000 which brought forth total takings of £10,125 for what had been a truly amazing tie. With the fourth round designated for the following Saturday, this Monday afternoon encounter had to be decided just to avert the chaos of fixture congestion. As they had done at Crystal Palace, it was the Lions who drew first blood with a somewhat fluky goal when Jack Cock's pass found its way to 'Chisel' Forsyth, whose miscue from 25 yards completely wrong-footed Howard-Baker who could only watch the ball just about creep into the net.

With typical stoicism, Corinthians countered to drag themselves level with probably the best goal of the game following a corner-kick. From the moment Robins crossed the ball, it did not touch the ground until it had hit the back of the Millwall net. Ashton's deft touch found Doggart, who, with his back to goal, sent in an excellent overhead-kick that left Millwall custodian Willie Wilson a mere spectator. With the teams still deadlocked at the interval, the thought of extra-time would have had occurred to many at this stage. But the scenario was to change through human frailty, when in the 53rd minute Howard Baker was at fault. A well-worked corner left Billy Corkindale the space to exploit the former Olympian and British high-jump champion's lack of positional sense to crack home from an acute angle. He had to shoulder the blame for Millwall's third goal, too, when he allowed Wadworth's soft effort to slip from his grasp, enabling the predatory Jack Cock to block Knight's attempted clearance which rebound into the net. The bold amateurs' resistance finally collapsed altogether when Cock scored the fourth following a fine individual run, before Corkindale completed the rout when he had all the time in the world to pick his spot for Millwall's fifth and his second.

Following the gruelling triumvirate of games against the Corinthians, Millwall had just five days to prepare physically and mentally for the fourth-round tie against Doncaster Rovers at The Den, and if offered beforehand Millwall would have accepted any sort of victory. But to gain a 4–0 win would have been beyond their wildest dreams. However, in reality it was a very flattering result, and the final score was a tad harsh on the gritty northerners. Prior to the kick-off, skipper Jack Graham had received a telegram from his Corinthian opposite Graham Doggart whose sincere gesture and encouraging words were 'Best luck to you all this afternoon and next rounds'.

Millwall looked very tired and jaded in what had been a drab first-half, and they were thankful for the lead given to them by Jimmy Hawkins, a recruit from Barking Town, who scored just before the break when he converted Wadsworth's centre. Missing from the Lions team were the likes of Joe Lansdale, Dick Hill and Wilf Phillips, and so it appeared that the scratch team were going to scramble through by the only goal. In the last 15 minutes, however, they finally broke loose to extend the scoring with three further goals against their hard-done-by opponents. If the profligate Hawkins had any composure he would surely have added to his two-goal haul, and he was grateful for Jack Cock's persistence in obtaining his second. Jack was

The Times published some excellent photos for the Millwall versus Corinthian replay at The Den, and the one here shows goalkeeper Howard-Baker punching clear a Millwall threat.

again heavily involved when setting up Corkindale for the third before the fourth followed Forsyth's mazy run and dribble, which gave Wadsworth the simple task of netting.

Having reached the fifth round for the second time in three years, Millwall would now revive their rivalry of old with West Ham United, for the first Cup meeting since December 1899 when the Hammers were then known as Thames Ironworks. Since those heady days of Millwall claiming the East End bragging rights, West Ham had moved ahead of the Lions in status. The Hammers were current members of the First Division, having been elected into the Football League in 1919, and had contested and lost the initial Wembley Cup Final in 1923 to Bolton Wanderers. Millwall's form, however, had not been too bad leading up to the game, but after conceding four first-half goals with three of them in a devastating four-minute spell there was no way back for the Lions.

The windy conditions also had a bearing on the game. The wind was blowing directly down the Upton Park pitch, but West Ham adapted so much better and therefore gained the early advantage. The Hammers got quickly into their stride to open the scoring with the best goal of the game when Tommy Yews swung in a low cross from the right for Viv Gibbins to drive powerfully past Joe Lansdale. The outcome was decided conclusively 20 minutes later when Vic Watson touched home Jim Barrett's deceptive free-kick before Lansdale fumbled for Yews to scramble home a third. The 240 seconds of mayhem ceased when Watson, with his eighth Cup goal of the season, added a fourth from virtually the restart, reaching a bouncing ball before Lansdale to head past the stranded Lion.

The referee then came to Millwall's aid to deny Watson his hat-trick when he ruled out what would have been a fifth for West Ham as they continued pile on the misery. For Millwall and their disheartened fans the half was brought mercifully to an end. The second period saw the wind get stronger and the temperature dip even further as Millwall set out to soothe their bruised pride. They were rewarded when Harry Wadsworth scored the Lions' consolation goal. Cashing in on 'keeper Ted Hufton's weak clearance, Harry left the forlorn Hammer a sorry figure as he scored into an open goal. Millwall created some other chances which were not taken before a snowstorm in the closing minutes sent many fans scurrying for the exits. By virtue of their 4–1 victory, West Ham had for the third time in successive home ties registered four goals, after beating Notts County and Leeds United 4–0 and 4–1 respectively.

By the second week of January 1931 the Lions got no further than the third round after slipping up in a disappointing 3–1 defeat at Third Division Southport. This came after a heart-warming display against Charlton who were sent packing by six goals to nil the week before. All the gloss and polish garnered from that win dulled to insignificance after they conceded two goals in the first 15 minutes. Poor displays at full-back from the usually reliable Sid Sweetmen and Jimmy Pipe afforded Southport's wingers so much room it beggared belief, and despite these deficiencies Jimmy Poxton could and should have reduced the arrears before half-time, but the hard-hitting winger saw his penalty-kick saved by Baker. Jim did manage to find the net in the second half when he and Wadsworth provided the only bright spots during Millwall's only threatening passage of play in which they may have forced an equaliser. Hopes of bringing Southport back to New Cross were dashed when Cowan restored the two-goal advantage with his second of the tie.

It was just as well that centre-half Frank Hancock was on form by keeping a tight rein on Southport's leading scorer Waterston, and had Southport's shooting been on a par with their approach work Millwall could have ended up suffering a far bigger embarrassment. The outcome may have come as a shock to the Millwall fans, but later results would show it was no flash in the pan. Southport would go on to knock out their First Division neighbours Blackpool and Bradford before crashing out to Everton 9–1 in the quarter-finals.

As with Huddersfield Town in the 1920s, it was Manchester City who were the team to face the Lions most often in the decade leading up to World War Two. They met on no less than four occasions, which included a replay, with all the original games being played at Cold Blow Lane. The first in this mini-saga was a third-round match which took place in January 1932, a game that brought the premature end of Millwall centre-forward Les Smith's career, who up until then had scored 16 goals in 22 League games. Les had been signed in 1930 from Redhill FC, where his sharp shooting skills in and around the box had turned him into a prolific goalscorer.

It was Brighton-born Les who gave Millwall an early lead, before John Landells nearly added a second, but it was Lions goalkeeper Willie Wilson they had to thank for keeping the score respectable as Halliday, Marshall and Tilson all threatened to overrun a beleaguered home defence. Unruffled by the 'keeper's display, City managed to turn it around before half-time when Halliday pounced twice to put the visitors in command. Following a typical battling display in the first 20 minutes of the second half, Millwall gained an opportunity to equalise after 65 minutes. It was City's former England man Sam Cowan who handled in the area, which allowed Jimmy Poxton to restore parity when he slotted home the penalty. There was to be no fairytale ending this time, however, as with five minutes remaining Toseland's spurt into the Millwall area put him in an excellent position to convert Eric Brook's centre for the winning goal. A depressing week was made harder to bear when a Smith-less Millwall went down to their record League defeat of 8–1 at Plymouth, with seven of Argyle's goals arriving at regular intervals during the second half. George Bond, Les Smith's replacement, was the scorer of the Lions' only goal.

Through a Jimmy Poxton penalty and a Bert Bloxham strike, Millwall appeared to be home and dry with a two-goal lead over Reading at The Den in the third-round tie in 1933, before another wretched fog intervened with just 15 minutes to go. As galling as it was, the conditions left the referee with no alternative but to abandon the game. Four days later, the teams reassembled at New Cross, and following a goalless first-half Poxton, not to be denied his obligatory Cup goal, nudged the Lions ahead after 70 minutes with a fine effort following some bright and enterprising play. But with 10 minutes to go the unthinkable happened as Reading drew level with a stroke of luck. The unfortunate Jimmy Pipe, one of Millwall's better players on the day, was left with egg on his face when his own-goal secured the Royals' equaliser. The frozen pitch at Elm Park made the replay a lottery, and Reading's good fortune finally ran out. By adapting better to the conditions Millwall recorded a 2–0 success. Quick release of the ball became the order of the day, and it nearly brought the Lions an early reward. With just a minute gone, it seemed easy pickings for George Ivory, who was left all alone in front of Reading's goal but contrived to miss from six yards. The first-half appeared to be heading goalless, but with just seconds remaining Bert Bloxham

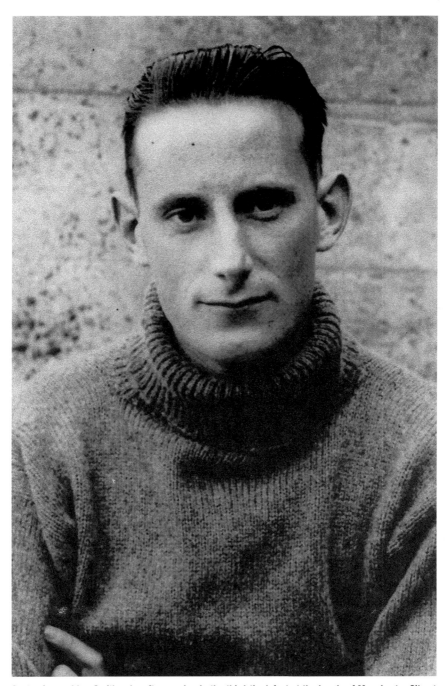

Centre-forward Les Smith, who after scoring in the third-tie defeat at the hands of Manchester City at The Den in 1932 sustained an injury that was to finish his career. [Mike Smith]

scored. A Millwall throw-in caught a statuesque Reading defence flat-footed, and, timing his leap to perfection, Bert outjumped a posse of players to nod home the first goal just as the whistle sounded.

Bloxham the scorer became Bloxham the provider as Millwall clinched the tie after 70 minutes. His fine individual run and centre caused Reading's Dick Mellors and Matt Forsters to dither over responsibility, allowing George Bond to punish their indecision with a smart header for goal number two. Shortly afterwards, the home team were given a chance to reduce the arrears when Hancock was adjudged to have fouled Palthorpe in the box; however, the Royals' misery was made complete when the pressure proved too much for the taker, Charlie Barley (I kid you not), who fired his effort straight at Wilson as Millwall went on to complete a deserved win. The replay had given the watching members of the Aldershot team the chance to preview what to expect in the following Saturday's fourth-round tie as they spied from the Elm Park stands.

The Shots, newly elected into the Third Division South, in reaching this stage had beaten both Clapton Orient and Accrington Stanley away before taking the scalp of Bristol Rovers in the third round. Millwall faced a formidable task of breaching a defence that had conceded only one Cup goal thus far. A crowd of 8,661 assembled inside a cramped Recreation Ground to see an Aldershot victory by a narrow one goal to nil. Despite their marginal loss, however, the Lions had been well beaten.

Aldershot's game plan was simple. Long before the Wimbledon team of the late 1980s and early 1990s, who were branded as 'long ball' merchants, the Shots had perfected the tactic, and it ultimately led to success in this tie. As well as launching the ball as often as possible down the middle, they also toyed with playing long balls down the flanks to great effect. It was the former West Ham and Brentford player Fred Gamble whose main job it was to harass the Lions defence, which he did surprisingly well, and he was aided and abetted by Jack Lane and the Surrey and future England cricketer Laurie Fishlock, who struck the only goal of the game in the 42nd minute when thumping home McDougall's free-kick.

The result of a football match can be rectified almost immediately, but the loss Millwall suffered two months later on 28 March 1933 was a much mightier blow when the shattering news came that the manager, the great Bob Hunter, had died. This bore a striking similarity to man he had replaced, Billy Lindsay, who had collapsed and died while preparing the team for a Cup tie in 1897. So Bob, who had been the club's guiding light for 36 years, was no more, and the devastation felt by the club was be immense. Although the team would go on to finish in their highest League position, gaining a credible seventh place, following the win at Charlton four days before Bob's death the team became a rudderless boat without the steadying hand of their skipper. Lacking the motivation to kick a football, the rest of the season tailed off as the team picked up a mere four points from the 16 available. Had Bob Hunter lived, who knows where his beloved Millwall may have finished in the final reckoning.

Following Bob's passing, the alarm bells started clanging long before his replacement's, the legendry Irishman Billy McCracken, first full season of 1933–34 was over. The stop-start campaign imploded, and McCracken could do little or nothing about it, and the club's poor form had far-reaching repercussions. The quest for survival hinged on the last game of the campaign against Manchester United at The Den with Millwall needing just a point to survive, while United required both. The teams played out a tense and fraught encounter, in which United prevailed with a 2–0 win to condemn the Lions to their first unpalatable dose of relegation.

The two Cup ties Millwall played during McCracken's initial season were both played at home, the first of which saw them take on northerners Accrington Stanley in the third round. Without too much trouble the Lions saw off the Lancastrians 3–0, despite Stanley reaching half-time still on level terms; however, the inevitable finally occurred after 56 minutes when Jimmy Yardley, who had made the short journey to The Den after signing from Charlton the previous November, sent in a glorious cross-shot for the first, before George Phillips added a second soon after and Yardley's header clinched a meeting with First Division Leicester City.

A gate of over 34,000 welcomed the Foxes for the fourth-round encounter in which Millwall made one change from the team that had beaten Accrington a fortnight earlier, with Stan Alexander replacing George Bond at outside-right. For the neutral or a City fan this game was full of attacking football and incidents and was the sort of a match you would not want to end. Millwall's only consolation after the dust had settled was the part they played in an enthralling nine-goal thriller. Unfortunately, Millwall had no one to match the class of the visiting quartet of Arthur Maw, Arthur Lochhead, Hugh Adcock and Septimus Smith, who led City to establish a match-winning lead of 5–1 in the second half.

It was Smith who got Leicester on their way, who after rounding Pipe surprised everyone by driving the ball in-off the far post rather than putting in the expected cross. Jimmy Pipe then blocked a goal-bound effort from Lochhead. Millwall found a quick remedy a minute later when summer recruit Laurie Fishlock provided a pin-point centre for George Phillips to head home the equaliser. The action continued unabated as Arthur Chandler, one of City's best pre-war strikers, took advantage of some dreadful marking to force home Lochhead's knock-down. Fishlock then sent in a screamer which went narrowly wide before Stan Alexander had the Lions fans screaming 'goal', but his effort smacked the Leicester crossbar, with Foxes 'keeper Jimmy McLaren clutching at thin air.

Following this brief spell of pressure, Millwall fell further behind when an unsighted Willie Wilson was beaten by Maw's dipping volley into the top-left-hand corner. A mild piece of controversy then occurred when Danny Liddle claimed City's fourth after he appeared to kick the ball out of Wilson's hands with his left foot before driving it home with his right. The second half had barely started when Maw paved the way for Adcock to send in a pin-point cross for Chandler to head home number five. Jimmy Yardley set up a barnstorming finale when he reduced the arrears with an excellent strike before the Maw-Adcock pairing gave Lochhead the opening to score the sixth. This provoked some swift retaliation from Millwall. Roared on by the crowd, the fur began to fly when Bert Roberts gave Yardley a chance but shot wide, only to make amends moments later when obtaining Millwall's third with another fine goal to make it 3–6. The exchanges continued to flow from end to end until the referee, Mr F. W. Reeve of Devon, brought the pulsating Cup tie to its conclusion. It was now back to the weekly grind of League football. Despite the

The Millwall team and club officials have time for a photograph before their departure from Euston Station in readiness for the FA Cup the following day at Wigan, with centre-half Frank Hancock modelling the latest line in plus-fours. [Chris Bethell]

gallant display against Leicester, however, the desired boost failed to materialise as Millwall failed to win another game for over two months. This led to an inevitable slide down the table as they meekly surrendered their full-member status of the Football Association after just six seasons.

Hopes were high for the 1934–35 season, however, especially after an opening run of six straight victories, and it seemed McCracken and Millwall had turned the corner. But when a slump kicked in it yielded just three victories in the next 17 games, and Millwall had to settle for mid-table mediocrity with a 12th-placed finish. During the course of the next two seasons the FA Cup brought little cheer; although it did throw up something of a novelty when Millwall were drawn away to an unknown quantity in non-League Wigan Athletic up at Springfield Park.

As expected, Millwall gained a victory by four goals to one, but the final result did not tell the whole story and was a bit flattering. Wigan attacked for two thirds of the game, but it was the Lions who held the aces in all facets of the match, especially when they needed to defend. It was following Millwall's fifth-minute goal from Jim Yardley that Wigan began their onslaught on the visitors' goal; however, their forwards, when the occasion rose, preferred to pass instead of shooting, but they did manage to equalise when Roberts planted his header beyond Yuill after 26 minutes. But Wigan's celebrations were short-lived when Jack Thorogood restored the lead three minutes later, a lead Millwall held until the break. Wigan kept up their incessant attacks at the start of the second half, before they ran out of steam in the final 10 minutes.

It was then that Millwall's stamina came into play to hit Wigan with a double whammy. Jimmy Yardley put the match beyond their reach with the third after converting Jim McCartney's excellent cross, and with the home defence at a standstill Stan Alexander ran in an easy fourth. In the fourth round the Lions faced the shorter trip to Elm Park to face old rivals Reading. This encounter compared to the tie against the Royals two years earlier was a dour match that lacked the usual sparkle of a Cup game. Endemic of the campaign was the malfunctioning of the Lions' forwards, who never looked pulling back Tommy Tait's 40th-minute goal, which proved to be the winner.

Needless to say, Millwall's interest in following the season's competition got no further than the third round when they entertained First Division Stoke City, who included among their ranks Stanley Matthews, England prospect Freddie Steele and the first player of Chinese extraction to play League football Frank Soo, who was later to play wartime football for the Lions. Millwall's inability to break down a rock-like City defence combined with their own equally defiant rearguard resulted in an inevitable goalless stalemate. The replay was a real let-down for the Lions as they never showed any of the resilience that earned them a draw in the first game, and Stoke won at a canter, with Steele scoring three of their four goals in a win which earned them the right to face Manchester United in the next round.

Following manager Bill McCracken's resignation at the end of March, Millwall wasted no time in replacing him by hastily handing the job to man who would revolutionise the club from top to bottom, namely Charlie 'Captain' Hewitt, who took charge for the first time for the Good Friday fixture against Brighton at The Den on 10 April.

7. Charles Hewitt Esq.

Charlie Hewitt came with a fine track record when he was appointed as the secretary-manager of Millwall, following his arrival from Chester. He was trained as an accountant and as such he was always banging on about the finances and the effect they had in the transfer market. Nevertheless, he breezed into Cold Blow Lane and swept away the despondency that had hung around since Hunter's death and which had spread during McCracken's reign. His innovative showmanship came to the fore when he changed the colour of the players' shirt to royal blue that would incorporate a badge for the first time. The continuance of Millwall's Scottish association was aptly supplied with the lion rampant dominating the new badge. This was done to instil a sense of pride into his new charges. Another flash of inspiration was the erection of a giant clock on the then uncovered north terrace at The Den.

The engagement of Hewitt appeared to have caught the imagination of the diehard fans and those malcontents who had fallen by the wayside. An eager and expectant crowd of 35,000 turned up for opening match of the 1936–37 season, but typically Millwall managed to fluff their lines to lose by the odd goal in three against Bristol Rovers. Despite that minor hiccup, the die had been cast as team-building started in earnest with the mercurial centre-forward Dave Mangnall and left-back Tommy Inns joining from West Ham, along with other newcomers Ken Burditt, Ted Smith and Jimmy Wallbanks. These new faces along with some of McCracken's captures such as Jim McCartney, J.R. Smith, Tom Brolly and the old stager Jimmy Forsyth were to be the bedrock of the team that would give Millwall and their fans something to remember over the course of the next couple of years.

Inconsistency in the League was still Millwall's Achilles heel, but in the FA Cup the supporters got their fulfilment as the Lions steamrollered a path to reach their third semi-final, scoring 23 goals in the process. Being favoured with a string of home ties, five of them to be exact, was only one of many vital elements in Millwall's fortunes.

For the first round the Lions had to visit Aldershot and as such were presented with a perfect chance to erase the memory of the 1–0 defeat suffered in the garrison town four years earlier. Although leading by the only goal at the break from a Dave Mangnall strike, Millwall stepped up a gear in the second half to completely shatter any Aldershot hopes of a repeat success. The second half brought a continued barrage from Millwall, which saw the floodgates finally open when Bob Thomas found Jack Thorogood to convert the second after 65 minutes. Toying with the opposition with impunity, Millwall scored three more times in quick succession when Thomas and Mangnall twice, with one from a penalty to complete his hat-trick, put the Lions out of sight and in cruise control. Aldershot lost George Summerbee (father of the future England player Mike) with a knee injury, and following a spirited response they reduced the arrears slightly when Lions full-back Ted Smith put through his own goal following a manic scramble in the area. But it was skipper Dave Mangnall who capped a fine display by obtaining his fourth to give Millwall a spectacular 6–1 win and send out a definite signal that the Lions were back and roaring.

Following Aldershot's mauling, the run of five successive home ties commenced when Gateshead entered the Lions' Den for the second round. The visitors, who reached Cold Blow Lane by beating Notts County in the previous round, put up no more resistance than Aldershot and were unmercifully swept aside by a brand of fast-flowing and enterprising football that had the crowd purring.

Millwall made Gateshead look very pedestrian as they were left to chase shadows all afternoon. Not that the visitors could see any, of course, due to the foggy conditions that threatened to spoil Millwall's demolition of the Geordies. Apart from a Bob Thomas penalty, which enabled the entire forward line to register a goal, the other six goals had an air of the wonderment about them. The first, after 12 minutes, came when Mangnall headed home Thomas's superb centre, and the second arrived when Burditt pushed the ball past Conroy in the visitors' goal, only to see his thunder stolen by Thorogood, who smashed the loose ball into the corner of the net. More purposeful and exhilarating play saw Millwall go four up before the break when Jim McCartney and Burditt added further discomfort to an already punch-drunk Gateshead defence. Did I say break? No chance. Both teams forsook their half-time cuppa, as in a bid to beat the weather they changed ends the moment the whistle was blown. Three more goals were plundered in what descended into a total mismatch as McCartney, Burditt and Thomas saw a bemused Gateshead run up the white flag. This victory remains Millwall's highest FA Cup score since they became members of the Football League.

It was Second Division Fulham who followed Millwall out of the hat for the third round, and they duly went the same way as Aldershot and Gateshead. Millwall had just too much about them, and Fulham could find no answer to the home team's craft, skill and the seemingly high levels of energy and fitness. The vanguard of the Millwall attack was the excellent Ken Burditt, and it was he who put the Lions one up after 28 minutes by directing his effort past Alf Tootill, before skipper Mangnall's low shot made it two. There were no more goals to comment on in the second half, and the nearest anyone came was when

Football is a team game, and although the forwards get the glory a side would be nothing without its defence, and their work is perfectly illustrated here with goalkeeper Duncan Yuill and left-back Tommy Inns ushering away a Fulham shot during the third-round match at New Cross. [Chris Bethell]

Fulham's Trevor Smith hit a post, but generally Millwall were the far better team, with every member playing to the top of his game.

The draw for the fourth round on the following Monday gave Millwall another 'plum' when Fulham's west London neighbours Chelsea were paired with the Lions, reviving memories for the older fans of the two Cup games played before World War One. As in 1914, the colour clash saw Millwall change to play in an Arsenal-style red-and-white strip. They had warmed up nicely for this tie with a 3–0 success over Brighton, and if Chelsea had any misgivings about entering Cold Blow Lane they were soon underlined with a tentative opening that hardly filled their fans with any optimism. The Lions gave another inspirational display which had their opponents reeling from the word go as they revelled in the heavy conditions, toying with an illustrious side containing the likes of Sam Weaver (later to become a post-war coach at The Den), who along with goalkeeper Vic Woodley and Deptford-born George Mills was a future England international.

The Pensioners, going reasonably well in Division One, began the match but from the outset appeared not to be up for it, and after falling behind after 25 minutes any ambitions they had for an extended Cup run were doomed. Vic Woodley's point-blank stop earned Millwall a corner that Jimmy Daniels sent in to find the leaping Ken Burditt, who by straining every neck muscle managed to head the ball down and past Woodley's unsuccessful dive for the opener.

At last Chelsea instigated some decent approach work, but it was blown away when Millwall speedily broke through Thorogood, whose tantalising cross was met on the full by the onrushing Burditt who powered home a second header past Woodley. With two goals in

Another hero in the epic 1937 run was Ken Burditt. He is seen here scoring one of his two goals against Chelsea, whom they defeated 3–0 in the fourth round. [Chris Bethell]

the bag, Millwall appeared more than content to contain Chelsea in the second half, and so good was the defence that the visitors' attack had not given Lions 'keeper Duncan Yuill one telling save to make in either half. The nearest Chelsea came to scoring was when Dick Spence thumped his shot against a post. This effort emphatically summed up Chelsea's performance to a tee, which was, in a word, ineffectual. It was left to the dynamic Jack Thorogood to administer the last rites with the third, which put the cherry on the cake with still half an hour to go.

Millwall had now reached the fifth round for the first time since 1930, and as the interest began to gain momentum many pundits were speculating that the Lions could be the first club outside the top two divisions to make it to a semi-final. Into the last 16, the hope was that Millwall would draw fellow Third Division club Exeter City, but they got Derby County instead for an eagerly awaited contest that would bring in a record attendance at The Den of a seam-busting 48,762.

Such a gathering created an enormous crush, but following some frantic loudspeaker appeals the crowd got themselves into some sort of order to await the commencement of hostilities. Any discomfort the fans felt evaporated once the game got underway as Burditt and Mangnall made their present felt early on. This attracted the trips and the pushes from a pressurised County defence, and the crowd's reaction to these dubious tactics was to crank up the noise a further notch to create a deafening wall of sound. The Den went silent after

14 minutes, however, when Derby took the lead against the run of play when Keen took a free-kick some 35 yards out and the ball sailed unassisted over Lion and Ram alike into the net past an unsighted Johnny Burke.

Derby could barely hide their delight; however, it lasted just a minute as Millwall piled forward in answer to Derby's temerity. The hard-running Dave Mangnall latched on to Tom Brolly's sublime through ball and from the edge of the box thundered home into the roof of Ken Scattergood's net to send the crowd delirious. Millwall were like a rash all over County, who gave away more and more free-kicks in their vain attempt to disrupt Millwall's flowing football. No prizes for guessing which team were the more relieved to hear the half-time whistle. Millwall continued to take the game to their opponents in the second half as Scattergood was twice called upon to deal with goal-bound efforts from a totally dominant home attack.

It was during one of their better periods that County should have taken the lead, when Duncan's cross was met by Dai Astley, whose point-blank header was travelling at a rate of knots and looked certain to score. But somehow Lions goalkeeper Johnny Burke became the hero by producing a miraculous save to deny the Welshman. Given Derby's dubious tactics of earlier in the game, the Den patrons had little, if any, sympathy for Derby as they redoubled their efforts. They forged a procession of clear-cut chances from Napier, Astley

The crowd makes a wonderful backdrop as Millwall's skipper and centre-forward Dave Mangnall closes in on Derby County goalkeeper Scattergood. This encounter was witnessed by 48,762 spectators, a record attendance at the old Den. [F.J. Worcer]

and Stockill, all of which hit the frame of Burke's goal as for the first time during the run Millwall began to ride their luck.

Derby's attacking sojourn was countered by Millwall storming back on the offensive, and they thought they had earned their place in the next round with five minutes to go. The crowd's joy was stifled when the effort was ruled out for offside. Undeterred, Millwall were not to be denied, and the goal which guaranteed their passage into the quarter-finals was one worthy of winning the FA Cup itself. There were two minutes remaining when the outstanding Jim McCartney capped a memorable and magnificent team performance when he fired in a stunning volley to defeat the side destined to finish fourth in the First Division that season.

It has often been said that Cup football is a great leveller, with playing conditions and the fact that the underdog has nothing to lose being just two of the reasons. For Millwall it was having the good fortune to play all but one of their Cup ties at home, which was the main factor in their march to the semi-final; however, when champions elect and the strongest side left in the competition Manchester City were pitted against Millwall in the sixth round, even the most blinkered of Lions fans must have feared the worse. City had been winners of the competition in 1904 (ex-Lion Sammy Frost was a member of this team) and again 30 years later in 1934. Their path to The Den had seen them beat Wrexham 3–1 in North Wales and then Accrington Stanley at home 2–0, before crushing Bolton Wanderers 5–0 at Burnden Park in the previous round.

With history beckoning, to cite Jim Murray in his *MILLWALL Lions of the South,* 'The omens could not have been better. In previous rounds Gateshead, Fulham, Chelsea and Derby had all worn white: now it was City's turn for they, like Chelsea, found their colours clashed with Millwall's blue.'

Millwall were forced to make one change from the team that had beaten Derby, with J.R. (Reggie) Smith filling in at the last minute at outside-left for the injured Jack Thorogood. The fears the Lions fans had about the visitors upsetting the apple cart were dispelled as early as the 14th minute. Having totally dominated a City team lying in fourth place in their own division, Millwall reaped the reward from their whirlwind start. City's cause was not helped by the loss of Rogers with a cut over his eye after just 10 minutes, and it was during his absence that they fell behind following a barrage of Millwall corner-kicks. It was from one of these that Burditt found Mangnall, who rose above the throng to plant his header out of the reach of City's giant goalkeeper Frank Swift.

The crisp tackling and rapid distribution of Brolly and Forsyth kept the forwards constantly supplied, and if City threatened there was Wallbanks to win the aerial battles that mattered. A slightly smaller crowd of 42,474 began to fancy that another high-flying scalp was on the line. It was Millwall's threat from wide positions and the aerial dominance of both Mangnall and Burditt that were the causes of all the Mancunians' problems. The amiable Swift was at his best in dealing with the majority of threatening centres and crosses that Millwall fired in from all angles. City's response after conceding the goal was an effort from Toseland that Wallbanks blocked, before Burke saved a long-range effort from Jack Bray as the first half drew to a close.

But the history-making moment that set the Lions supporters roaring came after 57 minutes when the effervescent Mangnall's head connected with another excellent cross, this

Manchester City goalkeeper Frank Swift denies another effort from a rampant Millwall attack in the sixth-round tie at Cold Blow Lane. [Chris Bethell]

time from the equally superb McCartney, to put the game beyond City's reach. The visitors' reaction, as one would expect, was one of sharp retaliation, and they were unlucky when Alec Herd found some space to rattle the underside of Burke's crossbar, a strike which City claimed had gone in. The ball bounced down behind Burke but in front of the line, however, and despite City's protestations a disinterested referee waved the play on, as Burke again retrieved the situation by emerging with the ball from the rugby-style scrum. City belatedly realised the predicament they faced but could not break down Millwall's resistance, and the last meaningful effort came from Eric Brook whose terrific shot Burke foiled with an excellent save.

The final whistle brought expected delight and jubilation as the Lions fans cascaded down the terraces and onto the pitch to mob and congratulate their heroes. After such scenes New Cross would never be the same again as it began to sink in what the team had achieved. The talk in the local pubs over the rest of the weekend was who Millwall would draw in the semi-final. Would it Preston, West Brom, Wolves or Sunderland? Where would it be played? Monday's draw could not come around quick enough, and when it did the Lions would face either Wolves or Sunderland.

The venues chosen would be Leeds Road, Huddersfield if the men from Wearside were successful, or Liverpool's Anfield if Wolves won through. The thought of playing at either ground brought an immediate protest from Millwall, who fired off a letter of complaint to the FA stating if was unfair to both the club and its supporters in terms of locations and finance. But in their infinite wisdom the FA rejected it out of hand, which probably came as no surprise to anyone connected to Millwall Football Club. So, following a protracted tie Sunderland finally gained the right to confront the Lions on 10 April 1937 in West Yorkshire.

Since reaching such dizzy heights Millwall's League form dipped, and they recorded just two wins, which did not come as a surprise given the effort the players had put in to become the first side from the Third Division to reach such a stage. But more of concern was the injury to Dave Mangnall, incurred from the crude tackling of the Clapton Orient defenders in their 0–1 defeat in the middle of March, and Millwall's latest international, Tom Brolly of Ireland, was also doubtful for Sunderland game.

If the injuries were not enough to be going on with, the preparations for the big day were well and truly underway when the directors decided to reward the players with a few days in Blackpool as a thank you for their exploits and efforts during the campaign. This added distraction did not fully meet with Charlie Hewitt's approval, as he preferred the squad to remain in familiar surroundings with family and friends, and after seeing their promotion hopes blown out of the water with Easter losses at Luton Town 5–0 and Swindon 3–0, he had some justification.

An injury to captain and centre-forward Dave Mangnall was of great concern to Millwall prior to the semi-final with Sunderland, and it was touch-and-go whether he would make the team. But the healing hands and the treatment Dave received from Otaker Steinberger saw him line up on that historic day. [Chris Bethell]

Dave Mangnall's 10 goals from seven matches during the 1937 run certainly brought him and Millwall to the nation's attention, and here is some memorabilia he received during that memorable run, including the now defunct telegram. [D.J. Mangnall]

With promotion virtually written off, the main aim was to get Mangnall fit for the Cup. Having missed the last six games, there followed some extensive treatment on the injured striker. An X-ray had not shown any breakages, but all known treatments to repair the damage appeared to be in vain as the injury was not responding. As a last resort Millwall arranged for local herbalist Otaker Steinbegger to apply some of his 'magic' powers, and low and behold it appeared to do the trick in what was nothing short of a miracle. The talismanic Dave Mangnall was declared fit to play just hours before the team left on the Friday to travel to their base in Harrogate.

An allocation of just 10,000 tickets at various prices was Millwall's allowance, which seemed

Huddersfield Town
A.F.C. ———   600

F.A. CUP, 1936-37. SEMI-FINAL TIE.
Saturday, April 10th, 1937,
ON THE GROUND OF THE
HUDDERSFIELD TOWN FOOTBALL CLUB.
Kick-off 3-0.

SUNDERLAND v. MILLWALL

This portion to be retained.

H. Beever.   **Stand E**
                Admission 7/6
                (Including Tax)

Row **S**   Seat No. 16
This Ticket Admits through
TURNSTILE No. 16

A rarely seen ticket from the semi-final at Huddersfield in April 1937. Note the entrance fee of 7/6d [37p]. [Andy Sullivan]

Dave Mangnall's opening goal in the 1937 semi-final versus Sunderland got the Lions fans dreaming of Wembley, but two goals by the Mackems shattered the illusion. [Chris Bethell]

rather meagre considering Leeds Road held nearly 70,000 spectators. But whatever the circumstances, the Lions fans made their way north in good spirit and with a fair amount of optimism, having adopted Billy Cotton's version of Bing Crosby's popular 1936 tune *Shoe Shine Boy* as their anthem. Those who failed to obtain a ticket had to content themselves by attending a reserve-team fixture at Cold Blow Lane, where a gate of over 20,000 would hear tannoy announcements blurted out every 15 minutes on how the game was progressing up in Yorkshire.

Without the ferocious backing of the fans at The Den, Millwall's mettle and resolve were severely tested by a Sunderland side that were excellent going forward, but with their commitment to attack they were liable to concede a goal or two. The Lions, having given high-octane displays in the previous rounds, found that there were not too many scribes willing to discount them completely. Now that Mangnall was back in the team, and having seen off the League champions in waiting Manchester City, Millwall were eyeing up a double of their own and do the same to the current holders Sunderland. Led by Horatio 'Raich' Carter, Sunderland had a very imposing attack with Bob Gurney, Len Duns, the Scot Pat Gallagher and Eddie Burbanks. For Millwall, Hewitt dropped Burke and brought back Yuill in goal for reasons he could only justify, with Bob Thomas returning at outside-right.

Unfortunately all good things have to come to an end, and so it passed for Millwall, whose gallant efforts to be the first club outside the top two divisions to reach the Final fell at the last fence. There was no disgrace in this defeat, however, as Sunderland gained a well-merited victory to earn the prize of a place at Wembley. They even missed a hatful of chances that on another day may well have found the back of the net. As it was, the Lions kept their record of scoring in every round when the took a surprise 10th-minute lead with a gem of goal. Using the tactic that worked so well against City, left-back Tommy Inns sent in a long, diagonal pass into the Sunderland box which Mangnall controlled in an instant, swivelling to shoot past Mapson. The goal clearly rattled the champions, and Millwall's keen and quick-tackling defence kept the Makems at bay for next 20 minutes before Sunderland levelled. It was Bob Gurney who slotted home a rebound after Yuill had blocked Carter's original effort.

The second half was a tale of Millwall being overwhelmed by the Roker men's class as much as anything else. Being penned back on the defence for most of the time, their resistance finally eroded when Sunderland grabbed the winner. Looking back, Millwall could hardly complain about luck as they had been totally outplayed, but Sunderland's decider in the 70th minute did have two touches of good fortune about it. The first arose when the referee Mr Davies penalised Wallbanks for what seemed an unintentional handball. When the debated free-kick was taken the intended target, Pat Gallagher, appeared to miss-time his jump as his header took an unnatural bounce which left his fellow Scot Duncan Yuill a mere spectator as the ball looped in an arc into the net for the second stroke of luck.

Millwall's attack had been rarely seen in this half as the defence took all the honours as they battled against a succession of Sunderland corners. Twice Yuill came to the rescue with some magnificent full-length stops, and when Gurney's header appeared en route for the net up popped Tom Brolly to complete a splendid clearance. Millwall's response was very spasmodic, but an incident near to the end became the subject of much debate in the post-match analyses. The incident that caused much tongue wagging came when Thomas was flattened by Gorman in the area, but the official (another bone of contention for the fans to chew on afterwards) failed to spot the obvious and gave nothing. But at the end it was all academic; the dream and the run were over, Sunderland went through and would go on to defeat Preston North End 3–1 in the Final.

Millwall's team on this groundbreaking and emotional day should be recorded for posterity: Duncan Yuill; Ted Smith, Tommy Inns; Tom Brolly, Jimmy Wallbanks, Jim Forsyth; Bob Thomas, Dave Mangnall (captain), Ken Burditt, Jim McCartney, Reg (J.R.) Smith. Thanks must also go to the other players who preformed so admirably during this epic run, including Johnny Burke, Frank Hancock, Jack Thorogood, Don Barker and Jim Daniels. But Millwall's day in the sun would come, although they would have to wait 67 years to avenge this particular game.

Following the Sunderland defeat Millwall had to fulfil a League fixture on the next Monday night at Cardiff City. There appeared to be no hangover after Reg Smith scored the only goal of the game, but this was the only victory gained in the last five games of what had been an exhilarating period. Millwall finally finished in eighth spot, 12 points behind the champions Luton Town. With money in the bank Hewitt embarked on reshaping the team for the following season of 1937–38 by mainly bringing in some extra forwards, with the defence remaining very much the same.

After losing both the opening games Millwall put together some very useful runs, and by winning exactly half of their fixtures they fell just one short of averaging two goals a game as they took the Third Division title by a single point from Bristol City. During what was another exhilarating season, the FA Cup took something of a back seat. The opening Cup game saw the Lions lay down the welcome mat to a weakened Manchester City team. There was to be no giant-killing act on this occasion, however, as the teams shared a 2–2 draw at The Den. Millwall might have recorded a victory to progress to the fourth round had Billy Walsh, one of Hewitt's new recruits, taken a couple of gilt-edged chances offered to him.

A pulsating game saw City draw first blood after seven minutes when Herd, with a second bite of the cherry, scored after Yuill had parried his initial effort. Then, straight from kick-off, Millwall broke away to win a free-kick some 40 yards out. With City preparing their defence, Wallbanks, later deemed Man of Match, found Reg Smith darting in from the wing to put the finishing touch for the equaliser. Barely had the cheering died down before Herd restored the visitors' lead to score the game's third goal in as many minutes. Millwall's second goal came around the 55th minute when a magnificent shot from Jim McCartney all but deceived Frank Swift who managed to deflect the ball onto the crossbar, only for it to fall invitingly for his fellow Lancastrian Walsh (both were born in Blackpool) to tap home.

The one disappointment to arise out the replay at Maine Road was the margin of Millwall's defeat by three goals to one in what was another spirited performance from the Lions. City had Brook and Heale back in their team, and it was these two who made the difference. Up until the interval City played some sparkling football, especially after Heale's header had given them the lead after three minutes.

Millwall hit back in the only way they knew, and their attack led to Mangnall's goal-bound effort being blocked by Dale, more by accident than design, before Burditt, who had been preferred to Daniels, came inside to drive home the equaliser in the 11th minute. City were back in the lead seven minutes later when Brook rounded Yuill for the second, and when the half-hour mark was reached Herd extended City's lead with the third. Beaten but not disgraced, Millwall bowed out with heads held high, and with the 1937 encounter with City still fresh in the memory the Lions had given the reigning champions three matches to remember them by. With this blessing in disguise the Lions could now concentrate on reclaiming their rightful place in the Second Division, which they achieved in great fashion by winning their last six matches.

The last full season before the outbreak of World War Two was 1938–39 and saw the Lions make a devastating start in their Cup campaign when facing York City for the first time ever up at Bootham Crescent in round three. The tie had already fallen foul of the weather the previous Saturday and was rescheduled for the following Wednesday. Even then, the pitch had to be cleared of early morning snow before heavy rain threatened a further delay, and there were suggestions that the match could be postponed yet again. The weather relented a bit and despite a convincing looking 5–0 scoreline the match was not the stroll it appeared. The win, although deserved, was probably a wee bit flattering, being played in deplorable conditions that suited neither team.

Excellent build-up play by Sid Rawlings and Jimmy Richardson earned Millwall a corner, from which Johnny McLeod converted to give the Lions the lead at the break. The game was perfectly poised and could have gone either way until three terrible lapses in the York defence gave Millwall the chance to score three more times in a devastating seven-minute period around the hour mark. McLeod collected another pair to complete his hat-trick before Rawlings followed with the fourth. As most of the City fans were making their way home McLeod burst through a weary York defence to secure his fourth of the afternoon and thereby equal Billy Keen's four-goal haul from 1922 and Dave Mangnall's quartet against Aldershot in 1936.

Millwall then drew a team to whet the appetite when Grimsby Town, then a more than respectable First Division club, came to visit Cold Blow Lane. What is more, Millwall could and should have won but non-adherence to the old maxim of playing to the whistle cost them dearly, having held a 2–0 lead with just 10 minutes to go. Wrongly assuming that the ball had gone out of play, the Lions defence switched off. They were left appealing in vain when Grimsby's Boyd got to the goal line on the right to send in a cross which Howe headed home for the first. Four minutes from time it was Howe who secured the Mariners a draw when he scored with another header following a corner. Analysing Grimsby's contribution in the previous 80 minutes did not warrant such an outcome, but they took advantage of what was on offer to Millwall's detriment.

Previously everything had gone swimmingly for the Lions, and they deserved the lead given to them after 30 minutes when Rawlings, who had teased the Grimsby left-back all afternoon, floated in a centre for Richardson to knock down for the unmarked McLeod to slam home while Grimsby stood looking for an offside flag that never came. The second half was a repetition of the first, with Millwall running the show and only the combination hard-luck and good goalkeeping keeping the score down to one. At last the pressure finally paid-off with a second in the 78th minute when Reg Smith, the latest player to join the ranks of Millwall's internationals, put in a centre that gave McLeod the opportunity to seal the game with another header. With Millwall so much on top, a nagging doubt crept in that Grimsby, although outplayed for most the match would get something from it – and unfortunately they did.

One anonymous scribe who entered the Grimsby dressing room after the game looking for a post-match quote, asked 'What would you have given 10 minutes from the finish for your chances of getting a draw?', the shortest odds he was quoted were 100–1, and that summed it up precisely. Needless to say, the replay at Blundell Park was lost, and the players were left rueing those fateful 10 minutes at New Cross. Millwall made one change, with Freddie Fisher, later to lose his life in the ensuing war, replacing Sid Rawlings.

Following a placid opening 25 minutes in which neither goalkeeper had been seriously tested, the tempo increased when Lions 'keeper Bob Pearson was brought into action to block Swain's powerful drive as Grimsby set about to make good their escape from The Den. Grimsby's Boyd, the man who instigated the fightback at Millwall, followed in his corner-kick, which had only been half-cleared, to drive in a fierce cross-shot that Pearson hardly saw let alone was able to save in the 31st minute. After Tweedy had punched clear from Reg Smith the Lions drew level three minutes before half-time when a loose ball was seized upon by McLeod, who won the race against the onrushing Tweedy to play the ball to Jimmy Richardson who fired into an empty net.

Grimsby regained the lead following a long punt out of defence that saw Boyd fasten onto the ball, who slung in an excellent cross for Howe to nod home. The game was opening up, with Millwall making strenuous efforts to get level, before Howe clattered the Lions' woodwork. It was all-square again moments later when Smith caught the Grimsby defence all at sea, and McLeod found an opening to smash home the second equaliser. Millwall's luck finally ran out minutes later when Hall's pass found Jones to blast the Mariners into the next round. The most galling thing to come out this match was that Grimsby made the most of their reprieve and went on to reach the semi-final that year. We can only surmise what would have happened if Millwall had won. One thing is certain, though – the title of this book may have been very different.

The war clouds that had been hovering over Europe since the mid-1930s finally came to a head when Germany invaded Poland. Politically it left the British government no choice but to follow the same path as their predecessors in 1914 and declare war on Germany. Unlike the earlier conflict, the football season had already commenced, and Millwall had already fulfilled three fixtures, which were ultimately expunged by the authorities following Prime Minister Chamberlain's announcement.

Professional football had been pilloried for what was seen as inactivity in getting the players into uniform at the start of World War One, but this time the game was encouraged by the powers that be who commented that morale could be maintained by football as fans could congregate (air raids permitting) for a couple of hours to forget the troubles of the world for a while. In a matter of weeks football had been organised on a regional basis to avoid the extra long journeys. Cup football was also introduced, which had been totally halted in the previous conflict.

8. Watcha Cock

As many fans will know, Millwall appeared in one Wartime Final at Wembley in April 1945. This was a month before VE Day, and they lost to Chelsea 2 0 in a match that was not very exciting and was described in one match report as one of the poorest Finals ever staged at Wembley. What the future Queen, watching from the royal box, thought about it is not recorded, but the best thing said about the game was that at least Millwall got to play at the Empire Stadium, as it was then named.

The 1945–46 campaign was the last of regionalised football and saw the welcome return of the reinstated FA Cup, although for this season only the rounds would be contested over two legs. Millwall were managed by their former Lions centre-forward Jack Cock at that time, himself the scorer of six goals in 11 Cup games for the club. Gone forever were the halcyon pre-war days under Charlie Hewitt, who had resigned in disgrace in 1940 following inquiries into financial irregularities; although this was not the last Millwall would hear of him.

Although Britain was on the winning side at the war's end, the country faced an austere time, with rationing on virtually every home comfort, along with the basic requirements such as coal and sugar. Back on the football front, competitive football lay just around the corner, and with the FA Cup back on the menu there was something to look forward to. Facing the Lions in the third round was Northampton Town, and the first leg staged at the County Ground ended all square at 2–2, with pre-war Lion Reg Smith and Dave Ridley scoring the goals. This result set up an intriguing return match at The Den two days later, which turned into a stroll for Millwall, who were given an early lift when Town's right-back Tom Smalley was caught in two minds and dallied, then panicked, and sent his over-hit back-pass wide of his 'keeper Dave Scott into his own goal. Northampton then had a goal disallowed when the referee should have really played the advantage. Early in the second half some lovely football from Tommy Brown gave Russ Phillips the chance to extend the lead before Reg Smith pounced on another Smalley error to add a third.

Following the game, a report appeared in the *News Chronicle* stating, somewhat surprisingly, that Millwall were so impressed with a number of the Northampton side that they tendered an offer of five figures for a same number of their team plus a separate bid for centre-forward Alf Morrall. This audacious offer brought back memories of the alledged bid of £50,000 for the entire Raith Rovers forward line back in the 1920s. Whatever the media speculation, nothing materialised as none of the Northampton players arrived at The Den.

The Lions' reward in the fourth round was two money-spinning matches against Aston Villa, the first Cup encounter between the clubs since 1901. Villa had of late been scoring goals for fun, recently passing the 70-goal mark in no more than two dozen matches. Millwall would certainly see the potency of their attack over the next two games, with the first leg set for New Cross. Against opposition like Villa, Millwall needed their full compliment but were handicapped by the loss of left-back George Fisher with a cut eye after 20 minutes.

Following Fisher's departure, a gaping hole appeared in the Lions defence, which was the avenue Villa exploited to score twice in six minutes. The first goal came when stand-in full-back Tom Brolly mis-kicked, allowing Billy Goffin an easy chance to open the scoring before he provided the cross for George Edwards to make no mistake for the second. Never the

Millwall's first FA Cup for seven years saw the Lions take Aston Villa in January 1946 where 30,0000 football-starved fans saw six goals scored, Millwall's two coming from a Jimmy Jinks brace. The Lions lost the second leg 9–1, their heaviest loss in the Cup. [Author]

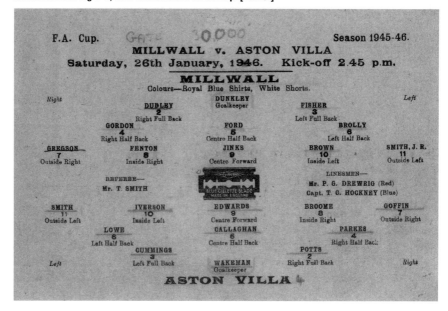

Millwall faced mighty Aston Villa when the FA Cup proper resumed in 1946, and uniquely rounds one to six were played on a two-legged basis. In the first-leg at The Den Villa triumphed 4–2, and one of their scorers, Billy 'Cowboy' Goffin, is seen being tackled by Tom Brolly. [Keystone]

team to let the big guns have it all their own way, Millwall gamely fought back to score the best goal of the game when J.R. Smith began the move that Jimmy Jinks finished. Goalkeeper George Dunkley and fellow defenders Fred Ford and George Dudley all gave sterling performances, with Ford more than holding his own against the prolific Edwards. The inspirational Tommy Brown was initiating some elegant moves, and it was during this period that Millwall managed to draw level when Jinks netted his second.

Goalkeeper Jimmy Purdie's only Lions appearance in the FA Cup saw him concede three goals when Port Vale caused a shock at The Den in January 1947. [Author]

Nonetheless, Villa still held all the aces and played their full hand to take a 4–2 lead back to the Midlands after further goals from Edwards and Les Smith had completed their tally. The daunting prospect of facing Villa on their home ground turned into a nightmare in reality, as six Villa players (including all the forwards) found the net. Reg Smith's token effort barely covered the embarrassment of the 9–1 result – Millwall's heaviest defeat ever in a competitive match.

If the Villa Park result was gruesome, worse was to come in the 1946–47 season as Millwall flirted with relegation, but despite two excellent results over Chesterfield and Newcastle at Christmas they found Third Division Port Vale too hot to handle at The Den as they succumbed in the third round to a morale sapping 3–0 defeat. Vale's first summed up the day perfectly when after 24 minutes Bob Kelly's intended pass hit the referee and fell to Eric Prince, who found Don Triner, who beat Jock Purdie with a low cross-shot. Following Purdie's partial save from Triner's cross, Bill Pointon was on hand to thump home Vale's second in the 56th minute, with the same player adding a third near to the end.

Trouble continued to beset the Lions during the following 1947–48 season, their last in that particular division for 18 years. The FA Cup saw the visit of Preston North End to The Den, who included in their team Bill Shankly, who became the legendary manager of the great Liverpool team in the 1960s, and Tom Finney, the Preston plumber who later became a knight of the realm for his services to football.

North End were one of the leading lights in those early post-war seasons and would go on to finish seventh in the First Division that year. With nothing to lose, Millwall went straight for the jugular against a North End defence that did not look too confident and were further rattled when Norman Smith scored, but his effort was disallowed.

Following a Preston move in which Anders tested Millwall custodian Charlie Bumstead, it was the Lions who took the lead after nine minutes when the former Royal Navy combatant Ronnie Mansfield took advantage of a hesitant Preston defence to nip in to score from close range. The joy was short-lived, however, when moments later Preston were back on terms when Len Tyler misread a long punt up field which Harry Anders seized upon to run and beat Bumstead.

But on 30 minutes North End took an undeserved lead when Scottish international Andy McLaren netted what proved to be the decisive goal. Try as they might, Millwall just could not find that little bit of luck they needed to force even a draw. Relegation was confirmed later that year, leading to the inevitable departure of manager Jack Cock. Jack remained in the New Cross area to run the White Hart public house. The new incumbent in the Millwall hot seat was none other than the pre-war messiah Charlie Hewitt.

9. A Familiar Face

Upon his return from Leyton Orient, Hewitt set about the task of restoring the club back to their pre-war prominence, and in some ways he succeeded, and despite one season in which Millwall finished in 22nd place Hewitt had them regularly attaining a position in the top half of the division by being placed eighth, fifth, fourth, second, 12th and fifth. But Millwall's interest in the FA Cup got no further than the fourth round during Hewitt's second tenure at Cold Blow Lane.

For first time since 1936 Millwall entered the FA Cup at the first-round stage, and they drew their local amateur neighbours Tooting & Mitcham United – and what a hard time they gave the Lions. In the end Millwall were thankful for Walter McMillen's thumping header 12 minutes from time from a Johnson corner after countless Millwall attacks had floundered on United's rock-like defence. It ended Tooting's spirited display and a frustrating afternoon of missed Millwall chances. They gratefully took the solitary goal success (Walter's only strike for the Lions), but the all the glory went to Tooting, who brought with them 60 coachloads of fans.

Millwall's reward, if you can call it a reward, for toppling gallant Tooting was a trip to Crewe Alexandra; although the Lions entered the match with four straight wins, including a remarkable 6–5 victory at Walsall. But the Cup encounter left a bad taste in the mouth of one the *South London Press* reporter, Dave Caldwell, who stated 'The game at Crewe was the dirtiest and most diabolical game of football that was ever played'.

Maybe it was, but such confrontations at the time between northern and southern teams always had an added an extra bit of spice, even more so when there was a potentially lucrative place in the third round at stake. The raw aggression and intent were there for all

Millwall made very hard work of beating near neighbours and leading amateur club Tooting & Mitcham United in the first-round match in 1948. It took a goal from Walter McMillen to break the amateurs' stubborn resistance. [Chris Bethell]

to see from an early stage and a stronger referee than Jack Sherlock of Sheffield would have taken a firmer grip of the proceedings. Left-winger Ronnie Mansfield was left limping after 10 minutes, and according to Caldwell Ron's colleague on the right Johnny Johnson was hardly seen in the second half.

More vitriolic condemnation from Caldwell stated that Lions 'keeper Finlayson was deliberately kicked while lying on he ground after making a save and Frank Reeves was kicked on the right leg with the ball yards away; however, in between the kicking, biting and rollicking, a football match broke out in which some fine goals were scored, including Millwall's opener from Constantine whose solo effort saw him cut in from the right to drive the ball past Ray Evans after 14 minutes. But Crewe were soon level when the unfortunate Simmonds was adjudged to have handled when to most observers it appeared to be ball to hand.

It was the former Tottenham player Ralph Ward who stepped up to take the kick, which Finlayson could only parry, allowing Crewe's McCormack to fire in the equaliser after 39 minutes. Sixty seconds later the home team were ahead when Crewe gained possession from the restart to set up a move which Frank Mitcheson finished with a fine shot for his first goal since moving from Doncaster Rovers.

Finlayson was injured in a goalmouth scramble following his save from Basford, but 20 minutes into the second half Millwall found themselves back on terms when Lindsay, Crewe's centre-half, mis-kicked a Johnny Evans free-kick that left Jimmy Constantine the simple task of tapping home. Crewe regained the lead once more eight minutes later when Mitcheson scored with another fine shot to beat Finlayson.

As the teams entered a final hectic phase both goals had narrow escapes, but the last five minutes determined the final outcome for Millwall as both Willie Hurrell's and Frank Reeve's efforts rattled the Crewe crossbar. By going out of the competition the Lions missed out on an attractive home game and the chance to even the score against Sunderland in round three.

Millwall's lead-up to their one and only Cup game of the dreadful 1949–50 season, the worst in Charlie Hewitt's reign, saw them gain just one win in seven. A crowd of 19,487 were hoping of for change of fortune in the FA Cup, but Millwall's history at times has been a catalogue of misfortunes, and so it came as no real surprise when the first-round tie against Exeter City produced a highly charged but nauseating 5–3 defeat at The Den, which again featured some questionable refereeing.

Three of City's goals were hotly disputed which infuriated the home support so much so that a group of around 200 of them lay in wait for the match officials as they left for their journey home. Mr Meade, the referee, claimed he was hit on the back and that missiles had been thrown, and the outcome of the resulting Football Association disciplinary committee meeting was the closure of The Den for seven days.

The game itself, however, contained every emotion associated with Cup football; thrills by the bucket load, goals and drama as disputes were followed by grievances. Millwall took an early lead after eight minutes when Constantine converted a Johnny Johnson centre, but they found themselves trailing 2–1 minutes later. A quick double from City's Dick Smart in the ninth and 11th minutes turned the game completely on its head. The Lions then suffered another blow when goalkeeper Ted Hinton was carried off after collapsing on 20 minutes, after which Chris Simmonds donned the 'keeper's jersey. By half-time the Lions were 4–1 down and reeling as Smart completed his hat-trick on 30 minutes, which was followed by Regan's effort nine minutes later.

Not a team to take all this adversity lying down, 10-man Millwall flew at City at the start of the second half as Ernie Forrest took over in goal as Morgan and Constantine both went close before Connie reduced the arrears with a header 10 minutes into the half, and two minutes later, following a free-kick, Tom Brolly pulled another goal back. The crowd were ecstatic; roaring on the team as they went in search an equaliser, only to be caught on the break by Archie Smith's clincher in the 80th minute.

Naturally, the press thought the referee had done a good job, and maybe he did, but Lions manager Charlie Hewitt thought otherwise. Highlighting the contentious points that had so irked the crowd in the following week's match programme against Leyton Orient, he said 'City's first two goals involved handling offences by City which were ignored […] Connie was then alleged to have fouled an opponent when he was the victim and the free-kick was given against him amazingly, from which Exeter scored their fifth goal which put paid to Millwall'. Strong words indeed, but Millwall were out after City had claimed their first-ever

Selhurst Park was the starting point for Millwall's Cup campaign in the 1950–51 season where they defeated local rivals Crystal Palace 4–1 in which Jimmy Constantine (kneeling) beats former Lions goalkeeper Charlie Bumstead. [Unknown]

victory at The Den. Millwall's day of woe had started before a ball had been kicked when Johnny Short was sent home before the game suffering with pneumonia, and on the pitch they came up against an inspired opponent in City's goalkeeper, Bert Hoyle.

Leading-up to the first-round FA Cup tie against the old adversaries Crystal Palace at Selhurst Park in November 1950, Millwall had been in reasonable form, having failed just twice in finding the net during the previous 19 League matches and felt quietly confident. But all the preparation went of the window when the game was abandoned after 34 minutes due to fog, with the score standing at 0–0. The following Wednesday was scheduled as the new date and saw Millwall give a devastating display by running out 4–1 victors, which more than made up for the contentious defeat suffered when the sides last met in the Cup back in January 1929.

The outcome of the match may have turned out a lot differently had Jones converted a 17th-minute penalty for Palace instead of hitting a post, from which Millwall took comfort to take the lead 10 minutes later. It followed an excellent save by ex-Lion Charlie Bumstead from Constantine at the expense of a corner, from which Johnny Jones supplied Johnny Johnson to snap up the opening goal. From thereon in the Lions never looked back.

Palace provided some neat, intricate football from Noel Kelly and Les Stevens, but they were never allowed the space to exploit it, with Gerry Bowler keeping it tight at the back. Millwall cashed in again when Palace centre-half Bill Whittaker underhit a back-pass to his goalkeeper and Stan Morgan nipped in for the second after 38 minutes. It was 3–0 four minutes into the second half when the enterprising Frank Neary finished off a move started by Frank Reeves before the formidable Constantine made it four with his 17th goal of the season with an exhilarating shot on the run in the 75th minute.

It was not all one-way traffic as Lions goalkeeper Ted Hinton would testify, who had to dive bravely at the feet of Charlie Rundle to save a Ted Broughton cross before diving spectacularly to save Rundle's header before Kelly reduced the arrears just before the end for a Palace consolation.

The success at Palace brought Bradford to The Den, who were always referred to as Bradford Park Avenue, mainly outside of their native Yorkshire to differentiate them from their neighbours from across town, Bradford City. Riding high in the Northern section of the Third Division, Bradford, having won their two previous away games, arrived at Cold Blow Lane attempting to lower the Lions' colours, who was this stage remained unbeaten on their own patch.

On a fine afternoon, Millwall started the game and straight away gained a free-kick on the edge of Bradford's area after Jones had been brought down with a heavy tackle. From the kick, Neary's effort was deflected for a corner which came to nothing. After some ineffectual attacks from the visitors Millwall moved forward once more and this resulted in Bowler's follow-up shot being charged down by Arthur Wheat. Surprisingly, Millwall were given ample space by the visitors, allowing both Constantine and Morgan to test Mitchell Downie's abilities in the Bradford goal.

The one major scare to the home team came when Bradford's speedy Dennis Brickley hit his cross hard and low, aimed for the lurking Bobby Crosbie, who was foiled by Gerry

The FA Cup second-round clash in 1950 brought Bradford of Third Division North to The Den. They gained a 1–1 draw after Bob Crosbie gave them the lead. [PA Reuter]

Millwall's equaliser against Bradford proved to be a contentious point when Frank Neary was accused of handball, doubly so when the Lions won the replay 1–0. [Chris Bethell]

Bowler's alert interception. This only delayed the opening goal by a few minutes when the persistence of Billy Deplidge paid off after his original shot was blocked, as Crosbie was on hand to fire past Ted Hinton in the 17th minute.

A highly invigorated Bradford confidently took the game to Millwall and gave their travelling support something else to cheer about as they carved open the Lions defence once more. It was George Fisher's fine positioning that denied Brickley from increasing their lead as both Brickley and Deplidge were becoming the main threats. An emphatic point was made when the dangerous pairing had to receive treatment as Millwall fought to curb their lively play in and around the Lions penalty area. The latter left the pitch when a hard-hit clearance caught him in the stomach.

Finally clicking into top gear, Millwall drew level six minutes before half-time with a goal that came from some uneasiness in the Bradford defence. Hesitancy by Jack Haines and Charlie Currie let in Millwall's Welsh duo of Jones and Morgan to gain a corner from which Frank Neary forced home through a ruck of players. The equaliser brought vigorous protests from the Park Avenue players who claimed Neary had fisted the ball into the net. They pleaded with the referee Mr Iliffe of Leicester to consult a linesman, but to their annoyance he let the goal stand. Both teams spurned later chances that came along in the second half, but there was no further scoring. Both sides would face a replay on the following Wednesday.

The incentive for the winners was a trip to Second Division Queen's Park Rangers, but first Millwall had to overcome a very fine Bradford side and a frozen pitch. In such conditions it is usually the team making the least mistakes that succeeds, and this was the way it turned out for the only goal of the game arrived in such a manner. The unfortunate chap was Bradford's Charlie Currie who sliced his clearance, which fell nicely for Stan Morgan to slam a crisp drive past Downie after 21 minutes. Millwall relied heavily on their Irish backbone of Gerry Bowler at the heart of the defence and 'keeper Ted Hinton to keep Bradford at bay, with Hinton dealing bravely with some acutely embarrassing moments caused by the vagaries of the pitch.

By virtue of their win at Bradford, Millwall would now pay a visit to their old West London rivals Queen's Park Rangers, managed by none other than Dave Mangnall – one of many heroes in Millwall's 1937 Cup run. Having scored eight in their last two League matches, Millwall had the firepower to cause a third-round upset. If it was goals you were looking for, then this was the game for you as the Lions gained a thrilling 4–3 victory, at one stage holding a 4–1 lead during the second half.

Millwall were first out of the blocks and in the opening five minutes pummelled their hosts, with former Rangers player Frank Neary shaving a post with a shot, while at the other end the dithering Bert Addinall gave Malcolm Finlayson the chance to clear. The Lions came again when Les Jones forced Rangers' goalkeeper Reg Saphin to concede a corner, from which Constantine headed just over before Millwall's exceptional start was rewarded with a goal in the 26th minute. The initiative was all Les Jones's as he drew the Queen's Park Rangers defence, giving Neary the space to find the corner of the net; however, the joy was extinguished six minutes later when Rangers levelled through Addinall. His decision to dribble rather than pass was rewarded when he skipped past two tackles to shoot past Finlayson.

Despite the setback, Millwall continued to be in control and remained so into the second half. The half was just eight minutes old when Constantine laid the ball back for Neary to send his piledriver screaming into the net, and moments later the 'Brown Bomber' should have completed his hat-trick but somehow screwed his shot wide. Play began to get overheated, with both trainers working overtime with the amount of injuries accruing. Around the hour mark Millwall must have thought the game was won after they secured two further goals within a minute. Johnny Johnson put in a fine drive from the edge of the penalty box for the third, and before Rangers gathered their thoughts they conceded a fourth when Constantine netted from close range.

But the home side rallied to reduce the arrears after 65 minutes when Alf Parkinson scored through a crowd of players after Finlayson had parried Addinall's point-blank effort. Parkinson heightened the tension with his second goal eight minutes from the end to set up a nervewracking last few minutes. Incredibly, Rangers should have brought the game level in the 87th minute, but with Finlayson lying prone on the deck Ernie Shepherd missed when he should have scored, and with that chance missed Rangers' hopes of a replay went with it.

When Millwall drew Fulham out of the hat for the fourth round it no doubt brought comparisons from the golden period under Hewitt prior to World War Two. But there was no repetition of that dazzling 1937 victory over Fulham. Just as Millwall benefited at Bradford from the frailties of human error, it was Fulham's turn this time to become the beneficiaries.

Even the combination of the Millwall strikers Jimmy Constantine (left) and Frank Neary could not stop the Lions slipping to a disappointing 1–0 defeat in the fourth round at The Den. [Chris Bethell]

An uninspiring match at The Den was settled by one of just a few exciting moments after 23 minutes. It followed Fulham's Arthur Stevens's touchline-hugging run that left the Lions defence totally bemused and saw the Fulham man despatch a harmless-looking cross that nine times out of 10 the dependable Johnny Short would have dealt with. But on this occasion poor old John could only divert the ball to Archie Macaulay, who put in Johnny Campbell for the Irishman to score the only goal. Incidentally, Fulham faced Chelsea in the next round.

The win at Rangers was Millwall's last FA Cup success on the road for 22 long years. Now that the Lions were plying their trade in the lower reaches of League football, their appearances in the third round during this era only came in 1953, 1955 and 1957, with some horror shows laying in wait.

Millwall's start to the 1951–52 season began with two losses in the first four games, but they then settled down to something resembling a promotion bid and suffered just one defeat before the FA Cup appeared on the calendar. That loss occurred at Plymouth, who themselves were striving for a place in the Second Division. By a strange twist of fate the Cup paired the Lions against the Pilgrims for the first-round tie at The Den a week after Argyle had given Millwall a 5–0 trouncing at Home Park. This gave the Lions an instant chance of rectifying that mauling down in Devon, and so a splendid attendance of 26,544 at Cold Blow Lane came to witness what should have been a classic.

Gerry Bowler won the toss on a very dull afternoon as both teams set out to justify that expectant label, and early on the fans were not disappointed. Millwall's Johnny Hartburn

Another single goal success in the FA Cup came in 1951 when Arnie White scored his only Millwall goal in the 1–0 victory over Plymouth Argyle. Arnie is seen in the thick of the action during the first-round tie at The Den. [*Daily Graphic*]

and Arnie White combined, only for White to shoot over, while Argyle responded with Astall hitting straight at Ted Hinton, before Argyle's Tadman shot narrowly wide.

The ever-alert Hinton was called into action once again to foil George Dews after Argyle had carved Millwall open with a five-man move. As play switched from one end to the other at a fair rate old rate, the Lions retaliated with the lively Hartburn just off target, before Frank Neary brought Bill Shortt into action with a fine save.

Despite the many efforts by both attacks, it was the defences who were the masters as they repelled everything thrown at them. That was until the 35th minute when Millwall took the lead. It followed a concerted bout of pressure, but the goal itself was out of kilter with what had preceded it. Lions winger Johnny Johnson slung over a centre that caused an almighty mêlée in the Argyle area before Arnie White emerged to scramble home the decisive goal.

Argyle's attack faded early in the second half as the game went a bit flat. Their danger man, the ex-Charlton player Maurice Tadman, had been kept at arm's length by the immaculate Gerry Bowler. When Argyle eventually caught their second wind, Tadman at last got free of Bowler to test Hinton with a cross-shot before Astall sliced another chance wide.

Tempers began to fray as Argyle tried but could not find an equaliser; however, Neary should have settled the game beyond doubt after breaking away but shot straight into the hands of Welsh international 'keeper Bill Short. That was about it, although the visitors did mount some thrusts towards the end but were either caught offside or were let down by the final pass.

Millwall's Northern Ireland international goalkeeper Ted Hinton kept a clean sheet in the goalless draw against Scunthorpe United during the second-round match at New Cross in December 1951. [PA]

The preparations for the second-round tie against Scunthorpe were severely hampered by an injury to Gerry Bowler that he picked up in his part-time job, which so infuriated manager Charlie Hewitt that he went public in his condemnation of his skipper. In a thinly veiled threat to other members of the playing staff contemplating similar actions of foolhardiness he promised there would be serious repercussions. The final score of 0–0 in the second round hardly tempered Hewitt's mood, despite the game having everything but goals. There were plenty of missed chances, and Scunthorpe could and should have despatched Millwall at the first attempt as they constantly had the Bowler-less Lions defence at sixes and sevens. Irons' outside-left Horace Cumner had the hearts of the Lions fans in their mouths after 20 minutes, but he contrived to miss an open goal following Ted Hinton's excellent stop from Ray Powell's flying header.

Although Millwall's rearguard came under severe pressure, it held out to give their forwards a slim chance to create an opening, but invariably their attacks petered out on the edge of the Scunthorpe area. Jimmy Constantine did manage to have one effort cleared off the line as the thrills and spills continued. A Johnny Hartburn header was too high, and to add to the fans' frustration he missed another straightforward chance a moment later as the home attack began to stir. Frank Neary hit a post before Constantine, of all people, eclipsed Cumner's earlier miss by failing to hit the target with all of it to aim at.

For both teams going into the replay the carrot dangling in front of them was the rewarding prospect of entertaining Tottenham Hotspur, the then Football League champions, famed for their 'push-and-run' style under manager Arthur Rowe. The match would have surely filled The Den, but the Lions' hopes were dashed with a three-goal reverse, as Scunthorpe romped into the third round for the first time in their 41-year history.

It would be another 15 years before Millwall would get the opportunity to face Spurs in the Cup. The margin of defeat was hard on Millwall, who had fought well but fell to three excellent goals, with United's centre-forward Ray Powell obtaining two of them. It was Billy Rudd who fired them ahead following Alex Jardine's foul on Cumner that led to Scunthorpe taking a half-time lead, when Jackie Brownsword's free-kick found its way back to Rudd to score with a low drive through a crowded area.

It seems that these Scunthorpe and Millwall players have changed the game—but this was the position when, with goalkeeper Hinton on his knees, his centre-half colleague, Reeves, leaped over Powell of Scunthorpe to clear.

28/12/51

Just making sure. Millwall goalkeeper Ted Hinton and his centre half, Frank Reeves, jump together to clear in the replayed second round Cup clash at Scunthorpe yesterday. These defenders were hard pressed throughout the entire second half. Scunthorpe won 3—0.

This is how Powell got his second goal. The ball has cleared Jardine's head and with Hinton out of position he was on the spot to nod home Mosby's centre.

F.A. CUP - 2ND ROUND - REPLAY.
ATT. 13,580.
SCUNTHORPE UNITED. 3. MILLWALL. 0.
POWELL 2. RUDD.

F.A. CUP - 2ND ROUND - REPLAY.
ATT. 10,434.
NEWPORT COUNTY.
MOORE 2. BEATTIE.

BEATTIE—he's not on the picture—shot beats emergency goalkeeper Vic Groves to score Newport County's first goal of three in the Cup replay. Vic, really a centre-forward, was filling the breach in goal till J. Hughes could get to the ground after missing a train connection.

The second-round replay at Scunthorpe United in December 1951 resulted in a 3–0 loss for the Lions, and here are some action shots taken from the game. [Chris Bethell]

Millwall had an earlier scare when both Hinton and Jardine nearly collided with one another after Cumner had lobbed the ball into the area, but fortunately Hinton got to it first to clear the danger without further ado. Poor Jimmy Constantine, so often the hero, missed a great chance to put the visitors ahead but failed to convert Hartburn's hard, low centre from five yards. Lacking leadership and the commanding presence of Gerry Bowler, they nearly lost another key component when Ted Hinton was injured at the start of the second half following Jardine's under-hit back-pass which forced the Irishman to make a brave save at the feet of Powell.

Millwall steadily improved, but when Connie again failed to register when heading tamely into Thompson's hands their resistance collapsed. The dangerous Powell finished off Harry Mosby's great run and centre with 10 minutes remaining. The Lions' last hurrah saw them force three late corners which all came to nothing before Powell put the game to bed in the 88th minute with his second, a header from another fine Mosby cross.

The opening salvo in the Cup in the 1952–53 season saw Millwall take on their divisional opponents Aldershot, where the Lions had already claimed a 2–1 victory in September through an Alan Monkhouse double. But on this occasion Millwall had to thank goalkeeper Malcolm Finlayson for preserving the status quo, especially in the first half when he rescued two desperate situations when all seemed lost. The first Aldershot chance came when a harmless-looking shot from Paddy Bonnar ricochetted off George Fisher's leg, and the ball spiralled towards the net, inducing Finlayson to leap to tip over the bar. The other scare came when Tommy Wright blasted his effort straight at the Lions' 'keeper, when had he put it either side of him Millwall's participation could have ended there and then.

Conditions underfoot were wretched, but this could not be used as an excuse for the lack of style from both attacks, despite a subdued Frank Neary narrowly missing after firing in one of his specials. Millwall's best effort came from Johnny Short, who let fly from 20 yards which caused home 'keeper Joe Houston to gather at the second attempt. But overall the Lions were more than happy to be given a second chance following a 0–0 draw. They knew they would have to play a lot better if they were to progress, although they might have had a penalty near the end when a push on Johnny Short went unnoticed.

Poor weather, combined with an early kick-off on a midweek afternoon, were the causes that kept the attendance to below 7,500 for the game in which Millwall completely overwhelmed Aldershot to the tune of seven goals to one. It was two youngsters who illuminated a gloomy Den when 22-year-old Alan Monkhouse and John Shepherd, 20, claimed a hat-trick each. If Millwall looked lethargic down in the garrison town, they shook it off to dominate from start to finish in a convincing display of fast, open football that was bright and inventive. A fact confirmed as early as the ninth minute when some excellent play down the right came when Willie Hurrell collected a miskick to put in Aldershot-born Frank Neary who, without breaking stride, powered home.

After saving efforts from George Stobbart and Shepherd, Houston was beaten again on 28 minutes when another error in the visitors' defence allowed Monkhouse all the time in the world to head home. It was he who snapped up the third from a rebound 12 minutes later after Hurrell's shot had been blocked on the line. The one-way traffic theme continued as rain descended from the ever-darkening skies as Millwall rained in shot after shot, two blockbusters from Neary narrowly missing before Monkhouse scraped a post with another.

Aldershot's sporadic attacks, when they materialised, were instantly snuffed out by a hard-tackling half-back line, in which the returning Gerry Bowler excelled. Monkhouse completed his well-earned treble when fastening on Shepherd's short pass to swivel around to shoot past the advancing Houston after 62 minutes. John Shepherd then got in on the act with Millwall's fifth when he headed home Neary's centre, but straight from the kick-off Aldershot netted a consolation through Kenny Flint. Monkhouse then hit the bar and the ball fell very nicely for the former polio victim Shepherd to net number six from a yard out. As the weather closed in Shepherd claimed the seventh when pinging home a drive of immense power and accuracy to deceive Houston with virtually the last kick of the game.

The second round pitted Millwall against northern opposition in Barrow at Holker Street for the first-ever meeting between the clubs. There ensued a fitting 2–2 draw which the local press described as a thrilling Cup tie, in which Barrow shaded the first half, with Millwall the better team in the second 45 minutes with their superior football. The pre-match entertainment was provided by the Barrow St Andrew's Pipe Band, with fans from both clubs bringing their non-human mascots out to the centre-circle.

Charlie Hewitt made four changes, three positional, but dropped Willie Hurrell from the team that cantered home against Aldershot. The rearranged forward line read Neary, Stobbart, Shepherd, Monkhouse and Hartburn. It was Barrow in their new claret-and-blue strip that nearly took the lead when Alan Keen sent in a cross that cleared Finlayson's crossbar by a whisker. Keen then got through on to Gordon's pass, but his shot lacked venom and was easily cleared.

Millwall's tactic of playing through the middle seemed ideally suited to both the marauding Shepherd and Monkhouse, but the main threat to Barrow came from Frank Neary who was warming to the task as play switched from end to end. But despite a lively opening half, the interval was reached with no goals scored.

At the start of the second half the referee, Mr Sherlock, provided a new white ball that seemed to induce the one missing factor, a goal. The new leather made the required impact after 50 minutes when following Alan Layton's corner Billy Gordon headed home via a post to give Barrow the lead. This got the home crowd cheering wildly, but the din had hardly faded away when Millwall equalised within a minute. From the restart George Stobbart went on one of his typical solo runs and fed Neary, who supplied a dangerous centre which Barrow failed to cut out. It was left to Stobbart to complete the move he started by beating Hindle from close range. The goal made Barrow change their approach with the long ball through the middle as their main threat.

Millwall were now imposing their undoubted class, with danger man Neary showing his intentions with a snap shot that went just wide, as did an effort from Hartburn. But Frank was not to go home empty handed when in the 63rd minute his run deviated inside and he fired home an unstoppable left-foot shot that Jack Hindle hardly saw to put Millwall ahead. Barrow came storming back as Keen forced Finlayson into a smart save, before Monkhouse raced away to test Hindle from 20 yards. Following some persistent Barrow pressure, they drew level after 72 minutes when Willie Buchanan's free-kick was only partially cleared, allowing the Scottish international Andy McLaren to hook the ball home from 15 yards.

The remaining quarter of an hour could have seen either side nick it, with Barrow relying on spirit more than anything else. Backed by their biggest crowd of the season, they sought a winner but were reminded of Millwall's potency when Hartburn sent in a screamer from 25 yards, which Hindle did well to keep out. The excitement continued to the very end as the home team gained a last-minute corner, which resulted in McLaren's effort being deflected to Bill Hannah, who just failed to connect. That was the last meaningful action of the game.

After the third-round draw was made, the prize awaiting both these combatants was the mouth-watering prospect of entertaining the current League champions Matt Busby's Manchester United just after Christmas. But first things first, Barrow had to be disposed of. Millwall made one change for the replay, with Stan Morgan coming in at inside-left and Monkhouse reverting to the wing in place of Johnny Hartburn.

The lanky Johnny Shepherd was the Lions' hero with his third hat-trick of the campaign. His first had come on his debut at Leyton Orient when he had scored all four goals in a 4–1 success the previous October. In addition to his three goals against Barrow, Shepherd also hit a post with another effort, missed a sitter and had other countless chances with feet and head to have claimed six goals, never mind three. He and the rest of the attack treated Hindle's goal as a shooting gallery. A flurry of three goals in an eight-minute spell midway through the first half kept the replay simmering until the last 10 minutes.

George Stobbart opened the scoring after getting the merest touch on a Neary corner, but four minutes later Barrow drew level after Malcolm Finlayson dropped Layton's cross giving Gordon an easy goal. Johnny Shepherd restored Millwall's advantage, which they held deep into the second half. The expectant supporters, seeing the finishing line in sight, had their anxiety lifted after 80 minutes when George Stobbart lost possession in one of his now familiar runs, and the ball fell to the supporting John Shepherd, who in an instant hit the back of Hindle's net with a stinging drive, despite the gallant 'keeper getting his hands to it. Two minutes later the scene was set for The Den to stage its biggest match since United's neighbours Manchester City came to town for a sixth-round tie in 1937.

The enigmatic Man of the Match Frank Neary sent over another of his many fine centres for Shepherd to nip in front of Hindle to flick home with his right foot for number four as fans started counting the days for the Busby Babes' visit. The watching United manager Matt Busby clearly had something think about, as he stated afterwards 'Millwall will give us a hard match at The Den on 10 January. Forget the Division One versus Division Three tag. The Lions have a fine side'.

By the time United paid what was to be their first of three visits to The Den in a calendar year, Millwall had hit a rich vein of form. Going well in the Third Division and unbeaten in their last 11 Cup and League matches, they had racked up 30 goals into the bargain. After 90 minutes Millwall must have wondered how they had managed to lose, because for three quarters of this match Manchester United were outplayed, outmanoeuvred and outfought by an excellent Millwall side.

Lose they did, however, in such circumstances that must have left manager Charlie Hewitt wringing his hands in despair as he saw a replay payday slip over the horizon when

Millwall goalkeeper, Malcolm Finlayson, foils a Manchester United attack in the third-round tie at New Cross in 1953. Over 35,000 fans saw United grab a fortuitous 1–0 victory with a late goal. [PA]

United scored a most fortunate 83rd-minute winner. United's John Berry collected a throw-in from Aston, who then sent in a high cross that Finlayson seemed a shade slow in reacting to. The ball dropped over his outstretched right hand for Stan Pearson to head home at the far post. Finlayson and his teammates protested the ball had gone out of play before Pearson scored.

All this should have been academic as Millwall had carved out enough openings to put themselves out of sight as Shepherd, Hartburn and Morgan all spurned easy chances. Ray Wood was brought into action time and time again, and when he was eventually beaten the crossbar came to his rescue when a goal seemed inevitable.

Millwall were more than a match for their illustrious opponents who, other than the faultless Johnny Carey, their best player on the day, were superior in every department. The two wing-halves Johnny Short and Pat Saward were exceptionally solid, with the other honours going to Stobbart, Morgan and Gerry Bowler, who did not deserve to be on the losing side.

Following their near miss for promotion when finishing second to champions Bristol Rovers and the galling departure from the FA Cup, the Lions' involvement in the competition for the coming season of 1953–54 was rather low key in comparison and did not advance beyond round two after becoming the victim of a giant-killing act. Colchester United provided the opposition at Layer Road in the first round, where the consensus was that a replay should not have been necessary if the U's had kept their first-half form going in the second. Millwall had their defence to thank that they went into the break just one goal behind. The reports relayed from Colchester stated that Gerry Bowler had played U's danger-man Kevin McCurley better than any centre-half that season, which was just as well given Millwall's impoverished attack.

However, the big Irishman could do nothing to stop United taking the lead in the 41st minute when John Harrison sent in a deep free-kick which saw McCurley free himself of Bowler's shackles to loop his effort high over Finlayson and into the net. United paid for their tentative approach after the break when Millwall drew level in the 58th minute to earn a replay. A sloppy clearance from a Lions corner was snapped up by Alex Jardine, who floated over a perfect centre for George Stobbart to net from close in.

Millwall's performance at Layer Road had displeased manager Charlie Hewitt greatly, and in response he made two changes for the replay. In came Frank Neary, who had missed the first game due to a heavy cold, to replace Johnny Shepherd and at left-half Irishman Pat Saward took over from Jack Heydon, while one of United's changes occurred at right-back where 'Digger' Kettle took over from the injured Harrison.

Hewitt's minor blood-letting had the desired effect as the replay turned into a stroll in the park for the Lions, opening the scoring as early as the ninth minute when Colchester's goalkeeper Wright went down in instalments in an attempt to stop Stobbart's low 20-yard shot. Six minutes after the break, the hapless Wright was again at fault when he careered out of goal and collided with his teammate Bearryman, leaving Stobbart to shoot into an empty net.

Apart from some isolated bursts from United's McCurley, it was plain sailing for Millwall, who made it three five minutes from time when Johnny Johnson was played onside after the ball cannoned off Fred Lewis for him to pull the ball back for summer-signing George Hazlett to score what turned out to be his only FA Cup goal for the club. It was Johnson again who created the fourth, with another excellent centre that put in Neary to score on the run with the best goal of the game two minutes from time to complete the rout.

If the Colchester game turned out to be a cakewalk, the opponents for the second round proved to be made of sterner stuff when non-League Headington United (later to become Oxford United) arrived at Cold Blow Lane in early December. Evergreen George Fisher and half-back Jack Heydon were declared fit to face the Southern League champions, who, if they had sensed any nervousness among the Millwall ranks, made them more edgy by taking the game to the Lions straight from the kick-off.

Visiting centre-forward Ken Smith set Headington's stall out early on when he breached the Millwall defence, and only the bravery of Malcolm Finlayson denied Smith from giving them the lead. Finlayson then stopped a long-range effort from the busy Smith before the Lions 'keeper cleared from the feet of Duncan as the visitors buzzed around the Millwall goal.

It was the former Charlton full-back Peter Croker who was the stumbling block to Millwall before they finally got moving, with Neary popping in three of his trademark rockets; although sadly all were off target. At the other end a Smith effort cleared the bar, and with half-time beckoning Millwall took a fortuitous 40th-minute lead. Somewhat against the run of play Shepherd took Neary's pass in his stride to whip home a vicious strike. It was Millwall who settled the better at the start of the second half as Shepherd and Alex Jardine both went close, and in another storming move the United 'keeper Ansell was injured.

Despite Millwall looking the more threatening, Headington refused to buckle and came back through Smith, who had an effort disallowed before they deservedly equalised. Eventually they forced yet another corner, which Maskell sent over for Peart to head home in the 55th minute, and this goal stopped Millwall in their tracks. Worse was to follow within minutes when Headington outside-right Steele put them ahead with a stunning shot on the turn from 30 yards. United's pace, especially in attack, was unnerving the Lions' rearguard,

As Cup upsets go, this one Millwall suffered at Headington United in 1953 is up there with the worst. They lost this replay by the only goal, scored by Jack Smith, seen here beating Lions goalkeeper Malcolm Finlayson. [The Press Association]

In the decade from 1950 the FA Cup will not, with a couple of exceptions, be fondly remembered by the Lions fans, and in that period they fell to non-League sides 1953, 1958 and 1959 and shown here the covers of the match programmes of those infamous occasions at Headington (now Oxford) United, Worcester City and Bath City. [Author]

and it came as no surprise when they extended their lead with a third. It was another header, this time from Maskell after 73 minutes that put the skids under Millwall, who were now perilously close to getting knocked out. The situation looked hopeless, but professional pride made them go on all-out attack for the remainder of the game. Frank Neary reduced the deficit before the 'Brown Bomber' gave an astute pass for Johnny Short to the pull the game out of the fire with Millwall's third.

The replay following the 3–3 draw at New Cross was tough and uncompromising as Millwall's attempt to unsettle the non-League team with some overzealous play backfired. Headington took the intimidation in their stride to play what little football there was on show and earned the right to meet Stockport County in the third round. During the course of the game United's rampaging striker Ken Smith was spoken to on four occasions by the referee, but he became the Headington hero after scoring the game's only goal in the 20th minute, stooping to head Maskell's free-kick to send Millwall tumbling out of the Cup.

Afterwards Lions manager Charlie Hewitt could not hide his disappointment when he stated very succinctly in his post-match comment 'Sorry, we played badly'. The game would not be the last Millwall were to see of Ken Smith, as five years later he came back to haunt the Lions again when a Gateshead team secured a 2–0 win at The Den in February 1959.

Following the previous season's disappointing League place of 12th, an improvement was made during the 1954–55 campaign where the team climbed to fifth in the table, added to which was a small run to the third round in the FA Cup. Drawn at home Exeter City in the first round, Millwall could set the record straight by reversing that controversial first-round defeat by the Grecians five years earlier at Cold Blow Lane.

A player who would make his mark over the course of the next few seasons was the ungainly looking Dennis Pacey. Signed from Hewitt's old club Leyton Orient in the October, he scored the only goal of the game on his debut against Bournemouth and went one better in his first FA Cup outing when he bagged a brace. Dennis was a most unlikely looking footballer with his laboured running action, but he was as deceptive as he was effective, having scored 46 times in 120 games for the O's.

After a quiet opening 15 minutes, Millwall booked their place in the next round after instigating some devastating and exhilarating football in the remaining 30 minutes leading

Third Division rivals Exeter City were victims in the first-round tie at The Den in 1954. Here City's 'keeper Hugh Kelly foils Millwall's Freddie Ramscar and Dennis Pacey, who scored twice in a 3–2 success. [Keystone]

up to the interval, a period in which they could have scored half a dozen. Securing a 3–1 lead, Millwall became complacent in the second half and nearly paid the price. In that splendid half-hour the Lions were virtually unplayable as their enterprising approach stood out against City's more direct style, with Pacey threatening to tear City apart on his own. He was ably assisted by the pinpoint centres and crosses from Kenny Prior and George Hazlett. Pacey unlocked the Exeter defence after taking Freddie Ramscar's neat flick, evading a tackle to coolly beat Kelly in the City goal with a low ground shot after 20 minutes. Twelve minutes later the second arrived when the grind of the training ground paid dividends when Johnny Short chipped a free-kick for the onrushing Alex Jardine to slam the ball home from way out past an astonished Kelly. Then, three minutes before the break, the Lions obtained their third and probably the best goal of the game when Hazlett flashed in free-kick after he had been fouled. It appeared that the ball was going wide until Pacey emerged from a ruck of players to meet it with his head to score with an unstoppable header.

In between, City had reduced the arrears when Murphy latched on to a long through-pass and, despite the attentions of a young Charlie Hurley and goalkeeper Finlayson, fired home after 35 minutes. Millwall's pallid display in the second half was mainly down the wing-halves Short and Heydon failing to regain their dominance of the first half. Millwall became over-reliant on Charlie Hurley snuffing out the Exeter threat; however, the brawny Irishman was powerless to stop Angus Mackay heading home City's second goal to leave Millwall facing a nervy final 10 minutes.

For the second round Millwall fielded an unchanged side for the Accrington Stanley tie, who were making their second visit to The Den for a Cup game, their first coming in 1934. Millwall's play, reported one sage, was as dull and grey as the December skies, with only the display of Malcolm Finlayson and some weak Accrington finishing stopping them from taking a more commanding lead at the break. Stanley had gone in front when Bob Scott scored inside the first seven minutes. After that shock, play was entirely in Stanley's half and saw the Lions force 11 corners to the visitors' one. But Millwall's failure to score was down to Accrington's solid defence and an inspired display by their excellent goalkeeper Jimmy Jones.

Millwall's patience finally bore fruit when pocket dynamo Freddie Smith got the crowd roaring when supplying the pass for Kenny Prior to equalise after 58 minutes. This was a welcome shot in the arm for the Lions. It perked up their wing-halves no end to reproduce some of their old brilliance and finally take command. They gained the lead for the first time with a header from Pacey, whose aerial prowess had been wantonly neglected through lack of supply from his cross-shy colleagues. Close to the end, two goals arrived in two minutes when Ramscar took Prior's pass to side-foot home the third before Harry Bodle registered Stanley's second, but it came too late to stop Millwall sneaking into the third round.

Millwall were again paired with Lancastrian opposition in the third round when they drew First Division Bolton Wanderers at Burnden Park, rekindling memories the first Cup meeting 40 years earlier. The Lions took 10 coach-loads of supporters to cheer them on, including Mr W. McCrossen, a Millwall fan for more than 50 years who was accompanied by his home-made model 'Lion' manufactured from canvas and filled with sawdust. He and fellow day-trippers saw Charlie Hewitt make some positional changes to the line up, with

Johnny Summers retaining the left-wing spot, a role he had filled in the last two League games. Freddie Smith kept the number-seven shirt, with the regular outside-right George Hazlett filling in at inside-left.

Fog was threatening when Dennis Pacey got the tie underway, but Bolton gained instant possession to mount the first serious raid on the Lions goal when Doug Holden and Johnny Wheeler combined to put Dennis Stevens through before the danger was cleared. Johnny Summers retaliated for Millwall in their first meaningful attack but was robbed by Bolton right-back Johnny Ball, before Pacey fired in an effort that went wide. A foraging run from Pat Saward was terminated when Hanson saved the Irishman's effort as Millwall sought the early breakthrough. But it was Bolton who opened the scoring following a number of promising raids with a very simplistic goal in the 16th minute when their Scottish international Willie Moir was in the right place to tap-in a Nat Lofthouse cross.

Lions 'keeper Malcolm Finlayson was called into action at the start of the second half when saving Lofthouse's header, while at the other end his opposite number, the veteran Stan Hanson, had to fist away Alex Jardine's tempting free-kick after Pacey had been fouled. Millwall then began to move freely and were quicker to the ball, but their creative football was sadly let down by some woeful finishing. When Lofthouse narrowly missed with a header Millwall broke at pace to draw level with a goal that their entertaining play deserved when the quick-thinking Jack Heydon's cute pass left Bolton's Malcolm Barrass red-faced, leaving Freddie Smith the formality of equalising after 51 minutes.

With their star in the ascendancy, Millwall, led by the excellent Pacey's example, continued to press an anxious Bolton defence in search of a knock-out goal. So concerned were Bolton they made the tactical switch that eventually turned the tide in their favour, bringing Ray Parry in from his left-wing berth and putting Stevens into Parry's position. Nonetheless, the game appeared to be heading for a draw when Parry's move inside paid dividends. He produced the one piece of magic to secure Bolton's victory with a tantalising cross which had Lion's 'keeper Finlayson back-peddling. The big Scot got the merest touch, only to see the ball clip the crossbar and drop for the waiting Moir to tap home with 10 minutes to go. Any hopes Millwall had of forcing a draw were finally crushed five minutes later when Parry capped a fine, inspirational 20-minute spell to put away Bolton's third.

In defeat the Lions had given an impressive display of football which had been appreciated by the fans and opponents alike, and they had these comforting words of the victorious captain Willie Moir to accompany them on the journey south: 'I have never played in a cleaner tie or one where the football was better'. High praise indeed.

10. Parting of the Ways

W ell before the 1955–56 season was completed the autocratic Hewitt would be gone from The Den. His ways and manner were of a bygone age, and society was changing, leaving the likes of Charlie and his ilk behind. Never high in the popularity stakes, his esteem had plummeted further after he accused George Fisher, of all people, of being a malingerer. This may have been acceptable in the forelock-touching Edwardian era but was totally unjust in post-war Britain. Hewitt's probable rejoinder would have been that he was here to win football matches not make friends, but poor old Charlie was losing the few he had.

After four wins in the first nine games, there followed a desperate run of six consecutive defeats that culminated in the 6–2 thrashing at Ipswich that would fuel a sombre ambience at The Den. Victories over Walsall and Queen's Park Rangers were interspersed with more losses, including the one in the Cup at the hands of Northampton Town, which led to more unrest. The continued absence of Charlie Hurley in the heart of the defence did not help, and with Millwall struggling Hewitt had been unable to fill the big man's position adequately.

Young Hurley had learnt the night before the tie at the County Ground that he had been called up by the Irish Republic for their match against Spain the following week; however, the elation of selection was deflated in a most ungracious way as the 19-year-old Charlie and his Millwall team went down 4–1, and to cap it all (no pun intended) poor Charlie knocked-in an own-goal and picked up an injury.

It was the return of Northampton's Jack English to their team who undid the Lions. He had been out of action since September but his manager, Dave Smith, decided to risk him, and his faith was amply justified when English hit a hat-trick. His first arrived when Hurley was off receiving some treatment to open the scoring in the 43rd minute when he struck home following a corner. Early in the second half Malcolm Finlayson distinguished himself with two excellent saves before Hurley's mishap made it 2–0 as he attempted to cut out a cross from the rejuvenated English. The Cobbler completed his treble with a fine header and then a tap-in for Northampton's fourth when Finlayson could only parry Ray Yeoman's shot. Millwall's token reply came in the final minute from their most impressionable forward Dennis Pacey. The injury to Charlie Hurley was now compounded by the insult that was to force him to withdraw from the Ireland squad, thus delaying his international debut until May 1957, some 18 months later.

So with New Year hardly underway, Charlie Hewitt was dismissed as manager. When Alex Jardine heard the news he immediately withdrew his transfer request, with most if not all of the playing staff raising a glass in celebration. Ron Gray took charge of first-team affairs as what was already a traumatic season ended in Millwall seeking re-election. They finished with a brief flurry, however, by winning the last three games (all at home), including two by 5–0 margins over Norwich City and the champions Leyton Orient.

It was not just the team's inconsistency the suffering fans had to put up with but also the tendency to ship goals with alarming regularity. That scenario continued into Gray's first full season (1956–57). They continued to record heavy losses, with seven goals leaked at Walsall, half a dozen at Bournemouth, four along the coast at Southampton and five more at Brentford.

During this gloomy period in Millwall's history, it was little wonder the fans looked to the FA Cup to inject some cheer into what was already a flagging season, and on this score they were not let down. Millwall embarked on their finest run in a generation that commenced by the sea in good-old Sussex when facing Brighton at the Goldstone Ground. A splendid display from Millwall's inside trio of Joe Tyrrell, Dennis Pacey and John Shepherd (one of only two ever-presents) was the foundation in gaining a spirited 1–1 draw, whereas Albion on the other hand had a day where they just could not fathom Pacey's multi-tasking role. His deep-lying position and probing caused Albion plenty of problems, as did his outstanding display when in the vanguard of the attack.

If Dennis was Millwall's main man, Albion's continuance of switching positions impressed nobody and confused no one other than themselves. But they did manage to take the lead when Dennis Foreman teed up Glen Wilson to smash his drive past Bill Lloyd. Albion's lead lasted no longer than two minutes when Shepherd rose to head home Hazlett's corner to send the teams in level at the interval. Nothing really happened in the remainder of the game except for some ill temper that crept into the play which saw Wilson and Tyrrell square-up to one another before Anslow became target of the Brighton boo-boys when he sent Foreman sprawling on the cinder track with hefty tackle. Other than that it was one to forget.

Brighton's refusal to play under the Cold Blow Lane floodlights reduced some much needed 'readies' into both clubs' coffers. Both teams remained unchanged from the Saturday encounter, and had their finishing been better Millwall would have won more handsomely than the 3–1 scoreline suggests. The Lions gave an imaginative display of football that was full of youthful zest, which had rarely been seen in the League. Quicker to the ball and a lot sharper in passing, Millwall achieved some telling thrusts in and around the Brighton penalty area.

So poor were Albion that Lions 'keeper Bill Lloyd was unemployed for much of the time, which could hardly be said about his opposite number Eric Gill. Although three of the four goals came from penalties, the game was hard fought but never got out of hand, which was mainly due to the excellent handling of the game by the referee, Mr J.W. Hunt of Hampshire. Albion started briskly enough but were astounded when Millwall gained an eighth-minute lead, when Tyrrell's neat header put Shepherd in the clear to lob Gill for the opener. Tyrrell was again instrumental for the second after 24 minutes, when Jim Langley handled Joe's powerful drive to allow Stan Anslow to put away the spot-kick.

Brighton's half-hearted response at the start of the second half was countered by Millwall's third goal in the 66th minute. It was John Shepherd's alertness that paved the way when Albion's Ken Whitfield took an eternity to clear only to be caught out by Shepherd's eagerness, and in the ensuing tussle Whitfield was adjudged to have fouled the Lion. Anslow's second penalty went the same way as his first, giving the hapless Gill no chance. Brighton finally gave their fans something to cheer about in the 80th minute, when Alex Jardine, the most polished player on the field, blotted his copybook after bringing down Foreman in the area. Up strode Langley to hammer the ball into the roof of Bill Lloyd's net.

Millwall were then given an excellent opportunity to reach the third round for the second time in three years when they were drawn at home to Kent League club Margate, who had knocked out the Hellenic League side Dunstable Town in the previous round. The final score of 4–0 to the Lions appeared comfortable enough on the surface, but it was a close-run thing, with Margate giving as good as they got well into the second half. Millwall served up some delightful football and deserved their success, but it could have been a lot different had a Margate effort not been disallowed three minutes before half-time for a tight offside decision.

Millwall's hero of the day was the effervescent Johnny Shepherd, who registered his fifth Cup goal of the season with another hat-trick (he also had another three efforts disallowed). He opened his account in the 15th minute when heading home Hazlett's free-kick, but not before Johnny Roche, later to join Millwall, sent in the first shot of the game which grazed Bill Lloyd's crossbar. Margate's 'keeper Pete Peters was then forced to make a couple of tremendous stops in quick succession as Millwall went about building on their early strike. Despite the constant attacking, Millwall reached the interval with only one goal to show for their efforts in a very open game.

Margate's illuminating start to the second half went unrewarded, and they fell further behind in the 61st minute when the deadly Hazlett sent another excellent centre over, which found Shepherd's head to put Millwall two up. Eleven minutes later John completed his hat-trick when snapping up a loose ball after Tyrrell's shot had been cleared off the line by Terry Joyce. It was tough on the gallant Kent side that were deprived of a deserved goal when the dangerous Roche hit a screamer that cannoned off a post to safety. Millwall rounded off a decent afternoon's work when left-half Colin Rawson took advantage of the failing light to move forward and unleash a terrific shot from 35 yards to complete the scoring.

For the third round Millwall were fortunate to receive another home draw. It was not the plum tie they had hoped for but was perhaps the next best thing – a local derby against Crystal Palace. The Lions' pre-match preparations got off on the wrong foot when skipper Colin Rawson got stranded in a major traffic jam, which allowed Roy Summersby to make his FA Cup debut. Rawson's absence did not seem to affect the team too much, however, as they obtained a vital early goal. It came in the fifth minute when Paccy's low header took a vicious spin off the pitch, which forced Palace's left-back Gordon McDonald to handle on the line. Up stepped chunky Stan Anslow to utilise one of his powerful tree trunk-like thighs to blast home the spot-kick.

Just after the break Shepherd nearly increased Millwall's lead when he ran unchallenged through a square Palace defence, but the danger was averted by Ray Potter's well-timed save. The Lions striker was not to be denied a second time, however, and sure enough after 62 minutes his persistence was rewarded. Gordon Pulley's acrobatic overhead-kick caught the Palace rearguard on the back foot and, sensing the kill, Shepherd veered in from the left to fire home the loose ball into the far corner of the net. This fairly convincing success saw Millwall enter the fourth round for the first time in six years, and this time they really struck gold when mighty Newcastle United were drawn to face them at Cold Blow Lane at the end of January.

The fine start to the New Year continued with Millwall winning all four home games played in January. A belated Christmas present for the fans came when manager Ron Gray, in a flash of inspiration, decided to place the sturdy full-back Stan Anslow up front in an effort to beef up the attack. Stan's response exceeded all expectations. In his first game in

One of Millwall's better days in the 1950s came when they beat the decade's FA Cup team Newcastle United at The Den 2–1. Here is the cover and teams from the official match programme for that auspicious fourth-round occasion. [Author]

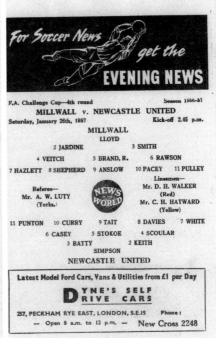

Another rarity is the match ticket for Millwall's giant-killing act over Newcastle United at The Den in 1957, when a Stan Anslow brace saw off the Magpies 2–1. [Andy Sullivan]

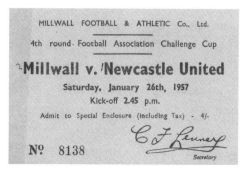

MILLWALL FOOTBALL & ATHLETIC Co., Ltd.

4th round · Football Association Challenge Cup

Millwall v. Newcastle United

Saturday, January 26th, 1957
Kick-off 2.45 p.m.

Admit to Special Enclosure (including Tax) - 4/-

No 8138

Secretary

the number-nine shirt he thumped home a hat-trick, as did John Shepherd again, in the 7–2 thumping of Torquay United. Stan had already notched three goals in the Cup, including one against Palace in the third round. He then registered another against the same opposition a fortnight later, but he saved his finest hour in football for when he hit both the goals that saw Newcastle's interest in the FA Cup melt away.

When the Magpies visited The Den on that famous occasion they had taken on the mantle as England's greatest Cup team by monopolising the tournament in the first full decade since the war. Having won it in 1951, they retained it in 1952, before taking it back to Tyneside once more after defeating Manchester City 3–1 in 1955. Besides these fantastic achievements they had also won it in 1910, 1924 and 1932 and had been runners-up four times before World War One. Against a team with such an excellent pedigree, Millwall knew would have to pull out the stops and more if they were going to cause an upset, as the gulf in class between the teams was wider than the distance Newcastle and their fans had to travel to south-east London.

But cometh the hour cometh the man, well two actually in Millwall's case. Stan Anslow stole the headlines with his brace, but the unsung hero was none other than Dennis Pacey. In a plaudit-gaining display he marked and thwarted at every turn the moves by the Geordies' influential playmaker Jimmy Scoular. To say Dennis accomplished his task would be an understatement as he carried out his orders to the letter, as many of the 45,646 spectators crammed into the rafters could verify. Newcastle began the match bent on winning the pot for the fourth time in six years, and for first 10 minutes or so the question was how many they would win by? But the Lions defence, suspect for most of the season, had tightened up considerably of late and showed great resilience against the threat of United's inside triumvirate of Tait, Curry and Davies.

After Newcastle's early dominance, the pendulum now swung Millwall's way, and as Anslow began to feed off Pacey's diligence United felt the unease to the point of becoming ragged, before the unlikely happened in the 33rd minute. Scoular was robbed by the niggling Pacey, who despatched the bullish Anslow on a run to fire past Ronnie Simpson for the opener. Unsettled by the turn of events, Newcastle nearly conceded again moments later when a header struck the bar before the Irishman Dick Keith cleared the danger. With Pacey linking well with the stylish Colin Rawson, Millwall had taken full control in midfield, and no one would have been surprised if they had reached the interval with the two-goal lead that their spirited play merited.

The question was, could Millwall keep up such a display? Barely seven minutes into the second half the question was partially answered when Stan Anslow wrote himself into

Millwall folklore. He raced on to another excellent through ball, this time from Shepherd, and United's centre-half Mal Scott was in frantic pursuit but could only watch as Stan hammered home his second goal past the advancing Simpson.

With Newcastle's Cup reputation looking tarnished, they finally decided to do something about it and went full throttle with some powerful attacking play. It was Millwall who nearly scored again when the energetic Pacey agonisingly missed. But when another Lions attack broke down Alex Tait hopefully chased down a long punt upfield. By doing so he caught the Lions defence unawares to tuck the ball under Bill Lloyd's body to reduce the arrears after 58 minutes. With just half an hour to survive, Millwall's team of battlers regrouped to confront the expected Newcastle onslaught. To be fair, the Geordies did have chances to save the day, but their over reliance on Jimmy Scoular proved their downfall. The falling rain began to make the pitch very muddy, and as the robust encounter entered its final stages Alex Jardine scraped one United effort off the line before Johnny Shepherd retaliated with two efforts that nearly brought another goal. The enthralling tie eventually came to an end soon afterwards, with Millwall worthy winners.

It was a pity that such a happy occasion for the Lions was spoilt by two events that soured an historic day. The first was the crush in which over 50 fans were overwhelmed, mainly through fainting, and the second was that 100 or so ticket holders, including a few from Newcastle, failed to gain admission and demanded their money back on the day. But let us

Millwall reached the fifth round in 1957, and prior to the game against Birmingham City mascots of both teams paraded around the pitch at The Den, a scenario that would never take place today. [The Press Association]

After beating Newcastle in the fourth round Millwall entertained Birmingham City in the next phase but were generally outplayed as City strolled to a 4–1 win. This shot shows Lions 'keeper Bill Lloyd and left-back John Smith failing to stop the third goal from Noel Kinsey. [PA]

finish the report of a momentous day with the comment from Lions skipper Alex Jardine, who summed up the key reason for the win thus: 'Pacey looked after Scoular according to plan, and Scoular was played right out of the game'.

Do you know the old saying of what follows the Lord Mayor's show? Well, normally it is the dust cart, and this is no less appropriate in Millwall's case. After the scintillating display against Newcastle the roof caved in against the previous year's FA Cup runners-up Birmingham City, who visited Cold Blow Lane for the fifth round. The Lions, in their own indomitable way, began brightly enough but were gradually worn down by a stronger and more skilful team to finally go down by four goals to one. It was Dennis Pacey who put in the first telling shot after the former Millwall amateur Ken Green mis-kicked and Gil Merrick went full length to save the low drive.

Millwall were again at City's throats when Gordon Pulley's snappy header from Shepherd's splendid cross tested Merrick before he was called into action again when collecting the Lions' first corner. It was against the run of play when City took the lead in the 14th minute when Noel Kinsey nodded home Govan's centre. The goal and a slight knock to Stan Anslow took the sting out of the Lions' tail as Birmingham began to take a firm grip. It took a miraculous save from Bill Lloyd to save Millwall from going further behind when he saved Kinsey's blistering drive from 10 yards.

A second City goal was not long in coming when Gordon Astall defied all logic after chasing a lost cause when he not only reached the ball before it ran out but somehow

Millwall's consolation goal against Birmingham from Johnny Shepherd (not in picture). [PA]

managed to screw back a superb centre for Govan to head home after 35 minutes. A further disaster to undermine Millwall's confidence came in the very first minute of the second half when the normally dependable Jardine erred twice. Initially he lost possession and, when given the chance to redeem the situation, tried to play himself out of trouble, only to lose the ball a second time to Brown, who set up Kinsey to snap up number three.

Millwall were dead and buried before the hour was up when City scored their fourth in the 59th minute. The excellent Astall and Kinsey combined to carve open Millwall's now ragged defence for Brown to score. To their credit the Lions kept plugging away seeking a consolation goal, and when it arrived it had a touch of the *Keystone Cops* about it. City 'keeper Gil Merrick's imitation of a drunk trying to catch a balloon was at least comical, but he was not laughing as the ball bounced off Ken Green's head to fall invitingly for Johnny Shepherd, who tapped into an empty net for his seventh Cup goal of the season.

Following the Birmingham defeat Millwall had to wait eight long seasons before they got another look-in at the latter stages of the FA Cup. But in the barren years in between they astounded the fans with a catalogue of horror shows which were as embarrassing as they were unpalatable, and setting the tone Millwall won just four more League games (all at home) to finish in a disappointing 17th place.

11. Shocks and Scares

Optimism is rife at the start of any new football season, and Millwall felt this even more after they were boosted by four wins in the first five games of the 1957–58 campaign. However, the hopes and dreams gained from those early wins had all but disappeared by the end of the year, and the position began to look grim. That season and for a period over the course of the next six years, the FA Cup could offer no solace for the suffering fans.

With their sixth successive home draw, Millwall were set to take on west London rivals Brentford in the first round. What interest the Cup held for both clubs at the time is unknown, but Millwall were definitely looking at the sanctity of the top half of the Third Division to save them ignominy of Fourth Division football while the Bees, who had won at Cold Blow Lane a month previously by a single goal, were upwardly mobile and seeking promotion. But whatever direction the two were taking in the League, it did not prevent the old adversaries putting on a very entertaining match. From the outset it appeared one goal would settle the tie, with Brentford beginning the brighter. But as their star faded, Millwall's began to brighten, and they produced some fine attractive football, which was in stark contrast to the dross that had been served up in the match at The Den four weeks before.

Two contentious points arose in the lead-up to Millwall's winning goal in the 35th minute. The first came when Bees' super goalscorer George Francis was allegedly fouled, leading him to say after the match: 'I was fouled. I saw a linesman flagging. I expected the whistle from Mr Barradell.' But the Leicester official saw nothing wrong and allowed Millwall the advantage of playing on. The second controversy came when George Hazlett was brought down by Kenny Horne, and Lions full-back Alex Jardine sent over his free-kick that was smartly headed home by fellow Scot Angus Morrison. His timely run had sprung the visitors' offside trap, and they appealed in vain to the referee, who waved aside the protests as Brentford's sense of injustice intensified.

Boosted by this fillip, the Lions swarmed around Gerry Cakebread's goal, and only his fingertip save from Rawson's header prevented Millwall doubling their lead before the interval. The second half saw the teams go hammer and tongs, and it was surprising that no more goals were scored. It was during those frantic final moments Brentford came close to equalising while the referee was being urged by the home fans' 'whistles' to blow for full-time. Their penultimate effort made Millwall hearts miss a beat when the excellently positioned George Bristow fired his effort straight into the grateful arms of Bill Lloyd, who soon afterwards was equally relieved to see Johnny Rainford send his last-gasp strike narrowly wide before the official finally called it a day.

The second round saw Millwall come out of the hat first, followed by another old rival, Gillingham. Another intriguing match saw Millwall take the lead with Johnny Shepherd's 18th-minute goal. In today's football climate, however, John would have been booked at best, or possibly even red-carded, for the scoring incident. When Ron Heckman's long pass put Gordon Pulley away down the left, he reached the by-line and put his centre into the waiting arms of Gill's 'keeper Chic Brodie. But before he could take any evasive action he was bundled into the back of the net still clenching the ball by the bustling Shepherd, who received an injured eye for his troubles. A thrilling Cup tie in which the teams created many chances saw Millwall hold out until the 77th minute, when a well-taken goal from Jim Fletcher brought Gillingham a deserved equaliser after Brian Payne and Ron Saunders had penetrated the Lions rearguard.

However, Millwall's interest in that season's FA Cup did not extend beyond the replay four days later. On an extremely difficult surface Gillingham had no trouble in giving a scintillating display and inflicting on Millwall their biggest Cup defeat since Villa put nine past them in 1946. The outcome had been more or less settled in the first 20 minutes after the Gills scored three times in a devastating 10-minute spell. But spare a thought for Millwall's full-backs Ray Brady and John Smith, up against two wingers in Brian Payne and Wendell Morgan who on the day were unplayable. The impetus of this pair steeled the rest of the Kent side to give one of their most impressive performances of the season.

It was the Lions who began what Gillingham carried on so emphatically, when a Phil Hayes cross was nearly deflected into his own goal by Les Riggs before Ronnie Heckman went close from 25 yards. But when the livewire Payne opened the scoring with crisp left-foot drive in the ninth minute the writing was on the wall. Three minutes later it was 2–0 when Fletcher converted after Bill Lloyd had turned Morgan's shot against the bar, before the rampant Payne pounced on Fletcher's knock-down to hammer in the third after 19 minutes.

Millwall tried to adapt, but they just could not stem wave after wave of Gillingham's attacks, relying too much on the overworked Bill Lloyd who in rapid succession denied both Fletcher and Morgan. Gillingham's fourth came in the 41st minute when both Rawson and Smith failed to clear the danger on the edge of the penalty area, leaving Saunders with a clear run in on goal. Seconds before the half-time whistle sounded, the heroic Lloyd prevented a fifth when he saved Joe Hutton's shot from point-blank range.

Resting on their laurels somewhat, Gillingham let Millwall produce some tidy football in the second half without giving too much away, but in a couple of forays Parry cleared a George Veitch effort off the line before Summersby got free to shoot narrowly wide. The Lions' persistence finally paid off when they managed a consolation goal after 72 minutes when Summersby took Hayes's pass to slam home from 15 yards. A minute later, however, Gillingham made sure of a visit to First Division Nottingham Forest in the third round when Hutton fastened on to Saunders's through ball to notch the fifth, and with 12 minutes to go Bill Lloyd was beaten for the sixth time when Fletcher ended his solo run to complete the scoring with a fine goal.

The chastisement at Gillingham could have had two outcomes. One would have been that Millwall rolled up their sleeves to engineer enough points to avoid finishing below the cut-off line. The other outcome was a feeling of doomed resignation and, by winning just three more games after the mauling at Gillingham, Millwall got the second option and the unwelcoming prospect of basement football in the new Fourth Division after finishing bottom.

The club's stock was threadbare, and the inevitable cull of players was more than justified. The turmoil brought other casualties too, as disquiet among the few decent players was highlighted by the departure of Johnny Shepherd and Gordon Pulley in the ensuing close season. If this upheaval was not bad enough, the sad news was released that the playing career of the excellent Alex Jardine was over. His mountainous injury problems were the cause given for his retirement. Talk about putting the boot in, could things get any worse?

Another New Year, and yet another managerial departure; Ron Gray's resignation came less than a year after he had led Millwall to the fifth round and two years after he had replaced Charlie Hewitt. Filling the caretaker role was coach Johnny Short, the man to hold the fort until a new gaffer was appointed. The new boss was a surprise for many as it was 62-year-old Jimmy Seed, the man who had led neighbours Charlton Athletic to some of their greatest moments in the game either side of World War Two. Jim had played for England and had been an FA Cup-winner with Spurs in 1921. If his appointment had not been universally endorsed, the horrendous start his new charges made was certainly gave the doubters all the ammunition they needed. After taking over at the end of January, Seed's team did not win a game for nearly two months until they defeated Gillingham 3–1 to end a run of nine matches without a victory.

The doom and gloom merchants were ready and waiting to pounce at the start of the 1958–59 campaign, and following four defeats and two victories in the first six games at the start of Jimmy Seed's one and only full season at the club the pressure began to mount, which was only partially lifted by a seven-game unbeaten run which ended in a single-goal defeat at Coventry City. Millwall's attempt to regain their place back in the Third Division saw Seed give youth its head as Millwall had some talented youngsters waiting in the wings. The locally-born duo of Dave Harper and Joe Broadfoot, along with Jeff Howells and Ray White, had or were waiting to make their first-team debuts, and this created an air of wary optimism around the club.

After 13 games Millwall lay in second place, and following the win over Palace they were just two points behind leaders York City. But their preparation for the first-round Cup tie against the amateurs of Hitchin Town (J.R. Smith's former club) hit the buffers as they slumped to their heaviest loss thus far, a 4–1 drubbing at Crewe. Following the shambles at Gresty Road,

Millwall were mightily relieved to reach the second round after two gripping games, but this fact does not convey how close they were to getting unceremoniously knocked out. For in the very last minute of the first match Hitchin's Peter Hammond sent a splendid header crashing against the Millwall crossbar, only for the ball to fall to a thankful Lions 'keeper.

With everything to gain and nothing to lose, Hitchin produced a high-tempo game full of commitment, and after a nervy opening 15 minutes they matched and at times bettered Millwall's effort. The visitors' listless attack was bolstered with centre-half Ray Brand moving up to add some punch to a fretful looking Lions. Having survived until the last quarter of the game, Millwall deservedly went a goal down in the 64th minute when Brian Figg tapped a short free-kick to Hammond, whose lob deceived Davies. The home cheers that welcomed the goal were deafening, and with Millwall's attack malfunctioning an upset looked very likely.

Millwall, however, were given a fortunate lifeline six minutes later with a more-than-generous penalty award. Hitchin's full-back 'Tubby' Allin was, according to the referee Mr Dennis, guilty of bringing down Ron Heckman. The task of saving Millwall's blushes was given to Roy Summersby, who gleefully slammed the spot-kick home as the Lions collected their get-out-of-jail-free card. Despite the setback, Town's spirit was far from diminished; although Millwall's rarely seen attack nearly nicked a win when two goal-bound efforts were cleared of the Hitchin goalline, but it was they who had the last word when the crossbar intervened.

The Monday night replay attracted Millwall's biggest gate of the season, with 18,865 spectators turning up to see if the minnows could match their performance of 48 hours earlier. Those who did turn up saw another excellent display from Hitchin Town, and their 2–1 defeat was looked upon by their officials and supporters as a moral victory as they again matched the Lions to keep the issue open until the very last kick. Millwall, who had been lacking in every department in the initial match, looked much stronger and faster, but more significantly they looked the better team. Nonetheless, credit must go to Hitchin defender Bruce Spavins and goalkeeper Peter Edwards, whose rock-like resistance kept Millwall at bay for long periods. Just before Millwall opened the scoring, the lively Brian Figg got away to sweep in a low centre that Reg Davies pushed away from the onrushing Watts who, had he connected, must have surely scored.

This scare was just the rocket Millwall needed to move the ball swiftly up field, where Alex Moyse gained possession and in turn found Ronnie Heckman, who blasted home an unstoppable drive past the gallant Edwards after 35 minutes. With seconds remaining of the first half Joe Hutton, one of the tormentors in Millwall's 6–1 replay thrashing at Gillingham the year before, increased the Lions' lead with the very last touch. If the Lions thought Hitchin were there for the taking, however, they were to be given a rude awakening. The second half was barely two minutes old when Hitchin reduced the deficit after Watts created the opening for Figg to strike a splendid goal. Flushed with adrenalin, the brave amateurs could not find an equaliser to force extra-time, while Millwall were more than content to play out the game until the final whistle.

Once again Millwall were asked to face non-League opposition in the second-round tie against Worcester City. Millwall had tuned themselves up nicely with the 5–2 demolition of promotion candidates York City the week before. But what evolved at Worcester's St George's ground would had Millwall's least passive fans voicing their displeasure. A

These two tickets highlight Millwall losses against non-League opposition in successive seasons. Although the results were terrible at the time, they were softened somewhat when Worcester beat Liverpool in the next round while Bath defeated Division Three runners-up Notts County. [Andy Sullivan]

sensational start saw City, captained by the former Manchester City Cup-winning skipper of 1956, Roy Paul, take a first-minute lead. To their cost, Millwall left Tommy Brown unmarked, and he tricked Ray Brady to fire into the opposite corner of the net to send the home fans delirious. Millwall pushed for an instant equaliser, but none was forthcoming. Instead, there followed the second shock of the game. After forcing a corner, the ball was switched swiftly down to the Millwall end, and unbelievably they found themselves two down after just five minutes. The goal came when Tommy Skuse took full advantage of Brown's and Knowles's excellent approach work that left him the simple task of prodding the ball home from virtually on the goalline.

By conceding two goals so early on Millwall never fully recovered their composure, which was highlighted when Joe Broadfoot got free to put in an inviting cross that was totally wasted as none of his fellow forwards were in position to take advantage. That seemed to sum up Millwall in a desolate first half that could not end quickly enough. Whatever Jimmy Seed said to his team at the break it appeared to have sunk in initially, for at the start of the second half a Ronnie Heckman snap-shot brought Worcester 'keeper Kirkwood into action, before Johnny Roche reduced the arrears after 48 minutes from close range after Heckman had done the spade work. For the first time Millwall began to look dangerous, as a promising attack was halted when Broadfoot's powerful drive just cleared the Worcester bar.

A tactical switch by Worcester saw Brown and Knowles swap roles, and this brought them instant reward in the 59th minute. The foraging Skuse's run was halted by a tackle which led to the ball running on to Knowles, who in turn evaded Redmond's tackle to fire in a shot, which Reg Davies got a hand to but could not stop crossing the line. The Worcester fans had more to cheer about after 70 minutes when another fine move involving Bryceland, Brown and Follan found Knowles, who rode a half-hearted tackle to blast home from 12 yards.

Bemused, ragged and thoroughly beaten, the agony continued when City, displaying a supreme air, inflicted further humiliation on a nonplussed Lions support with a fifth 12 minutes from time, when Brown beat Davies with an unstoppable shot. Even Alex Moyse's excellent run and shot after 87 minutes to make it 5–2 failed to lift his dispirited colleagues as he schlepped back to the centre-circle a lone forlorn figure. At last the merciful blast of the referee's whistle brought an end to the torment as a shell-shocked Millwall trooped off after what had been their heaviest defeat from a non-League side in the FA Cup.

One could forever ponder on the reasons why the wheels came off at Worcester, but whatever soul searching and looking in mirrors achieved in the seven days that followed it certainly had a desired effect on the ensuing Saturday. Port Vale, the champions elect, were the visitors to New Cross, and an unrecognisable Millwall astounded all and sundry by beating them 4–2 in a highly entertaining game. The more sagacious of the Millwall fans merely put the Worcester debacle down to a bad day at the office. The ignominy of the defeat was put into perspective early in the New Year when Worcester despatched Liverpool, then of the Second Division, 2–1 in the third round.

The final 11 fixtures, in which too many points were dropped in drawn games, condemned Millwall to missing out on promotion for a ninth-placed finish. Manager Jimmy Seed stood down from his role to become an 'advisor' to the new hot-seat incumbent whenever he was appointed. The rumours that had been circulating turned into fact when former Lion and member of the 1937 semi-final team Reg Smith was appointed as manager in the summer of 1959. Reg (J.R.) had achieved some minor miracles in Scotland with Falkirk, whom he guided to Scottish Cup Final success against Kilmarnock, and now Millwall were hoping his run of success would rub off on them.

Smith's team, including newcomers Sammy Wilson from Celtic, Dennis Jackson from Aston Villa, who was installed as the new skipper, and former Palace striker Barry Pierce, who had been exchanged for Johnny Roche, got off to flying start at the beginning of the 1959–60 season. The new-look team embarked on an unbeaten run of 19 games, although 11 of those fixtures ended in draws. The run came to an end at Notts County, who were destined to finish runners-up that season. But a week later the FA Cup first round brought them up against another non-League outfit, this time Bath City at Twerton Park.

If J.R.'s thoughts were of more Cup triumphs, then his bubble was about to burst in the very first instance as the Lions failed again to master supposedly one of the lesser lights of football. Bath's attack had been galvanised by the arrival of Scotland's Charlie Fleming, who led City to victory in an incident-packed, full-blooded encounter. Surely after the previous season's nightmare at Worcester, Millwall would not underrate Bath – would they? Bath's spirit, courage and determination would surely be matched by the Lions'. Would it not?

Well, in the event it appeared Millwall had neither the heart or the fight to equal that of the Southern League leaders, who took a 25th-minute lead through Peter Wilshire who converted Fleming's astute through ball. Almost immediately, former Celt Sammy Wilson caught the home defence napping to race in and score from 15 yards. Now was the time to put these Somerset upstarts in their place. There was some frantic action in the Bath area as Millwall went for the kill as clearances were hacked to safety with the Lions threatening a second. But after failing to build on their goal, Millwall were caught cold when with just three minutes of the first half remaining Wilshire was brought down just outside the box. This range was well within Charlie Fleming's (62 goals in 107 matches for Sunderland)

capabilities, where he could live up to his nickname of 'Cannonball'. The Lions' wall stood its ground but Fleming beat Davies with a powerful shot that took a slight deflection to put Bath City 2–1 up.

Wound up by J.R.'s interval chinwag, Millwall clearly meant business at the start of the second half as Moyse and Alf Ackerman both tested the home team's resolve. But the only strike to hit the target came when Sammy Wilson thumped Bath's O'Neill, whose retaliation saw them both sent off by referee Bill Clements. The dismissals seemed to spur on Bath more than Millwall, and it was the part-timers who confirmed their passage into the next round when Davies, susceptible to the lob, was beaten by Frank Meadows's effort for number three in the 79th minute. Bath then achieved in the next round what Millwall could not when they went to Notts County and won by a goal to nil. As for the League, Millwall were again left to rue all those drawn games, 17 in all, which denied them one of the four automatic promotion places, leaving them in fifth.

During the close season of 1960, manager Reg Smith boosted the goalscoring department at The Den with the capture of Peter Burridge from Leyton Orient, who over the course of the next two seasons would show a high consistency of producing goals of rare quality. But with one win in the first seven games, it confirmed to the fans that going forward Millwall were superb, but defensively were decidedly suspect, conceding 17 against the 14 scored.

The lead-up to another away draw in the FA Cup first round at old rivals Reading had been very encouraging. The Lions had handsomely won the previous three games when defeating Hartlepools 5–2 and Carlisle 4–2 at home, which sandwiched a 1–0 victory at Wrexham. This put the team in fine heart for the short trip to Elm Park, but almost immediately things started to go awry. Heavy flooding in the Thames Valley delayed their arrival at the ground, and along with 'keeper Reg Davies still being unavailable in goal the omens did not look promising. Davies's replacement was the summer signing from Swansea Bill Waters, who had played in those three earlier victories.

Poor Bill must have wondered what he had done to deserve the deluge Reading inflicted upon him, which was all done and dusted in the first 10 minutes as inadequacies in defence proved catastrophic. Hardly had the whistle gone when Millwall found themselves one down when John McIlvenney angled home his shot without a Lion touching the ball after 25 seconds. The Royals doubled their lead after five minutes when Lacey and McLuckie combined for Jimmy Wheeler to shoot home. It was 3–0 after 10 minutes when Wheeler became provider for Bill Lacey to touch home, and after 36 minutes it was good night Vienna when Wheeler headed the fourth.

Saying Millwall were second best would be understating the fact, but they did have the satisfaction of scoring possibly the best two goals out of the eight scored. Not surprisingly, Burridge instilled some pride into a flagging situation by bagging a brace of what were fast becoming trademark finishes. His first on the hour was a venomous left-foot volley from the edge of the area, and his second was an equally fine bullet header that flashed past Dave Meeson in the blink of an eye. In between, Wheeler completed his hat-trick with Reading's fifth, and in the dying seconds Evans headed home number six. One Reading player who stood out was the flaxen-haired Jimmy Whitehouse, a performer who four years later was wearing a Millwall shirt. So, Millwall fell at the first hurdle once again, and in the space of four weeks they had conceded 13 Cup goals. Besides the six lost at Reading they had also been humbled in the first round of the inaugural League Cup by First Division Chelsea 7–1 at The Den in October.

While in the promotion stakes Millwall were again faltered by finishing in sixth spot, they were encouraged by scoring an incredible 97 goals and some outstanding displays; however, the team's weakness was there for all to see as they conceding nearly as many, 86 in all. This meant a massive total of 183 goals scored involving the Lions in the League, a total bettered only by champions Peterborough United's 199 (134 scored/65 conceded). A bigger sensation occurred the following January, however, when after thumping Chester 5–1 Reg (J.R.) Smith was sacked due to the club's financial situation, which led to the assistant manager, the loyal Ron Gray, stepping into the breach yet again.

In the summer of 1961 Ron Gray made one seemingly insignificant signing from West Ham United when he captured the signature of a young Harry Cripps. Harry made just three first-team starts the following season but was an enthusiastic skipper to the reserve team that year. But his love of the game, exuberance and never-say-die attitude would gain 'Arry boy iconic status among the Millwall fans over the course of the next 13 years. But for the forthcoming 1961–62 campaign the energies at Millwall's disposal would be directed at ridding themselves of the burdens of Fourth Division football. Their commitment to the League was highlighted fully with first-round exits in both Cup competitions.

With Millwall's attention being focused on promotion, the first round matched them against Third Division Northampton Town in yet another away tie. This game itself was dominated by both rearguards, and as such the encounter became a grim, colourless struggle, as the early promise of both sets forwards came to very little as they floundered on rock-like defences with chances at a premium. It came as no surprise that the first 45 minutes failed to produce a goal. In such circumstances, games like these can be settled with a blinding piece of skill or something freakish occuring, and it was the latter that played part in Town's first goal when Lions 'keeper Reg Davies damaged his shoulder. This injury was Millwall's undoing, as Northampton left-winger Barry Lines sent in a shot that to many looked like a cross. Whether he meant it, only he would know, but had Davies not been incapacitated he would have surely cut it out.

From the restart Peter Burridge took over in goal as Davies went off to receive further treatment, but the Millwall goalscorer was powerless to prevent Northampton's second when Pat Terry chipped him after Pat Brady had made a rare error on the edge of the box. The record books will show the final result as 2–0 to Northampton, but there will no mention of Millwall's superior football style in the second half, in which they created some excellent chances but failed to take any of them. Whereas Town's direct approach was meat and drink to Ray Brady and Co. for the majority of the game, it is goals that count and Town had scored them. The one good thing to come out of this defeat was that the following February Pat Terry joined the Lions to boost their successful run-in to promotion with an impressive input of 13 goals in 17 appearances.

The gloss of Millwall winning the Fourth Division Championship in 1962 was sullied somewhat by the sale of ace goal-getter Peter Burridge to Crystal Palace that summer. Burridge's replacement was the ex-Brentford and Queen's Park Rangers player Jim Towers, who admittedly had had a phenomenal scoring record with Bees. It was hoped that Jim would continue in a similar vein with the likes of Pat Terry, Dave Jones and Joe Broadfoot. The Lions gained a couple of points in their two opening away games at Bristol City and Port Vale, before dismantling Watford 6–0 at The Den, with Towers getting a hat-trick. A great 0–0 draw in the return game with Port Vale attracted 20,533 spectators, who witnessed a pulsating Monday night encounter, which was followed by the thumping of Hull City, who crumbled 5–1. Another thoroughly entertaining game was the 3–3 draw with Coventry at New Cross, before the buffers were well and truly hit at Boothferry Park in the return match with the Tigers, who nearly reversed their 5–1 mauling at The Den by winning by 4–1 to end Millwall's unbeaten start to the season.

After that flurry of excitement, Millwall's form dipped alarmingly, and by the time the FA Cup came around in early November they had not won in any of the previous five League games. The home tie against Southern League leaders Margate bore the hallmarks of an upset. The previous season they had dumped Bournemouth out with a convincing 3–0 win down at Dean Court; they then took Notts County to a replay before losing. No wonder Lions boss Ron Gray had a furrowed brow leading up to the game, as the current League form was nothing to write home about, nor was their recent Cup record against teams from the non-League arena.

Its easy after the event, but Ron need not have fretted unduly, as once Millwall got into their stride, with Harry Obeney returning to steady the ship, along with new skipper Ray Brady ably marshalling the defence, play went all the Lions' way. Millwall took command from the moment Towers chased a lost cause by retrieving the ball, which he squared back for the waiting Pat Terry to dive in low and head home after 10 minutes. Margate then had a couple of decent chances, which Cyril Jeans and Alan Jones missed when they should have done better.

Five minutes after the break Millwall's Dave Jones scrambled home the second, with Margate protesting that the ball had not crossed the line, but this was academic 20 minutes from time when Margate fell through the trapdoor. When the Lions' form had dipped earlier in the season after an exhilarating start, manager Ron Gray had delved into the transfer market in late September to bring the Blackburn Rovers and former Arsenal winger Joe Haverty back to London. It was the tiny Irishman who put paid to Margate's interest when he skilfully hooked home the third to all but end the tie. Overall, Margate were out-paced and out-played for most of the game, although they did manage to pull a goal back through Jeans. But there was never the fear of a shock as Millwall eased in round two.

Millwall's good fortune continued with another home draw in the second round when high-riding Coventry City called in at The Den for only their second visit to Cold Blow Lane. Following the six-goal thriller the previous September, Millwall were hoping to get the better of City, who had conquered Bournemouth in the first round courtesy of a goal from the ex-Reading man Jimmy Whitehouse.

Foul weather kept the attendance down to less than 15,000 as continuous rain further hampered the team's progress on a muddy surface, but despite the conditions a decent game was played, which was a finely balanced affair. City had the better of the first half with their Welsh winger Ronnie Rees the main threat, and it was he who after skipping past his compatriot Dennis John fired in fierce shot that Reg Davies expertly held. The visitors had a narrow escape when Joe Haverty beat Peter Sillett with a certain amount of ease to cross for the waiting Broadfoot, whose shot was too tame to test Wesson. But five minutes later Broadfoot made amends when he burst through and sent in a teasing chip that caused the back-tracking Wesson to tip the ball to safety.

The rain was coming down in torrents and turning the pitch into a morass, which nearly proved fatal for Millwall when Pat Brady underhit his back-pass, and it held up in the mud to let in Terry Bly, but he was just beaten to it by Davies's alertness. At the start of the second half Millwall sought that illusive breakthrough in which they forced three successive corners and nearly scored from one of them; however, Pat Terry's weak effort from a few yards out allowed Wesson to smother the ball on the line. Further Millwall pressure forced City to have all 11 men back in defence, and after 65 minutes the game really got frenzied when goals seemed likely at either end. Firstly Broadfoot managed to scoop the ball over the bar with the goal at his mercy, and this was followed by a solo run from Terry Bly that ended when he fired narrowly over. It appeared as though Millwall's run was over with two minutes left when City's Hugh Barr gathered enough energy to shoot through Davies's legs, but his effort was ruled out for offside and a muddy and very entertaining game finished 0–0.

In front of a crowd of 22,583, some 250 short of their biggest gate, Coventry City gained the second-round replay victory by the odd goal in three. The Sky Blues had the better of first half after taking a two-goal lead into the break, the first of which arrived after 25 minutes when the persistent Barr managed to keep his balance while being tackled to hammer the ball past Davies. It was 2–0 three minutes later when Millwall's nemesis Jimmy Whitehouse, the best forward on the field, dived to flick home a looping header from a Billy Humphries' cross. In keeping with the first game, both goals had escapes as Mick Kearns diverted a Haverty shot away from danger with Alan Spears (replacing Joe Broadfoot) waiting to cash in, while Dennis John denied City a third after clearing Roy Dwight's header off the line.

Millwall did grab a lifeline just after the interval when left-back Johnny Gilchrist made a surging run into the City penalty area which induced a rash challenge from George Curtis.

Dave Jones's impeccable despatch of the 49th-minute penalty into Wesson's net gave them the launchpad to pen City back in their own half for really the first time in the game. No matter how much they pressure they applied in this period, however, they found Coventry 'keeper Bob Wesson in tip-top form as he inspired his team to weather Millwall's attacks to earn a place in the third round.

As autumn turned into winter, Millwall's last competitive match of 1962 came at Selhurst Park, and the 3–0 defeat by Palace on Boxing Day was to be their last until 16 February the following year. The 'Big Freeze' came in with a vengeance and hit Britain with the worst winter conditions seen since 1947. It caused havoc across the country, throwing all manner of sporting fixtures into utter chaos. Given Millwall's perilous standing in the table, the enforced break came as blessing in disguise; although it did nothing to aid the financial situation.

After climbing to the safety of 16th spot, Millwall were looking forward to pushing on and establishing themselves as a decent Third Division side, but after an opening day home win over Reading they did not taste victory again until a 3–2 success at London Road against Peterborough six weeks later. Eight defeats in the first 11 fixtures put the pressure on manager Ron Gray, and many fans took their grumbles a bit further and began to display banners and hold pre and post-match demonstrations. The mood of the supporters, including the Dockers, was blackened further by the sale of terrace favourite Joe Broadfoot to Ipswich Town. Nothing Gray attempted seemed to work, with the only respite coming in the League Cup, in which they reached the fourth round before losing at Rotherham United. But typically, out of all this mayhem Millwall addressed a perilous situation temporarily by gaining an excellent (if unexpected) 2–1 double over table-toppers Oldham Athletic in the space of five days.

But in the FA Cup issues came to an head; after beating the previous season's non-League 'bogey' Margate, Millwall were drawn away to face Kettering Town in the first round. The visitors took an early through Pat Terry in the 15th minute when he lashed home Millwall's only decent chance against the tough-tackling Kettering defence. The Lions may have thought Pat's goal would be enough for victory, especially after Kettering striker Derek Randall became the main culprit for not taking the Poppies into a substantial lead at the break. He missed two glaring chances as Millwall rarely threatened before half-time, with their best efforts coming from long-range strikes by Dave Harper and Harry Obeney.

It was mainly due to the sterling work of goalkeeper Alex Stepney and centre-half Bryan Snowdon that the Lions held out for as long as they did. Kettering went full-tilt in the second half and piled on the pressure, which finally paid-off when the unfortunate Snowdon intercepted Derek Hogg's shot, only to hit his back-pass wide of Stepney in the 80th minute. However, Kettering's euphoria was eclipsed by the death of an elderly spectator who collapsed and died while watching the match.

The replay was an accident waiting to happen and had been put back a week due to adverse weather, although this only delayed the inevitable. Kettering made it to round two after an excellent 3–2 win as the spectre of Millwall's Worcester and Bath nightmares reappeared with a vengeance. Kettering became the first non-League club to win at Cold Blow Lane since Lincoln City back in January 1921, and the poor result only added to the deepening crisis. The rot had well and truly set in, and following this excruciating defeat many were left

Millwall's first post-war FA Cup defeat at home to a non-League side came in 1963 when Kettering Town won a first-round replay at The Den 3–2. After obtaining a 1–1 draw, the Lions' agony was prolonged for a further week, as this ticket illustrates, when the replay was postponed due to heavy rain. [Andy Sullivan]

Nº 0755

MILLWALL F.C.

GRAND STAND

MILLWALL
v.
KETTERING

Monday, 18th Nov.
1963

UNRESERVED
SEAT

Price 6/0

This portion to be
retained by Holder

wishing that Millwall had bowed out in the original game at Kettering. The Lions spluttered their way through 90 minutes of purgatory in a truly awful performance of mind-numbing proportions. Any of the football played came from the part-timers, with many of the 9,000-plus crowd having seen enough and streaming out long before the final whistle on night of abject disgrace. A crowd of around 200 disgruntled fans gathered after the game to vent their anger by echoing the now familiar 'Gray must go' chant.

The amazing thing was that Kettering, managed by the ex-England warhorse Tommy Lawton, were themselves struggling in their League and were not even rated a decent non-League side. Whatever their standing, however, they were still too good for the Lions. They had taken a 34th-minute lead when Derek Hogg's pass split the Millwall defence and Armour shrugged off a tackle before shooting past Stepney. However, Kettering's joy was shortlived as they were caught dozing two minutes later when Harry Obeney found some space to fire home the equaliser. It was Hogg, the former West Bromwich and Leicester City player, who masterminded their second after 51 minutes when he dummied Dennis John and the rest of Lions defence to set Daldy up to score with a header, who for his pains was knocked unconscious after colliding with Alex Stepney.

If poor old Ron Gray ever made a panic buy then it had to be the novice Gordon Fraser from Cardiff City, who could not hit a barn let alone its door in his five League games but in three Cup matches managed to score three times. It was the young Scot who pulled Millwall back from the brink when heading home a free-kick for equaliser number two. But there was to be no silver lining for Millwall, as with 10 minutes remaining they sank into the abyss when Kettering struck the hammer blow. Following a corner, Millwall came charging out to deny Daldy the space, who instantly shot from 30 yards to find Stepney's net via a post to seal a spectacular night for the non-League side. The fallout of this depressing embarrassment saw Ron Gray relieved of his duties two days later. Even before the hot seat at The Den started to cool down, the board ushered in Billy Gray, the former Chelsea and Nottingham Forest inside-left, as the new supremo within days of his namesake's departure.

12. Fulham and Spurs

In the close season of 1964, Gray wielded the axe by releasing Dave Jones, Pat Terry and Joe Haverty, who despite being a full Irish international was dammed by the manager of having just one foot. Also shown the door was the Scottish pair of Des Anderson and John McLaughlin and the part-time taxi-driver Gary Townend.

Keeping faith with most of his defence, Gray secured newcomers in Dover's Barry Rowan and Southend United's Kenny Jones, who were added to Gray's signings from the end of the previous campaign Hugh Curran, Billy Neil, Jimmy Whitehouse and Roy Senior. The new manager's promise of promotion got off to a great start when the Lions scored four times at Stockport County on the opening day, but two disappointing home draws against Torquay and York City muted the enthusiasm; however, this was the prelude to the run of 59 unbeaten home League matches that would stretch until January 1967.

By the time the draw for the first round of FA Cup was made, Millwall had only lost once in 17 matches, and they were given a quick-fire opportunity to avenge the Kettering fiasco when they were paired with the Poppies for second season running. Two goals from new-boy Barry Rowan in the first 15 minutes blew away any chances of another disaster. But Rowan failed to claim an impressive hat-trick when he blazed wide with only Ted Smethurst to beat, who, it must be said, was the main reason the Lions did not add to their tally. Near to the end of the first half the referee, Mr Setchell of Luton, threatened to abandon the game if the 'phantom' whistle blower in the crowd did not stop his shenanigans. To be honest, the 2–0 result was about right as Millwall won the game at a canter. Their best forward by far was Jimmy Whitehouse, the Lions' chief tormenter at Reading in 1960 and Coventry two years later.

Lion Barry Rowan, arms raised, celebrates one of his two goals against Kettering Town in November 1964. Barry's direct opponent that day, John Harding, is seen retrieving the ball from the net. This pair was reunited some 42 years later when the author arranged a reunion at the 'new' Den in 2006. [Mercury]

During November the Lions went goal crazy, slapping Halifax Town all around The Den for a 5–1 win, then Kettering, which was followed by a third consecutive home win when a resilient Chesterfield side went down 4–2; however, the last Saturday of the month saw the team brought down to earth following a resounding 4–0 loss at Doncaster Rovers. This reverse was not the ideal way to prepare for the second-round meeting with Third Division Port Vale at The Den seven days later. Were Millwall holding something back for that particular game? It appeared so. With Vale struggling, the time was right to take advantage of their plight. For one of their team members his return to The Den would be a baptism of

fire in the face Millwall's superb display, and that player was none other former Cold Blow Lane favourite, goalkeeper Reg Davies.

After crushing Port Vale, Millwall made it to the third round for the first time in eight years as they marched boldly on following a marvellous second half display. The margin of their victory would have been far greater if it had not been for the gritty show of the aforementioned Reg. Among his saves was one early in the game to deny Len Julians when he somehow managed to juggle Len's header over the bar. Moments later, Len burst through, only for Davies to save at his

Half-back Ray Gough made his debut for Millwall in the second-round tie against Port Vale at The Den in December 1964 when the Lions ran out 4–0 winners. [Author]

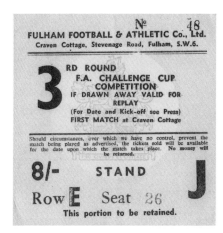

The calendar year of 1965 saw both sides of the coin in regards the FA Cup. The two tickets here are for the 3–3 draw at Fulham, and later in the year was the defeat at non-League Hereford United. [Andy Sullivan]

feet, and Millwall threatened Vale's goal over and over again. Burly Barry Rowan brought Davies to his knees with some stinging drives before Millwall finally took a deserved lead on 40 minutes when Whitehouse's mazy run left three defenders in his wake, and he sent in a vicious cross which saw Julians nip in front of Davies to score.

Vale showed a bit more spirit at the start of the second half but fell further behind after 63 minutes when Whitehouse chested the ball down in an attempt to set up Julians. In his effort to block Julians, Vale's centre-half John Nicholson inadvertently sent the ball into his own net. It was now the ghostlike figure of Jimmy Whitehouse who took over the show when four minutes later he cottoned on to Julians's pass to beat a couple of defenders before firing home the third, and then with 10 minutes to go the superb Whitehouse seem to glide over the sodden pitch to lash home the fourth after Vale's defence had been sliced open.

With Millwall battling for promotion, an extended run in the Cup might have derailed their aim of an instant return to the Third Division, as most of their fellow contenders had got no further than the first round. Millwall, having now reached the round where the big clubs enter, found themselves paired with First Division Fulham at Craven Cottage. Unfortunately the League form, especially away from home, had dipped, with just one point from eight on the road meaning that Millwall had slipped out of the top four by the time they faced Fulham. However, the overriding concern of many Lions fans was hoping their team would not get overwhelmed or embarrassed. This could well have been the case against a Fulham side containing England players George Cohen, Bobby Robson and the elegant Johnny Haynes.

Those concerns came flooding back after 12 minutes when Fulham took the lead when Alex Stepney, for once, misjudged a Stan Brown cross which left Fulham's Johnny Key the simple task of heading into an unguarded net. If that goal was below the belt then Fulham's second was surely the knock-out punch. Millwall went down to 10 men when right-back Johnny Gilchrist was carried off following an accidental collision with teammate Len Julians, and it was during Gilchrist's absence Fulham increased their advantage when Stepney's reaction was not the quickest and left Reg Stratton to put Fulham two up after 33 minutes to leave Millwall reeling on the ropes.

Alex Stepney, who had saved Millwall on countless occasions in the past, finally had something to smile about four minutes later when the bullish Hughie Curran, famed for his hard shooting and bullet-like headers, was on hand to tap home a loose ball after Macedo failed to gather a free-kick. With their tails up, Millwall ripped into Fulham at the start of the second half to ultimately gain their reward – or so it seemed. When the industrious Jimmy Whitehouse entered the Fulham area in the 57th minute only to be sent sprawling by Fulham's left-back Jim Langley it gave skipper Harry Cripps the chance to restore equanimity, but in front of Millwall's baying fans he sent his spot-kick tamely into the grateful hands of Macedo. Let off by Millwall's generosity, Fulham virtually put one foot in the next round when Reg Stratton scored his second to finish off an excellent move started in his own area by George Cohen for their third goal.

All hope appeared lost, but then 8,000 travelling Lions fans commenced their famous incessant roars of encouragement. The team started to respond as the sound of 'Millwall, Millwall, Millwall' shook Craven Cottage to its foundations. Picking up on the vibes, Jimmy Whitehouse began to weave his Cup magic from wide on the right wing. After receiving an inch-perfect pass from the unflagging Dave Harper in the 66th minute, Jim cut inside looking to feed in the killer pass, but Fulham's rigid man-to-man marking left Jim no option but to go it alone. Spotting Macedo slightly off his line he set his sights, and from 25 yards sent his vicious dipping drive over the stranded 'keeper to reduce the arrears.

Millwall, then of the Fourth Division, took on Fulham of the First Division in January 1965, and despite missing a penalty and being 3–1 down managed to draw 3–3 at Craven Cottage, and here Hugh Curran is seen taking on the home defence. [Chris Bethell]

The cover of the match programme for the historic victory of Fourth Division Millwall over First Division Fulham in the third-round replay. [Author]

All hell broke loose at this awesome strike, and sensing a recovery the fans cranked up the decibels as Millwall battered Fulham for the next quarter of an hour. Then, 10 minutes from time, they scored the equaliser that had seemed so unlikely 30 minutes before. Fulham were now holding on for dear life, and when they failed to close down yet another promising Lions move down the right flank they paid the price. Lion Bryn Jones, relishing the space, fired in hard and low, causing Macedo to blunder for a second time. Fumbling the Welshman's cross, he allowed Whitehouse to pull the game out of the fire by running the ball into an empty net to make it 3–3. Scenes of total ecstasy pervaded the large open terrace at the Cottage end, where the Millwall's supporters were congregated, who were more than happy to take the replay. Afterwards Fulham's acting manager Arthur Stevens bemoaned his own fans' timid backing by lamenting 'They never seemed to cheer us. That's just one of things we have been fighting against at Craven Cottage this season. Millwall might just as well have been playing at home'. While Millwall manager Billy Gray enthused 'It was wonderful to hear them cheering us on'. And so say all of us.

The events and result from Craven Cottage captured the imagination of everyone connected to the club as Cup fever gripped New Cross for the first time since the Newcastle game of 1957. For the replay the streets at both ends of The Den were a throng of tidal humanity as latecomers, hoping to gain entrance, forced open the main gates in Cold Blow Lane to bolster what was already a packed arena. The official attendance of 31,339 was in excess of 35,000 but probably nearer the 40,000 mark. Included in this mass of bodies was a new generation of supporters poised to see a rerun of the 1937 encounter, and they were not disappointed as the Lions roared to equal that famous 2–0 victory in what was the season's first major FA Cup upset.

Again the crowd were in fine voice, there to encourage and play their part with their well-rehearsed ear-shattering cacophony of chants and songs, which before the start must have reached the ears of the Fulham players down in the dressing rooms. Now they knew what was in store for them and that anything less than 100 per cent commitment would see them fall by the wayside. If Fulham had underestimated Millwall in the initial game then the Cottagers took the replay a lot more seriously and should have taken a healthy, if not unassailable lead into the break. With a couple of first-time efforts from just outside the box, Haynes went perilously close, before both Marsh and Stratton missed when it seemed easier to score. The Lions, for their part, looked menacing on the break but were let down by an erratic final ball.

Millwall had been down to 10 men since the 37th minute following the unfortunate Dave Harper's hip injury, who on his return was moved up-front more for nuisance value. But his teammates, having harassed Fulham at every turn began to find some space, although the game was still goalless at the interval. The vital breakthrough Millwall craved and sweated blood for came as a bolt out of the blue. There appeared no danger when Barry Rowan gained possession on the right, and whether he meant to cross or shoot it matters not; however, Fulham failed to heed the threat as the ball fell nicely for the hobbling and unmarked Harper to prod home after 57 minutes. Engulfed by his ecstatic colleagues, poor old Dave must have been in agony. The volume of noise increased with the resonant chant of 'Millwall, Millwall' filling the January night as the intoxicating scent of victory began to fill the nostrils and the fans willed their team on with more bellicose support. The visitors, however, were not finished just yet, and their last chance came with three minutes left when Haynes and Robson broke through, but the future England manager was foiled by Alex Stepney's excellent save. Fulham must have sensed then they had shot their bolt.

The fans had a similar inkling too and began coaxing their heroes to one last mighty effort to the finishline. Dipping deeper into what seemed a bottomless well of spirit, resolve and willpower, Fulham were given the last rites as Millwall sprung forward to score a second in the dying embers. It was Saturday's hero Jimmy Whitehouse whose superb use of the ball placed another peach of a pass for Barry Rowan to slide home in the 89th minute. The headline writers and reporters of a euphoric press had a field day, and one of post-match quotes from the people who mattered came from Fulham's Bobby Robson and had a tinge of sour grapes about it when he bleated to the assembled scribes 'It was thoroughbreds against donkeys'. This was answered with one of the most illuminating putdowns ever from Lions boss Billy Gray, whose fabulous riposte was 'You're right; the donkeys had two tries…and still lost'.

After that epic victory Millwall would receive either Shrewsbury Town or Manchester City at home, who were due to replay the following Wednesday. Much disappointment was felt when Shrewsbury gained a 3–1 victory, mainly down the fact that City would have drawn a bigger gate. After the heartwarming joy of beating Fulham, Millwall were brought back down to earth with a loss at Brighton and then could only earn a point after they pulled back a two-goal deficit against Oxford United with two penalties from Hugh Curran. As injuries and weariness began to deplete Gray's squad, these excesses caused Millwall to drop off the pace in the promotion chase.

The loss of form and lack of goals was highlighted in the Shrewsbury Cup tie when full-back Dennis John was used in the centre-forward role to beef up a shot-shy attack. Dennis gave Millwall a half-time lead with a thumping header from Barry Rowan's 14th-minute corner, and by the break against an unhurried, if unspectacular, Shrews side they looked a fair bet to reach the fifth round.

But within two minutes of the restart Shrewsbury were back on level terms when George Boardman fired home Taylor's pull-back following a decisive move involving Brodie and Wall. Millwall responded with some lively attacks from Barry Rowan, and from one cross Whitehouse narrowly failed to get his head to it. Kenny Jones then sent in a long-range effort which the alert Alan Boswell kept out, before palming a Harry Cripps free-kick over the bar, but he was helpless as a Dennis John piledriver scraped the wrong side of the post. Shrewsbury had not been idle either, threatening to score again with some excellent teamwork and finally securing the lead in the 78th minute when Taylor, their main architect, sped in from the left and had two options open to him. Shoot or pass? To Millwall's detriment he chose the latter and found Trevor Meredith to crash home the winner.

Despite losing out on a money-spinning tie with Leeds United, the Lions hit all the right notes to thump Barrow at Holker Street 5–0, with four of the goals arriving in the last 12 minutes. But the old failings in front of goal saw the Lions gain just three points out of the next eight. The Lions needed a super-human effort to stand any chance of going up, and with just four games left to play they needed to win all of them with the other candidates dropping points. Thankfully they achieved it by winning the quartet of matches to pinch the runners'-up spot. In doing so they deprived Tranmere of their place in the Third Division, who had looked certain of a promotion place for most of the campaign.

Millwall's elevation took on a new meaning, for after a splendid start to the 1965–66 season consolidation was of no concern, but a second successive promotion was. However, but the old problem of scoring enough goals continued to gnaw at the Lions' aspirations. A total of 76 were two less than the previous season's tally of 78, but defensively the total of a miserly 43 goals conceded was two better than the year before. The FA Cup exit at Hereford, along with the fourth-round defeat by Peterborough in the League Cup, had given the Lions a free run from early December to concentrate entirely on League football.

Millwall's first-round opponents in the FA Cup came from non-League football in the shape of the Isthmian League amateurs Wealdstone. They hardly caused a problem to Lions 'keeper Alex Stepney, whose one excellent save came from teammate Tommy Wilson's awkward back-pass and was dealt with by Stepney's usual efficiency. But after some wayward shooting Millwall got their noses in front after 31 minutes when Jones and Curran paved the way for Mickey Brown to ease Curran's precise lob past Brian Goymer. The Stones goalkeeper was beaten again when close-season signing George Jacks headed smartly home from John Gilchrist's centre three minutes before the interval.

There were two talking points early in the second half, both involving Johnny Gilchrist. The first came when he flattened winger Bernie Bremer in the box, but amazingly referee Aldous gave nothing, and then on 53 minutes the official awarded Millwall a spot-kick when Gordon Sedgeley tripped Brown outside the area. Up stepped Gilchrist with the chance to extend the lead further. But justice was forthcoming when the Scot blazed hopelessly wide. 'Trying too hard', was Gilly's explanation afterwards. These two events could have seen Wealdstone buckle, but to their credit they gave it a go and were rewarded when striker Jim Cooley pounced on a rare Wilson mistake to beat Stepney with a fine 67th-minute effort.

Any thoughts the amateurs had of taking Millwall back to Lower Mead were dispelled 10 minutes from time when Lennie Julians's astute through ball found Barry Rowan sprinting in to send his deft header past the advancing Goymer to make it 3–1. Unimpressed, Millwall boss Billy Gray praised Wealdstone but thought his team made had hard work of it.

Millwall's Cup interest ended on a wet and dismal day at Edgar Street, where they faced Southern League Hereford United, who themselves had beaten Isthmian League opponents in the shape of Leytonstone in the first round. Conditions had a massive influence on the proceedings in which Lennie Julians rarely got going on a cloying pitch. Hereford took full advantage of the mud and were aided in no short measure by some strange refereeing decisions, the official booking both Bryan Snowdon and Barry Rowan during the course of the match. It was Ron Fogg, who had also been cautioned, who scored the game's only goal on the hour mark when he cashed in on Man of the Match Rodgerson's clever pass and Snowdon's slip to slot past Stepney. It was Stepney who later stopped his team from going further behind with two stunning saves to further enhance his burgeoning career. Millwall's best chance fell to Mickey Brown in the 85th minute, when for once he got the better of the former Arsenal and Wales centre-half Ray Daniel with a spontaneous flick that squelched against a post.

The mood among the supporters was a bit downbeat following the defeat as they trudged back to the station for the long journey home. Also entrained were the team, and the

This Millwall team photo was taken just before the kick-off for the second-round tie at Hereford United which ended in a 1–0 defeat on a very muddy Edgar Street pitch. [*Football Monthly*]

This defeat at non-League Hereford United in 1965 was seen as a blessing in disguise as Millwall marched to their second successive promotion. In this shot Lennie Julians tests the Hereford defence during the 1–0 defeat.

question most of them were asked was what went wrong today? Tommy Wilson spoke to the fans and said he thought the loss was a blessing in disguise. 'Just watch us go for promotion' was the Scot's prediction, and true enough the Lions did just that the following May, and by the time the Cup came around again Millwall were a Second Division club, still unbeaten at home in the League and with a new manager.

Billy Gray's resignation came as a shock to one and all, and it arose over differences of opinion with one of the directors after the 6–1 mauling at promotion rivals Queen's Park Rangers the previous March. Although Bill agreed to stay until promotion was achieved, there was no turning back, and sadly with Millwall on the cusp of something substantial they had to find a new manager. As with the appointment of Gray himself back in 1963, the powers that be wasted no time in hiring the former player Benny Fenton, whose last appearance for the club had been a home FA Cup defeat by Port Vale in 1948, a game that ultimately cost Fenton a place in Charlton's winning team later that year.

If Benny's appointment did not exactly set the pulses racing, he did bring a great deal of stability to the club that had changed managers every two years over the last decade. Although Fenton made Millwall into a formidable Second Division side, his record in the FA Cup was at best mediocre. His best run came in the 1972–73 season when the Lions reached the fifth round; however, he did kick-off with a very high-profile encounter when Tottenham Hotspur followed Millwall out of the hat for the third-round tie at Cold Blow Lane in January 1967.

Two momentous games with Tottenham Hotspur in 1967 resulted in a 1–0 success for Spurs after a titanic struggle as Lion Tommy Wilson rises to clear another Spurs attack in the first game. [Associated Press]

After 25 games Millwall were lying in third place behind the Midlands duo of Coventry and Wolves, but they took their eye off the ball and promptly lost their next two matches, including one against Plymouth, who finally lowered Millwall's colours to become the first team to win at The Den since Bristol City back in April 1964. It halted Millwall's magnificent run of 59 League games unbeaten. These defeats and a loss of form did not deter over 41,000 from squeezing into The Den on a wet and gloomy afternoon to see if one of football's glamour clubs could achieve what Plymouth had accomplished a fortnight earlier.

This game and the replay that followed will be remembered by those Millwall fans fortunate enough to see them as two highly charged confrontations. The goalless draw at The Den was down to the two exceptional goalkeepers on show, Millwall's Lawrie Leslie (a close-season signing to fill the void left by Alex Stepney) and the outstanding Pat Jennings, Tottenham's Irish 'keeper. But Spurs, with an array of talented internationals, found it hard to break through when confronted by the barrier Snowdon and Wilson had erected, which blunted many of their assaults, as tackles abounded on a giving but muddy surface.

The pitch may have been paradise for the defenders, but Millwall's main playmaker, the lightweight Eamon Dunphy, was probably the most composed player on the morass, who, along with Lennie Julians, made light of the conditions. They gave Spurs some uncomfortable moments in midfield as they effortlessly glided past some robust challenges from the tormented Spurs half-back line of Alan Mullery, Dave Mackay and Mike England. The game took off immediately when Alan Willey forced Jennings into making a decent save in the opening moments, but it was Leslie who brought the applause from the crowd when he confidently held Greaves's stunning shot on the turn, before denying Gilzean's powerful header with another smart save.

Millwall's most telling effort, however, came from Billy Neil when he forced Jennings into a back-breaking save, as Dunphy continued at his imperious best by breaking forward at every opportunity with some neat and tidy dribbles, while would-be challenges slithered past his slender frame. But on chances created Tottenham should not have needed a replay, as Millwall's stamina began to wilt close to the end and provided Spurs with three great chances from which Greaves, twice, and then Gilzean failed to clinch the tie.

The White Hart Lane replay was Millwall's first visit there for a Cup match in 56 years and saw them give a much better performance on a night of glorious failure. The official attendance

MILLWALL F.C.

v

TOTTENHAM HOTSPUR

F.A. CUP THIRD ROUND

SOUVENIR

CUP PROGRAMME

Another spin-off for the FA Cup ties and other big-match games was the 'Pirate' programme, and these are rarely, if ever, seen nowadays, but these covers illustrated here (and overleaf) are from the two Millwall versus Tottenham encounters in 1967 and for the Leicester City game at The Den two years later. [Author]

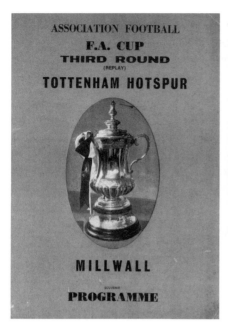

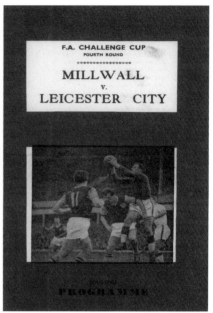

given was 58,189, with thousands more locked out. Even the Paxton Road stand, the one designated for the Lions fans, saw many more spectators admitted who were neither ticket holders nor Millwall fans.

Millwall took a battering on the night, with Spurs scoring the only goal, who after creating so many chances at The Den were grateful to score from one not of their own making. It occurred when another of their attacks was nullified by the calm efficiency of 'Mr Cool' Tommy Wilson, who having snuffed out the danger intended to roll the ball back to his goalkeeper. Unfortunately, Tom failed to notice the lurking presence of Tottenham's own artful dodger Jimmy Greaves. The England striker was only too pleased to pick Wilson's pocket to end Millwall's gallant defiance. But Greaves could only watch in disbelief as Leslie denied him again. Alas for the despondent Wilson, the ball spun into the air for a grateful Gilzean to send Tottenham through with a 70th-minute decider.

I make no apologises in quoting extracts of Brian James's excellent match report in the following day's edition of the *Daily Mail*, which was typical of the passion and even the prose of FA Cup football. He opened his copy with these profound words 'With the embarrassed gratitude of a millionaire who begged for a light, Spurs accepted from Millwall last night the simple goal they simply could not get for themselves'.

The tackling, especially in the second half, at times bordered on the reckless, but Millwall, backed by their raucous support, whose relentless chant of 'Millwall, Millwall, Millwall' echoed around White Hart Lane, were never going to be intimidated by their more illustrious foes. They clashed head-on with Dave Mackay and Co., who not only dished out some meaty challenges but were also on the receiving end of some that originated somewhere along the Old Kent Road. Millwall's chances, as expected, were few and far between, but what they did create invoked James to pen 'For Millwall, succeeding in breaking down Tottenham's loose lines only rarely, still managed to provoke from Jennings two fine saves and still managed to create the situations in which full-back Knowles and Kinnear had to clear from the goalline'.

Millwall's valour was magnified tenfold in the second half as Tottenham's grip tightened, and it took the Lions around 20 minutes to test Jennings purposefully. In contrast, Leslie had saved from Robertson then fell on a Greaves effort after Gilzean had set it up, before tipping over Mackay's piledriver to concede a corner. Terry Venables, Greaves and Gilzean pinged in shots that all went wide. James again, in his penultimate paragraph, wrote 'Finally came that dreadful Wilson mistake. It seems a pity to name him, so well had he played in such a good defence until that split-second of wrong decision'.

A highly relieved Spurs manager Bill Nicholson was quoted at the end as stating 'That was a hard one! Millwall must be certainties for promotion. The goal was a tragedy for them – they gave it to us on a plate.' Unfortunately Bill's prophecy never materialised as the Lions had shot their bolt, but they did finish in a creditable eighth place.

13. Fenton's Failures

Millwall's goalless run in the FA Cup continued in the 1967–68 season when they crossed swords with Aston Villa in Birmingham in the third round. This was the second of three defeats Millwall would suffer at the hands of Villa that season. Inconsistency was a fellow traveller throughout the campaign, as missed chances proved very expensive. At Villa the Lions fell behind in the 26th minute when Brian Godrey's strike from just inside the area beat Leslie all ends up after it took a deflection off Barry Kitchener. But Millwall had only themselves to blame for an early exit after threatening to overrun Villa. The ineffective Dunphy (with a pale shadow of his displays against Spurs) was hauled off and replaced by Harry Cripps, as Fenton shunted Kenny Jones into the attack in a move that seemed very likely to pay off.

By exposing Villa's weakness at full-back, the Lions held the upper hand but were flattened by a double whammy 15 minutes from time. It was the former Arsenal winger Johnny McLeod who swung in a cross into the Millwall goalmouth where Beatle-lookalike Willie Anderson swept it past Leslie, and then three minutes later Godfrey played a harmless-looking ball into the area. The scenario that followed was lamentable when the Lions defence gave Villa's Woodward an easy third to finally extinguish Millwall's fire.

A fine start to the 1968–69 season coincided with ex-Tottenham players Derek Possee and Keith Weller commencing their second season at The Den, and they soon began to establish themselves as outstanding performers. But theirs and the team's efforts were derailed by a blip in the autumn from which they never recovered, leading the club to finish in a disappointing 10th place after an excellent start. The Cup offered little distraction, but Millwall did manage to overcome another old adversary from the past in the guise of

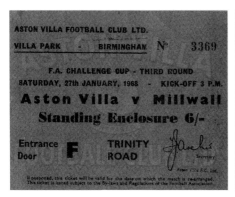

After knocking out Aston Villa in 1900, Villa Park became a veritable graveyard for Millwall's FA Cup aspirations, and this pair of tickets shows the loss of 3–0 in 1968, and virtually 22 years to the day previously Villa inflicted upon the Lions their heaviest defeat ever of 9–1. [Andy Sullivan]

Middlesbrough. Having beaten Boro with two Derek Possee goals earlier in the season, it was the nippy little striker who gave Millwall the half-time lead at Ayresome Park when he met Weller's excellent cross to send his glancing header just inside the post after 40 minutes. Moments later Gordon Bollard was denied a second when he picked up a poorly taken free-kick and hammered his 30-yard effort against Maurice Short's crossbar.

Given this stroke of good fortune, the home side came out fired up after manager Stan Anderson's interval team-talk and were back on level terms after 57 minutes when Dave Chadwick fed Michael Allen, whose slow-motion effort seemed to take an eternity to cross

Like their two previous visits to Villa Park in the FA Cup in 1901 and 1946, this third-round tie in 1968 went the same way, as Villa ran out 3–0 victors, with John Woodward scoring their third past Lions 'keeper Lawrie Leslie. [*South East London Mercury*]

the line. Boro's equaliser saw them go all-out for the winner with all guns blazing, forcing Millwall to withdraw into their shell and leaving Possee and Bolland to fend for themselves up front. In weathering Boro's frantic attacks Millwall managed to hold out for the draw but had to rely heavily on Bryan King, who gave a splendid exhibition in goal and displayed all the qualities which made him the ideal replacement for Lawrie Leslie.

A visit from First Division Leicester City or Third Division Barnsley was the incentive for the winners, but Millwall first had to overcome Boro in what turned out to be a tight and tense affair which from early on had extra-time written all over it. The game had been played in a very sporting manner, but when Frank Spraggon committed a reckless tackle on the hour that left the recipient, Billy Neil, badly injured, all propriety went out of the window. Suddenly the game degenerated into a tit-for-tat contest, with some very questionable tackling becoming the order of the day; however, Middlesbrough's continued hectoring and bullying was ultimately their undoing. Neil's departure through injury meant an FA Cup debut for Tottenham-born Ronnie 'Butch' Howell.

Up until Ron's introduction, Millwall's attacking momentum had hit the buffers, but Butch flew into the fray with youthful exuberance and had hardly warmed-up when Bill Gates bundled him into the retaining wall and was promptly booked for his actions. But six minutes later Ronnie exacted revenge in the most meaningful way possible by scoring the winner. It was Keith Weller who initiated the opening when he chased a deep ball out on the wing. His intended cross was for the waiting Eamon Dunphy. But the Irishman's immaculate control momentarily deserted him and the ball ran fortuitously to Butch Howell, whose swivel and placement was perfect to beat Maurice Short for what was to be his only senior goal for the Lions. But before Millwall could count their chickens there was one more piece of drama that came in the dying seconds. With Millwall vainly appealing for offside, McMordie nearly equalised when he flashed in a header that King tipped away to safety and so prevented extra-time.

For the fourth-round visit of Leicester City the local constabulary had insisted on a ceiling of 42,000 for the all-ticket clash, which in the end attracted fewer than 32,000 spectators. For the first quarter of an hour or so Millwall were equal to anything City had to offer in attack, but the shape of the game hinged on one mistake that occurred in the 19th minute. Poor Johnny Gilchrist relived the agonies suffered by his fellow Scot Tommy Wilson two years earlier when he under-hit his back-pass to Bryan King, allowing Kennington-born Len Glover to scamper in and steer the ball past King for the only goal of the game. This knocked the stuffing out of the Lions who could not respond with anything positive for the rest of the tie. Millwall's woe continued 15 minutes into the second half when the hapless Gilchrist's day was made complete when he was carried off with a twisted knee. Mulling over his thoughts after the game, John described it as 'the most miserable weekend of my life'.

Despite Keith Weller's ingenuity (a trait that would serve Leicester well in the future), Millwall tried to force themselves on City's defence, but adherence to a rigid 4–4–2 formation left them with no other options. With nothing to lose they never took a gamble to chance their arm, and as such they never looked like troubling the Foxes. If Millwall had given it a go they might have given a young aspiring goalkeeper, a certain Peter Shilton, something to worry about. For their part City would go to on to complete a unique double that season by getting relegated and losing the FA Cup Final to Manchester City.

Over the course of the following two seasons, Millwall's departure from the FA Cup came at the first hurdle, and in 1970 Fourth Division Scunthorpe maintained their unbeaten Cup run over the Lions with a 2–1 success at the Old Show Ground. Millwall, having gone 19 years since they last won an away tie, extended their dismal record and never looked like ending it, as not only did they lose but agonisingly were also outclassed. Missing flu victim Derek Posse was hardly an excuse for Millwall after they were felled by Stephen Deere's 30-yard volley past a surprised and static Bryan King.

One goal became two in the 57th minute when Kerr centred for Cassidy to head on to the approaching Terry Heath, who sent his stinging drive into King's net. Feeble Millwall had not tested Barnard at all in the Scunthorpe goal until midway through the second half when the bar came to his rescue when he was beaten by Weller's thumping drive, although George Jacks screwed the rebound hopelessly wide. A goal then may have lifted Millwall from their slumbers, but they had to wait until two minutes from time, when Scunthorpe substitute Mike Atkin was robbed in the area by Gordon Bolland who hammered home a goal that did not even raise a cheer from the totally disinterested travelling support.

The inevitable sale of Keith Weller materialised during the close season of 1970 when he signed for Chelsea. Finding a replacement took a while longer when they signed the pacey Barry Bridges from Queen's Park Rangers in September. Millwall were to pin their goalscoring hopes on the speedy pairing of Derek Possee and the former England striker. The mindset of the club was geared on promotion, leaving both the Cups way down on the list of priorities, especially as Millwall had a smallish squad. At the time the lesser lights in football who engaged in elongated Cup-runs would see their resources stretched to the limit, and Millwall were no different. So it came as no surprise when a third-round defeat at First Division Stoke City occurred, a team the Lions had already dumped out of the League Cup earlier in the season.

There was to be no repeat of that success, however, despite Derek Possee's 10th goal of the season in the 2–1 loss. With this defeat Millwall inadvertently took over Stoke's mantel of being the holders of an unwanted record of not winning an away tie in the FA Cup for a Football League club, in this case 24 games. But that weekend's football was overshadowed by the harrowing news of the deaths of 66 fans on stairway 13 at Ibrox Park following the New Year clash between Rangers and Celtic.

In the 1971–72 season Millwall almost discarded one of football's most unwanted records, that of being the only London club never to have savoured the delights of First Division football. They had to tote this burden for another laborious 16 years, as in the end they finished the campaign in third place behind promoted Norwich and Birmingham. The manifestation of delight when news filtered through that Birmingham were losing following the Lions' final game against Preston turned into abject dismay moments later when the message was relayed that Birmingham had won. City needed to win their last game at the Orient to pip the Lions for promotion, which they did. It was a bitter pill to swallow in a season that had promised so much.

Back in January, however, everything seemed rosy in the garden when struggling First Division Nottingham Forest visited Cold Blow Lane for a third-round encounter. Following Millwall's stunning 3–1 victory, many saw this result as a yardstick of their progression as they were ideally placed to take over Forest's place in the higher division. The outcome could have been more embarrassing for the visitors who, had it not been for goalkeeper Jim Barron, could have easily conceded double figures. Forest's woeful defence included the former Lisbon Lion Tommy Gemmell, a goalscoring hero in Celtic's 1967 European Cup victory, but as a unit they were constantly exposed by Millwall's breathtaking attacks. Even before Millwall took a deserved 19th-minute lead, both Harry Cripps and Derek Smethurst could and should have scored. But once the lead had been established there was only going to be one winner. The opening goal arrived when Doug Allder headed on Dennis Burnett's long through ball, forcing Forest skipper Peter Hindley to handle. It was left to Gordon Bolland to register his 10th goal of the season from the penalty spot.

Forest did threaten to make a game of it when Richardson stabbed home a surprising equaliser, but the Lions were in no mood to play second fiddle and took the lead once more. As Forest prepared to spring the offside trap the influential Burnett produced an exquisite chip to pick out Derek Smethurst's well-timed run through the visitors' rearguard for the South African to execute a sublime finish by hooking the ball over a stranded Barron. A splendid win was sewn up when Possee got the goal he deserved in the 71st minute by heading home Allder's cross following a superb run. Possee was then denied a second when Barron defied all logic as he turned the Millwall man's point-blank effort around the post.

A dress rehearsal for the fourth-round tie against Middlesbrough at The Den came the week before when the League meeting was settled by Barry Kitchener's 59th-minute goal to give his team a 1–0 win in what had been a ding-dong encounter. The appetite duly whetted, the Cup game seven days later was one to savour too, in which Boro looked home and dry when leading 2–0 with just 10 minutes to go. The chances of Millwall getting anything out of the game looked very remote. But then Millwall's Possee and Smethurst turned the game on its head to earn a replay in the most dramatic way. Having dominated most of the second half, Millwall had not found too much joy.

One former player, W.I. (Billy) Bryant, had been invited by the club to attend the game, which was played some 45 years after the two teams had clashed in a fifth-round tie, in what was regarded as one of The Den's most memorable matches. Unfortunately, Bill had to pass up the invitation to visit the scene of one of his many triumphs to attend a family gathering in Essex. As head of a family that consisted of four sons, two daughters and 22 grandchildren, the 72-year-old had to make his kith and kin the priority.

Boro's two goals came in breakaways; the first in the 44th minute from a corner saw the ball bounce between Kitchener's legs to give John Hickton an easy opportunity to score. Millwall threw everything at them after the break, but it was the visitors who increased their lead when Derek Downing sent hundreds of Lions fans scurrying for the exits after a Hickton effort had been blocked. Had those supporters remained, they would have seen a miraculous turnaround. It was Derek Smethurst who started the fightback, when having seen an earlier effort ruled out for offside he was rewarded when he squeezed his shot between goalkeeper and post. With referee Clive Thomas eyeing his watch, the game entered injury time with Boro looking ready to advance to the next round, when in roared pocket dynamo Derek Possee to send the tie to a replay with an 89th-minute equaliser.

Millwall played Middlesbrough twice in a week at The Den in the 1971–72 season, and the second meeting was an FA Cup fourth-round tie which finished in a 2–2 draw. This excellent photo depicts Millwall's Gordon Bolland attempting a cross, despite the close attentions of Boro's John Craggs and Nobby Stiles. [The Press Agency]

The carrot dangling in front of both teams could not have been more tempting, and so the chance of entertaining a star-studied Manchester United team in the next round attracted over 36,000 spectators for the Ayresome Park replay. Millwall were immediately put on the back foot when 'keeper Bryan King was left dazed after a 13th-minute clash with Boro's Derek Downing. The treatment lasted some three minutes before King bravely, if somewhat foolishly, carried on playing, despite his teammates telling him he should go off for a spell. Millwall managed to hold out until the interval, despite not being at their best, and they eventually went a goal behind after 57 minutes when Downing was allowed to dive and head low into the corner of the net.

The goal that earned Boro their trip to Old Trafford came with a disputed 70th-minute penalty when match official Clive Thomas unbelievably allowed play to continue following Brian Brown's crude lunge at Derek Downing. He then compounded one bad decision with another by awarding a spot-kick for Kitchener's innocuous nudge on Hickton. King went full length to save Hickton's powerful shot, but a linesman signalled he had moved. Waving aside Millwall's protests, Thomas ordered the kick to be retaken, which Hickton did to score via the underside of the bar. Dennis Burnett hit a consolation in the 89th minute before Harry Cripps came close to nearly repeating Saturday's result by heading narrowly wide just before the final whistle went.

If being deprived of a money-spinning tie against United was not bad enough, the bitterest pill to swallow came when the Lions failed by a one point in their quest for First Division football when they lost out in the most heart-breaking of ways. Millwall were looking forward to pushing on and going one better in the 1972–73 season, but they would do so without Barry Bridges, who contentiously left to join Brighton. Replacing the fleet-footed Bridges was the more pedestrian, but no less effective, Alf Wood from Shrewsbury Town for £45,000. Alf was an entirely different kettle of fish to Bridges, who had hit a record 40 goals in all games the previous season for Shrewsbury; however, this campaign was in stark contrast to the one that preceded it, and following a 2–3 defeat at Nottingham Forest in early November Millwall found themselves bottom of the table.

Following a run one of one defeat in 10 matches, Millwall clicked into gear, and Derek Possee eventually equalled and then passed Jack Cock's club goalscoring record of 77 goals. Derek's feat was somewhat diluted, however, when after scoring a brace against Bristol City he was transferred to Crystal Palace, leaving him clear to play for the Eagles in the up-coming FA Cup. Without Possee, Millwall faced a veritable banana skin in the shape of Fourth Division Newport County, who were doing reasonably well lower down in the League chain, for the third-round tie at Cold Blow Lane.

The final score of 3–0 to the Lions seemed comfortable enough, but initially Millwall had to match County's work rate, early thrusts from midfield by Len Hill and the pace of tricky winger Wayne Hooper, which were unsettling for the Lions. A further endorsement came when Willie Screen's shot clattered a post. Hard-working Newport's ethic was shown to great effect when Millwall broke at speed through Doug Allder and Alf Wood, only to find themselves outnumbered after seven County players combined to halt the move.

It was from an unlikely source that Millwall took the lead after 38 minutes when transfer-listed skipper Dennis Burnett provided the breakthrough. Frustrated by his forwards' lack of progress, he surged forward with a penetrating run that took him past two defenders and then got lucky with a rebound off a third which saw him slip the ball past the advancing Macey for the first. One up, Millwall's midfield began to show the class that had been missing for the entire first half, and the tide turned in their favour. County were fortunate when Sprague was booked for tripping Alf Wood as he prepared to shoot, when the advantage may have been better applied.

Millwall's domination of a now subdued Newport attack forced their manager Billy Lucas to make a change. Eight years after playing his part in Fulham's downfall in 1965, former Lion Bryn Jones made another appearance at The Den, this time as a substitute for Newport. But within a minute of Bryn's cameo appearance Millwall scored a second with what was described as a 'picture perfect' goal. Gordon Bolland sent full-back Brian Brown foraging down the right, and his superb cross found the returning Derek Smethurst (playing his first game in four months) to stoop low and head home into the corner of the net. 'We've been practising that move for six weeks and that's the first time it's worked' enthused Lions boss Benny Fenton afterwards. Following Harry Cripps's disallowed header after 80 minutes, Alf Wood put the game to bed a minute later when Man of the Match Burnett centred for the burly striker to head wide of Macey for the third.

A much sterner test awaited Millwall in round four, with a visit to Merseyside to face Everton. Going into this game, the Lions had to shoulder the burden of not having tasted victory in an away game in the FA Cup since they beat Queen's Park Rangers in 1951. But against all the odds that particular ghost was finally exorcised as the wearsome millstone of a 22-year wait was finally lifted, and what a place it was to achieve it. Everton's Goodison Park was the scene of the historic occasion which saw Benny Fenton's pride of Lions inflict a massive 2–0 defeat over one of the First Division's glamour clubs. The opening 20 minutes saw the Toffees throw everything at Millwall, who rarely got into the Everton half, and had it not been for goalkeeper Bryan King's string of superlative saves the tie could have been lost very early on. However, his gallant display gave his team the boost they needed to defend with an increasing confidence. Another factor was the cool and commanding presence of skipper Dennis Burnett, whose intelligent play of turning defence into attack was not only galvanising his team but also spurring on the many Lions fans who had travelled up to Merseyside.

The turning point came when Joe Harper netted early in the second half. The linesman on the far side (Mr Hamil) failed to raise his flag, and a lesser referee than Harold Hackney of Barnsley may have been convinced to award the goal. But the Yorkshire official was excellently placed to correctly disallow Harper's effort for offside. As Millwall's resolve got stronger, Everton's huffing and puffing started to waiver, and in a rare moment of breath catching the Toffees conceded. A swift Millwall move was halted by a foul, and without compromising his defensive duties the buccaneering Harry Cripps found himself untroubled to meet Eamon Dunphy's delightful free-kick to despatch his header beyond Dave Lawson. As the minutes ticked by Everton's attacking became frantic, only to be met by Millwall's fierce, robust tackling, which they decided to meet head-to-head with some of their own meaty tackles. With soaring confidence, Millwall channelled back to protect their lead as Everton pressed harder and harder but still could not find the elusive goal against a fully composed Millwall defence.

In their pursuit of an equaliser Everton were caught with a classic counter as Millwall chivvied out a second goal. A rapid switch from the back found Gordon Bolland, no mean goalscorer himself, and he became the provider as he found space down the right to whip in a pin-point cross that was met by the marauding Alf Wood's head to seal a most historic and epic victory at one of the shrines of English football. But the gloss of victory at Goodison was somewhat tarnished when news filtered through that four Millwall supporters had been attacked by some rival fans. The outcome was that one fan, 17-year-old Kevin Stoker, required two operations after being stabbed by some disgruntled Evertonians following the game. Kevin survived, thankfully, but had lost five pints of blood.

In getting past Everton, Millwall's reward was a visit to another of English football's giants Wolverhampton Wanderers in the fifth round. Some might say the Lions had expended their good fortune against Everton, but they they could still count themselves decidedly unlucky against the Molineux men. The reason the Cup run came to an end was mainly due to Millwall's inability to convert their chances after Wolves had opened the scoring with a goal worthy to win the Final itself, with a John Richards strike after seven minutes. Following this early setback, Millwall remained calm and as a result they more than matched

Millwall had high hopes of a decent run in 1973, especially after an historic fourth-round win at Everton. Drawn away to another First Division team in Wolves, they lost 1–0 despite having a fair share of possession. Here Lion Alf Wood contests an aerial challenge with a Wolves defender. [*The Mercury*]

their opponents in all areas, and from a footballing point of view they were performing much better than they had at Goodison Park.

The Wolves goal came after Eamon Dunphy conceded a dopey free-kick, which Frank Munro pumped over for Derek Dougan to nod on for Richards to blast an unstoppable shot past Bryan King. When the Lions stopper denied Richards on the hour it was last threat Wolves were to mount upon the Lions goal. Frustratingly for the fans, however, Millwall just could not get the equaliser that their play and possession merited, and this ultimately cost them at least a replay. Wolves had the rub of the green all the way to that year's semi-final,

The three-day week in the 1973–74 season highlighted the austerity normally associated with post-war Britain, as depicted here with a rare single-sheet programme for the replay at Scunthorpe United. [Author]

SCUNTHORPE UNITED FOOTBALL CLUB

PRICE 2p.

F.A. CUP THIRD ROUND REPLAY
Tuesday, January 8th, 1974. Kick-off 1-30 p.m.

UNITED v MILLWALL

UNITED (ALL RED)	MILLWALL (ALL WHITE)
1 BARNARD	1 KING
2 LYNCH	2 BROWN
3 WELBOURNE	3 JONES
4 SIMPKIN	4 DONALDSON
5 BARKER	5 DORNEY
6 HOUGHTON	6 ALLDER
7 COLLIER	7 BOLLAND
8 PILLING	8 CLARK
9 WARNOCK	9 WOOD
10 DAVIDSON	10 SAUL
11 KEELEY	11 HILL
Sub.	Sub.

Referee :	Linesmen :
A. W. GREY (Gt. Yarmouth)	B. Baker (Sheffield) Red Flag J. S. Hackett (Sheffield) Yellow Flag

Due to the present Emergency we very much regret it is impossible to publish a full programme for this F.A. Cup Replay

nearly fulfilling Lions right-back Brian Brown's post-match comment of 'With their luck I might have a few quid on them'.

Benny Fenton's last full season of 1973–74 was undistinguished in many ways, although it did give him his best run the League Cup by reaching the fifth round before going out to Norwich. But two of the most influential performers, Dennis Burnett and the impish Eamon Dunphy, would depart to Hull City and Charlton respectively after both had appeared for the last time in a Millwall shirt in the home defeat by promotion-chasing Middlesbrough.

Scunthorpe United proved to be the fly in the ointment once again in 1974 when forcing a draw as they had 22 years earlier. [*Shoot/Goal*]

1973/74 ... Millwall (white strip) could only draw with Scunthorpe at The Den. The Fourth Division club triumphed 1-0 on their own ground in the replay a few days later.

The FA Cup was a non-starter in the New Year, when having drawn their last four League matches Millwall made it five on the spin when Fourth Division Scunthorpe United denied the Lions further progression. Apathy seemed ingrained in both the club and supporter. As for United, they had conceded seven goals at Gillingham a few weeks before but were in no mood to be so generous on this trip south, and as the Lions could only muster just one goal they were fortunate to gain 1–1 draw. The Iron took the lead after Frank Saul had been substituted in the 55th minute. It was poor Frank who had been left high and dry by Eddie Jones's misplaced pass that allowed United's all-action man Graham Collier to run on and beat Bryan King with ease.

Millwall's equaliser caused a fair amount of consternation, with United claiming the ball was over the line when Gordon Hill crossed it for Brian Clark to flick on for Alf Wood to apply the finishing touch. Geoff Barnard, Scunthorpe's 'keeper, was livid, and he irately stated later: 'As I protested Wood grinned and said "We have extra wide white lines at The Den."' If that had been a reprieve, then Millwall were to get none on the following Tuesday.

With industrial relations and economical strife at a very low ebb, the three-day working week had been enforced and was causing havoc with people's leisure time, and the replay at Scunthorpe was no exception, being forced by legislation to start with an early afternoon kick-off time.

The light that had barely flickered on Millwall's progression was finally doused within seconds of the start at the Old Show Ground as United settled the tie when Stuart Pilling picked up a loose ball and sent his dipping drive over a back-peddling Bryan King from 30 yards. The many fans still queuing outside to gain admission missed what was the game's only goal. So after five FA Cup meetings against the Iron, Millwall still had not won.

The inevitable parting of the ways with manager Benny Fenton came when his main benefactor on the board, chairman Mickey Purser, resigned in late September. Fenton followed him out of the door on 3 October just weeks before his 56th birthday, leaving coach Lawrie Leslie holding the baby until Gordon Jago was appointed to the hot seat a fortnight later. Jago, who had worked miracles at his previous club Queen's Park Rangers, saw Millwall as similar sort of challenge. Another departure from all the debris was the sad conclusion of 'Arry Boy Cripps's' career at The Den. The fans' 'man on the pitch' was transferred to Charlton.

14. More Horrors

Once settled in, Jago's attempt to alter Millwall's image by suggesting a change of both the name of the club and that of Cold Blow Lane put him on a collision course with the traditionalists, which in truth was nearly if not all of the support. All the fans wanted to see was change on the playing front, but sadly the team could not put any substantial runs together and ultimately suffered relegation. Gordon's first sample of the FA Cup with Millwall came at Gigg Lane, Bury, where Millwall rekindled memories of those competitive encounters either side of World War One.

It took Third Division Bury three games to destroy Millwall's hopes of earning some much-needed funds. They fought out a 2–2 draw, a score which came as surprise given the first half had been a complete waste of time. The second half contained every facet one would expect from an FA Cup match. When a football match eventually a broke out it featured two penalty dramas and a pitch invasion. The tie sprung into life after 58 minutes following a mêlée in the Lions goalmouth, during which the unfortunate Barry Kitchener was adjudged to have handled while prone on the ground.

The penalty was the spur for a group of young Millwall fans to menacingly head towards the referee, but a quick response by the police saved what could have been a nasty incident and ushered the malcontents back behind the barriers. After a couple of minutes' delay George Hamstead hit his kick straight at Bryan King but managed to force home the rebound. Within 60 seconds Millwall got their chance to score from the spot when Thomson clearly handled an awkwardly bouncing ball, leaving Gordon Bolland the task to draw the teams level. The Lions went for the kill, and in one swift attack Bolland lifted the ball over the Bury defence for the onrushing Gordon Hill, who had just replaced Doug Allder, to lob it over Bury's stranded 'keeper John Forrest.

The Shakers retaliated in the same way Millwall had by equalising within a minute in a rather fortunate manner. Their Irish striker Derek Spence took a pop shot that appeared to be hurtling towards the corner flag when his teammate Brian Williams managed to get his head in the way of the ball and divert it past a startled Bryan King. The replay was a dour match that replicated the first half at Gigg Lane, and not surprisingly it was still goalless after 90 minutes, during which Bury had for more than an hour played with just 10 men and really should have been beaten out of sight. It was Jago's signing from Huddersfield Town Phil Summerill who finally gave the Lions the lead in the 97th minute, but gutsy Bury refused to lie down and were recompensed for their efforts right at the death to silence The Den in the 120th minute. Bryan King could only half stop Hamstead's shot that left Bury's big defender John Thomson the easy task of earning them a second replay.

The solution the FA eventually put in place to alleviate an already congested fixture list and to prevent Cup ties going on until a winner was found was the introduction of the penalty shoot-out. This would be activated following the replay and extra-time; however, before that ruling became the norm a third meeting with Bury was destined for The Hawthorns, the home of West Bromwich Albion, where a meagre crowd of 3,041 caused little excitement. Unfortunatly for the Lions, the game saw Bury earn the right to face Mansfield Town in round four. After a tentative start Bury went on to control the game to run out deserved 2–0 winners over a below-par Millwall. They just were not at the races for the majority of the game, and the soulless surroundings and a small attendance probably favoured the Shakers a lot more. Even Bryan King, who was being watched by Wolves manager Bill McGarry, gave a hesitant display and was well below his best.

Following their one and only bright spell, Millwall did produce some clever moves involving Dougie Allder and Summerill, and from one of them their best chance fell for Brian Clark, who narrowly

A rarity now is a second replay in the FA Cup, with ties now being decided by extra-time and penalties if necessary in the first replay. This programme, produced for the second replay between Bury and Millwall at West Bromwich, was attended by just 3,041 fans and was no doubt a factor in ending prolonged ties at such venues. [Author]

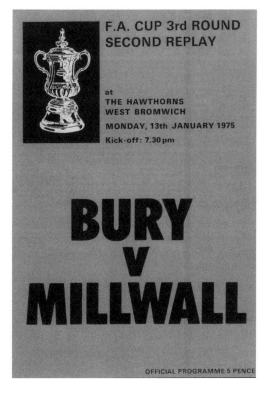

F.A. CUP 3rd ROUND SECOND REPLAY

at
THE HAWTHORNS
WEST BROMWICH
MONDAY, 13th JANUARY 1975
Kick-off: 7.30 pm

BURY
V
MILLWALL

OFFICIAL PROGRAMME 5 PENCE

failed with his header. That was about it before the wheels came off when Williams sent in his cross for Spence to nip in front of Barry Kitchener to set up Hugh Riley, who hammered home after 33 minutes. The unhappy Clark was replaced by Gordon Bolland, whose attempt to capitalise on a weak back-pass saw him lack composure at the vital moment and the chance go begging. The second half belonged solely to Bury's direct football, with goalkeeper Forrest launching a barrage of long-range punts upfield whenever the opportunity arose.

Bury added another victory to their list of Cup wins over Millwall when they sealed progression after 77 minutes after the former Manchester United player Jimmy Nicholson found George Hamstead, whose silky touch set up the unmarked Chris Duffey to turn the ball home for the second. The early exit failed to ignite Millwall's fight against the drop, however, as the Lions were finally relegated after spending nine seasons in Division Two. The irony, or was it just bad timing, was that had they finished in 20th place two years previously they would have survived, but the Football League had since re-jigged the relegation rules. This meant that from the end of the 1973–74 season the bottom three clubs went down instead of two. It was neighbours Crystal Palace who were first to suffer this indignation.

Gordon Jago's team would enter the FA Cup at the first-round stage from that point, and there was another trilogy of matches for the fans to endure when the Lions were paired with the renowned giant-killers Yeovil Town in November 1975 down on their famous sloping pitch. That was not Millwall's main worry, as more of a concern was the woeful finishing that nearly sent them home empty-handed and red-faced, with a result summed up so aptly by manager Gordon Jago who remarked 'It took a defender to show my forwards how to score.'

The defender in question was none other than big Barry Kitchener, who ambled up for a corner 10 minutes from the end to thump home a header to save the blushes. If the shooting had been as crisp as the build-up play, then there would have been no need for a second game, let alone a third. A Frank Saul near miss, Alan Welsh's stinging effort that brought a great save from Mike Franklin, plus a Tony Hazell shot that was cleared off the line deserved better. But after these scares it was Yeovil who began to grow in confidence as their forwards, who had not seen too much of the ball, began to look the business on the break. It was from one such move they took the lead on 30 minutes when the unmarked Ken Brown converted Housley's pass.

The Glovers clung to their lead for the majority of the second half, their goal having a charmed life, with Millwall's scalp looking very likely to be added to Yeovil's impressive list of victims. That was until 'Big Kitch' made his presence count. Yeovil's skipper Stan Harland was sporting enough to say the Lions deserved a draw. If the performance at Huish Park had been just about acceptable, then the display Millwall gave in the replay was an absolute shambles and horror show, which left Gordon Jago firing both barrels at his team by publicly lambasting them. 'Disgraceful,' he uttered. 'It was the worst performance I have seen by any team I've managed. This is the first time I've ever criticised any team in public, but that's how I feel.'

But he was 100 per cent right, for Millwall could count themselves extremely fortunate to be still in the Cup after this insipid, disjointed and totally inept display. Initially it had the fans scratching their heads, before they started hurling barrel-loads of abuse the team's way.

All the honours and praise went rightly to an excellent Yeovil side that after 120 minutes of gallant football merited more than the 2–2 draw. It was Yeovil's generosity that meant Millwall managed to score their goals, and even then they could not hold the lead as the West

Country team pegged them back twice. On the previous Saturday the Lions had at least on a few occasions looked capable of scoring, but at The Den they continually failed to offer anything in the way of positive marksmanship. Alan Welsh and Eddie Jones were the first of many culprits to miss rather that hit the target, before Franklin, one of Yeovil's heroes in the first match, made a right dog's dinner in the 10th minute when Barry Salvage's shot went through his arms for the opener.

Eight minutes later, Yeovil hit back with a cheeky goal when centre-half Terry Cotton, playing up front in place of the suspended Dick Plumb, caught Lions goalkeeper Ray Goddard in no-man's land. After initially chipping him, Cotton had the awareness to run round the stranded Goddard to head into an empty net. Millwall, who had run most of the first game down in Somerset, never really looked comfortable, despite going ahead again in the 40th minute when Steve Flay's throw-in was way too short to his goalkeeper, who could only head clear. The ball came out to Terry Brisley, whose pass left Alan Welsh with the easy task of rolling the ball into an empty net with Yeovil's custodian left high-and-dry.

Millwall's main threat was Barry Salvage, who carved out another splendid opening for Eddie Jones just after the restart. But with the whole of the goal gaping in front of him, Eddie managed the impossible by missing all of it. That should have been curtains for Yeovil but they stuck at it and got their reward when another attack of indecision by Goddard allowed Cotton's cross to reach Stuart Housely, who headed home after 66 minutes. Dave Donaldson nearly won it for Millwall at the death but was foiled by Franklin as normal time ran out.

As a comparison, Millwall's painful plodding in extra-time was like wading through treacle as Yeovil could and should have had the game sewn-up when they created two excellent chances. The first ended with Goddard's last-ditch save at the feet of the enterprising Brown, and secondly Cotton's header looked a winner until Kitchener cleared off the line. Then in the dying stages Millwall could have achieved daylight robbery when Saul put Welsh away, and with Yeovil appealing for offside the Scot rounded Franklin, but in keeping with the rest of the game he shot wide of an empty net. Boos greeted the final whistle as Millwall fortuitously lived to fight another day.

The neutral setting of Aldershot was the scene for the second replay, where on a bitterly cold night just 3,309 turned up – hardly surprising given Millwall's previous performances. The Lions eventually clinched a meeting against local rivals Crystal Palace in the next round, but again it took them an eternity to get going against the part-timers, many of whom had been to work prior to the match. It was the experienced Frank Saul who imposed himself as the instigator of all things good, as Millwall on two occasions in the first half had efforts disallowed by referee Ken Salmon of Barnet, who decreed Franklin had been fouled.

Yeovil had a great start to the second half with two marvellous chances involving the prominent Cotton, who outwitted Kitchener to find Clancy who brought an excellent save from Goddard, and he further excelled to deny the lively Cotton moments later. However, the Lions prospered again from a Yeovil error when player-manager Stan Harland, who had looked very assured in all three games, failed to control a Franklin throw-out. As the ball ran loose it was snapped up by Phil Summerill, who fed it through for Alan Hart to fire into an empty net for the winner after an hour's play.

A local derby in the FA Cup should have got the juices flowing, but the second-round tie against the Palace was as bleak as the December weather. What followed was a bruising encounter that not only chilled the bones but also the heart. In the end a hard-fought 1–1 draw was about the right result anyone could ask for. It was Palace, managed by Terry Venables, who was beginning to carve a niche in the game as a forward-thinking coach, who took the lead with a goal that had Venables's fingerprints all over it.

Lions boss Gordon Jago had emphasised before the game that Millwall's intention was not to concede free-kicks in or around the 18-yard box. So what happened? Millwall did not heed their manager's concerns and conceded a free-kick in that exact area. In Peter Taylor, Palace had a player who could exploit the situation and when the early opportunity arose the Eagles man was on hand to capitalise. It was Taylor who had been fouled just outside the penalty area, and he then sent over the perfect cross to the far post for Jim Cannon to head back for Dave Swindlehurst to finish after 11 minutes. Some over-zealous tackling from both teams was overlooked by lenient referee Ron Crabb, who booked just one player when he cautioned Lions skipper Barry Kitchener for clattering Jeff Johnson. Millwall found it hard going as Palace came close to adding to their lead through Chatterton's effort in the 27th minute, and seven minutes before the break Cannon saw his goal chalked-off.

Five minutes after the break Millwall were given a chance to draw level when Alan Hart wriggled free in the area, only to be floored by Ian Evans's tackle. The onus now lay with Barry Salvage, but he sank to his knees in disgust after blazing wide before Palace had

The Lions played local rivals Crystal Palace three times in a week in late 1975, including two Cup matches. Despite the conditions at a frosty and cold Selhurst Park in the second-round replay, tackles were still evident as Terry Brisley here can vouch. The other Millwall (in white) players are Jon Moore (number three) and Barry Salvage. [The Press Association]

another effort disallowed after 89 minutes when Mr Crabb ruled Swindlehurst had fouled Goddard. However, the twist in the tail appeared in the additional five minutes the referee had added on after play had been held up on three separate occasions by excitable youngsters running on to the pitch. Most other games around the country had finished when Millwall struck at the death of a very spirited second half performance. It seemed that all Millwall's attempts were going to be in vain, but with two minutes to go Ray Evans pumped a long ball forward, which Hart neatly flicked for Summerill to place his shot wide of Paul Hammond for a deserved equaliser.

The replay at a freezing Selhurst Park saw Palace skate through – almost literally. On a slippery, frozen pitch both teams did well to produce any sort of football on an evening when the arctic conditions numbed every part of the anatomy. The players showed commendable common sense as tackling was out of the question. As the Scarborough manager Colin Appleton (the winner's next opponents) observed: 'On this frozen surface, it was difficult to judge the quality of either side. I wouldn't have wanted to play on it'.

But play on it they did, as Palace went on to win 2–1. They were comforted with an early lead after 15 minutes when David Kemp burst through onto Dave Swindlehurst's pass to lob the ball over the advancing Goddard. The Eagles then doubled their tally after 40 minutes when Kitchener was penalised for handball, but even so it took Peter Taylor two attempts to convert the penalty, rifling home at the second attempt following some encroachment. By forcing a string of corners at the start of the second half, Millwall refused to give up the fight, and when Hammond failed to collect one of them full-back Jon Moore was able to hook the ball home. Despite Millwall's brave attempt to even things up, Palace weathered the storm through to the end to book their passage to sunny Scarborough.

After their Cup exit Millwall's fortunes turned for the better. Facing Palace for the third time in a week, they reversed the 2–1 result from Selhurst in a vital League match at The Den and then went on to gain a much unexpected promotion at Palace's expense. This was made all the more remarkable following the transfer of goalkeeper Bryan King to Coventry City and Manchester United's swoop for Gordon Hill. If the fans' enthusiasm had been dampened initially by the sales, a resurgent second half to the campaign confirmed Second Division football would be on the agenda in the ensuing season.

Having escaped the clutches of rounds one and two of the FA Cup, Millwall were given a strenuous-looking tie at First Division Coventry City in the third round. This was a second high-profile meeting against a West Midlands club they faced that season, having gone out to Aston Villa in the quarter-final of the League Cup a month previously. This run contained a protracted spell of nine games in the competition, which had included three against both Colchester United and the Orient. But there was to be no lengthy participation in England's premier tournament, as despite giving a good account of themselves Millwall fell at the first fence as City scored the only goal of the game.

The 1976–77 season was a topsy-turvy one, but during its course manager Gordon Jago was reasonably satisfied with the club's progress, despite some inconsistent results. However, the result against Coventry in the third round at Highfield Road had many fans muttering 'We were robbed' at the end. But the old failing in not taking the gilt-edged chances on offer was one of Millwall's downfalls. The other reason they could offer up for their loss was the display by City's Scottish goalkeeper Jim Blyth. The Lions matched their opponents for the best part of an hour, and at times often outplayed them, and as early as the ninth minute Blythe did well to blocked Trevor Lee's effort.

City's best spell came during the middle part of the game when Irishman Donal Murphy and City's Welsh international Terry Yorath both went close. The first 20 minutes of the second half saw the Lions pile forward, testing Blyth's capabilities once again as he excelled in stopping Dave Donaldson's diving header. But he was rooted to the spot when Millwall's other full-back, Ray Evans, pinged his shot into the side netting. Then calamity struck. Millwall's hopes were dented when City's overlapping left-back Bobby McDonald was on hand to fire home Barry Powell's right-wing cross high into Goddard's net after 66 minutes. Lion's defender Tony Hazell claimed he had been pushed when going up for the ball.

Unfazed, Millwall went in search of an equaliser but were lacking the one flash of inspiration that could fetch a hard-earned draw. When chasing the game they were dealt another cupful of misfortune when skipper Barry Kitchener was carted off seven minutes from time with a damaged ankle. City, however, managed to cling on to their solitary goal, leaving the visitors to lick their wounds on the journey home. Coventry's goalscorer Bobby McDonald summed up his team's feelings when he stated afterwards 'I for one didn't fancy going down there. Millwall made it very hard for us.' Sadly for the Lions, this defeat cost them a money-spinning tie against rivals of old in the next round, Arsenal.

After two fairly presentable campaigns, manager Gordon Jago had stated that his team were nearing the point they needed to be at if promotion was to be achieved. To this effect he went out to sign two vastly experienced midfield performers named Hamilton: John from Glasgow Rangers and Bryan, the Northern Ireland international, from Everton. It appeared on the surface that ambition at The Den was in full flow, and with the addition of one or possibly two new strikers, Millwall might find success. But an opening-day horror show against Palace at The Den shattered more than a few illusions as the team went down 3–0.

Despite victories over Southampton and Burnley and an excellent 2–0 victory at Newcastle United in the League Cup, the cracks began to appear long before the autumn was out, and by Christmas Jago had gone too, the infamous BBC TV's current affairs programme *Panorama* being the straw that broke the camel's back. Lured to the US, where he could fulfil his further ambitions that were now sadly out of reach at Cold Blow Lane, Jago's departure evoked a siege mentality on an embattled Millwall, as the team nosedived towards relegation.

George Petchey's appointment as manager came just in time to oversee Millwall's assault on the FA Cup but was as unpopular as Benny Fenton's had been back in 1966. The board, never sensitive to the fans' feelings, had a club to run, and whether Petchey's appointment appeared to be a knee-jerk reaction mattered not as time was running out. Petchey's remit was to avoid a quick return to the Third Division. His first game in charge to run the rule over his new charges came at Rotherham United in the FA Cup third round. Just 48 hours into the job, Petchey, it appeared, was not only to suffer just a defeat but also the ignominy of crashing out of the Cup. This appeared very likely until the evergreen Barry Kitchener, once again the lifesaver, scored an injury-time equaliser when he leapt to meet Bryan Hamilton's excellent free-kick to quieten Millmoor into near silence.

United had taken a 10th-minute lead when Richard Finney had time and space to fire home his 20-yard shot high into Nicky Johns's net. For the rest of the first half Rotherham held sway as Millwall hardly threatened following John Seasman's blocked effort in the fifth minute. Seventeen-year-old Peter Nix, making his Rotherham debut, should have put his team two up when an open goal beckoned, but he preferred finesse to power and paid the price. If the efforts from Jon Moore and Brian Chambers had heartened the travelling fans then the only other chance to come Millwall's way was midway through the second half, when skipper Bryan Hamilton had the fans either crying or laughing. The scenario could have come from the comedy slapstick manual when Hamilton became the deserved recipient of an in-the-face custard pie. Standing all alone on the penalty spot, for no apparent reason he fell over and missed an even easier chance than the one young Nix had frittered away.

For the replay George Petchey recalled the out-of-favour Trevor Lee, who responded handsomely with both goals to break Rotherham's stiff resistance. The Lions, much to the manager's liking and the fans' surprise, created a hatful of chances with some very attractive and enterprising football. But their weakness in front of goal was there for all to see and showed why they were in such a perilous position in the League. Bryan Hamilton, having recovered sufficiently from a troublesome Achilles tendon (probably the reason he fell over at Millmoor), looked the part when supplying the vital spark in midfield for Millwall to take a 24th-minute lead. Reacting to a punt down the middle, Lee in greyhound fashion went in hot pursuit and caused a touch of panic in the Rotherham defence as he managed to hook the ball past an advancing Tom McAllister.

United, so dominant on Saturday, were rarely seen but were given a chance to draw level two minutes later when the well positioned Dick Finney shot wide. Generally Millwall were in complete control, as Jon Moore tested McAllister with a fine header after 68 minutes before Brian Chambers worked a nice one-two with Seasman, only to drag his effort wide. Millwall settled the tie in the 76th minute when Barry Kitchener would have done Twickenham proud when he lofted an up-and-under that McAllister dropped under pressure, leaving Trevor Lee the simple task of tapping home his second of the night into an empty net. McAllister made amends for his howler five minutes from time when he blocked Hamilton's stinging drive. For probably the first time in the season, Millwall won with something to spare. An elated George Petchey was now looking forward to a home tie against Luton and was beaming when he excitedly said afterwards 'We played some good football tonight, and that's the pleasing thing.'

Due to Saturday's postponement Millwall were given the extra incentive to defeat old rivals Luton and face Notts County in the fifth round if victory over the Hatters was forthcoming. As it turned out, Millwall gained victories in both these games against teams from their own division, and at the end of 90 minutes against Luton half of the job in reaching the last eight for the first time since 1937 had been accomplished with a 4–0 demolition.

The match was also a personal triumph for Lions' Yorkshire-born striker Ian Pearson, a former physical education teacher who had only turned professional a month before after joining from Wycombe Wanderers back in August, who claimed a hat-trick. But it was Luton who started the better, with confidence borne from an unbeaten run since the middle of

The Lions' League form had no bearing on their FA Cup run to the sixth round in 1978, and on the way they beat Luton Town in the fourth round, with one of the goals coming from John Seasman, seen here scoring in the 4–0 victory. [The South London Press]

autumn; however, despite the promptings of midfield general Lil Fuchillo and Phil Boersma's threat out a wide, Luton's strikers were misfiring, putting pressure on their shaky-looking defence. Millwall, for their part, began to exploit Luton's uneasiness and explored the gaps that were forming through the middle. The first Lion to show was the ex-Luton star John Seasman, who outpaced the returning Paul Futcher only to be thwarted by Alan Knight's save. A few moments later Futcher's lack of match fitness was exposed when he was dispossessed by Pearson, who then rounded Knight, only to see his shot cleared off the line by Graham Jones's outstretched leg.

Luton's relief was shortlived when another former Hatter, Brian Chambers, dropped his corner into a crowd of players, onto which Pearson pounced to give his side the lead in the 37th minute. It was Seasman who added the second on the stroke of half-time, sending his volley wide of Knight after Trevor Lee's cute little flick set him up. Luton's best effort came from Ricky Hill early in the second half, whose powerful shot was brilliantly foiled by Nicky Johns, who then got down well to save from Fuchillo. Millwall advanced into the next round with another two goals from Ian Pearson. Firstly he rose to meet Seasman's centre after 70 minutes, before completing his treble when the hapless Futcher was caught in possession by Pearson, who the held off Carr's challenge to despatch Millwall's fourth into the far corner of the net.

The Lions were confidently eyeing a quarter-final place, thanks to Ian Pearson's hat-trick, the first in the Cup by a Millwall player since Johnny Shepherd's threesome against Margate 21 years before. But first they had to surmount the obstacle of Notts County that barred

The Lions' best FA Cup run for over 20 years occurred in 1978, and one of the victims was Notts County, who were beaten 2–1. Here Phil Walker scores one of the goals and then celebrates with the fans. [Millwall FC programme]

their way. The hype and euphoria that accompanies a run was put into the shade before the match against County got started, as a sombre minute's silence was observed and floral tributes were laid on the centre-circle in memory of the eight young Millwall supporters tragically killed in an automobile accident the previous week while on their way to the game at Southampton.

The County game was a tense affair, and to be fair Millwall did not have a look-in during the opening 30 minutes, and the goal that broke the deadlock was contentious to say the least. Ian Pearson managed to find some room on the right to send in a cross that hit County skipper Sammy Chapman on the arm, and to everyone's amazement referee Alan Robinson of Hampshire pointed to the spot. Up to then Millwall had not tested McManus in the visitors' goal, but he found himself picking the ball out the net after Brian Chambers squeezed home the disputed penalty in the 31st minute with Millwall's first meaningful shot on target.

County, much to the fans' discomfort, had dominated the first 20 minutes by forcing six corners, but fortunately the twin threat of Les Bradd and Mick Vinter were kept under admirable control by the experienced duo of Tony Hazell and Barry Kitchener. Following the goal, Millwall assumed command for the rest of the half to take a one-goal advantage into the break. They were two to the good seven minutes into the second half when the inspiring Phil Walker started and finished an excellent five-man move when racing from the halfway line. Taking Chambers's pass in his stride, he skipped past Pedro Richards to slam the ball under McManus's body as The Den went delirious. The visitors pulled a goal back after 60 minutes when penalty victim Chapman gained some personal consolation when he headed home Steve Carter's corner-kick.

This left Millwall a nervy half-hour to negotiate and, although County did offer some menace, the nerves were mainly down to Millwall's self-inflicted edginess in which the normally imperturbable Barry Kitchener got caught up in the chaos. County, with the outstanding Arthur Mann, never looked like regaining their early poise to force a replay as Millwall finally reached the sixth round. The post-match comments from County manager Jimmy Sirrell were scathing of the penalty award when he fumed 'We were cheated. They weren't even in it until that penalty. The ball may have hit skipper Sammy Chapman's arm, but it was never deliberate.' Even Millwall boss George Petchey agreed when he piped up to say 'I would not have liked that decision against us.' It was a pity that just 12,176 fans turned up to see Millwall create another little piece of history.

Millwall had been given an excellent opportunity to reach their first semi-final in 41 years with another home tie in the sixth round to face Bobby Robson's much-fancied Ipswich Town. However, the match was overshadowed by the scandalous crowd trouble during and after the game that made the 6–1 trouncing Millwall got pale into insignificance. It left Millwall facing another ground closure, once again to become English football's pariahs.

So what should have turned out to be an exciting Cup tie played in an equally suited ambience became irrelevant as the off-field shenanigans took centre-stage when some of Millwall's more notorious fans excelled in their illogical and ill-founded moment of notoriety. The game itself not only became a sideshow but also a very one-sided one as the Tractor Boys skated home to repeat the pre-season friendly result of 6–1 (odds of 100–1 were on offer

The weather in early 1978 affected the football fixtures, and this Millwall ticket for the sixth-round tie depicts two opponents who the Lions could have faced. [Andy Sullivan]

MILLWALL FOOTBALL CLUB
AT THE DEN

F.A. CUP 6th ROUND

Saturday, March 11th, 1978

MILLWALL v.
BRISTOL ROVERS
/IPSWICH TOWN

Kick-off 3.00 p.m.

D.G. Borland
SECRETARY

THIS PORTION TO BE RETAINED
Should this game be postponed
this ticket is valid for the
re-arranged fixture

FORECOURT
£1.50
INCLUDING VAT

ROW   SEAT

A 15

BLOCK

H

against this happening again) to reach the last four for the only second time in their history.

Full-back George Burley got the ball rolling when he blasted home from 30 yards in the 10th minute. Surprisingly this remained the only score of the first half, but with the distractions during the break it appeared Millwall had already given up the game as a bad job. Ipswich, with their slick and graceful movement, went three up before substitute Dave Mehmet latched onto the rebound from Paul Cooper's legs to make it 3–1 with just five minutes left. With Millwall's bubble already deflated, Ipswich with impunity scampered embarrassingly through a virtually non-existent Lions rearguard to score in the 87th, 88th and 89th minutes through Wark, Talbot and Mariner, who completed his hat-trick. The reasons given for the outbreak of violence during the game were many and not all one-sided, but Millwall being the home club bore brunt of the FA commission's findings, for which they were severely punished. With the obligatory fine came a ground closure, and added to a lengthy indictment sheet was

Barry Kitchener's attempt against Ipswich Town in 1978 provided Dave Mehmet with Millwall's only goal on a sorrowful day in which they lost 6–1 to the ultimate winners. [Jim Standen]

The Den saw disgraceful scenes of football violence which marred the sixth-round tie with Ipswich Town (the eventual winners) in March 1978, in which the Tractor Boys ran out comfortable winners 6–1. [Unknown]

that Millwall over the next two seasons, if drawn at home, would have to play their FA Cup matches on the ground of their opponents.

Despite the fallout from the Ipswich fiasco, the team remained focused on their precarious League position, managing to survive the drop by winning their last six matches. Now looking to consolidate their piece of good fortune, manager George Petchey was given some money to bring in a bit of quality and class. To his credit, three of his signings looked promising, with John Mitchell arriving from Fulham in the summer and two splendid recruits coming in the autumn. Tony Towner joined from Brighton, but a more surprising import was that of Nicky Chatterton from nearby Crystal Palace; however, despite this infusion of new blood, Millwall continued to struggle, and by the time they met Blackburn Rovers at Ewood Park (the first beneficiaries of the FA's dictate) for a third-round match, both teams were languishing in the relegation zone.

The 2–1 defeat was hardly unexpected, but once again the wounds were self inflicted, and even if the Lions had managed to hold out for a draw the replay would have still been staged in Blackburn. It was Rovers who dominated play virtually from the start, with Millwall's equaliser something of a surprise. A covering of snow affected the playing surface as the Lions battled hard to overcome not only the conditions but also a rampant Blackburn attack, which not only clattered the woodwork on three occasions but also saw two other efforts cleared off the line. Millwall's survival at this stage owed much to the defensive partnership of Dave Donaldson and Barry Kitchener, who strode manfully to stem the Rovers tidal wave.

Rovers' greater determination saw them rewarded in the 66th minute when the former Spurs player Noel Brotherston timed his run to perfection to head Metcalfe's angled centre past Pat Cuff. Phil Walker was the man who dragged Millwall back level with 11 minutes to go when he and Towner initiated the move which completely wrong-footed the Blackburn defence, leaving Walker to fire home from 10 yards, despite being surrounded by a posse of Rovers defenders. But five minutes from time Blackburn clinched their fourth-round place when another former north London hero, John Radford, the former Arsenal striker, latched on to Paul Round's header to score past a hesitant Cuff. A further blow to the Millwall coffers came when Blackburn were drawn away to Liverpool in the next round. At the campaign's end Millwall failed to replicate the Houdini act of 1978 as they sank back down to Division Three in the company of their FA Cup conquerors Blackburn Rovers.

The FA's embargo on Millwall having to play their Cup ties on their opponents' grounds rebounded on them in a perverse sort of way; not once, but uniquely twice in successive rounds. After being drawn away to Salisbury in the first round, the tie was switched to The Dell at Southampton, a venue more familiar to the Lions than their Wiltshire hosts, which seemed to be proven when Millwall went ahead after 15 minutes. A Tony Towner effort was blocked, giving John Mitchell plenty of time to crack in a low drive from all of five yards for his first Lions FA Cup goal.

Twenty minutes later Millwall were given a splendid opportunity to really finish off the part-timers when Salisbury goalkeeper Bob Wilshire, all 6ft 4in of him, flapped at a Dave Donaldson's swerving free-kick from 25 yards which flew through his outstretched arms and into the net. Salisbury's best chance before the interval came five minutes later when Lions' new goalkeeper John Jackson came out to bravely smother a dangerous cross that had been intended for Salisbury striker Paul Christopher. But the Wiltshire team were back in contention within a minute of the restart when Tony Kinsella disregarded the first rule of defending when he cleverly won possession but then tried to be overly clever and dribble his way out of trouble, only to be robbed by Salisbury player-manager Dave Lennard. It was he who found Christopher, who in turn left Mike Hibbs in the clear to rifle his drive wide of Jackson's dive.

Salisbury's expected revival came but was hardly threatening as they rarely tested Jackson. Both teams came close to scoring again, but an effort from Millwall new-boy Johnny Lyons was disallowed, while for the home side Christopher got clean through but shot too hastily, making John Jackson's job a lot easier.

After successfully clearing the Salisbury hurdle, Millwall were drawn against another non-League club, but this time a lot nearer to home when they were paired with the Isthmian League side Croydon. Once more the venue was changed to accommodate a police request when Selhurst Park was selected. But a disappointing crowd of less than 10,000 attended what was a turgid encounter ruined by a high wind, in which Millwall struggled to make any impression whatsoever.

Sluggish and inert, Millwall not only had the blustery conditions to put up with but also had Croydon putting the wind up them, when from their first corner of the game they took an eighth-minute lead. Rod Ward received a pass from his namesake Andy to volley over a helpless Jackson, back on his old stomping ground, from just inside the penalty area. Millwall's first real chance came on the half-hour when Mitchell saw his shot through a crowd of players cannon off the Croydon 'keeper Dave Cobb. But 10 minutes later they were level when John Seasman picked up a loose ball to cut inside Barry Constable and skip past another two opponents and fire in a low cross which was only half-cleared, leaving another Palace old boy, Nick Chatterton, to lash home from 15 yards.

With the wind in their favour, the Lions nearly capitalised in the opening minute of the second half when Johnny Lyons latched onto Jackson's long punt upfield, only to shoot wide. Croydon responded well and were coping much better with the blustery conditions than Millwall had earlier. It was the visitors who had the best chance of winning when Seasman's dipping volley thudded against Cobb's crossbar in the 76th minute, with Croydon's best effort in this period arriving seven minutes from time when Ray Sunnucks broke free only for the bulky frame of Dave Donaldson to block his drive. Millwall's showing at Selhurst and their faltering form in the League attracted a crowd of less than 5,000 for the replay, and with Christmas on the doorstep the shrewder fans kept their money in their pockets as the Lions struggled to overcome a resilient opponent who forced Millwall into some unwanted extra-time.

How Croydon managed to lose the game will remain one of the enigmas of FA Cup history. Relishing the thought of upsetting the apple cart, they took the lead when Barry Constable slammed home a free-kick from 20 yards past Millwall's defensive wall, giving 'keeper John Jackson the task of picking the ball out from the back of the net. It was Lions' teenage sensation Kevin O'Callaghan who brought his team back from the brink when he fired home a 73rd-minute equaliser, some 15 minutes after replacing Nick Chatterton.

Croydon boss Ted Shepherd was livid with referee Alan Gunn, who awarded Millwall a very dubious penalty when Barry Walker was judged to have handled Dave Mehmet's close-range shot after 81 minutes. Amid Croydon's vehement protests, Tony Towner, the subject of a recent £150,000 bid from Blackpool, coolly slotted home the spot-kick. Justice seemed to be done six minutes later when Constable slammed home his second of the game from the spot following Dave Mehmet's foul on Andy Ward, sending the tie into extra-time.

Fate dealt the tired, mud-splattered heroes of Croydon a cruel blow in the first period of added time when John Lyons saw his shot deflected in by John Mitchell past a startled Dave Cobb, who could only stare in horror as the ball trickled into the net. This blow knocked Croydon sideways and they could offer no more as Millwall wrapped up what had been, for the most part, 210 minutes of blood-and-thunder Cup football. Croydon's manager, Ted Shepherd, was still fuming at the injustice of it all as he waded into Alan Gunn's handling of the game when he said afterwards 'I am convinced that his decisions robbed us of a home tie against Shrewsbury. Tonight nothing went for us – only against'.

As in 1965, when Shrewsbury last visited The Den for a Cup match they were in a division higher than Millwall, but there was to be no repeat victory for the Shropshire team on this occasion. Millwall, still grateful to be in the competition after the Croydon scare, entered this game with a renewed appetite and much vigour. Not only did it produce a goal glut, but also a team performance that was totally unrecognisable from the showing in the previous round. Much of the exuberance displayed came from Millwall fielding five teenagers from the side that had won the FA Youth Cup the year before.

Millwall gave a scintillating display that had Shrewsbury Town player-manager admitting 'Millwall taught us a lesson in finishing and how to defend. They played as if their lives depended on it'. Drooling praise indeed for a team missing key players in Chatterton, Donaldson and Mitchell, all out injured. Such was Millwall's command over their Division Two rivals, these lads were hardly missed as the summer recruit from Wrexham John Lyons repaid a huge slice of his £60,000 transfer fee with a hat-trick. If it was Lyons who stole the headlines, it was Tony 'Tiger' Towner he had to thank for his second half treble, which he claimed in an explosive 17-minute spell.

Outside-right Towner and his young colleague O'Callaghan on the left between them terrorised the Shrewsbury backs, and along with the marauding Alan McKenna, making a miraculous return from a cartilage operation, sought the early goal. It duly arrived after 15 minutes when Phil Coleman's drive was cleared as far as Kevin O'Callaghan, whose swerving drive appeared to be going wide until the alert McKenna altered the course out of 'keeper Bob Wardle's reach for his first senior goal in a Millwall shirt. It was 2–0 when the invigorated Tony Tagg headed home a Mehmet cross in the 28th minute.

A brief Shrewsbury recovery saw them force eight corners in the space of 10 minutes before Towner set off on a 50-yard diagonal run that took him past five defenders before he was foiled by Wardle to bring an entertaining first 45 minutes to a close. If the first half had been a pleasure to watch, then the second was to hold more wonderment for the fans. They were cheering another Millwall goal after 58 minutes when Colin Griffin fouled McKenna. Up stepped Johnny Lyons to produce a goal of stunning velocity when from fully 35 yards the Welshman's awesome strike soared into the top corner of the net.

Five minutes later Towner broke away from the tormented Griffin to send in a low cross that showed Lyons at his predatory best when he stabbed home at the second attempt. Within minutes Mel Blyth kept Millwall's goal in tact when clearing a rare Shrewsbury effort off the line. But generally it was the Lions who were calling the tune with one attack after another. From one of these John claimed the match ball with a lethal volley, this time from six yards out. Chances were coming by the barrow load as Millwall went in search of their biggest victory of the season. That looked on the cards until Paul Maguire got in on the act with another stunning goal for Shrewsbury's consolation. After such a barnstorming display Millwall fancied a crack at one of the big boys in the fourth round but got Chester away instead, who themselves had impressively knocked out Newcastle United 2–0 at St James' Park in the previous round.

In many instances the fixture list throws up an anomaly of teams meeting in the Cup who will clash against one another within days for a League match. This occurred when, having beaten Chester 3–1 in a Cup rehearsal at The Den the week previously, the Lions were hoping get a draw at least from the trip up to Cheshire; however, Chester, despite losing at New Cross had let Millwall know what lay in wait seven days hence.

The fillip Chester gained from an early goal was a blow from which Millwall never recovered to make the tie a decent contest – a huge disappointment to the army of fans that made the trip. The home side's unquenchable enthusiasm and efficient all-round display left the Lions deflated, and they failed to respond to the challenge and could not muster the fighting qualities needed to pull back a two-goal deficit. Any advantage Millwall accrued from The Den encounter had vanished after Chester's goal that came in front of their largest crowd of the season. Their inspiration was their player-manager, the 37-year-old veteran Alan Oakes, whose performance got him a standing ovation at half-time as he led his troops off with a two-goal lead.

The constant thorn in Millwall's side was Chester's winger Peter Sutcliffe, whose crosses provided headed goals for Trevor Storton after five minutes, and then 11 minutes before the break the highly rated 18-year-old Ian Rush planted an effort wide of Jackson. As Towner had proved too hot to handle for the Shrewsbury defence in the previous round, Sutcliffe similarly ran Millwall ragged, who conceded numerous free-kicks in an effort to curtail his threat. The result was that both skipper Dave Donaldson and John Lyons (from nearby Buckley) were booked by referee Keith Hackett.

The downside to losing out on much-needed revenue from a Cup run saw the sale of Dave Donaldson to Cambridge United for £50,000 just five days after the Chester defeat. To boost a flagging promotion bid, George Petchey brought in defender John Sitton from Chelsea in February and the following month striker Chris Guthrie arrived from Brentford. These signings did not have the desired effect, however, and missing the promotion boat would cost Millwall dear. Gone before a ball was kicked in the 1980–81 season were Tony Towner and John Seasman, both joining Rotherham United, and by the end of September the fans' favourite and top scorer Johnny Lyons was sold to Cambridge United, where he linked up with former skipper Dave Donaldson. More irritating was the sale of the young starlet Kevin O'Callaghan, which left manager George Petchey under pressure and ever more reliant on his remaining younger players.

These were dreadful times for Millwall, with gates rarely rising above 5,000, and with no money to spend they were well and truly on the ribs. The FA Cup was the only thing that might offer a lifeline to the parlous looking bank balance. But Millwall's first step in that season's competition was nearly their last when they were drawn away to Kidderminster Harriers in the first round. George Petchey was not around to see it, however, as his reign ended following the 3–0 defeat at Tony Towner's Rotherham, where his last signing, Welling United's John Bartley, made his debut.

Assistant manager Terry Long took charge of a youthful-looking Millwall team to face the Harriers, with the Lions having lost all but one of their previous nine away games. Given Millwall's recent struggles against non-League opposition, this did not bode well, and a defeat on the road would not have surprised anyone. This initial match with Kidderminster and the replay offered the Lions two priceless opportunities which they could not garner themselves. The game in the West Midlands saw Millwall clinging on by their fingertips during the last agonising minutes and were so hard pressed they should have sunk without trace.

Millwall's dreadful away form must have been on the players' minds as their passing was shoddy, and anything resembling a straightforward move seemed totally alien. Passes were overhit to the hard-working strikers, whose shrugging shoulders illustrated the mounting frustration. It was just as bad at the rear when a lack of concentration led to Harriers opening the scoring. Thirty minutes had elapsed when Tony Tagg miscued a simple pass back to John Jackson that let in the former Walsall and Everton striker Bernie Wright to rifle home from an acute angle. This wakeup call saw Millwall finally redouble their efforts, and from the restart they put their first decent move together. The much sought-after equaliser may never have materialised had a pass reached its intended target, Tony Kinsella, instead of finding Harriers defender Mick Williams. His attempt to clear saw him clip the ball against a post before entering the net for lucky goal. Up until then the Lions had only threatened on two occasions. Firstly when Chris Dibble's raking cross caused Steve James to head over his own cross bar, before Nicky Chatterton's effort from 25 yards whistled over the same piece of timber. Despite their ineffectiveness, Millwall had an excellent opportunity to take the lead just before the interval when Dave Mehmet swivelled from six yards to fire in a point-blank range effort which forced home 'keeper Brian Parry to make an outstanding stop.

An ill-tempered second half saw Chatterton and Tagg join Williams, Gavin and Chambers of Kidderminster in referee Mr Newsome's notebook. After 79 minutes Harriers introduced

Phil Mullen for Gary Fleet, whose immediate involvement was to brush aside Paul Robinson's challenge to fire inches over the bar before testing John Jackson's resolve in the 88th minute. Fortunately the Harrier fluffed a clearer chance from the resultant corner as Millwall were more than happy to be given another crack.

The replay was not a foregone conclusion by any means, but the unattractive incentive of a home tie in the next round against Exeter City made the Kidderminster game one to miss, and a little over 4,000 attended. Millwall's progress was down to one man, the veteran goalkeeper John Jackson, as non-League Harriers had just as much of the play if not more than their hosts. It was shortly after an early flurry of Millwall attacks, which saw headers from McKenna and John Sitton clear the visitors' crossbar, that Jackson began his heroics. He began with a superb save from Mullen, as Harriers, and Mullen in particular, started to dominate as they had in the first game. Gary Fleet should have put them ahead moments later but completely missed his kick in front of an open goal while standing in splendid isolation.

Jackson's one-man show and Fleet's miss added further distress to the visitors, which finally came to a head when Millwall were gifted the winner after 69 minutes. When Travis dispossessed Mehmet he committed the cardinal sin of playing the ball across his own area, and the ball found Chatterton loitering with intent. Needing no second asking, he blasted home his seventh goal of the season via the underside of the bar for Millwall's second lucky break.

Millwall's hopes of pulling a plum tie in the third round were dashed by a moment of madness against Exeter City in the second round at The Den. Young midfielder Andy Massey, who was making his first FA Cup start, failed to reach goalkeeper John Jackson with his back-pass that allowed the lightening-quick Peter Rogers to slam the ball high into the net for the only goal after 71 minutes. Millwall responded in typical and determined fashion, with Barry Kitchener giving his all as usual by forcing Len Bond into a good save, but it was all to end in tears. The dressing room was like a morgue after the game, with poor Massey inconsolable, but in his misery one must spare a thought for big lionhearted Barry Kitchener for whom this was his 31st and last appearance in the FA Cup, a record for Millwall. As for Exeter, who included former Lion Ian Pearson in their team, they went on to reach the quarter-finals that year by defeating both Leicester City and Newcastle United.

15. Some Dark, Some Bright Days

With George Petchey's replacement Peter Anderson now in charge of Millwall's fortunes, the League form improved marginally when they claimed ninth place in the 1981–82 season. A slight increase in attendances was a mini boost, and the club also had a new chairman in the guise of Alan Thorne, a descendent of Tom and Fred Thorne, a family link that went back to the days when Millwall were based on the Isle of Dogs. It seemed things had taken a turn for the better, especially when Anderson was given some funds to reinforce the team. He recruited Sam Allardyce from Sunderland for £90,000, intended to be the natural successor to Barry Kitchener, and the gifted midfield player Alan West from Luton Town.

From the start, however, the team's form was a bit up and down, echoed by one amazing result that occurred down at Exeter where Millwall hit four goals but still managed to lose by the odd goal in nine. For the second season running, Millwall were pitched against a team from their own division when they were paired with Portsmouth at Fratton Park for the first time ever in the FA Cup. This is a surprising stat considering the number of times Millwall had opposed Pompey's deadly Hampshire rivals Southampton. It turned out to be a bruising encounter, and considering the events that happened post-match between warring sections of the teams' supporters it was just as well they had not drawn one another that often.

As a spectacle the game was not great, but one bonus for Millwall was the coming of age of their talented youngsters in a team that should have seen them through to the next round at the first attempt. They fought a brave fight in typical knockout fashion, even though their goal caused uproar with a controversial penalty award. It was Pompey who drew first blood when Alex Cropley, one of three new signing in the home side, got in a cross from the by-line for Jeff Hemmerman to head home at the near post after 13 minutes.

The blame for the goal lay at the door of Nick Chatterton for allowing Cropley the room to cross, but then the Lions skipper more than made amends in the second half to produce another fine display, which drew this comment from a beaming Peter Anderson: 'He is always involved where the action is. He's very important to us.' The reason for Anderson's gratitude arose after Chatterton had gained control of the midfield, which gave the teenagers Dean Horrix and Andy Massey the opportunity to express themselves to the full. It was Horrix who had Millwall's best chance in the first half, 10 minutes before the break, when with space and time to steal some glory he tamely lobbed the ball into the grateful arms of goalkeeper Alan Knight.

Millwall's perseverance paid off with an equaliser after 51 minutes when Alan West's rasping drive was spilt by Knight, leaving the way open for the young Scot Alan McKenna to sprint for the loose ball. Just as Knight went down to save, the speeding McKenna tumbled over him, and in the referee's eyes (Mr Brian Stevens) it was a penalty. With great aplomb, Chatterton converted his 10th goal of the season, and he later became the victim of a well-executed tackle from a disgruntled Pompey fan who ran onto the pitch to confront a bewildered Lions skipper at the conclusion of the game.

After taking a 2–0 lead in the replay, Millwall should have gone to win by a few more but allowed Portsmouth to claw their way back and force extra-time for the right to meet Alliance Premier League side Dagenham in the next round. It was Sam Allardyce who got the Lions roaring with his first goal in the 34th minute when he powered home a header from Alan West's free-kick, and three minutes later Chatterton took Horrix's return pass to crack home a superb second.

Within a minute of the restart Bobby Doyle cleared just in time from West as Millwall set about wrapping up the game in style. Pompey reacted to Doyle's urgency to pull a goal back in the 59th minute when Mick Tait cracked home from 20 yards. Andy Massey then relived his nightmare of the Exeter match of the previous season when he conjured up another horrendous back-pass which left 'keeper Peter Gleasure stranded, leaving

Austin Hayes, whose sole FA Cup goal for the Lions turned out to be the winner against Portsmouth in 1981. [Press Association]

The Dagenham tie was finally played and won 18 days after original date in 1981 as this ticket shows, which forced Millwall to play two FA Cup matches on the spin when they hosted Grimsby Town six days later. [Andy Sullivan]

Jeff Hemmerman the simple task of bringing Portsmouth level. How ironic that Millwall's winner came from former Southampton player Austin Hayes, who had been signed earlier in the year and settled the tie with a dramatic goal in the 110th minute. The result of this goal was to ferment an undercurrent of hostility that was fortunately quelled by some forceful policing as both sets of fans prepared to confront each other at the final whistle.

The weather had been playing havoc with the fixtures, with Millwall having completed just two games during the whole of December (both defeats) and, for third time of asking, they finally got to meet Dagenham on the penultimate day of the year with the third round due in a matter of days. When tie finally got underway it was the Daggers who controlled the majority of the first half, with Millwall looking hard-pushed to retain any further interest. Dagger Ricky Kidd had already given the Lions more than one scare before Eddie Stein's corner-kick flew into the net unassisted to give the home team a well-deserved lead after 31 minutes.

Conveniently, Millwall evened up the scores right on the half-time whistle, when a combination of Alan West's boot and Sam Allardyce's head did the trick once again from a free-kick. But if there was one player you need in a crisis then Nick Chatterton was your man. Again it was left to captain fantastic to decide the outcome when he unleashed a rocket from 25 yards which left 'keeper and former Hammers junior David Danson clutching thin air to take the Lions through to face Grimsby Town at home.

The upshot of the unrelenting weather was another postponement of a Saturday game against the Mariners, which meant the third-round tie was rearranged for the following Wednesday night at Cold Blow Lane. For most of the 5,795 hardy souls who attended the game it turned into a complete fiasco, nearly as bad as the Ipswich match in 1978, for Millwall were out-classed, out-thought and out-fought by a totally dominant Grimsby. The final score of 6–1 could have easily been doubled, and even that only told half the story. Unlikely as it seemed, Millwall had miraculously gone in at half-time a goal up, scored by new signing Dean Neal in the 27th minute when he somehow initiated an unlikely trajectory on the ball by the near post that saw it arch over Grimsby 'keeper Nigel Batch and into the net.

Despite the lead, the concern for Millwall was not whether the Mariners would score but how many? The sense of foreboding was not helped by Grimsby's apparently unconcerned attitude. Having conceded, they could count themselves very unfortunate to not have at least a three-goal advantage at the break. Even before Millwall scored, Kevin Drinkell (twice) and Mick Brolly had spurned exceptional chances. Poor Andy Massey, after this nightmare, must have started to hate the FA Cup with a vengeance. Wantonly played out of position at right-back, he was given a torrid time by the speedy Brolly, who exposed his slow turning on the icy pitch time after time. Andy was never the quickest, and his lack of pace meant he was given a complete run-around. Grimsby pulverised the Lions in the second half as the Mariners threatened to overtake or at least equal Aston Villa's 9–1 FA Cup thrashing of Millwall in 1946.

Those fans fearing a deluge were not disappointed as goals looked likely every time Grimsby ventured over the halfway line. Scot Bobby Cumming equalised in the 48th minute when he raced on to a Mitchell pass to shoot hard and low past Peter Gleasure. The Lions 'keeper was picking the ball out of the net again 11 minutes later after Brolly had put the visitors ahead before Drinkell forced home number three on 63 minutes. Millwall's defence had been fragile at best, but it was totally non-existent when Sam Allardyce joined in the farce after failing to deal with Batch's long punt downfield, and Trevor Whymark lashed home from 25 yards for the fourth.

Millwall's torment and torture continued uninterrupted as Grimsby, with the throttle fully opened, claimed the fifth a minute later when Cumming followed up Drinkell's header, and four minutes from time the inquisition was complete when Drinkell waltzed through an AWOL defence to score a simple sixth. This mauling could have had a demoralising effect on the team, but once the weather improved they went on to claim ninth spot in the table. Peter Anderson's chopping and changing of the line up was hardly conducive to finding a settled team, however, and was mostly to blame for the demise of John Bartley's full-time career.

If the 1981–82 season had been one of missed opportunities then the ensuing one of 1982–83 was an unmitigated disaster, with one calamity following another. A new crop of players had been signed, including Bermondsey-born Trevor Aylott, who had performed so admirably at Barnsley, the experienced Scottish international Willie Carr and a young goalkeeper Paul Sansome who arrived from Crystal Palace. But just three League victories prior to the opening of the FA Cup campaign was not the ideal preparation to face a battling non-League side. There had been some improvement in the match performances, but Anderson was coming under pressure to produce some winning results. All of a sudden there was some intrigue for the supporters to get their head around when the club announced that both Anderson and his assistant Terry Long had been suspended for three days. Assuming control was Barry Kitchener, now a part-time scout for the Lions, and coach Roger Cross, another ex-player.

A further twist came on the Monday following the home draw with Wrexham when both Anderson and Long were given the sack. Needless to say, a dispirited and ragged Millwall went down at Wigan in their next match. Big Kitch had a massive job on his hands, with the instillation of some discipline into the team the top priority.

In 1937, when Sir John Betjeman published a collection of poems, one of which was named *Slough,* in which he protested at the building of some 850 factories there, he wrote 'Come friendly bombs and fall on Slough' and caused uproar among the locals. Well, some 45 years later the only bomb that went off was the bombshell which befell Millwall as they became the victims of yet another giant-killing act. Kitchener's preparation for the tie at Slough Town was not helped by the team he inherited. It was hopelessly lacking in character and self-control, which was clearly illustrated as the game descended into an ill-tempered brawl, with both Dean Neal and Dave Martin being red-carded.

Neal's dismissal came after just 15 minutes, when he exchanged blows with Town's Dave Yerby. Far from cooling everyone down, it had the reverse effect, and 10 minutes later Millwall conceded a harsh-looking penalty, which thankfully Slough skipper Keith White thumped wide. Then on the stroke of half-time Martin received his marching orders when he and Dylan Evans started swinging their handbags as the players trooped off to try and cool down. What's good for the goose is good for the gander, or so the so-called fans thought. Taking it upon themselves to show Slough what it was all about, hundreds of them stormed onto the pitch to get at their Slough counterparts who thought it better of it by decamping into some neighbouring fields, a much better option that getting mullered by the visiting yobs.

Now down to nine men, Millwall at last kept their composure to create a string of chances that should have seen the end of Slough's unbeaten home record. Thankfully the fans took a leaf out of the team's book, deciding to watch rather than fight. With the match seemingly heading for a draw, a disaster struck which underlined Millwall's ills of the season thus far. Gary Attrell, Slough's teenage striker, found a chink in Millwall's overstretched defence to snatch an 87th-minute winner. Despite all the openings they created, Millwall had only tested former Palace 'keeper Frank Parsons twice in the first half, who saved well to deny Aylott and then Slough-born Dean Horrix.

The Rebels (Slough's nickname) were under siege for most of the second half, but despite lengthy spells of ball retention and Trevor Aylott's sharp shooting Millwall could not breach Slough's stoic defence. Andy Massey continued his hate-hate relationship with the Cup in the 55th minute when he missed with a free header following a cross from the burly Aylott. He was at it again two minutes later when Parsons went full stretch to deny him, and then Allardyce set him up but Andy's shot flew just wide of the target as he sought atonement. If Massey could not score then Lawrie Madden should have, however. Five minutes remained when Horrix's cross was missed by Andy Massey, which left the onrushing Laurie Madden the whole goal to aim at, but he sent his bullet-like header wide from five yards for the miss of the match.

The multitude of missed chances – and Madden's especially – were to prove costly just two minutes later when Slough defender Joe Maloney chipped the ball forward for Attrell to send his low drive past the advancing Paul Sansome. If the result was hard to take, chairman Alan Thorne's chilling statement soon after about the fans' behaviour at the game and the events that followed made even less comfortable reading. He further added that if matters did not change then the bottom line was that he would threaten closure of Millwall Football Club once and for all before the Football Association did so. But as the fallout subsided, events in the League were of a more pressing nature as Millwall looked destined for the Fourth Division once more.

Sadly for many fans, stand-in gaffer Barry Kitchener did not take the manager's job full-time, but the former Arsenal and Scotland player George Graham did after being appointed in December 1982. He was a stern disciplinarian, who after his bedding in period went about dismantling a side of under-performing misfits that was perilously close to the drop. He wasted no time in restructuring the team by signing a bevy of new players who he hoped in the short term would bring about the club's survival. He did it, but only just, by winning on the very last day of the season at Chesterfield where Dave Cusack's penalty secured a 1–0 success. Graham's first objective had been achieved, and now it would be one of consolidation as he prepared his team to build upon a strong defensive foundation that would give him a launchpad to promotion in 1984–85.

Graham's first FA Cup encounter as the Lions boss was against non-League opposition in Dartford, a club that taken on many former Millwall players down the years. It would take stand-in skipper Dave Cusack to help him negotiate the first-round hurdle, and for once Andy Massey had a smile on his face during a Cup tie. He had shot Millwall into the lead after 10 minutes after becoming the beneficiary of a bad back-pass as he fastened onto Bobby Arber's most welcome error. Missing were regulars like the suspended captain Dean White, David Stride, Steve Lowndes and loan signing Steve Burke, which forced Graham to play Alan McLeary at left-back, Massey and Paul Robinson in midfield and Dave Martin in the forward line.

Millwall produced some quality football once they found a way to combat Dartford's suffocating approach. Kevin Bremner nearly increased the lead following a delightful five-man move, but his effort narrowly missed. The breathing space Millwall required with a second goal was not forthcoming, and the susceptibility to the breakaway found them pegged back after 62 minutes when Micky Nutton brought down Terry Sullivan in the box. Dartford's Joe Simmonds stepped up to coolly beat Peter Wells from the spot, which brought the game to life. From there on in the game became a gripping affair as Millwall sought a winner, with Dartford fancying an upset. However, six minutes later the Lions got their noses in front once more when following a free-kick Nick Chatterton rolled the ball into Dave Cusack's path, whose screamer from all of 30 yards put paid to Dartford's run.

Millwall were given a splendid opportunity to reach the third round when they drew Fourth Division Swindon Town in the second round for what looked a fairly straightforward win on paper. But typically Millwall shot themselves in the foot, much to George Graham's displeasure. The Scot could not hide his disappointment after being knocked out at The Den by the odd goal in five, and it showed in the after-match press post mortem when Graham raged 'I'm gutted. It showed our lack of professionalism. You shouldn't lose after twice being ahead at home. Too many of our players were off form at the same time. We'll have to buckle down and start again from Monday.'

But the afternoon began so well for the Lions when Swindon's Gibson floored Nicky Chatterton in the 22nd minute. Steve Lovell, after a hat-trick of misses from the spot, registered this time to put Millwall ahead. However, the joy evaporated seconds later when the Robins equalised when Gary Emmanuel crossed for Jimmy Quinn to nod home. Following the break Millwall piled on the pressure but could not add to their score until Dave Martin produced a piece of magic with a goal out of nothing when he headed home a Steve Lowndes centre.

But Swindon were back on parity within three minutes when Jimmy Quinn provided Paul Batty with a chance he could not miss. Graham then sent on Dean Neal with 20 minutes left in an attempt to secure victory, but four minutes later Swindon rewrote the script. It was that man again, Quinn, who was not closed down quickly enough and unleashed a magnificent shot from 30 yards to claim the winner. If Graham's new boys had let him down against Swindon, it was the old guard who would go on to lift the Football League Trophy when Millwall took the Final by 3–2 over Lincoln City at Sincil Bank. Whether Graham took any consolation from winning this piece of silverware is not known as none of the players he brought in were eligible, but more reassuring was the ninth place Millwall gained at the end of the season.

Now with a squad he wanted, all George Graham required was a few close-season captures to boost the competition for places in his team. Lindsay Smith, who had had a previous stint on loan at The Den in the 1977–78 season and whose aggressive approach would bolster the defence, and the hard-tackling left-back Bill Roffey, were joined by the feisty Les Briley from Aldershot who had been an exchange for Andy Massey. Also recruited was former Lion Tony Kinsella, who rejoined after being released by Ipswich. Millwall, under Graham's guidance, meant business, and they set about a promotion challenge as they contemplated their sixth season in the Third Division.

With just two League defeats before the FA Cup came around the Lions were sitting proudly at the top of the table after 14 games played. Even more remarkable was the goalscoring form of full-back-cum-midfielder Steve Lovell, who had boldly suggested to Graham to let him have a go up front. If George had not been too enthusiastic about the request he was certainly not disappointed by the outcome. Steve Lovell repaid his manger's trust and his own ability by netting 11 times, including two penalties. It was Kevin Bremner's lack of goals that was causing concern, as the Caledonian war-horse had not scored since the end of September. What was not a worry was Kevin's spirit and commitment to the cause, as he would run through a brick wall if it meant getting a goal. Bremner ended his lean spell when he managed to score one of the three goals that defeated Weymouth in a tricky-looking first-round match in Dorset. The final result of 3–0 may have flattered Millwall a touch as Paul Sansome did what all great goalkeepers do, produce saves at vital stages during a game. Manager George Graham confirmed as much when he ran on the pitch in a rare display of emotion at the end of the game to congratulate the young Lion on the two magnificent stops in the 65th and 68th minutes when Millwall were looking likely to surrender a two-goal advantage. The visitors had been fairly innocuous for the opening 20 minutes when Weymouth were on top before the Lions edged in front against the run of play. Terras defender Richard Bourne would have had nightmares after he tripped Kevin Bremner as the Scot powered his way into the area in the 33rd minute. The resultant penalty was neatly tucked away by man-of-the-moment Lovell.

The goal that really floored Weymouth came six minutes after the break when Bremner netted his first goal in seven weeks. He raced through in his indomitable way, shrugging off a couple of tackles to send a thumping left-foot drive past the ex-Bristol City 'keeper Len Bond. Millwall lost skipper Les Briley after 57 minutes when he was packed off to hospital with a broken nose, with Dean Neal coming on as his replacement. It was now that Sansome took centre stage, and when Weymouth threw caution to the wind the young Lion rescued his team with two outstanding saves from Weymouth's Mick Doherty.

After weathering the storm, Lovell, who had taken over Briley's role, fired in a 75th-minute shot that Bond did well to reach at the expense of a corner. With Millwall finishing the stronger, Neal's long-range effort was tipped over by Bond, who was brought into action again when he had to save at the feet of Lovell, before the Lions wrapped it up through Anton Otulakowski. Three minutes into injury time the Lion swerved inside a spent Terras defence to hit a splendid shot on the run to complete the scoring.

The second-round draw brought Millwall up against another non-League outfit, Enfield, at The Den. The tie was settled by Dean Neal's solitary goal in the 30th minute after the improving Steve Lowndes split the Enfield defence to leave Neal with ample time to pick his spot for his 10th goal of the season.

By the time Millwall entertained Crystal Palace in the third round they had added to their strike force by purchasing John Fashanu, a boisterous forward from Lincoln City, for £55,000. 'Fash the Bash', as he became known, would make himself a real handful for any defence, and his all-action knock-'em-out-the-way style upset opponents as well as officialdom. For the visit of Palace, in which Fashanu made his Lions FA Cup debut, his presence in the competition was nearly over before it began. Palace, having soaked up all of Millwall's pressure, gained the lead from Tony Mahoney's 25th-minute header that rounded off a scintillating move which involved ex-Lion Trevor Aylott. Had it not been for two superb saves from Paul Sansome, Mahoney, the former Brentford man, could have had a hat-trick.

At the other end George Wood twice denied Dean Neal with equally fine stops, before Fashanu had an effort ruled out for offside. Time was running out when up popped Neal to celebrate his birthday by bundling home Dave Cusack's flick-on in the 88th minute to salvage a deserved draw. An overjoyed birthday boy had this to say after game: 'Palace will have to come at us, and that will make it easier. They scored fairly early on Saturday and after that were very cautious. But it will all change in the replay.'

Those prophetic words from the 24-year-old striker became reality after 90 minutes of football. The Selhurst replay was something of reunion for many of the Millwall players as former Eagles Paul Sansome, Bill Roffey, Nick Chatterton and Steve Lovell, along with their former coach the Lions boss George Graham, made a triumphant return to Norwood. But not before Palace had opened the scoring after just 90 seconds when Trevor Aylott cashed in on a defensive mix-up between Dave Cusack and Sansome.

Palace's early edge was dulled somewhat when Millwall equalised after 25 minutes through skipper Les Briley, before it was completely blunted when Steve Lovell popped up to score the winner in the 66th minute. With his move to the striking role, Lovell had acquired the uncanny knack of appearing to hover in the air when meeting a high cross. He achieved the feat perfectly to score the winner when Steve Lowndes centred perfectly for him to head past a statuesque George Wood. Steve Lovell was naturally chuffed with his 20th goal of a fruitful season and was one to savour, as he revealled later it was 'The best and most satisfying goal I've ever scored.' Not only was Lovell happy, but so were the club and its supporters with a visit to Stamford Bridge to look forward.

Before the Chelsea meeting, Millwall needed to re-ignite their push for promotion. In the last seven League fixtures they had only picked up maximum points on one occasion, a 2–1 home win over Bournemouth. The very severe weather did not help, and on the date set aside for the fourth round Millwall were held to a goalless draw at The Den by Walsall, while opponents Chelsea made light work of tanning Wigan 5–0 in a delayed third-round replay. Two days before the scheduled tie at Stamford Bridge Millwall got back to winning ways again when a surprising brace from Dave Cusack saw off Newport County at Cold Blow Lane. This win saw the team embark on a splendid run of just one defeat in the next dozen games.

One stroke of luck came Millwall's way before the Monday face-off against the Blues, when Kerry Dixon, scorer of four of the goals against Wigan, cried off with an injury. Millwall, with the exception of Dean Neal who had fallen out with George Graham, were at full strength. Despite the loss of Dixon, Chelsea were expected to go through but had not allowed for the exuberance of John Fashanu, who on the night was at his belligerent best with his direct approach to goal allied with his aerial prowess a concern for Chelsea's defence all evening.

It was down to Fashanu's powerful running in the 18th minute that Millwall edged in front when he was sent sprawling by Darren Wood. From the free-kick, taken by ex-Chelsea junior Les Briley, Steve Lovell ghosted in to dispatch his header into the net. Chelsea hit back straight away when Pat Nevin sent a stunning drive that just cleared the bar before the home team were level after 54 minutes. A clearance from a corner fell into the path of Nigel Spackman (later to become Millwall's manager briefly in 2006) to drive home the equaliser.

Millwall now needed to hold their nerve against the First Division outfit and regroup, but Chelsea's blood was pumping and five minutes later went ahead with a Paul Canoville goal. Sensing the injustice of it all, Millwall set about putting the matter right by injecting some pace and producing some excellent attacking football which brought reward in the 61st minute. Dave Cusack's fine through ball found Fashanu shrugging off Joe McLaughlin's (another to find later employment at The Den) challenge to stop him to crash home a splendid half-volley past the advancing Eddie Niedzwicki into the roof of the net.

The jubilant Lions fans were in full voice and urging their favourites to complete the job without relying on a replay, and with 19 minutes left their hopes rose in when the exasperated Wood clattered the unstoppable 'Fash' in the box. The goal machine of the season, Steve Lovell, smacked home the penalty for a 3–2 lead. It was a lead Millwall's play had warranted, with the back line of Stevens, Smith, Cusack and Hinshelwood looking supremely sound. Chelsea by now were looking for a favour and were extremely fortunate to get one three minutes from time. Gordon Davies, Dixon's replacement, flopped over in the area to get a 9.9 for artistic impression, and for such an over-the-top piece of dramatics he was amazingly given a penalty – much to the disgust of the Millwall contingent.

David Speedie, the man Millwall fans loved to hate, made sure justice was done when he fired wide from the spot, Chelsea's 11th penalty miss in 17 games. The outcome at Stamford Bridge saw the Lions gain ample revenge for the League Cup defeat by the Blues earlier in the season. The match ranks alongside some of those earlier epic Cup ties such as Aston Villa in 1900, the Manchester City and Newcastle encounters of 1937 and 1957 respectively and the spectacular success at Everton in 1972.

A fortnight later Millwall hosted the visit of another Division One club, Leicester City, in the fifth round. The meeting was fuelled by the pre-match comments of City goalkeeper Ian Andrews, who stated that he had never heard of John Fashanu. Well, after 90 minutes he had more than a cause to remember him. On a treacherous night at The Den it was Leicester who nearly took the lead in the first minute when Alan Smith put Ian Banks in the clear but was thwarted by Paul Sansome's smothering save. With the future England striker Gary Lineker a continuous threat, they nearly cashed in when Lindsay Smith slipped on the icy pitch and gave City their best chance so far, but thankfully Steve Lynex drove powerfully across the face of the Lions goal.

That let-off gave Millwall added resolve and confidence to pave the way for them to take the lead on the stroke of half-time, with many supporters still waiting to get in. Fashanu's pace and strength, that had caused Chelsea so many problems, was similarly upsetting Leicester City, showing he was no Fash in the pan. He collected a Keith Stevens clearance to brush aside two challenges and score with fierce low drive from an acute angle. The Foxes, to their credit, came out in the second half to dominate for long periods with some direct intelligent play, with Lineker going close on two occasions before Sansome's impressive form of late was magnified with a stunning save from John O'Neill's header.

However, Leicester's interest was terminated for another season 10 minutes from time. When an O'Neill header hit the crossbar Millwall countered immediately, and when Fashanu's header found Alan McLeary in space he swept the ball past Andrews for number two that set the seal on an exceptional result. To cap an excellent February, the following Saturday Bradford City, the champions in waiting, were swamped 4–0 in yet another exhilarating display at The Den.

Millwall were in the sixth round for the first time in seven years and were drawn away to face either of those arch rivals of old, Watford or Luton Town. Recalling the scenes previously after the Ipswich tie in 1978, Millwall implored both Watford and Luton to make the game all-ticket. Watford concurred with this request but Luton, looking at the financial aspect, did not. Needless to say, Luton defeated the Hornets after a second replay. To their everlasting folly Luton saw their Kenilworth Road ground wrecked in what was one of the worst acts of mindless hooliganism the game has ever seen. For 13 March 1985 would go down as yet another day of infamy in Millwall's history.

The sheer weight of numbers, swelled by the arrival of a number of fans from other London clubs, led to a crush, which was not helped by police intransigent to the fans' problems. The ultimate blame fell squarely on Millwall's shoulders. Much has been written about this sordid event, which left the genuine punter sick to the pit of the stomach as the

The changing face of match tickets is dramatically shown with this pair, with the now usual computerised effort of Luton Town in 1985 and the traditional one of Scunthorpe United of 1970. [Andy Sullivan]

LTFC.	LUTON TOWN FOOTBALL CLUB LTD.	
	THE FACE OF THIS DOCUMENT HAS A COLOURED BACKGROUND	
MILLWALL.	LUTON TOWN V MILLWALL F.A. CUP 6TH. ROUND K.O.3-00 P.M.	
9-MAR-85. ADULTS. £3	SATURDAY 9TH MARCH 1985	
	ENCLOSURE	
JUVENILES &OAPS PRICE. £2	H.BLOCK	
	PRICE (INC. VAT) ROW SEAT	
1264	20 1264 £3.00 D 015	
	THE BACK OF THIS DOCUMENT CONTAINS AN ARTIFICIAL WATERMARK	
COUNTERFOIL	TO BE RETAINED See Reverse	

F.A. CUP—3rd ROUND

3rd JANUARY 1970

UNITED
v.
MILLWALL
Kick-off 3-00 p.m.

WEST STAND
WING END B

ROW and
SEAT No.   J   5

Entrance: Henderson Avenue
TURNSTILE 17

Ticket 7/6

This portion to be retained.

game was once again dragged through the mud. The disturbance and frightening scenes which were witnessed on television delayed the start of the match for 25 minutes, and in the coming weeks it would dominate the news as media frenzy went into overdrive.

This quarter-final tie, Millwall's third against opposition from the top division, was settled after 31 minutes when England striker Brian Stein scored the game's only goal. The intimidating atmosphere had obviously affected the players but once the whistle went they went off at pace with the Lions showing up well, nearly scored when the bullish Fashanu had a header cleared off the line by a multitude of frantic Luton bodies before Hinshelwood sent in another driving effort just wide after 28 minutes. But the mortal blow came three minutes later when Otulakowski's intended back-pass to Paul Sansome was way too short and Stein nipped in to fire a cross-shot in off the far post.

In the second half Mick Harford had a 56th-minute effort disallowed for a foul as Luton's class began to tell and Millwall's resistance melted away in a match that was becoming meaningless. The referee Dave Hutchinson thankfully brought the game to an end that had suffered several interruptions which at times looked doomed never to finish. Hauled before the FA again the following April, Millwall were fined £7,500, which they successfully appealed against the following summer. Nonetheless, all their FA Cup matches the following season had to be all-ticket, and they was also censured and warned as to their fan's future conduct.

Only the immense fortitude shown by the management and players by keeping their eye on the ball (so to speak) was the main reason the season was not derailed altogether by the awful events at Luton. Suffice to say, Brentford cancelled their match the following Saturday, but after the dust settled Millwall were back on track by the end the month with narrow victories over Gillingham and Swansea and a draw at Rotherham. The defeats in early April at Hull and Preston were the only losses sustained thereafter, as Millwall maintained their promotion push with six wins that accompanied two draws in their remaining matches. They eventually finished worthy runners-up to Bradford City. Except for a highly publicised evening of mayhem in March, the 1984–85 campaign would go down as an exceptional one.

So after an absence of six years Millwall were back in the Second Division, but the battling Dave Cusack would not be there to reap the benefits of promotion having left in the summer to sign for Doncaster Rovers, back in his native South Yorkshire. Fans' favourite Kevin Bremner was also on the move having joined Reading. Other than the purchase of Robert Wilson, the Fulham midfielder, and Cusack's replacement Alan Walker from Lincoln City, the playing personnel remained virtually unchanged from the squad that had served the Lions so well over previous two seasons. Millwall were given an early test of their advance at the start of the 1985–86 campaign when First Division Southampton were held to 0–0 draw at The Dell in a second-round League (Milk) Cup game which saw them come through with flying colours, only for the Saints to win the second leg at New Cross with the only goal of the game.

Despite this, Millwall could take heart from their performances against a vastly experienced Southampton side as they could now concentrate on establishing themselves at a higher level as the FA Cup would not infringe upon their time until the following January. Although their League position looked a tad scary around Christmas, especially following the 6–1 hammering at Norwich, a victory at Sunderland put them in the right frame of mind for the visit of high-flying Wimbledon a week later in the FA Cup third round.

On a freezing day at The Den, Millwall passed into the fourth round following the success in their first FA Cup tie since that riotous night at Luton. The outcome was more comfortable then they might have expected, especially as they lay a lot lower in the table than the Dons, who at the time were in third place. Wimbledon, by their normal standards, gave a very limp display, a view echoed by their manager Dave Bassett, who was not best pleased by his team when he stated 'Today we did not perform. Millwall performed well, and we were second best in everything.'

This game was a tame affair for a derby, with the Millwall crowd in good heart, and they were soon cheering when Steve Lovell made up for an earlier miss when he stabbed home his 14th goal of the season after Dons 'keeper Dave Beasant could only block a header on the goalline after 11 minutes. The Lions went keenly in search of a second and nearly got it when Alan Walker sent in a header that flashed just wide of the target. On a difficult surface the tackles became a bit reckless, with Wally Downs incurring the referee's displeasure as he was promptly booked for upending Fashanu, but Lovell was fortunate when the official took a more lenient view of his challenge on Beasant.

Wimbledon came into the game on the back of a New Year's Day defeat by Portsmouth and were unfortunate to see a Smith header go close, and they may have had a penalty when Robert Wilson appeared to handle. But it came as no surprise when Millwall increased their lead in the 36th minute. Striker John Fashanu had been targeted for a fair amount of stick but made the most of an opening just outside the area to send a thunderbolt into the right-hand corner of Beasant's net. Two minutes after the break Walker was denied a third after his header was deflected off Beasant's legs.

Evans then had a chance to reduce the lead but completely missed converting an inviting cross before Beasant was called into action to bravely block Steve Lowndes' effort, who could only watch in amazement as Otulakowski lobbed the loose ball over the bar. Not for the first time, Alan Walker made his presence felt in the Dons box and finally got his reward when he squeezed home Millwall's third after 76 minutes from Otulakowski's free-kick. Substitute Kevin Gage scored a last-minute consolation goal for Wimbledon but not before Beasant made two more great saves to deny Lovell.

For the fourth round Millwall faced another strenuous task when they were drawn to visit Aston Villa, who in the past had heaped some heavy Cup defeats on Millwall over the years, such as 5–0 in 1901 then 9–1 in 1946 and 3–0 22 years later on Millwall's previous trips to Villa Park. Thankfully on this visit there was no repetition of those horrors as Millwall gained a wonderful 1–1 draw with a gritty performance. It contained a fair amount of determination and robust play that highlighted Villa's shortcomings. Keith Stevens tackled as if his life depended on it, and with Alan Walker and Mickey Nutton effectively shutting out the dual threat of Andy Gray and Simon Stainrod, Villa could count themselves fortunate in earning a replay.

Alan McLeary provided an early boost after seven minutes following Alan Evans's needless foul on John Fashanu; although he needed two attempts to score from a Steve Lowndes free-kick. It was left to Steve Hodge to rescue Villa when he collected a pass from Gary Williams to run clear of the Lions defence and fire in a wicked cross-shot after 25 minutes. It was Hodge, however, who was at the centre of a penalty controversy when he appeared to bundle the ball over the by-line from Wilson's cross with his hand. Manager George Graham, himself an ex-Villa player, made light of the claim after the match when he comically quipped 'It only hit his one hand. It has to hit both to get a penalty away from home.'

Global warming became a threat to planet earth in the ensuing decades, but heat was the last thing on people's minds back in January 1986. It was bitterly cold at Cold Blow Lane, and the replay was fortunate to get a Wednesday night go-ahead after it had been postponed from the previous evening. The forecasts beforehand stating Villa would fancy their chances were proved groundless as Millwall recorded a victory. In fact, they should have beaten them by more than the one goal as their football richly deserved more. Millwall's route to a more emphatic win was barred by the excellent performance of Lewisham-born Paul Elliott at the heart of the Villa defence.

As it was, Millwall had to wait until the 56th minute to score the winner when Fashanu rose to meet Steve Lowndes's tantalising free-kick to thump his header past Kevin Poole. Poole, in for the injured Nigel Spinks, was a mere spectator in the first half as efforts from Fashanu and Otulakowski rebounded to safety after hitting the underside of the crossbar. They even allowed themselves the luxury of missing penalty after 19 minutes. Referee Keith Hackett awarded the spot-kick for handball after a goalmouth scramble involving as many as eight players, but Poole pushed away Lovell's attempt to safety as he tried in vain to keep his team from disappearing off the radar. Ultimately, the Villa 'keeper was powerless to stop Millwall on their march to the fifth round to face Southampton yet again.

The following Saturday Millwall beat Shrewsbury Town 2–0 at The Den for what was their sole preparation game before meeting the Saints two weeks later at The Dell. The tie was uncompromising affair and would be best forgotten, with the match official awarding 52 free-kicks for various misdemeanours, with 30 awarded against Millwall. But in the wake of all this filibustering, only three cautions were administered, to Les Briley and Alan Walker of Millwall and Kevin Bond of Southampton, which seemed very lenient. By their own recent standards, Millwall's play fell way too short, with too many below-par performances, and as such nothing tangible evolved in the way of chances. Despite the prevailing bad weather, Millwall managed to fit in the replay during early March, some two and a half weeks after the initial game, but on the night they could not produce any of the magic that saw them topple both Wimbledon and Aston Villa. Lacking the killer touch to seal the tie, Millwall fell to a 15th-minute goal from whippet-like Danny Wallace, another locally-born youngster the Lions missed out on, who converted Glen Cockerill's pass to take the Saints through to the next round.

Millwall finished the season in a respectable ninth place, but further improvement on the playing side would have to overseen by a new manager, as George Graham, having been touted for the Arsenal job, finally departed for the greener pastures of Highbury during the summer. One can only marvel at the thankless job he took on at Cold Blow Lane in which he pulled a club destined for the bottom tier of English football into a team that was resilient, hardworking and not short of skill either, and for that we must be truly thankful. One of George's last tasks was to sell the iconic John Fashanu to Wimbledon on transfer deadline day. This sale, purely financial, was a shock to most of the fans, but ready to take Fashanu's mantle was a young lad named Teddy Sheringham.

16. The Doc

The dismantling of Graham's team had already started even before he departed. After Fashanu's move around transfer deadline day was confirmed, Robert Wilson left after just one season and Steve Lowndes was also ushered through the exit door at Cold Blow Lane. Steve Lovell was now nursing a long-term injury that occurred while playing for Wales that made him a non-starter in new manager John Docherty's plans for new campaign. All in all, the 1986–87 season was one of transition and was entirely unrecognisable from the one that had just passed. The attractive football played under Graham had vanished, and at one the stage the club looked to be heading back down to the Third Division.

The FA Cup that year summed up the frustration in a nutshell when Millwall were drawn at home against Fourth Division Cardiff City, who held the Lions to 0–0 draw in which four likely goals were cleared off the goalline, three at Millwall's end. The first came within a matter of seconds when Keith Stevens was ideally placed to clear a City header to safety, then Alan Walker did likewise from Phil Brignull's looping header, and just before the break Walker again saved the day when Wheeler's cross looked destined for the net. Millwall did have some chances, the best when Darren Morgan robbed Wheeler in midfield and strode forward to power in a shot that brought a fine save from Cardiff 'keeper Mel Rees.

City were the first to show in the second half when Alan Curtis sent in a finely judged lob which Brian Horne, now Millwall's number one, only just managed to tip over. It was Darren Morgan who then set up Teddy Sheringham, who cashed in on a misunderstanding between Rees and David Giles but delayed his shot, allowing Giles to recover and block his effort on the line. Nicky Coleman then got in on the act to clear another goal-bound effort midway through the half, before the game fizzled out in a goalless stalemate. Ten days later the teams faced one another at Ninian Park for the right to play Stoke City in the next round.

It was Millwall's Welsh Youth international Darren Morgan whose late face-saver in the land of his fathers sent the tie to a third meeting, after the Camberwell-born youngster scored in the 85th minute. A further 30 minutes of extra-time saw nothing resolved, leaving the teams to battle it out for a third time. Millwall had taken a second-minute lead through John Leslie, who was only playing because of a freak accident to Danis Salman, who somehow managed to injure himself in the bath at Bradford the previous Saturday. Having failed to press home their advantage, they found themselves pegged back when Nigel Vaughan drew City level after 33 minutes, and it was totally against the run of play when Cardiff took a 68th-minute lead when Chris Marustick scored.

From then on it appeared that the Fourth Division side were poised to cause an upset until Morgan, whose father was from Barry Island, crashed home a beauty from 25 yards into the bottom corner of Rees' net. It was Cardiff who called correctly when the toss of a coin decided the venue of the third meeting, and it was they who progressed as Millwall slumped out to a team almost 50 places beneath in the League ladder. The only goal arrived in the 47th minute when Cardiff-born Chris Pike, on loan from Fulham, was left unmarked to head home Mike Ford's free-kick. Lions boss John Docherty stated afterwards: 'We've had three good close games with Cardiff but in the end they took their chance and we didn't.' Doc was probably referring to one in the 85th minute when Sheringham's glaring miss stopped the tie from going into extra-time for the second time in six days.

Despite their brief flirtation with relegation, Millwall did survive, and new chairman Reg Burr and his fellow directors made some money available for the manager to spend during the close season. Docherty's team building had already began in early 1987 when he recruited Terry Hurlock and Jimmy Carter, and he continued his remorseless search for new talent during the summer with some quality acquisitions. Striker Tony Cascarino arrived from Gillingham to partner Sheringham, and together they would go to form one of Millwall's best pairings up front since the war. They were joined by two wide players in George Lawrence from Southampton and former Lion Kevin O'Callaghan returning to the fold from Portsmouth. The defence was not neglected either when £80,000 changed hands to snag Steve Wood from Reading.

Even if the supporters were not convinced about Millwall's aims, everything at the club for the 1987–88 season was geared for an assault on the promised land of the First Division. The bedding-in period was short, with the team clicking virtually straight away, but despite a few blips along the way not only was promotion achieved but the Second Division Championship title was also annexed, with an exceptional 12-match unbeaten run which included nine victories.

In the Cup, however, Millwall were given the opportunity to gauge their improvement in the marble halls of Highbury when drawn away to George Graham's Arsenal. It was the clubs' first meeting in the competition since 1909, when a Dick Jones goal gave Millwall a 1–0 success. Here was the ultimate challenge to test the water for what could be a Division One fixture the following season. For whatever reason Millwall failed to show up; whether the crowd trouble outside the ground had filtered unnervingly through to the dressing rooms before kick-off or whether the 50-plus ejections during the course of the match had unsettled them, we cannot know. Arsenal's victory by two goals to nil was very comfortable, and Millwall appeared have an attack of stage fright. Their first goal attempt from Cascarino did not arrive until the 78th minute in what was very unproductive game for the Lions. By this time the Gunners were home and dry, with goals from Martin Hayes, who converted Richardson's pass after 10 minutes, and David Rocastle 12 minutes later when two south London-born players contrived to secure Arsenal's second goal. It was Millwall's inability to deal with one of Kenny Sansom's (from Camberwell) long throw-ins that enabled Rocastle (Lewisham) to score and so seal Millwall's departure long before the final whistle.

Whatever lessons Millwall had learnt over at Highbury were taken onboard, and after achieving promotion the next time the Lions visited the famous old stadium they were being touted as possible League Champions. This time around it was the Gunners who could count themselves fortunate in obtaining a point from a 0–0 draw. Les Briley saw his brilliant strike annoyingly ruled out because Teddy Sheringham was adjudged to have been interfering with play. If the First Division had been stimulating to both club and supporters, the FA Cup involvement in the 1988–89 season did not progress beyond the fourth round.

First up were Luton Town for a third-round tie at The Den, a team Millwall had beaten 3–1 in November, and this match had a touch of theatre about it. Unlike the carnage of Kenilworth Road four years earlier, the drama this time was centred on a floodlight failure with just six minutes remaining when a single pylon malfunctioned. The referee John Hunting then escorted the teams off the pitch while the fault was rectified. This action caused more frustration than panic, especially when rumours started circulating that the game would be abandoned if full power could not be restored.

It was last thing the club officials wanted, especially with Millwall leading 3–2. Thankfully, after a 28-minute delay the frantic attempts to solve the problem bore fruit, allowing play to resume. It was beyond comprehension that another 'Luton' scenario could break out if the tie could not continue. The referee's action cut no ice with the Millwall chairman Reg Burr (a former Luton director), who muttered 'I couldn't see any reason to stop play – there was only one pylon at fault, and matches have gone ahead in worse conditions'. It was an opinion that was backed-up by both managers Ray Harford of Luton and Lions boss John Docherty. All this fuss had not helped the nerves of the Millwall faithful, who had seen their side fritter away a two-goal lead and were thankful to Sheringham, who rose majestically from a ruck of players to convert Briley's fierce cross-shot after 72 minutes.

It was Teddy, watched by his old manager George Graham and Jimmy Carter, who had Luton in a continuous spin for lengthy periods in the first half, as two goals scored within a minute confirmed. The first, in the 14th minute, saw Kevin O'Callaghan slide a measured pass that took out a static Luton back four for Tony Cascarino to trap and turn in a single movement to place his shot under Sealey's dive. The normally reliable Steve Foster then fluffed a clearance which let in Carter to rifle home the second, before Luton pulled one back after 36 minutes when Kingsley Black crashed home via the underside of the bar. It was all square five minutes into the second half when Danis Salman upended Danny Wilson who, after regaining his composure, smashed home the penalty-kick past Brian Horne. There it stood until the emerging Teddy Sheringham, whose skill with head and feet throughout the afternoon and early evening was a pleasure to watch, rescued Millwall from what could have been a difficult situation.

The televised fourth-round home tie with Liverpool was hugely disappointing as once again Millwall failed to rise to the occasion. One of the very few positives to emerge from the game was the respect Liverpool showed the Lions by playing three centre-halves to combat the aerial threat of both Cascarino and Sheringham.

Millwall's biggest crowd of the season, 26,615, sportingly accorded the visitors an ovation at the end after they had completed a thoroughly professional job and showed they were the masters of coping with pressure. The goals that saw Liverpool home came within minutes of each other in the second half when John Aldridge soared above the Lions defence to crash home a header after 57 minutes from a John Barnes cross. The second arrived six minutes later when Ian Rush began and finished a move involving Barnes and Aldridge, to fire in off a post. Millwall did come close to reducing the arrears when Carter's shot spun off the pitch to hit a surprised Grobbelaar on the chest before the danger was cleared.

A couple other plusses for the Lions were the displays of central-defender Steve Wood and left-back Ian Dawes, whose series of interceptions and tackles were the inspiration to prevent Liverpool obtaining an early goal. This provided both Briley and Hurlock the stimulus to take control in midfield without really exploiting any weakness in the Reds' defence. Liverpool's years of experience in coping with all that was thrown at them eventually saw them go all the way to the Final. If Millwall's Wembley dream had been shattered, a respectable 10th spot in the League was obtained, and this despite them not winning any of the last 10 fixtures. But Millwall's continuance as a First Division club depended on Docherty's close-season transfer dealings. Doc was provided with suitable funds for that purpose, but his apparent reluctance to bolster the squad was to cost Millwall their hard-earned place in the top flight and ultimately John Docherty his job in February 1990.

After defeating Aston Villa 2–0 in mid-December, who ironically were the last side Millwall beat the previous season, the Lions failed to pick up maximum points in any of their remaining games, which included 15 losses. One of those defeats had come at Manchester City, and seven days later they were back at Maine Road to contest an FA Cup third-round tie. They achieved a pride-restoring 0–0 draw, with Keith Branagan taking centre stage with a excellent performance. So long Brian Horne's understudy, Keith had waited patiently for nearly two years to make his debut in which he more than made up for lost time. Keeping a clean sheet in a fiercely contested match earned him a standing ovation at the end and must have made the wait worthwhile. It was a lack of opportunities that had forced Keith to hand in a transfer request the previous November, and the only time he was beaten during the game was in the ninth minute. A Paul Lake header crashed against the angle of bar and post that came to his rescue, and after that early scare he dealt competently with all that City could muster, including two stunning full-length saves from the menacing threat of David White and Mark Ward.

Another showing his true form was Terry Hurlock, who had been so anonymous the week before but certainly made his presence felt on this occasion. His fine example engineered the same response from his teammates, including record signing from Derby County, Paul Goddard. The draw meant City would have to visit The Den for the first time since 1946, when a certain Jimmy Constantine scored a hat-trick in City's 3–1 win. Following 120 minutes of football, the deadlock remained with the teams still level at 1–1.

A delay of 10 minutes may have been one of the reasons why the first half's fare was very mediocre, compounded by City 'keeper Chris Dibble's schoolboy error when he allowed Jimmy Carter's powder puff effort from 10 yards to squeeze through his legs into the net. The Welsh international seemed unconcerned by his faux pas, however, and went on to deny Millwall with string of fine saves as City strived to retain a foothold. If the Lions had created most of the chances, it was City's midfield duo of Peter Reid and Gary Megson who enjoyed the majority of possession, but in Branagan they met a redoubtable barrier.

City's persistence finally paid off in the 80th minute when Colin Hendry scored his first goal for them, when glancing home Andy Hinchcliffe's cross to beat the brave Branagan at last to send the tie into extra-time. It was in this period that City should have wrapped up the game when the industrious Paul Lake pounced on a Steve Wood slip, only to shoot straight at Branagan. Following another stalemate it was Millwall who won the right to stage the second replay at The Den the following Monday. The successful team would meet Fourth Division Cambridge United in the next round, and both City and Millwall fancied their chances of further participation.

The third meeting started off a lot brighter than the previous two and became even more entertaining the further it progressed. City's employment of a sweeper system, that had only conceded four goals in their previous seven games under Howard Kendall, had already been pierced twice in the first 10 minutes by a rampant Millwall who went for the jugular from the off. It all began in the second minute when Paul Stephenson sped down the right to cross for Paul Goddard to thump home his first goal in five games since his arrival, after Dibble had blocked his initial effort. Eight minutes later it was two, when Lake, under pressure from Cascarino, could only half clear the ball which found its way to Sheringham. In an instant, Teddy left Redmond in his wake and scored with a superb low drive from 20 yards that left Dibble flat-footed.

City, however, refused to buckle, and following a prolonged bout of possession Mark Ward went very close with a clever attempt from a long way out. After Colin Hendry sent a header wide, they lost Clive Allen with a pulled hamstring, allowing Ashley Ward to make his City debut. It was Millwall who should have increased their lead when the exuberant Terry Hurlock, with one of many astute passes, found Goddard scampering away, and with City appealing for offside he fired his shot high over the bar. The visitors reduced the lead when the talented Lake pulled a goal back in the 55th minute as he demonstrated his undoubted skill with a peach of a volley from the edge of the area following Peter Reid's corner.

It was Lake again who nearly scored Millwall's third when his ill-judged header narrowly missed the goal by inches in the 63rd minute, but 60 seconds and two corners later Dibble was beaten again by Sheringham's fierce shot, which settled matters once and for all. Millwall now had to face Docherty's old club Cambridge United in the fourth round, a club he had taken to promotion to the Second Division in 1978 and one which Millwall appeared to have had difficulty in beating in the past. And this match was to prove no different.

John Docherty had spent seven happy years at the Abbey Stadium and must have feared the worse when his old charges gained a 1–1 draw at The Den. The first half proved as arduous as it was frustrating for Millwall, before Tony Cascarino edged his side in front after 43 minutes. The Irish international swooped upon a loose ball to sneak his shot inside the left-hand post. However, there seemed no apparent gulf in the three divisions that separated the teams with United giving as good as they got.

Millwall's lead was short-lived, when three minutes into the second half Philpot played an excellent pass down the left flank and Chris Leadbitter took up the running to deliver an inch perfect cross for the on-rushing Taylor to send his diving header flashing past Branagan for the equaliser. Just after the hour Paul Goddard was replaced by Jimmy Carter, who offered Cascarino and Sheringham the chance to slot into their old routine that nearly brought them a second goal. Millwall at last began to find some rhythm, in which Cascarino unleashed a thunderous shot from 25 yards that brought the save of the match from U's 'keeper Vaughan, who tipped Cascarino's goal-bound effort to safety. Millwall realised it was not going to be their day, and this was underlined moments later when Vaughan nearly bettered his earlier heroics by denying a Hurlock thunderbolt.

The least said about the replay the better, because Cambridge achieved what they threatened to do at The Den and knocked Millwall out to enter the fifth round for only the second time in their history. Having said that, it was a visiting player who scored the only goal. Former Lion Andy Massey had had an unhappy time in the FA Cup due to several under-hit back passes, but on this occasion the hapless Dave Thompson produced the flipside when he not only over-hit his back pass but also placed it wide of the stranded Branagan four minutes from the end of extra-time. Miserably Millwall simply failed to get going, leaving Cascarino and Sheringham to plough a lone furrow against an assured home rearguard. Millwall's one clear-cut chance on a doleful night came when they finally got to grips with the windy conditions. For once Teddy got free to set up Cascarino, who steered his header goalwards only for Vaughan to spin in mid-air acrobatically and paw the ball away from goal. It fell nicely to the unmarked Paul Stephenson, but he could only strike a post from an acute angle.

Lacking the injured Terry Hurlock and Gary Waddock, Millwall could offer up no excuse for such a woeful display as Cambridge ran out worthy winners. From thereon in the team went into freefall, and following Docherty's departure in February, Tony Cascarino also got on his bike and was sold to Aston Villa a month later. But Millwall managed to retain the services of Teddy Sheringham for one more season. Chief scout Bob Pearson was the surprise name to take on the manager's role, and in his brief tenure he added two vastly experienced internationals to a depleted squad when he signed Ireland international Mick McCarthy, who had been playing in France, and Welsh striker Malcolm Allen from Norwich City. Pearson appeared to be a mere stopgap and was replaced before the season's end by Bruce Rioch, the former Torquay United and Middlesbrough manager, who was appointed in April 1990.

17. Some Style

Rioch's new broom did not sweep too much away, especially on the playing front, but he did give some tried and trusted colleagues jobs on the managerial side, with Ian McNeill becoming his assistant. The former Watford and Blackpool player Steve Harrison was given the onus of coaching the first team. It was McNeill's deep knowledge of the game and its players north of the border that oversaw the arrival of two players from Scotland. Rioch invested £100,000 on Alex Rae of Falkirk and then bought Montrose's John McGlashan. These were the first Scottish imports to Millwall for a dozen years. Also joining the party was Jon Goodman, the human greyhound from non-League Bromley.

The 1990–91 season got off to a splendid start with three consecutive wins, followed by four draws and then another two victories, before Rioch suffered his first defeat at the hands of his former club Middlesbrough in mid-October as Millwall paraded some panache to their play at last. The month ended with an exceptional comeback against Sheffield Wednesday at The Den, which came after the Owls led at the interval with two well-taken David Hirst goals. There seemed no way back for the Lions but a scintillating display in the second half led by the enigmatic Jimmy Carter blitzed the visitors into submission with a frenzy of attacking football towards the Cold Blow Lane end to rattle in four goals from Carter, Sheringham, Malcolm Allen and new boy Alex Rae. It was a match in a million, but fate would decree that it was only the precursor to what would occur when the teams met later in the campaign.

Once the season had levelled out, however, Millwall became irritatingly inconsistent, elating and deflating in equal measure, but Teddy Sheringham's emergence as a thinking centre-forward was a plus, whose lack of pace was no hindrance as he began to not only score some important goals but was now introducing a more panoramic view in his progressive build-up play. At times his vision was a step ahead of anyone else's but it was very gratifying to all concerned when it all came together. The first FA Cup match under Bruce Rioch's stewardship saw his team drawn at home to Leicester City in the third round. Millwall had beaten them 2–1 at The Den on Boxing Day, but a repeat looked very remote, with City leading this particular battle. Going into the last five minutes, Millwall appeared to be on their way out after trailing for much of the game to a third-minute goal from Tony James. It was his height and battling qualities that caused Millwall problems they found hard to combat. So it came as no surprise when James was left completely unmarked to head home a Gary Mills cross. Moments later, his aerial threat was again evident as he came close to increasing City's lead by thumping another header against a post.

Millwall had hardly come close to scoring, and City were looking more than comfortable with their one-goal lead, when all of a sudden the face of the fiercely fought tie changed dramatically when the Foxes lost their composure. The game had intensified in the last dozen minutes when Leicester's Paul Ramsey was dismissed for thumping Keith Stevens. Just as it appeared Leicester would hold out with 10 men, Sheringham registered his 18th goal of the season with a sublime left-foot volley two minutes from time. The game had hardly restarted when Leicester failed to pick up Paul Stephenson (replacing Jimmy Carter) a minute later. The Geordie, fresh as a daisy, received the ball to pressurise a tiring City defence and was allowed to cut in from the left to despatch a delightful curler past the sprawling dive of Carl Muggleton from 20 yards to send the crowd into ecstasy. Indignant by this sudden change of fortune, Leicester's frustration manifested itself when in desperation Steve Walsh followed Ramsey to the dressing room for clattering Lions goalkeeper Brian Horne.

Millwall had certainly played their 'get-out-of-jail-free card' against Leicester, but they did so again when Sheffield Wednesday provided the opposition at Cold Blow Lane in the fourth round. Those fans who had witnessed the League encounter three months earlier could not in their wildest of dreams have envisaged what was to unfold in what must have been one of, if not the finest game seen at the old Den in living memory. The tie had everything, with two sides going all out to bust a gut in a cut-and-thrust encounter that saw fortunes fluctuate, as play switched from end to end without pause. An exemplary sporting affair without a touch of malice in any of the tackles was a joy to observe in an eight-goal extravaganza.

The match winner against Leicester, Paul Stephenson, got the ball rolling when he darted down the right to send over a cross which Alex Rae missed, and then Sheringham and Goodman both had efforts blocked before Stephenson finished off his own handiwork by guiding the ball into an empty net. Wednesday hit back 13 minutes later when the American John Harkes crossed hard and low for Hirst to claim his 21st goal of the season to beat Horne for the equaliser. All of a sudden the Lions had their backs to the wall when Nigel Pearson's cross spun up in the air allowing the veteran Trevor Francis to leap up and head home the Owls's second after 30 minutes.

Alex Rae had the Lions fans roaring four minutes before half-time when he stabbed home from close range following a spectacular overhead-kick from Sheringham. Millwall fell behind once more in the 56th minute when the maestro of the dead-ball situation John Sheridan found Pearson, whose touch put the Owls ahead for the second time. Still, Millwall would not lie down, and three minutes later Goodman's low cross found Sheringham, who was on hand to score goal number 20 for the season. It seemed all over for Millwall when Viv Anderson put his team 4–3 up after heading home Sheridan's corner four minutes from time.

But this pulsating thriller had one further twist for a captivated audience when Millwall piled forward to rescue what seemed a lost cause when Alex Rae squared the match in injury time by scrambling home a last-gasp equaliser. The young Scot said afterwards 'It was an extremely exciting match to play in. When they scored a few minutes from time I thought "that's it", but there I was on the spot. I am absolutely delighted.' It was an exceptional game, defensively it would have had the coaches pulling their hair out, but this truly remarkable encounter had all the ingredients fans would love to see every week.

The replay, however, failed to attain the heights of the Saturday encounter, but nor was it expected to for games like those only come along once in a blue moon. Millwall rolled over in a rather tame fashion as the Owls went on to claim a 2–0 victory. For their part, Millwall failed to heed the warning of Sheridan's accuracy from the dead-ball, and it was Sheridan who supplied the cross for Anderson to head home the opening goal. Chasing the game, the Lions left themselves vulnerable to the counter-attack, and from one such break Wednesday made the game safe in the 57th minute when David Hirst raced on to Nigel Worthington's through ball to calmly tuck away his 22nd goal of the season. Millwall's best two efforts came, not surprisingly, from the boots of Teddy Sheringham. The first had Owls's 'keeper Chris Turner groping to save a super 25-yard volley after 26 minutes, and with 18 minutes to go Sheringham unleashed a 30-yard free-kick that smacked against the Wednesday crossbar.

Following the loss against Wednesday the target now was to secure a Play-off place, which was duly obtained by finishing fifth. This brought them up against Brighton & Hove Albion, a side Millwall had taken four points off in the League. True to form, the Lions, after taking the lead in both legs, amazingly tossed away the opportunity to reach the final by losing both games, 4–1 on the south coast and then 2–1 at Cold Blow Lane. The missed opportunity of a possible promotion was a bitter pill to swallow, as was the impending prospect of losing leading goalscorer Teddy Sheringham, who had scored 37 in all competitions. Alas, the pill was duly administered during the summer when Nottingham Forest paid £2 million for Teddy's transfer.

The money from Sheringham's sale began to burn a hole in Bruce Rioch's pocket as he went on an unprecedented buying spree, bringing in no less than seven new faces, all of whom played some part in the opening day defeat at Middlesbrough. But a culmination of Sheringham's absence, injuries and the expected inconsistency meant that Millwall found it hard to gain any momentum, and so they failed to make any progress in the League. The final position of 15th in the lower half of the table was looked upon as a failure. The FA Cup should have offered some comfort, however, especially after destroying the Terriers of Huddersfield Town 4–0 at Leeds Road with a scintillating third-round display.

Millwall reverted to a flat back four after making the sweeper role redundant after it had let Rioch down in the previous match against Swindon. The option now was to place the extra man in the middle, a move which made all the difference. The exceptional Alex Rae proved a real handful in a midfield which was bolstered by the signing of the elegant Etienne Verveer. The pair were aided and abetted by Ian Bogie, and between them they ran the show from tip to tail, this against a team that had come into the game with best defensive record in the Third Division.

An outstanding team performance was matched by an exemplary attitude as every player performed to their peak. They punished every mistake Huddersfield made and were spurred by the luxury of an early goal, and thereafter there was only going to be one winner. The opening goal in the seventh minute was so simplistic in its build-up that it took just two passes to score. After gaining possession, Mick McCarthy fed Paul Stephenson, whose run and centre found his fellow Geordie Dave Thompson to head the Lions into a spectacular lead.

Recalled goalkeeper Aidan Davison was brought into action when he foiled Terrier's danger man Iffy Onuora before the visitors doubled their lead. Millwall gained a corner in the 25th minute, which Stephenson crossed for Thompson to flick on to Verveer, whose attempt to control was poor; however, the live-wire Bogie was on hand to return the ball for the Dutchman to force the ball over the line. Paul Stephenson was the leading role in Millwall getting a third goal on the half-hour mark. After giving the run-around to left-back Mark Wright, he centred for Rae to pick his spot from 25 yards with venomous left-foot drive.

The dynamic little Scot had nearly made it four after 23 minutes, but this time the Huddersfield 'keeper Tim Clarke's stupendous reaction to Rae's 30-yard piledriver stopped his side from dropping further behind. Still, Clarke was helpless to stop the Lions making it four just before the interval when the on-fire Stephenson seized upon Huddersfield's generosity at the back to exploit a gap that allowed the unmarked Alex Rae to score with ease from six yards.

The match was over as a contest as Millwall eased up considerably in the second half, but Huddersfield raised an unlikely gallop and, having seen his teammates hog the limelight, Lions 'keeper Aidan Davison thought it was about time for him to impress. Two fine saves denied efforts from Kieran O'Regan and Phil Starbuck as Town failed to address the deficit. But Millwall's overall dominance should have seen them add to their tally, with Verveer and Stephenson both guilty of missing close-range chances. Nevertheless, Millwall cantered to a comfortable win.

The delayed fourth-round tie against Norwich City at Carrow Road saw Millwall display pride, passion and determination, but unfortunately this counted for nothing as they frittered away chance after chance. Further advance in the competition was denied by a combination of wayward shooting and the performance of Norwich's goalkeeper Mark Walton. Etienne Verveer's defensive deficiencies were exposed after two minutes when he put it on a plate for Mark Bowen to give City an early lift. Despite the horrendous start, the Lions battled their way back into the game, with Colin Cooper thinking he had equalised with a blockbuster that was turned away in some style by the rookie Walton.

Psychologically Millwall had a wonderful opportunity to peg Norwich back in the 44th minute when a Mark Falco header was handled; however, Paul Kerr put his penalty too close to Walton, whose partial save fell to Alex Rae who, in his eagerness, could only blast the rebound against the 'keeper's legs. Buoyed up, the Canaries took full advantage of the 'keeper's double save to score a second goal in the 65th minute. City's Scottish striker Robert Fleck, who had been taunted all game by Millwall's travelling support, put further torment on hold as he turned Keith Stevens inside the Lions' half before holding off the challenge of Cooper to toe poke his shot past Davison. Even Kerr's finely struck volley two minutes from time could not save Millwall, and in a desperate late flurry Rae capped a personal night of misery when from close range he managed to fire over the bar, to complete a hat-trick of dreadful misses.

Rae was honest enough to admit afterwards 'We let this game slip away from us because we missed too many chances.' You can say that again, Alex. Despite Fleck's class and quality, Millwall blew it big time as the Canaries marched all the way to the semi-finals. With nothing much to play for, Millwall had to concentrate on getting enough points to stay clear of the drop zone, but their inconsistency continued unabated as a players' revolt was stirring down Cold Blow Lane that came to a head following a 6–1 hiding at Portsmouth. There was unrest within the squad, who were fed up with Rioch's dictatorial ways and protested at Fratton Park in a most passive way. Rioch, sensing their feelings, had one option open to him – resigning. After his departure, one of the senior pros, defender Mick McCarthy, took over in temporary charge of first-team affairs. He seemed a popular choice with the majority of the players and of course the fans, but opinions were to change on both sides at a later date.

The 1992–93 season was the last in which Milwall would call Cold Blow Lane home, after 83 years at the ground. The Den was sold for redevelopment and was replaced by a brand new stadium on Senegal Fields. With many of Rioch's signings remaining at the club, McCarthy got the team playing some attractive football, but hardly had a ball been kicked in anger when two players were sacrificed. Chris Armstrong was sold to Crystal Palace for £1 million, with Jamie Moralee coming to The Den as part of the deal. But one of Mick's few masterstrokes came a few weeks before when he convinced Bristol City to exchange David Thompson for his old Manchester City buddy Andy May.

Another of the casualties was goalkeeper Aidan Davison, whose failure to adapt to the new back-pass rule cost Millwall a 3–1 defeat on the opening day of the season at Watford. So the supporters' Player of the Year for the final season at Cold Blow Lane was cast adrift and never featured in the first team again. Aidan was replaced by another Rioch recruit, the American Kasey Keller. Millwall's FA Cup assault that year never got beyond the third round, going out 1–0 in a very frustrating Roots Hall showdown. Although promotion remained the priority, this was an awful dose of medicine to swallow.

Yet again Millwall dominated possession with some slick football and exquisite passing but could not find a way through Southend's well-marshalled defence. When they did they found Millwall old boy Paul Sansome an impassable barrier, who was rolling back the years to remind the Lions fans of his epic Millwall performances in the Cup ties of the 1980s. Paul was in outstanding form as he brought off a number of first-class saves to deny Ian Bogie from close in and then defied logic to tip away an Alex Rae screamer. The loss was not only down to Sansome but also rare error from Colin Cooper, whose failure to connect properly with a Sansome clearance could only direct the ball into the path of another player who was to become a hate figure with the Lions fans, Stan Collymore (who, incidentally, was the other player offered to Millwall when they sold Chris Armstrong), who drove unerringly past Keller for the only goal. Millwall had what appeared to be a stonewall penalty turned down by a totally inept referee Ian Borrett in the 86th minute when Andy Sussex sent Alex Rae sprawling in the box.

18. The New Den

The Lions finished in seventh place at the end of the season and were gearing up for their new surroundings in a state-of-the-art stadium at Senegal Fields that lay just within the Borough of Lewisham's boundary. To mark the new enterprise, an opening game was arranged against the Portuguese giants Sporting Lisbon, then managed by a face not unfamiliar to Millwall in the FA Cup, the former England boss Bobby Robson. Before a virtually full house it was Robson's team who recorded a 2–1 victory on an exciting and atmospheric night.

It was around this time that Mick McCarthy began his strange forays into the transfer market. Doubts would later emerge about his tactical ability, and as a novice in the managerial stakes Mick made some errors of judgement that were detrimental to Millwall. None more so than the Play-off semi-final first leg at Derby County, where he changed a tried-and-tested formation, and the decision ended with disastrous consequences. One example of his miscalculations came in regard to three players he added to the squad. Another American arrived in the guise of Bruce Murray, who joined his international colleagues Kasey Keller and John Kerr at the club, and Brentford's Lee Luscombe was also signed. Other than Kerr on occasions, none could be described as a roaring success. The other newcomer to join was the experienced if dour Tottenham defender Pat van den Hauwe (supposedly a Lions fan in his younger days), whose arrival was supposedly to fill the void left by Colin Cooper's close-season move to Nottingham Forest.

So with a squad containing some excellent players, and some not so good, they went all out to secure promotion, and if the fans were looking for omens then there was none better than when they drew Premiership big guns and FA Cup holders Arsenal. What a game to

One of Millwall's most remarkable results in the FA Cup came at Highbury in 1995 with the 2–0 defeat of the Arsenal. These photos show Lion Keith Stevens getting to grips with Alan Smith, and Mark Kennedy administering the *coup de grace* with Millwall's second goal. [Brian Tonks]

christen The New Den with, a third-round tie versus the mighty Gunners. This was the same stage as when the clubs had last met in the competition in 1988, the year Millwall reached the First Division for the first time. This match was as desperate as it was disappointing, with Arsenal creating what few clear chances there were and playing the role of spoilers to perfection. But with Millwall lying in fourth place, and with aspirations of joining the Gunners the following season, they were found wanting. Their usual fluency had deserted them when they needed it most, and the game's only goal summed up a pitiful night perfectly. Eddie McGoldrick sent over a 90th-minute corner, which Kasey Keller fumbled under pressure from Paul Merson to give the Arsenal skipper Tony Adams the chance to prod the Gunners into the fourth round.

Former Lions manager George Graham said after the game 'There have been a few shocks already in the Cup, and we were going to make sure that there wasn't another one.'

The Gunners were to lose out in the next round when Bolton Wanderers beat them in a Highbury replay, whose gaffer was none other than Bruce Rioch. As history will show, Millwall did reach the Play-offs again, but to the consternation of the fans they failed yet again. The first match at Derby, where McCarthy inexplicably changed the formation and tactics that had served him well over the course of the season, convinced many fans that he was not up to it, and the game was lost before a ball had been kicked. The return game at The Den will be remembered more for the post-match violence that erupted after Millwall lost 3–1 to finally go down 5–2 on aggregate.

It was back to the drawing board for Messrs McCarthy and Evans, as they plotted their bid in the 1994–95 season for another attempt at the big prize. But three wins in the first 14 fixtures was hardly promotion form, and pressure was mounting for Mick to turn it around. His soul searching came after a drastic defeat at Port Vale at the end of November. His prayers were answered two days later, however, when a welcome, if unexpected, League Cup victory at the City Ground, Nottingham, lifted the despondency when Greg Barry of all people netted both goals in a 2–0 success over Forest. The turning point in Millwall's season had been delivered.

An unbeaten run in December saw a sequence of five straight wins in the League that made the horizon seem a lot brighter and put the team in the right frame of mind to face Arsenal in a rerun of the previous campaign's third-round FA Cup tie at The Den. The Gunners, who were in the running for three Cups, had to be satisfied with a 0–0 draw on this occasion as Millwall made a much better fist of it. The Lions were unlucky not to have taken the lead in the third minute when Jason van Blerk's left-wing cross was met by Dave Mitchell (two of Mick's better signings), who stretched David Seaman to the limit with a glancing header.

Arsenal's Ian Wright (a self-confessed Millwall fan) was booed every time he touched the ball, after his alleged inflammatory pre-match comments about the Millwall supporters only heightened an already highly charged atmosphere. He got more of the same when he clattered Alex Rae and received no booking for what was a nasty foul, but referee Stephen Lodge deemed it necessary to caution Dave Mitchell for retaliating on his fellow Glaswegian's behalf. Arsenal's two efforts of note came early when Ray Parlour fired over after Alan Smith had played him in, and then much to the delight of the home fans Wright did the self same thing following Steve Bould's knockdown. It was left to Kasey Keller to upstage his opposite number when his acrobatics kept out a Stefan Schwarz free-kick. Just before half-time Wright got his comeuppance when he was booked for the 10th time of the season for another late challenge, this time on Ian Dawes.

Arsenal's disciplinary record was made worse when Schwarz was yellow-carded for an ill-timed tackle on Rae as Millwall, now sensing a gap in the Gunners' resolve, created the best chance of the game in the 56th minute when, after some excellent work by Richard Cadette, Rae was given a chance from 15 yards, but his shot just dipped over the bar following a deflection. That was the last meaningful action as the game finished all square.

The replay at Highbury was set for 18 January, a date which will go down as one of the most memorable in Millwall's history when they humbled Arsenal by two goals to nil. It was a fully deserved victory that deepened further the crisis facing Gunners boss George Graham as he sat and watched his former team play an high level of neat, precise football to gain a 2–0 victory. No one can ever take this splendid achievement away from the Lions despite Arsenal getting a bad press. Their predictable and ponderous approach was panned by many critics, who stated it was the worst seen in recent years at Highbury.

Arsenal's style may have been tedious to watch, but after Millwall took an 11th-minute lead they never looked back. The enterprising Jason van Blerk took his assist tally to four, from the last seven goals scored. The Australian worked himself free down the left to send in a precise centre that found Mark Beard shuffling in unmarked to shoot past Seaman from 10 yards. Ian Wright's ever-increasing tally of cautions was added to for going in late on Kasey Keller; however, the American 'keeper was fortunate to remain on the pitch himself when his momentum caused him to handle outside the box, earning him a booking, despite Arsenal protestations. A frustrating evening for the Gunners got worse when Tony Adams, a 65th-minute substitute, missed their best effort before Martin Keown wasted another clear-cut chance seven minutes from the end.

Arsenal's last throw of the dice had been played when Millwall gained possession through Mark Kennedy, who in a lung-bursting run reached the Gunners area. With teammates and fans screaming at him to take the ball into the corner, the young Irishman, having outpaced one England man, Tony Adams, set about embarrassing another for the *fait accompli*. Not one to mess around playing keep ball, the teenager offered the Millwall support seated at the old Clock End a better alternative by hitting his searing drive into the top right-hand corner of David Seaman's net to set the seal on a magnificent night.

In the fourth-round match with Chelsea, who included reinstated captain Dennis Wise in their line up, they achieved what Arsenal had in the last round by gaining a 0–0 draw in an encounter played against a backdrop of simmering aggravation from two groups of England's most notorious fans. They were kept apart by a strong police presence inside the ground with many on horseback, who fortunately managed to keep the lid on a volatile situation. As he had after the Arsenal game, Mick McCarthy spouted on after this stalemate that Millwall would have no fear going into a replay. History favoured Millwall, having twice beaten the Blues in the Cup at Stamford Bridge, with the most recent being in 1985 and a replay way back in 1914.

On the balance of play, Millwall should have secured a place in the fifth round at the first time of asking, with Andy Roberts and Alex Rae dominating midfield and coming close to scoring in the 21st and 40th minutes. Dave Mitchell was also denied in the first instance by Dimitri Kharine's plunge at the Australian's feet. It was the future Millwall player and manager Dennis Wise who became Chelsea's saviour when he headed Tony Witter's glancing header off the line when it seemed destined for the net. Alongside Witter in the heart of the Lions defence was the impressive 19-year-old Ben Thatcher, deputising for the suspended Keith Stevens. The pair formed such an excellent barrier that did much too blunt Chelsea's better display in the second half. The Blues' formation of having five at the back limited their attacking options, with their best chance of a goal coming from a dead-ball situation. They nearly prospered when Ben Thatcher tackled John Spencer in the area; however, had the referee awarded a penalty it would have been very unjust, not only to him but to Millwall who were clearly the better side, with Lion cub Mark Kennedy in outstanding form.

Chelsea's player-manger Glenn Hoddle remained upbeat afterwards but offered these cautionary words when he stated to the press 'I've told the lads we've still got the hardest bit of the job to do.' Hoddle was under no illusions of what lay in store for the replay, and he had the nagging thought that his team had not won at home for three months.

McCarthy and history were proved right as Millwall extended their unbeaten FA Cup record against Chelsea by defeating them 5–4 on penalties following extra-time when the score stood at 1–1. Chelsea's failure in the shoot-out saw the home fans take it upon themselves to start the mayhem seconds after Kasey Keller saved John Spencer's effort. Pandemonium broke out in the North Stand, but despite all the post-match bedlam and eight bookings the game had been played in an excellent spirit. The tie finally saw its first goal in the 71st minute when Mark Stein latched on to Dennis Wise's exquisite chip that caught the Millwall defence napping. Had Stein struck the ball cleanly Keller may well have saved it, but his mis-hit shot deceived the American and had just about enough pace to carry it over the line.

Chelsea, the beaten finalists the year before, held the lead for just eight minutes before Ben Thatcher crossed from the left and Chelsea failed to deal with it, leaving substitute Dave Savage to smash home from 10 yards. The equaliser sent many Lions fans onto the pitch for a light-hearted celebration, but to the Chelsea hordes it was like waving a red flag to a bull. The extra 30 minutes ebbed and flowed in the manner of the previous 90, in which Stein failed to capitalise on a free header and at the other end Kharine's fantastic tip over denied Andy Roberts' dipping volley the winner in the last minute. The stage was set for dramatic penalty shoot-out. Millwall converted their allowance with great aplomb from Savage, van Blerk, Stevens, Roberts and Rae. They were matched for Chelsea's by Stein, Wise, Burley and Lee before Keller sent the Lions fans wild with his vital save from Spencer.

Millwall's good fortune ran out in the fifth round in another London derby at Queen's Park Rangers when, in the two minutes of added time and with another replay looking inevitable, the long arm of Damien Webber intervened. With seconds remaining, Andy Impey floated over a cross which Webber seemed set to clear, but he misjudged the flight for the ball to hit his arm to give Rangers a chance of a goal. Previously this had been denied them mainly due to the brilliant performance of Kasey Keller. But up stepped Clive Wilson to despatch the spot-kick beyond the gallant custodian to bring the curtain down on an exciting game.

It could have been all so different, had minutes earlier stand-in skipper Andy Roberts's 82nd-minute effort from 20 yards hit the net and not Tony Robert's right-hand post. Overall, Rangers probably deserved their success, as they could have been out of sight had it not been for Keller's heroics and elasticity. Mick McCarthy thought the decision was harsh, complaining bitterly 'It was an immense body blow, and Damien has taken it badly. I don't think he meant to hit the ball with his arm, I think it was an accident. So I guess I am saying I didn't think it was a penalty.' As you can imagine, Webber, playing only his fifth senior game at the age of 26, was inconsolable.

Following their London Cup saga Millwall finished the League campaign in mid-table, and not for the first time money was tight which necessitated the sales earlier in the season of Kenny Cunningham and Jon Goodman to Wimbledon. If this was bad, then the events over the course of the next couple years would have a debilitating effect on the club. Within a year McCarthy was gone, to take up the job of national coach to the Irish Republic. His reputation built on his success at Millwall became a tad overblown and was getting publicised nearly every day, linking him with not just the Irish job but also to other clubs on the lookout for a new manager.

Millwall's downward spiral began virtually from the start of the 1995–96 campaign. McCarthy had brought in a couple of new strikers in Uwe Fuchs of Kaiserslautern, who had had a successful time at Middlesbrough, and Chris Malkin from Tranmere. Also venturing into The Den was the Palace pair of Ricky Newman and Bobby Bowry, and a complete unknown from Queen's Park Rangers called Maurice Doyle. If some of these buys had not caught the Millwall supporters' imagination, the excellent start would. Even if the opening matches were uninspiring, it found Millwall skipping along nicely at the top of the table. That was until Mick McCarthy brought in right-back Gerard Lavin from Watford in late November.

It was then that the wheels came off during a disastrous December, with one point gained out of 15 available, and although they managed to cling to top place at Christmas the writing was on the wall. A New Year boost was the cloak-and-dagger process surrounding the signings of two Russian internationals, Vassili Kulkov and Serguei Yuran from Spartak Moscow, which would have done credit to a John Le Carre novel. From that moment on the team imploded, and form and results went straight down the toilet, along with the hope of another run in the FA Cup by being knocked out by Division Two outfit Oxford United after a replay.

The thoughts of the Russians would have been interesting to know after they watched their new teammates stutter to an unconvincing 3–3 draw, during which Millwall were

outplayed for long periods of time. Leading 3–2 with seconds remaining, Kasey Keller allowed Bob Ford's last-gasp corner to pass unmolested into the net to give plucky United a more than deserved draw. Needless to say, manager Mick was furious, declaring a lack of character in some of his players and further questioning how a team, who six weeks earlier appeared invincible, could concede three goals like they did against Oxford?

The underachieving tone was set when Booby Bowry headed against his own crossbar bar, which illustrated perfectly what lay in store for the rest of the afternoon. This was confirmed when United took an 11th-minute lead. Big Paul Moody put Mark Angel away with a delicate back-heel, whose deep

It was Millwall's Scottish Under-21 international Alex Rae who gained the honour of scoring the Lions' first FA Cup goal at the 'new' Den in the 3–3 draw with Oxford United in January 1996. [Unknown]

cross to the far post found the onrushing Stuart Massey to head home. Millwall huffed and puffed for the rest of the first half without blowing anything down as Oxford held on to their goal advantage at the break. Straightened out, no doubt, by some tough talking, Millwall were back on terms within five minutes of the restart when Alex Rae scored with another header from an identical position as Massey's after Kerry Dixon had helped on Lavin's centre.

Alex Rae's equaliser steadied Millwall's boat, but it was sent rocking again eight minutes later when Les Robinson was not picked up on the overlap and found himself in acres of space to find Moody, who duly thumped home from close range. Millwall's fire was finally ignited when substitute Scott Taylor fed Ben Thatcher, whose fine centre was met by Malkin's leap after 65 minutes, again at the far post. Keller then denied Oxford with a fingertip save before Rae appeared to give the Lions an unlikely win when the Scot reacted first to a loose ball to send a looping header over Whitehead. It was Tony Witter's error in attempting to usher the ball out as he came under pressure to concede a corner from which Oxford earned their reprieve.

The replay at the Manor Ground resurrected the spectre of December 1954 when Oxford, then known as Headington United, had forced a draw in a second-round tie at Cold Blow Lane and then went on to win the replay by the only goal of the game. The heirs of Headington United must have been swotting up on their football history as they emulated their predecessors in winning by the same score in a fiercely fought, if often drab, match. It was settled by a stunning goal from Stuart Massey in the 55th minute from 25 yards, on a pitiful night for Millwall that was summed up by the match winner, who stated he could not remember them (Millwall) having a clear-cut chance or a decent strike all night.

With Millwall's plight worsening daily, the season went into a tailspin following McCarthy's defection to Ireland. His replacement was the Raith Rovers manager Jimmy Nicholl, the former Manchester United and Northern Ireland player. But poor old Jim landed smack in the middle of a maelstrom and could not arrest the slide that had set in. Needing to win the last game at Ipswich to survive, the team could only muster a goalless draw that confirmed their descent into the Third Division, despite amassing a total of 52 points. The biblical tale of the tumbling Walls of Jericho had nothing on Millwall's unique and utter collapse.

The harsh realities of relegation began to bite as Keller, Thatcher, Rae, Taylor, Fuchs and the uncommitted and unfit Russians all departed before a ball was kicked in the coming season. The club was heading for meltdown. Although chairman Peter Mead stumped up the funds for the new gaffer to bring some new blood from over the border, the faith Nicholl showed in his imported quartet of Steve Crawford, Paul Hartley, Dave Sinclair and Jason Dair was sadly misguided, with only Crawford at times and Hartley appearing the only two looking capable of achieving anything.

The diet of football dished up over the course of the next few seasons was plodding at best and not very pleasing to the eye, and if HM the Queen had her *Annus Horribilis* around this time then Millwall had theirs twice over in 1996–97 and 1997–98. The FA and League Cups were no better in either results or performances, as Nicholls's first Lions dalliance in the FA Cup on a televised Friday night first-round tie at Woking showed.

Millwall made very hard work of it when opposing a supposedly lesser light, as Woking, with the 39-year-old Clive Walker mastering the frost bitten pitch better than anyone else, dictated play virtually from start to finish. It was Walker who cheekily deceived Mickey Harle in the second minute to send in a cross that strikers thrive on, but on this occasion it was Woking defender Steve Foster who out leaped above the Lions defence to head home. Dave Savage put Millwall back on level terms in the 18th minute after picking up a clearance, and his crisp volley from 20 yards found the corner of the net. Unbelievably, Millwall were ahead seven minutes later when Crawford outwitted Steve Brown before rifling home a sweet shot from outside the area.

With Millwall appearing to take control, Woking equalised when Mickey Harle was adjudged to have pushed Junior Hunter, which left Walker the formality of converting the penalty after 54 minutes. Two Tim Carter saves in the last 11 minutes saved Millwall's bacon, the first a magnificent tip-over and then a second to deny Taylor at point-blank range. Jimmy Nicholls's post-match interview on Sky TV gave the appearance of a dead man mumbling whose facial expression was that of a condemned man. During his brief chat, the body language said everything, and anyone watching knew instinctively that the replay was an accident waiting to happen.

The incentive, if you can call it one, was an away trip to Millwall's old nemesis Cambridge United. But even if a visit to the Abbey Stadium was not alluring enough, it was still no excuse for the lamentable display served up by the Lions. It was one of ineptitude, lacking in passion, and was in truth a shameful exhibition. After falling behind to Clive Walker's calm finish in the ninth minute, Millwall's confidence, if there was any to start with, went rapidly downhill as they were outfought and outplayed. A chorus of boos was left ringing in the players' ears as they left the pitch in what was a shambolic affair and one of Millwall's most humiliating results. Nevertheless, had Steve Crawford converted a first-minute chance things might have turned out differently, but his failure to do so saw the ensuing approach and application go from bad to appalling.

Things could hardly get worse but they did, as the New Year was barely underway when the club went into administration and share dealing was suspended as a rescue package was sought to attract prospective investors to save the club from going under. The accountants' brief was to stop the financial haemorrhaging, and so they wielded the axe that saw club secretary Graham Hortop, manager Jimmy Nicholl and his assistant Martin Harvey all sacked. Taking over in the short term as manager was none other than John Docherty, who was brought out retirement to take charge for a second time. His mandate was to stop further freefall as relegation looked a distinct possibility.

Off the park, a saviour was finally found in Theo Paphitis, the owner of Ryman's, a large stationery concern, and several retail outlets for women's lingerie, whose Midas touch in turning around ailing companies into profitably run businesses was legendary in the City. Millwall managed to drag themselves over the finishing line to secure safety, but to win ugly had been painful to watch for the long-suffering fans. With Docherty's remit accomplished, the new man at the top brought in the former West Ham United player and manager Billy Bonds, himself a south-east Londoner whose father had been a Millwall supporter.

But under Billy things were no better during his one and only season (1997–98), in which the Lions finished five points above the relegation zone in 18th position. The FA Cup campaign was strangled a birth with a first-round defeat at Bristol City, with the only goal coming from Shaun Taylor in the 24th minute, which was enough to beat a shot-shy Lions. This defeat and the 9–2 aggregate mauling at the hands of Wimbledon in the League Cup earlier on in the season was to many fans the termination of what was an already dead-in-the-water campaign as gates hovered between the 5–6,000 mark.

But typically Millwall fought back to claim back-to-back wins over Gillingham and highly placed Fulham in March, but results alone were not sufficient to save Bonds's job come the end of the season. His replacement was something of an inspired choice for once when former Lions player and skipper Keith Stevens was given the position after he had been running the Millwall reserve team. Here was a man who knew what it was to play for the shirt, who gave his all and more for the cause, as did his assistant Alan McLeary. A marked improvement all round saw the Lions finish in 10th spot. But the club's participation in the two Cups was again minimal, going out in both at the first attempt. Millwall were thumped 3–0 down at Swansea City in the FA Cup in a game switched to a Friday night in a bid to divert any confrontation between the rival fans. The 13 November encounter was described as a horror show, in which the Lions gave another dispassionate display. Going a goal down after four minutes from Jason Price was an early blow, but before Millwall could recover sufficiently Thomas doubled the Swans' tally in the 34th minute. Had it not been for Nigel Spink's performance in the Lions goal, his team's humiliation would have been far greater. But even he was powerless to stop Julian Alsop, who was given the freedom of the Principality to add a third a minute from time with the Lions defence nowhere to be seen.

The gloom began to lift gradually as the team began to gel, with Neil Harris and Richard Sadlier looking like becoming a threat up front. Harris, a transfer deadline signing by Billy Bonds, hit 15 goals in his first full season as a professional after joining from Cambridge City. The emergence of Tim Cahill and Steven Reid from the academy was a great boost as their power and thrust from midfield not only looked promising but was also a source of goals. These ingredients and further embodiments of the Stevens/McLeary style of management saw the team reach Wembley for the first time since 1945. Alas, like their predecessors they too tasted defeat after reaching the final of the Auto Windscreens Shield, beaten by a last-minute goal as Wigan Athletic claimed a 1–0 victory.

At the start of the following season Alan McLeary's job was upgraded to that of joint manager along with Keith Stevens as they plotted a route to promotion. They had brought in some excellent players who would go on to become mini-legends, like Fulham's Paul Moody, Tony Warner from Liverpool and Sean Dyche of Bristol City, who along with Arsenal's Dave Livermore were added to a formidable-looking squad that already contained Matt Lawrence, Paul Ifill, Paul Shaw and Stuart Nethercott. At the culmination of one of the most exciting seasons for some time, Millwall gained a deserved Play-off spot after coming fifth in the table, a point behind fourth-placed Wigan. Unfortunately, Wigan were again the victors and took a Final place with a 1–0 aggregate win over the two games. The losing return up at Wigan saw Millwall give one of their most exhilarating and dynamic displays for some time, but they just could not find a vital away goal. But the promise was there, along with the ingrained virtues of both Stevens and McLeary, and it was the prelude of better things to come, which were just around the corner.

But FA Cup glory was to prove elusive once more, as for the fourth consecutive season they fell at the first hurdle with an undeserved first-round exit at Hartlepool United that kicked-off at a very inconvenient Sunday lunchtime. Lining up for the 'Pool was ex-Lion Paul Stephenson, revelling in his centre-midfield role. With the tie heading for a draw, the Lions succumbed to Gary Jones's last-minute goal when he leaped to head home a Sam Shilton cross. It was left to Keith Stevens to lament 'It was a sickening way to go out. We gave them too many chances during the course of the game, and the one in injury time proved to be one too many.'

Millwall at last seemed as though they were heading along the right road when a dramatic event occurred after six games into the 2000–01 season when both Keith Stevens and Alan McLeary were summarily dismissed from their jobs as joint managers. The catalyst appeared to be the home defeat by Northampton Town, after which the decision to fire the pair made at a regular Friday board meeting was unanimous. This came before the scrappy 1–1 draw at Brentford the following day and was confirmed at the chairman's home on the Sunday. It was a sad and depressing day for all connected with Millwall when the two stalwarts were given the boot.

The board wasted no time in making an appointment, and when the new man was unveiled it was the unemployed Mark McGhee. Among the fans he was the least favoured candidate, especially after the acrimonious way he had left Leicester City for Wolves. The bottom line in giving McGhee the job was promotion or else. But the doubts that surrounded McGhee's appointment were forgotten by the time Leigh R.M.I. arrived at The Den for their 'home' FA Cup first-round match, with the Lions sitting pretty in fourth spot just four points behind leaders Wigan Athletic. The reason for switching the tie from Leigh's Hilton Park ground to The Den was the old chestnut of crowd trouble; however, if Leigh's gameplan was to keep Millwall quite for the first 15 minutes, then it lay in tatters with barely 15 seconds played. From the kick-off the ball was swiftly moved into Leigh's penalty area, and when Neil Harris threatened Neil Durkin's rash tackle he upended the Millwall striker to concede a spot-kick.

Unperturbed, Harris picked himself up to lash home the award that effectively ended Leigh's ambition of any giant-killing act. Despite restricting Millwall to just the one goal at the interval, the Vauxhall Conference side's resistance was pierced once again after 67 minutes when Marc Bircham unleashed a superb 25-yard drive to make it 2–0. The tie was done and dusted with Paul Moody's exquisite chip in the 75th minute reflecting Millwall's overall superiority over their non-League opponents. Drawn at home again in the second round, the Lions faced a much stiffer task when facing Lawrie Sanchez's Wycombe Wanderers. Unfortunately the game turned out to be as dismal as the weather, which was damp and soggy. A 0–0 draw summed up the day perfectly. For Millwall, it seemed the expectant visit of the new Division Two leaders Walsall the following Saturday had playing on their minds.

A much better performance saw Walsall beaten 2–0, indicating where Millwall's priorities lay, before they headed off to the Adams Park replay in a fairly buoyant mood, holding the mantle as leaders of a fluctuating division. An additional run in the Cup, no matter how profitable it might be, could not hamper their promotion bid at any cost, and the last thing they wanted was the distraction of a lengthy run. Well it all came to a halt when the Chairboys of Wycombe won the replay 2–1, deservedly according to their manager Lawrie Sanchez, giving the Lions a 'footballing lesson' into the bargain.

Referee Uriah Rennie, however, had chalked off two Millwall efforts, one from Richard Sadlier and another from ex-Wycombe man Matt Lawrence. It was centre-back Joe Dolan who had brought the tie to life when he stabbed home a loose ball for the equaliser to stir the match into something resembling a proper Cup tie. It may have turned out a lot different had Neil Harris's glancing header gone in and not hit a post in injury time. That was the cue for many Millwall fans to depart Adams Park in the knowledge that the Lions' involvement was at an end for another season. That year Wycombe went on to reach the semi-final before losing to Liverpool.

Millwall did accomplish promotion by gaining the precious point required in a 1–1 draw at Wrexham. The icing on the cake came a week later following the trouncing of Oldham Athletic by five goals to nil. The Championship was clinched in front of a packed house at The Den with an exhilarating display of inventive and bright attacking football from the first minute to the last. The euphoria of what had been an excellent season was tempered in the summer by the desperate news regarding Neil Harris. In his hour of glory Neil was diagnosed with testicular cancer. Thankfully, this dreadful disease was caught early enough and was successfully operated on. It was still a blow, however, especially now that Millwall having gone up a division, were to start the ensuing season without their leading marksman.

The momentum built up with the swashbuckling performances carried forward into the new season after a thumping of Norwich 4–0 on the opening day, although Birmingham City brought the Lions back down to earth with a bump at St Andrews a week later with a similar result. But McGhee and his coach Ray Harford knew they had the players to compete in the Championship, and as the team made rapid progress in their new environment the FA Cup was again to take a backseat when it came to prioritising. When Scunthorpe United visited The Den for the third round, Millwall were occupying fifth place in the table, four points behind the leaders Manchester City.

Approaching the Scunthorpe game, Millwall had warmed with a 4–1 New Year's Day success at Watford, where Neil Harris made a fairytale return following his fight against cancer. A very emotional day became a lot better when Neil scored a marvellous fourth. Third Division Scunthorpe, a team Millwall had failed to beat in three previous FA Cup encounters, saw them go a goal down after 14 minutes. It was down to Neil Harris's superb vision that put Richard Sadlier in to open Millwall's account. But any hopes Millwall may have had of running away with the game were scuppered when United's Jamie McCombe levelled six minutes later.

Scunthorpe are not called the Iron for nothing, and they attempted put Millwall out of their stride with some intimidatory play, with one nasty challenge on Tim Cahill leading to the Australian being stretchered off. The Lions never rose to the bait, however, and held firm against the Iron's steely approach that went arm-in-arm with some incredulous and often erratic refereeing from Mr Parkes. The deciding goal was a creation of the sweet left-foot of the Belgian Christoph Kinet, whose pin-point cross found the waiting Sadlier to head home his second of the match to finally exorcise another FA Cup ghost after 63 minutes. With the toppling of the Iron, it brought Millwall up against the Premiership outfit Blackburn Rovers at The Den for a fourth-round tie, with Rovers making their first-ever visit to the New Den.

Included in the visitors' line up was Lucas Neill, who was making his first trip back to south-east London since his transfer to Rovers the previous September. Against a team just six or so places above them in the League standings, Millwall made most of the running, up until around the hour mark when Rovers had their first meaningful attempt as Gary Flitcroft forced a diving save from Willy Gueret.

Millwall's attacking options up front were severely limited, with both Richard Sadlier and Steve Claridge out injured and Neil Harris still on the road to recovery. The main threat was channelled through him, and the one chance that illustrated Neil's plight came when Paul Ifill set him up in the 56th minute, but he could only spoon his effort over the bar, when a fully fit Harris would have surely done better. Rovers had been over reliant on their goalkeeper Brad Friedel, who denied Darren Ward's powerful header and early in the second half punched Steven Reid's dangerous looking cross clear which fell to the lurking Dave Livermore, whose magnificent volley found the American perfectly positioned to save. Little had been seen of Rovers and their lethal striker Andy Cole, who for most of the game had been feeding off the scraps. But when the opportunity arrived Cole's calibre did not fail him, and it was no surprise when he rose to head home Alan Mahon's stunning cross at the far post in the 87th minute to put an end to Millwall's hopes for another year.

The desperate seasons of the mid-1990s were fast receding into oblivion, and from around 1998 the Lions were chasing either a promotion or a Play-off spot. So with the defeat by Blackburn it now gave them a clear path to pursue the dream of a place in the Premiership. But that realisation went up in smoke after they lost yet another Play-off semi-final following Birmingham City's last-minute winner at The Den to take their place in the Final with a 2–1 aggregate. The mindless violence that took place after the game has been highlighted many times, and this is not the time to dwell on rehashing all that mayhem again. The expected repercussions could have the seen the club go out of business and only now, many years later, are Millwall slowly recovering from those events of that dreadful evening. In the aftermath a lot of soul-searching went on by all concerned, from the chairman down to the ordinary punter. Theo Paphitis must have thought that it was not worth all the aggravation, as the events of that spring evening gave him something to mull over during the summer of 2002.

With the collapse of the ITV Digital TV deal in late 2001 and the failure to catapult the club into the Premiership, the players were left disgruntled over the loss of potential revenue. At the start of the 2002–03 season they showed their displeasure in not receiving part of the promised wedge by taking their grievance into the curtain-raiser against Rotherham at The Den. Their motion and body language gave the impression they were not up for it as the match resembled a pre-season kickabout. They let the Millers run riot in a 6–0 victory that became a personal milestone for their striker Darren Byfield (later to join Millwall in 2006), who bagged four of the six.

19. Mr Wise

T his campaign got off on the wrong foot for several reasons, and compared to the previous four years this one would be fairly ordinary. There were no new signings to put the fans in an upbeat mood, leaving them to ponder what would happen next. Following the wretched surrender against Rotherham, Millwall kick-started their season with two home wins over Grimsby and Brighton; however, another limp-wristed performance was given against visiting Walsall, who rapped in three goals without reply and swanned off with the points. Watching this debacle unfurl in front of him from the director's box was a player who will be remembered in Millwall's history as much as former manager John Docherty.

The man concerned was none other than the former Chelsea and England player, Dennis Wise, who signed (without, it must be said, manager Mark McGhee's knowledge) on the dotted line three days after the Walsall match. This followed the well-documented and much publicised falling out with his previous club Leicester City after Wise had tried to rearrange the face of a Foxes teammate. Capped many times by England, he had won a number of honours with the Blues, but his on-field antics and seemingly irksome habit to influence referees made him public enemy number one at most grounds around the country. But at Stamford Bridge his iconic status reached godlike proportions and he would evoke a similar situation among many of the Millwall fans. Right on cue, his debut brought his new team a surprising 3–2 success at Coventry.

Millwall were languishing in 16th place after Ipswich had handed out a New Year's Day 4–1 thumping on the first of two visits to East Anglia in the space of five days. Given their Cup record against third-round opponents Cambridge United, a Millwall win was was not a forgone conclusion as Third Division Cambridge nearly upset the apple cart once again. They had overwhelmed Millwall for most of the game but only managed a single goal through a Tommy Youngs 49th-minute header. It was left to United old boy Steve Claridge to save the blushes when he fired in Paul Ifill's cross on the hour to give the lucky Lions a replay. Post-match comments from Millwall boss Mark McGhee contained some expletives, but one that could be quoted was 'I expected a hard game, but I didn't expect a performance as bad as that.' That said it all.

A second bite of the cherry was the only assurance that Claridge's goal at the Abbey had given Millwall. But even that counted for nothing when Dave Kitson, a player watched on numerous occasions by the Lions scouts but deemed not good enough, opened the scoring for Cambridge in the 57th minute after what had been a mind-numbing first 45 minutes. Kitson's goal sparked a flurry of activity with five goals in the next 20 minutes, three coming in a four-minute spell. Once the ice had been broken the game flourished with a fair share of near misses and goals. It made the second half and ultimately the match a most memorable one. Following the red-headed Kitson's strike, Millwall hit back immediately when they sprung into action, culminating in Steve Angus flattening Steve Claridge in the box. The former U's man picked himself up to stroke home the penalty to put his current side level again. But 60 seconds later United were back in front again when Matt Lawrence and Tony Warner dilly-dallied over a clearance, which allowed Tommy Youngs to stab home from close range.

When the enormity of the situation dawned upon Mark McGhee he threw on youngsters Peter Sweeney after 62 minutes and then Charley Hearn five minutes later. Within moments Millwall were back on terms, and the injection of new blood was a welcome shot in the arm, for it stung Millwall into positive action. Steven Reid led the way with one of his piledrivers that was partially saved, as was Paul Ifill's follow-up that earned a corner. Over trotted Dennis Wise to take it, but he was ushered away by Sweeney's dismissive wave of the arm. The young Scot was vindicated when his inviting corner was met by centre-back Paul Robinson at the back stick for his first goal for the Lions. Inspired substitutions by McGhee, or was it just lucky? Nevertheless, it paid handsome dividends 15 minutes from time when Sweeney supplied another inch-perfect delivery for the late-arriving Ifill to plant home his header for the winner. The match had definitely been a game of two halves.

The fourth-round meeting with Southampton at the new St Mary's stadium brought the reunion of two former Aberdeen stalwarts in Gordon Strachan, the Saints manager, and Mark McGhee, who as players had enjoyed some great times under the then Dons manager Alex Ferguson. Millwall certainly needed to up the ante if they were to progress, while Southampton were buoyant after their 4–0 thrashing of Spurs in the previous round and were odds-on to progress to the fifth round.

Two years after being brought in as a stopgap, Steve Claridge was probably the first name manager Mark McGhee pencilled in on the team sheet. The 36-year-old veteran striker was still going strong and because of his Portsmouth connections was booed every time he touched the ball. Nonetheless, it was the evergreen performer who gave Millwall the lead in the 17th minute when he neatly tucked his effort under Niemi's body following Paul Robinson's knock down from Steven Reid's free-kick. It was just not the goal that had both managers singing Claridge's praises but also his work ethic in a 4–5–1 formation in which he played as the lone striker. His runs, twists and turns kept the Saints rearguard on their toes throughout, and he saw another effort cleared of the line by Benali before a completely knackered Claridge was finally substituted by Kevin Braniff in the 90th minute.

Millwall weathered Southampton's early assaults, in which they hit a post and had another effort cleared off the line by the rookie Robinson. Having gained the early breakthrough Millwall were untroubled for the remainder of the half and continued to frustrate their hosts in the early stages of the second. Given Saints' ineffectiveness up front, Strachan subbed his striking pair of James Beattie and Brett Ormerod after 78 minutes, with the pair having been mastered at every turn by the rock-like Darren Ward and his young sidekick Paul Robinson. This action added to the glow of expectation of seeing Millwall defeat the Saints for the first time ever in the FA Cup.

A matter of 90 seconds stood between Millwall and a highly sought scalp when Strachan's double substitution paid off, as his new strikers Jo Tessem and Kevin Davies combined to pull the game of the fire. Davies, who earlier in the season had scored three times in six matches while on loan at The Den, was on hand to blast home the loose ball after the Norwegian Tessem (later to join the Lions on loan the following season) had seen his low drive blocked by Tony Warner to deny the Lions their little piece of history. Watching the game being relayed back to The Den on the big screen, many supporters felt Millwall's best chance of finally ridding themselves of this particular hoodoo had been lost.

The inevitability and predictability of the replay was delivered by two efforts from Matt Oakley, the Saints midfielder whose finely struck pair of goals condemned Millwall to another Cup defeat at the hands of the Saints. His first after 21 minutes was superbly hit from 20 yards to find one corner of the Lions net. He then placed his second on the other side of Warner's net in the 112th minute, when Steven Reid lost possession to Chris Marsden, Oakley was on hand to steer home the winner. Despite the frantic pace and having a slight edge, Gordon Strachan's team was forced to fight every inch of the way. After their opener they were pegged back following an excellent 36th-minute move involving Charlie Hearn, Paul Ifill and Steve Claridge, which gave Steven Reid the chance to finish off at the second attempt.

In the extra period Millwall's game became ragged as tiredness crept in, and Southampton's extra stamina proved vital in their success. Nonetheless, manager Mark McGhee seemed fairly satisfied with his team's efforts over the two games having placed some funds in the kitty. He must have been highly encouraged and delighted by the emergence of Paul Robinson, who again kept a fairly tight rein on Beattie. Unlikely as it seemed at the time, Southampton, with ensuing victories over Norwich City, Wolves and Watford, made it all the way to the Millennium Stadium, where they lost to Arsenal. But Millwall's day in sun was not too far away.

20. The Road to the Millennium

During the summer of 2003 Mark McGhee initiated a cull, which saw his assistant, the popular Steve Gritt, and coach Joe McLaughlin leave the club. Also departing was the iconic Steve Claridge, who was taking the manager's job at Weymouth. Replacing Gritt as McGhee's number-two was the abrasive Archie Knox, who had worked in similar roles at the highest levels with Manchester United and Glasgow Rangers. But the season kicked-off on a sad note when prior to the opening game against Wigan Athletic at The Den, news came to hand that first-team coach Ray Harford had lost his fight against cancer and had passed away that morning.

Among the new players recruited at the start of the season were Noel Whelan from Middlesbrough, the former Belgian international Bob Peeters of Vitesse Arnhem and the Australian Kevin Muscat from Glasgow Rangers. All things considered, McGhee and his new assistant, the tough taskmaster Archie Knox, should have brought further progress. But after 14 games and with the Lions sitting in a handy eighth place, they produced a dreadful home performance against Preston that was followed by a bombshell. Following an emergency board meeting after the North End match the club announced that both McGhee and Knox were leaving 'by mutual consent'. Whatever the reasons were for the unexpected departures, they were kept in house, but one rumour doing the rounds was that Archie Knox had alienated the players with his regimented ways, similar to Bruce Rioch's circumstances in 1992. McGhee's situation was that he was 'losing the plot', as some of his erratic team selections seem to confirm.

Thrown in at the deep end and so setting him on the first rung of the managerial ladder, Dennis Wise was given the task of running playing matters on a temporary basis. He kicked-off the new regime with a splendid 2–0 victory over Sheffield United. This win started the ball rolling as Wise and his assistant Ray Wilkins began to weld Millwall into a solid combination with a ruthless streak that stood up to all comers. He had not only instilled his own will to win into the team but had also made them into one that could be successful in the pursuit of honours. In addition were the qualities the team already possessed that would see Wise lead them to not only challenge in a race to the Premiership but also to take the Lions to their first-ever FA Cup Final.

One of Wise's first steps was to make the volatile Kevin Muscat his captain in an effort to curb the Aussie's self-destruct instinct. A lot of fans and players around the country perceived Kevin as *persona non grata,* with the press seeing the Wise and Muscat pairing as the devil and his advocate. Wise suffered his first defeat at The Den when Gillingham continued their amazing run over the Lions with a 2–1 win just after Christmas with loan signing, Everton's Nick Chadwick, scoring the Lions' goal. This then was the prelude to Millwall's modest opening of their Cup campaign when Walsall visited The Den for the third round. The old adage of needing just six wins to reach the Final is within reach of most of the big clubs but for an organisation of Millwall's status it is no mean feat. Although they had reached three other semi-finals previously in their history, 2004 would gloriously see Millwall go all the way to the Millennium Stadium.

Another facet of a Cup run is luck, and Millwall's road was indeed fortuitous, but even the big-boys need it, and to draw a comparison one need look no further than Tottenham's success in 1967. After overcoming the Lions in the third round they faced no First Division team until the semi-final when they met Nottingham Forest before defeating Chelsea in the first all-London Final.

Back to Millwall's opening game with Walsall, who, as they had in the League match earlier in the season, took an early lead with a gift of a goal. Dave Livermore's futile attempt to chest his back pass failed to carry enough purchase to Tony Warner, whose reaction was not the quickest and this gave Jorge Leito the easiest of chances to steer the ball home after 12 minutes.

Stung by this, Millwall astutely applied some controlled football that was rewarded eight minutes later following a patient build-up that allowed Neil Harris to deceive the Saddlers's defence. Walsall's attention to Harris left the easy part of scoring to the unmarked Kevin Braniff, who shot and beat Jimmy Walker. With the managers preparing their half-time team talks, Millwall altered the scenario by snatching a dramatic 45th-minute lead. Another plush move saw Wise and skipper Muscat making headway down the right when the player-manager whipped in a deep cross that was begging to be put away. Tim Cahill duly obliged with one of his trademark leaps to thump home an excellent header. Continuing their impressive football after the break, Andy Roberts took centre stage with an excellent array of passes that kept Walsall penned back on the defensive, and with Cahill buzzing he nearly increased Millwall's lead with two further chances in as many minutes.

Unable to stem Millwall's dominance, Walsall's frustrations came to the boil in the 68th minute. The Saddlers goalscorer Leito must have had a death wish, as in the space of four minutes he clattered Dennis Wise not once but twice and was promptly sent off, more for self-preservation than the early bath. Their 'keeper Jimmy Walker, who near to the end was also given his marching orders for foolishly pushing Wise, had before his dismissal seen a Harris shot cleared off the line. One of Walker's last acts was to palm a Braniff effort to safety.

The fourth round was to be the only time during the run that Millwall found themselves drawn away when facing non-League giant-killers Telford United, who had already accounted for both Crewe and Brentford and were now looking to take a bigger prize. However, the tie set for the 24 January was postponed due to the adverse weather and following another cancellation the game finally got underway nearly three weeks later. During January Wise peeped into the transfer window and brought in goalkeeper Andy Marshall from Ipswich Town, who would later replace the injured Tony Warner. The unfortunate Scouser would miss the rest of the season and the big day in South Wales, and for the second time in his career Tony had watch from the sidelines as he had as a substitute for Liverpool in 1996 Final against Manchester United. Also joining the club was Raith Rovers goal-getter John Sutton, the younger brother of Celtic's Chris, along with another striker Danny Dichio who came originally on loan from West Bromwich Albion.

The euphoria of Telford's exploits had been diluted somewhat with the deferments by the time Millwall game got played. With Dennis Wise's determined focus there was no real likelihood of an upset at Millwall's expense. United's momentum was stifled by what the game's insiders like to call 'a professional performance', which Millwall accomplished in front of an appreciative 1,500 travelling fans who had trekked up to Shropshire. With new goalkeeper Andy Marshall unavailable, it was forgotten man Willy Gueret who made a rare outing for his first game for over two years. So much in control were the Lions that Willy had not had shot to save and could have done with some sun and a deckchair to go with a heavily sanded Buck's Head pitch. It took Millwall no time at all to test Chris McKenzie in the Telford goal, who was called into action as early as the 10th minute with what was the first of many fine saves. However, an encouraging display brought its reward when Paul Ifill was the beneficiary from Tim Cahill's surging run down the left when he fired Millwall into a 37th-minute lead.

The visitors continued to dominate after the break as Cahill, Dichio and then Ifill all had chances to increase Millwall's lead as their precise passing kept Telford pinned back for long periods. Nonetheless, United began to play a lot better in this half, but their search for an equaliser was leaving plenty of room which Millwall failed to utilise until the 83rd minute. Appropriately it was Wise who secured the result to wrap up the proceedings by taking Braniff's pass in his stride to hammer a second goal past the despairing McKenzie.

The delay in finalising the Telford game left only 48 hours to prepare for the fifth-round tie against Burnley the following Saturday, but Millwall's passage into the quarter-finals on St Valentine's Day came after a highly charged confrontation at The Den.

Match tickets have become prized possessions among some fans, and though many of the modern ones are computer-generated they still create much interest. Displayed here is the one issued for the replay at Tranmere. [Author]

The match referee Howard Webb did exceptionally well to keep a lid on the game that threatened to boil over as the teams, fired up by their respective mangers Dennis Wise and Stan Ternent, slugged it out toe to toe.

Millwall, not for the first time, should have secured the win long before Danny Dichio's unstoppable header from Muscat's excellent cross after 70 pulsating minutes of blood-and-thunder Cup football. There were four bookings and a sending off, for Burnley substitute Paul Weller, who had barely broken sweat, found himself back in the dressing room. During the course of the season it appeared habitual for opponents to try and get the better of Dennis Wise only to fail. Weller was the third such player during the run to be sent off after laying hands on the player-manager. It gave Burnley a mountain to climb as they hardly created a chance worthy of the name with 11 men on the field.

Burnley's best efforts of the first half came when Ian Moore lost out on a one-on-one with Willy Gueret, and the other was Glen Little's promising breakaway that was halted by Muscat's finely timed tackle. They had their goalkeeper Brian Jensen to thank for keeping the score respectable, whose saves and bravery could have earned them an undeserved replay. But despite being under the cosh for the majority of the game, it was their Irish striker Alan Moore who had a stunning opportunity to endorse his 'keeper's fortitude. With seconds remaining, Moore headed a feeble attempt past an unguarded net to condemn his team to defeat.

On reaching the sixth round Millwall's achievement was met by most of the press who reported on a feisty and at times a testy encounter.

Incredibly Millwall pulled out of the hat the only club they had not met in the competition before, Third Division Tranmere Rovers, for their quarter-final date at The Den. It was Millwall's first appearance at this stage since the infamous night at Luton, 19 years previously. Rovers, a team with a fine Cup tradition during the previous decade, was the hurdle the Lions had to clear to emulate their 1937 counterparts and reach a semi-final. Tranmere's conquests were legendary, and as recent as 2000 they had contested the Worthington Cup Final before losing to Leicester City by the odd goal in three.

Millwall's quest for glory was put on hold, however, as Tranmere held out for a 0–0 draw against a very accomplished Lions side, whose failure to take the chances when offered was compounded by the heroics of Rovers' goalkeeper John Achterberg, who capped a fine personal exhibition by saving Kevin Muscat's penalty. His team, however, after a subdued first 45 minutes began to show more enterprise after the break, when Andy Marshall, who had hardly seen the ball in the opening half, was twice called upon in quick succession to foil Tranmere's left-wing-back Gareth Roberts, whose forays down the flank started to look a threat.

The chance Millwall were given to score came after Ryan Taylor's push on Tim Cahill. The award of a penalty seemed a bit harsh, but with regular spot-kick taker Neil Harris already substituted it was left to skipper Kevin Muscat to take responsibility, only for Achterberg to push the Aussie's penalty over the bar. A pulsating finale ensued as Braniff, Harris's replacement, fired straight at the 'keeper, who then saved Dichio's header from a Peter Sweeney cross before time finally ran out. The one pleasing aspect to emerge from the game was the attitude of the Millwall fans at the end, who although bitterly disappointed by not getting the win took their frustration in good part, and thankfully there no repetitions of the awful events of 1978 and 1985.

Another collectable are the 'First Day' covers, and we have two here with one from Millwall's fourth semi-final appearance versus Sunderland and the other for the club's greatest day in their history, the Final against Manchester United on 22 May 2004. [Author]

The prize awaiting the victors at Prenton Park was a semi-final date with Sunderland at Old Trafford. The draw had been rather kind to both Millwall and Tranmere as they missed out on facing either Arsenal or Manchester United. As Cup fever began to take a grip the extra fillip, if one was needed, was the exciting prospect of European football, with a place in the UEFA Cup assured for a losing finalist. All the clubs reaching the sixth round had received notification of possible European involvement. But before any fans could start looking for their passports Millwall had to dispose of gallant Tranmere, who were hoping to add to their impressive list of Cup victims. However, to reach their day of destiny against the team who had burst the bubble back in 1937, Millwall had to make sure of taking their chances if their day trip to Old Trafford was to become a reality.

What they failed to do in whole of 90 minutes at The Den Millwall managed to do twice in the first 16 minutes by breaching Tranmere's defence with two excellent goals, which should have been enough insurance for Millwall to have both feet virtually inside Old Trafford. Two stunning strikes of high quality from Tim Cahill and Neil Harris should have settled the nerves, but when Gary Jones reduced the arrears four minutes before half-time to set up a nervy second half, the feeling that Millwall might blow it hovering uneasily in the Merseyside air. All the pent-up emotions from the first game had been released in the 11th minute when Cahill sent the travelling support into raptures when he first controlled and then steered Dichio's clever flick past the helpless Achterberg. The big Dutchman was picking the ball out of the net five minutes later when Harris let fly with a cracking left-foot volley following further involvement from the on-fire Dichio.

Big Dan was proving a real handful to the Rovers defence and nearly made it three when he got his head to Ifill's curling cross, only for Achterberg to bring off a fine save. Having hauled themselves back into the game Tranmere's revival in the second half was very spirited, while Millwall's resistance looked a shade precarious. What was surprising was Rovers' decision to leave their leading goalscorer Eugene Dadi on the bench until 17 minutes from time. When he did make his belated appearance he set Millwall hearts fluttering when he nearly scored with his first touch. After weathering Tranmere's response, Millwall, missing the influential Dennis Wise through injury, finally breathed a sigh of relief when they heard the peeps from referee Uriah Rennie's whistle to send a certain part of south-east London into unquenchable ecstasy.

As delightful and unexpected as it was to reach the semi-final, the main business of promotion had been marginally pushed to one side. But the Mother's Day massacre of West Ham United at The Den brought it back into focus, despite Millwall missing two penalties. They were now within a point of a Play-off place after putting the Hammers firmly in their place. Four more points were gained with a win at Wimbledon and a draw at Walsall to set them up nicely for the Sunday showdown in Manchester, with many a Millwall fans up at the crack of dawn to make sure they got to Old Trafford for the television-influenced, but a totally unsuitable, 1pm kick-off.

Sunderland, then managed by ex-Lions boss Mick McCarthy, had beaten Birmingham City after a replay in the fifth round and then saw off Sheffield United in the quarter-finals by the only goal, and they had been made slight favourites by the bookies, however, Millwall had beaten them

The FA CUP SEMI-FINAL

OLD TRAFFORD, MANCHESTER

TheFA.com

SUNDERLAND v TRANMERE ROVERS or MILLWALL
Sunday 4th April 2004, Kick Off 1pm
Adult   £55.00   03014356

South Stand Upper
ENTRANCE   BLOCK   ROW   SEAT
S 21   STH125   4   119
TRANMERE ROVERS or MILLWALL AREA

Two tickets many Millwall fans thought they would never see are the semi-final versus Sunderland at Old Trafford, which was their first-ever victory at the famous ground, and of course the big day at the Millennium Stadium, Cardiff. [Author]

twice in the League, with the January meeting at The Den turning into a testy confrontation, and would be the last-ever match the luckless Tony Warner would play for Millwall.

As kick-off neared, my thoughts went back to that April day at Huddersfield in 1937 and the names of those players of long ago; skipper and goalscorer supreme Dave Mangnall, the flying winger Reggie (J.R.) Smith, who was the last survivor of that team and who had unfortunately passed away in earlier in the year; the heroic defence that held Sunderland at

The FA CUP FINAL

MANCHESTER UTD FC V MILLWALL FC
MILLENNIUM STADIUM, CARDIFF
KICK OFF 15:00   GATES OPEN 13:00
Saturday 22 May, 2004
GATE 2   STAIR 21 LEVEL 4   AISLE 403
BLOCK M3   ROW 1   SEAT 6
MILLWALL F.C.
£ 65.00   MILLWALL AREA
00853438
ENTER BY GATE COLOUR (SEE OVER)

bay for so long, goalkeeper Duncan Yuill, the full-backs Tommy Inns and Ted Smith, who with stalwarts Tom Brolly and 'Chisel' Forsyth et al were watching from the grandstand in the sky to see if the class of 2004 could go one better this time around. The shrill of referee Paul Durkin's whistle, and the roar of the crowd signalled kick-off.

Sunderland threatened early on as the Lions had to negotiate an awkward start, but backed by their faithful, noisy and boisterous following they remained resolute. One early scare came when John Oster's free-kick thumped the underside of Andy Marshall's crossbar, before the same player then lifted Tommy Smith's inviting knockdown over the same piece of wood moments later. Oster then became provider, only for Jason McAteer to blast over, before the Lions hit back to catch them cold when George McCartney's under-hit back pass to former Lion Phil Babb was picked up by Paul Ifill in the 25th minute, who instantly sidestepped another Black Cat to fire in a tremendous left-foot drive, which goalkeeper which Mart Poom blocked. The big Estonian's save merely delayed Millwall's champagne moment, as Aussie Tim Cahill's contorted twist enabled him to drill the loose ball past Poom from 15 yards at the end where the Sunderland fans were congregated.

Whirling his shirt above his head, Cahill raced towards his own supporters to become only the second Lion to score a semi-final goal. No one can explain that moment of joy, but seconds later it dawned that we had scored first at Leeds Road in 1937 and most of us know happened afterwards. Two minutes later, the fans were brought back to terra firma when Paul Ifill was carried off on a stretcher, and within 15 minutes skipper Kevin Muscat went the same way after receiving a nasty tackle from McCartney as the dream began to turn into a nightmare.

Despite the injuries, Millwall kept their shape with Dennis Wise patrolling his patch in the only way he knew, as an inspired Matt Lawrence coped against the dangerous threat of Kevin Kyle to ride out the Sunderland whirlwind up to the break. Sunderland worked and wasted further chances to draw level when Arca could only find the side netting before Paul Thirwell, later booked for another atrocious tackle on Wise, sent another shot into orbit, as did Arca from Kyle's chest-down. The big Scot did get one effort on target with a well-placed header that was equalled by Marshall's diving save.

Tim Cahill celebrates his goal against Sunderland which sent Millwall through to the FA Cup Final and the UEFA Cup. [Brian Tonks]

On the hour McCarthy surprisingly yanked off Kyle, who had been their main danger, to be replaced by Marcus Stewart before McCartney wasted yet another good chance. With only Marshall to beat, the Irishman, who was set up by McAteer's feint of Matt Pier's pass, placed his shot wide. At the Millwall end Cahill placed a superb cross for Dichio to power in a bullet header that had goal written all over it until Poom brought off a spectacular save with 16 minutes left. With the clock ticking down Harris got free in the 86th minute and looked set to clinch a 2–0 victory when he was cynically pulled back by McAteer, who did not wait to see Paul Durkin flourish the red card, having previously been booked.

As the final whistle blew on their greatest day, Millwall had finally laid to rest the spectre of 1937 forever, and those giants from 64 years earlier could now sit back and relax as the burden of expectancy had been passed on to another generation. One of the best quotes of many in the post-match excitement came from one of Millwall's unsung heroes, Dave Livermore, who said 'If anybody had suggested we would be in the FA Cup Final, Europe and chasing promotion last August, it wouldn't have been believable. The FA Cup is the greatest competition in the world, and there have been some upsets before, so who knows what might happen?' David's statement encapsulated what everyone else connected the club was thinking. Another curio to arise out of this victory was that Millwall had won at Old Trafford for the first time, but if you want to split hairs the Lions' Youth team had managed to put one over United in 1993 when they beat their hosts 2–1 in a two-legged FA Youth Cup semi-final.

Now that the Final had been reached the main concern was how the players would approach the vital League games in the run up to the big day? A period of seven weeks lay ahead until they stepped out on to the Millennium pitch. Claiming a majority of the 24 points available from the eight remaining games would not only define the club's season but also show the fans the commitment of the players by not holding back in fear of missing the Final. But the norm generally after achieving one aim is that it can retard other aims, and in this Millwall were no different. Three days after the semi-final the Lions suffered a hangover and were held to a stultifying 0–0 draw with Cardiff, in which Sunday's hero Tim Cahill became Tuesday night's villain by getting sent off in the final minute.

Worse was to follow on Easter Saturday when Coventry City thumped them 4–0, and on Bank Holiday Monday another draw at home to promotion challengers West Bromwich Albion saw Danny Dichio maintain his record of scoring against his former clubs. After sharing a 2–2 draw at Nottingham Forest, Millwall kissed their chances of rubbing shoulders with the Premiership elite goodbye with three defeats. Two came at home to Watford and Reading, and these topped and tailed the game at Derby, who won 2–0. The additional downside in these losses was Danny Dichio's dismissal against Watford, who despite appealing against the red card would miss the Final. Millwall wrapped up was a disappointing end to the League campaign with nothing more than a morale-boosting 1–0 win over Bradford City, courtesy of a Neil Harris penalty.

So with two weeks to prepare and plan their strategy, Dennis Wise and his assistant Ray Wilkins would have to do without the experience of the skipper Kevin Muscat and the main striker Danny Dichio. This would be an onerous task at the best of times, but to face the might of Manchester United with two vital players missing gave Wise an unwanted

The players emerge from the tunnel at the Millennium Stadium for the FA Cup Final. [Brian Tonks]

headache. By their very nature, both Wise and Wilkins were prepared to make the Final a damage limitation exercise from the start. To the majority of the Millwall fans this was all academic as tactics were for the professionals to worry about. They were going to enjoy themselves no matter what, as it was their day as well – they just hoped the team would not be embarrased.

A lovely spring day welcomed both sets of fans to Cardiff, with nearly every member of a Millwall-supporting family in attendance, or so it seemed. The Lions fans had no misconception of what the outcome would be, but for United this was their chance to pick up their only piece of silverware of the season – a fact they seemed to relish. This was despite certain people at United showing scant respect for the world's oldest knock-out competition by stating it was a spent force. For Millwall and their supporters, many who had not seen them play for a while and had come from far and wide to watch the biggest game of their lives, nothing was going to spoil it.

To see the Lions walkout side by side into the Millennium Stadium with Manchester United, a club, nay institution, so evocative that they draw support from around the globe, who take more revenue in programme sales than most clubs make with gate receipts, was incredible. They have an honours list that fades into the distance, and to step out alongside them filled many Millwall fans with an immense amount of pride. But the phenomenon that is Manchester United was also begat of humble stock originally, and question any Reds historian what game or event in their magnificent history was it that changed their fortunes and they would tell you it was not any of their FA Cup and League Championship triumphs,

Action from the FA Cup Final. [Brian Tonks]

nor the success in the Europe or the terrible loss in the Munich Air Disaster, but the last game of the 1933–34 season against Millwall at The Den on 5 May 1934.

Millwall needed just a point to survive as a return to the Third Division beckoned, while United had to win to save themselves from relegation. Well, it was the Reds who prevailed by winning 2–0, but had they gone down it would have the death knell for United, and if history had been different, who knows, Millwall may have been the big club opposing a team playing in their first FA Cup Final. So in some way, albeit a small one, the Lions have helped shape United's destiny to become the footballing leviathan they are today.

Sadly, for reasons already explained above, Millwall failed to turn up, unlike the fans who gave it their all. Wise fielded a team that would not win but that would not be beaten too heavily. He himself was looking to become the first player to win the Cup with three different clubs. Initially Millwall did reasonably well, and in one opening spell Harris and Ifill combined to create a chance, but Harris was given offside, which looked debatable. But sadly assaults on the United goal were far and few between. The first alarm for Millwall came when Andy Marshall made a spectacular save from United's skipper Roy Keane, who then narrowly cleared the Lions crossbar with a dipping volley after 22 minutes. With half-time looming Ronaldo, with only Marshall to beat, saw the former Ipswich 'keeper's save take enough pace off his effort to allow Darren Ward to complete the clearance.

Despite one or two scares, Millwall had kept United reasonably quiet, and when it appeared the first-half's work had been done their resistance was broken right on the whistle. A Gary Neville cross was floated in from the right to the far post for the onrushing Ronaldo to become the first Portuguese national to play and score in a Final, powering his header down and wide of the gallant Marshall. Wise, when fully fit, had been an inspirational and a motivational figure during the run with his cajoling and general busy-bodying. But on the day he was not 100 per cent, and had the Lions fielded what had been their regular line up he may not have played. There was no doubt in some fans' minds that he was out to satisfy his ever-growing ego as he crassly admonished poor Neil Harris for the opening goal.

The game ended as contest when Dave Livermore was adjudged to have tripped Ryan Giggs as he weaved his way into the Lions area in the 65th minute, giving Ruud van Nistelrooy the chance to tuck away what should have been the game's second penalty. Around the 26th-minute mark a similar incident had occured at the other end when Sylvestre flattened Ifill, but nothing had been given by referee Jeff Winter. With nine minutes remaining the Dutchman poked home his second of the game from what looked suspiciously like an offside position.

When the final whistle went the result did not seem to matter as Millwall got as many cheers as United. To the neutral it may have been a dull affair, but there was no mass exodus by the Lions support as had happened the year before when most of the Southampton fans decamped before Arsenal had even picked the trophy up. Millwall were criticised in some quarters for their showing in such a one-sided game, but such was the chasm in class that Wise had no option but to play that way. The other choice could have seen Millwall on the end of an absolute tanking, and that would not have done for a winner like Dennis Wise.

In the end United got the silverware they craved and Millwall got the glory, especially the fans, whose exemplary behaviour was commented on for a change by many observers in

The players salute the fans after the 3–0 defeat to Manchester United. [Brian Tonks]

the media. Although they were the runners-up, the Lions did manage to create one record by introducing substitute Curtis Weston, who became the youngest player to appear in an FA Cup Final at 17 years and 119 days. Still, at least Millwall had Europe to look forward to, with Wise now looking to the chairmen to support his original target of promotion to the top flight when he took over as player-manager six months earlier. But Millwall fans, if nothing else, can be a tad sceptical at times, with most of them suspicious of all this grandeur, and could only see a downside.

Within the year the cracks began to appear, and when Theo Paphitis handed over his role as chairman to Jeff Burnige it was to be seen sooner rather later as a gross misjudgement. When Jeff, a long-time fan, was announced as the future chairman in February 2005 he became a victim of an indiscreet verbal campaign within days and was being ridiculed by people who should have known better. Despite reaching their first Final, the club's money pot was never robust at the best of times, and it was clear that it would have to be larger than it was to fulfil the ambitions of Dennis Wise. Finishing in 10th place at the end of the season, and after the 0–0 at home to Burnley, Wise bade his farewells to The Den and Millwall, leaving the new chairman to look for a new manager.

Now in the hot seat, Burnige took some unpalatable decisions that his predecessor had seemed unwilling to take. He had to balance the books by off-loading the high earners such as Paul Ifill, Darren Ward and Danny Dichio. If that was not bad enough, the performance in naming a manager during the summer made the club a laughing stock, as candidates who thought they were in the frame were then pushed further down the short list when someone with a bit of pedigree was linked to the vacancy. Events became more farcical when iconic former Lion Steve Claridge was appointed the new gaffer in June. But when a number of

The players are greeted by crowds of fans. [Brian Tonks]

the senior players voiced their disapproving opinions over pre-season preparations Theo Paphitis stepped in, not only to undermine Burnige's position but to illustrate where the real power still lay. He unceremoniously sacked Claridge after just 36 days in the job, citing the reason that had the manager remained at his post Millwall would have been relegated. One has to wonder if Paphitis's words still resonate with him. Jeff Burnige, his position now completely untenable, left soon after having held the chair for just three months. His poor old dad Herbert, a former Millwall chairman, must have been turning in his grave.

With such upheaval, it was no wonder the team hit the road and fell flat on its face. Events began to quicken as the situation went further downhill, as the club imploded, and instead of making tracks for the big boy's League, the reverse happened as Millwall tumbled to relegation at the end of a turbulent 2005–06 season. Managers and chairman came and went at regular intervals in what was a futile attempt to paper over the cracks that began to appear weeks after Millwall's greatest day.

Epilogue

That epic, ground-breaking date of 22 May 2004 down in Cardiff seems light years away today, for within two years Millwall suffered relegation in 2006, condemning them, as a third-tier club, to commence their Cup trial from the first round. However, before their demotion, they got no further than third round in 2005, when a trip to Molineux saw them beaten 2–0 by Wolves; The Wanderers have now won all three Cup ties between the teams.

The season the Lions went down (2005–06) saw them entertain Premiership Everton, Tim Cahill and all. Millwall maintained (albeit very briefly) their unbeaten run against the Toffees in the Cup when Marvin Williams opened the scoring in a match that finished in a 1–1 draw. The replay at Goodison Park was settled in the 72nd minute by none other than Tim Cahill, the goalscoring hero of Old Trafford.

From the great stadia of Goodison and Molineux, Millwall were to see the other side of the coin in the autumn of 2006 when they were drawn away to minnows Havant & Waterlooville, where they won a hard-fought battle 2–1 with Ben May and Alan Dunne scoring the goals that saw the Lions advance into round two. Valley Parade was the Lions' next venue for a second-round tie versus Bradford City which ended the way it began, 0–0. The replay was best forgotten as it dragged on into extra-time before it was finally settled in Millwall's favour by Nathan Doyle's own-goal. Millwall's interest in the 2006–07 competition ended at Stoke City, whose two goals came in the last six minutes, one an own-goal from Marvin Elliott.

The following term the Lions went a round further, reaching the fourth round only to go down 2–1 at Coventry City after putting an exceptional display. Jay Simpson, a season-long loanee from the Arsenal, scored Millwall's goal. To reach such a stage Millwall had to travel up to non-League Altrincham for the first round, which was Kenny Jackett's debut as the club's new manager. It was a lucky start for the new man as he saw his charges register a 2–1 success with goals from Alan Dunne's penalty and one from Will Hoskins.

It was the same result when Bournemouth was beaten at The Den in the second round when two strikes in four minutes from Ahmet Brkovic (51) and another from Hoskins (55) saw off the Cherries' challenge. A goalless draw at Walsall in the third round brought the teams back to South Bermondsey in which Millwall squeezed through again by a 2–1 margin. Strikers Ben May and Gary Alexander, with his sixth goal in five games, did the honours to set up a trip to Coventry.

Millwall again reached the fourth round in the 2008–09 season that commenced with two successive 3–0 wins, at Chester City in round one and then a second against Aldershot Town at home, newcomer Ashley Grimes scoring in both these games. Just before Christmas Crewe Alexandra gained a League point at The Den in a 0–0 draw, and it was they who contested the third round at the same venue in early January. This encounter also finished all square, this time in a 2–2 draw. After falling behind to a Dennis Lawrence goal after 12 minutes, Millwall hit back with two goals in the five minutes before half-time. The unlikely sources of the goals were defender Andy Frampton (40) and midfielder Marc Laird in the 45th minute.

The replay victory at Gresty Road by 3–2 contained a significant landmark besides the result when Neil Harris became Millwall's overall all-time leading goalscorer when he put the Lions ahead in the 54th minute to overtake Teddy Sheringham's mantle. Scott Barron and Zak Whitbread's winner three minutes from time completed the win. It was Premiership new boys Hull City who put paid to further progress with a 2–0 success at the KC Stadium in a tie that was sadly marred by a reoccurrence of crowd trouble. This brief resumé brings the Lions' Cup record up to date.

Millwall's FA Cup Record 1887 to 2009

1887–88	Qly Comp	1	Casuals	h	w/o	
		2	Old Westminster's	a	1–8	Oliver
1888–89	Qly Comp	1	Lancing Old Boys	a	0–4	
1899–90	Qly Comp	1	Schorne College	h	0–4	
1890–91	Qly Comp	1	Ilford	h	2–3	Edwards, Butler
1891–92	Qly Comp	1	Rochester	a	2–1	Banks, McCullough
		2	1st Battn. Highland Lt. Inf.	h	3–4	Withington, E. Jones, Banks
1892–93	Qly Comp	1	Folkestone	h	6–1	J. Lindsay 3 (1 pen), Ingram, McCullough, E. Jones
		2	West Kent Regiment	h	2–0	Banks, McCullough
		3	Woolwich Arsenal	a	2–3	E. Jones 2
1893–94	Qly Comp	1	Ilford	a	3–1	J. Lindsay 3
		2	Woolwich Arsenal	a	0–2	
1894–95	Qly Comp	1	Folkestone	h	5–0	J. Matthew, Geddes, Robertson, H. Matthew, McKenzie
		2	Royal Engineers	a	4–1	McKenzie 2, Geddes, Robertson
		3	New Brompton	a	2–0	Geddes, W. Jones
		4	Royal Ordnance	a	3–0	King, Geddes, McKenzie
	Proper Comp	1	Sheffield United	a	1–3	Geddes
1895–96	Qly Comp	1	New Brompton	a	1–0	Geddes
		2	Folkestone	h	5–0	King, J. Matthew, Whelan, Geddes, Leatherbarrow
		3	Sheppey United	h	4–0	King, Malloch 2, Leatherbarrow

		4	Royal Ordnance	a	2–1	Leatherbarrow, Geddes
	Proper Comp	1	Liverpool	a	1–4	Geddes
1896–97	Qly Comp	3	Sheppey United	a	3–3	Gettins 2 (1 pen), Calvey
		R	Sheppey United	h	3–1	Gettins, Calvey 2
		4	Northfleet	h	6–1	McKenzie 2, Geddes 2, King, Calvey (pen)
		5	Woolwich Arsenal	h	4–2	McKenzie, Geddes 2, Gettins
	Proper Comp	1	Wolverhampton Wanderers	h	1–2	McKenzie
1897–98	Qly Comp	3	Sheppey United	a	0–5	
1898–99	Qly Comp	3	Brighton United	h	3–0	Calvey 2, Gettins
		4	Gravesend United	a	1–3	Gettins
1899–1900	Qly Comp	3	Clapton	h	7–0	Banks 4, Nicol, Brearley, Robertson
		4	Chatham	h	3–0	Banks 2, Brearley
		5	Thames Ironworks	a	2–1	Goldie, Banks
	Proper Comp	1	Jarrow	a	2–0	Brearley, Banks
		2	Queen's Park Rangers	a	2–0	Gettins 2
		3	Aston Villa	h	1–1	Nicol
		R	Aston Villa	a	0–0	– after extra-time
		2R	Aston Villa	n	2–1	Banks, Gettins – at Reading
		SF	Southampton	n	0–0	– at the Crystal Palace
		R	Southampton	n	0–3	– at Reading
1900–01	Proper Comp	1	Aston Villa	a	0–5	
1901–02	Intermediate		Bristol Rovers	h	1–1	Watkins
	Replay		Bristol Rovers	a	0–1	
1902–03	Intermediate		Bristol Rovers	a	2–2	Astley, Moran
	Replay		Bristol Rovers	h	0–0	– no extra-time bad light
	2 Replay		Bristol Rovers	n	2–0	Hulse, Moran – at Villa Park
	Proper Comp	1	Luton Town	h	3–0	Watkins, R. Jones, Hulse
		2	Preston North End	h	4–1	Moran, Gettins, Hulse, R. Jones
		3	Everton	h	1–0	Watkins
		SF	Derby County	n	0–3	– at Villa Park
1903–04	Proper Comp	1	Middlesbrough	h	0–2	
1904–05	Intermediate		Bradford City	a	4–1	Maxwell 3, R. Jones
	Proper Comp	1	Southampton	a	1–3	Opp own-goal (Hunter)
1905–06	Proper Comp	1	Burton United	h	1–0	Heaton
		2	Sheffield Wednesday	a	1–1	Hunter
		R	Sheffield Wednesday	h	0–3	
1906–07		1	Plymouth Argyle	h	2–0	Milsom, Dean
		2	Bristol Rovers	a	0–3	
1907–08		1	Bury	a	1–2	R. Jones
1908–09		1	Luton Town	a	2–1	Dean, Tellum
		2	Woolwich Arsenal	a	1–1	Twigg
		R	Woolwich Arsenal	h	1–0	R. Jones
		3	Nottingham Forest	a	1–3	Shand

1909–10	1	Derby County	a	0–5	
1910–11	1	Tottenham Hotspur	a	1–2	J. Martin
1911–12	1	Bury	a	1–2	Davis
1912–13	1	Middlesbrough	h	0–0	
	R	Middlesbrough	a	1–4	Wilson
1913–14	1	Chelsea	h	0–0	
	R	Chelsea	a	1–0	Davis
	2	Bradford City	h	1–0	Davis
	3	Sheffield United	h	0–4	
1914–15	1	Clapton Orient	h	2–1	Moody 2
	2	Bolton Wanderers	a	0–0	– after extra-time
	R	Bolton Wanderers	h	2–2	Moody, Davis – aet score 1–1 after 90 mins
	2R	Bolton Wanderers	a	1–4	Davis
1919–20	1	Notts County	a	0–2	
1920–21	1	Lincoln City	h	0–3	
1921–22	1	Ashington	h	4–2	Taylor, Keen 2, Moule
	2	Crystal Palace	a	0–0	
	R	Crystal Palace	h	2–0	Dorsett, Moule
	3	Swansea Town	h	4–0	Keen 4
	4	Huddersfield Town	a	0–3	
1922–23	1	Clapton Orient	a	2–0	Hannaford 2
	2	Huddersfield Town	h	0–0	
	R	Huddersfield Town	a	0–3	
1923–24	1	West Bromwich Albion	h	0–1	
1924–25	1	Barnsley	h	0–0	
	R	Barnsley	a	1–2	
1925–26	3	Oldham Athletic	h	1–1	Chance
	R	Oldham Athletic	a	1–0	Parker
	4	Bury	a	3–3	Amos 2 (2 pen), Parker
	R	Bury	h	2–0	Parker, Moule
	5	Swansea Town	h	0–1	
1926–27	3	Huddersfield Town	h	3–1	Phillips, Gomm, Black
	4	Derby County	a	2–0	Parker, Phillips (pen)
	5	Middlesbrough	h	3–2	Gomm, Black, Chance
	6	Southampton	h	0–0	
	R	Southampton	a	0–2	
1927–28	3	Derby County	h	1–2	Cock
1928–29	3	Northampton Town	h	1–1	Phillips (pen)
	R	Northampton Town	a	2–2	Cock Readman – aet score 1–1 after 90 mins
	2R	Northampton Town	n	2–0	Landells, Cock – at Arsenal Stadium Highbury

	4	Crystal Palace	h	0–0	
	R	Crystal Palace	a	3–5	Cock, Landells, Black
1929–30	3	Corinthians	a	2–2	Forsyth, Phillips
	R	Corinthians	h	1–1	Poxton – aet score 1–1 after 90 mins
	2R	Corinthians	n	5–1	Forsyth, Corkindale 2, Cock 2 – at Stamford Bridge
	4	Doncaster Rovers	h	4–0	Hawkins 2, Corkindale, Wadsworth
	5	West Ham United	a	1–4	Wadsworth
1930–31	3	Southport	a	1–3	Poxton
1931–32	3	Manchester City	h	2–3	Smith, Poxton (pen)
1932–33	3	Reading	h	1–1	Poxton
	4	Reading	h	1–1	Poxton
	R	Reading	a	2–0	Bloxham, Bond
	5	Aldershot	a	0–1	
1933–34	3	Accrington Stanley	h	3–0	Yardley 2, Phillips
	4	Leicester City	h	3–6	Phillips, Yardley 2
1934–35	3	Wigan Athletic	a	4–1	Yardley 2, Thorogood, Alexander
	4	Reading	a	0–1	
1935–36	3	Stoke City	h	0–0	
	R	Stoke City	a	0–4	
1936–37	1	Aldershot	a	6–1	Mangnall 4 (1 pen) Thorogood Thomas
	2	Gateshead	h	7–0	Mangnall, Thorogood, McCartney 2, Burditt 2, Thomas (pen)
	3	Fulham	h	2–0	Burditt, Mangnall
	4	Chelsea	h	3–0	Burditt 2, Thorogood
	5	Derby County	h	2–1	Mangnall, McCartney
	6	Manchester City	h	2–0	Mangnall 2
	SF	Sunderland	n	1–2	Mangnall – at Leeds Road, Huddersfield
1937–38	3	Manchester City	h	2–2	J.R. Smith, Walsh
	R	Manchester City	a	1–3	Burditt
1938–39	3	York City	a	5–0	McLeod 4, Rawlings
	4	Grimsby Town	h	2–2	McLeod 2
	R	Grimsby Town	a	2–3	Richardson, McLeod
1945–46	3	Northampton Town	a	2–2	J.R. Smith, Ridley
		Northampton Town	h	3–0	Opp own-goal, Phillips, J.R. Smith
	4	Aston Villa	h	2–4	Jinks 2
		Aston Villa	a	1–9	J.R. Smith
1946–47	3	Port Vale	h	0–3	
1947–48	3	Preston North End	h	1–2	Mansfield
1948–49	1	Tooting & Mitcham United	h	1–0	McMillen
	2	Crewe Alexandra	a	2–3	Constantine 2

1949–50	1	Exeter City	h	3–5	Constantine 2, Brolly
1950–51	1	Crystal Palace	a	4–1	Johnson, Morgan, Neary, Constantine
	2	Bradford	h	1–1	Neary
	R	Bradford	a	1–0	Morgan
	3	Queen's Park Rangers	a	4–3	Neary 2, Johnson, Constantine
	4	Fulham	h	0–1	
1951–52	1	Plymouth Argyle	h	1–0	White
	2	Scunthorpe United	h	0–0	
	R	Scunthorpe United	a	0–3	
1952–53	1	Aldershot	a	0–0	
	R	Aldershot	h	7–1	Neary, Monkhouse 3, Shepherd 3
	2	Barrow	a	2–2	Stobbart, Neary
	R	Barrow	h	4–1	Stobbart, Shepherd
	3	Manchester United	h	0–1	
1953–54	1	Colchester United	a	1–1	Stobbart
	R	Colchester United	h	4–0	Stobbart 2, Hazlett, Neary
	2	Headington United	h	3–3	Shepherd, Neary, Short
	R	Headington United	a	0–1	
1954–55	1	Exeter City	h	3–2	Pacey 2, Jardine
	2	Accrington Stanley	h	3–2	Prior, Ramscar, Pacey
	3	Bolton Wanderers	a	1–3	Smith
1955–56	1	Northampton Town	a	1–4	Pacey
1956–57	1	Brighton & Hove Albion	a	1–1	Shepherd
	R	Brighton & Hove Albion	h	3–1	Shepherd, Anslow 2 (1 pen)
	2	Margate	h	4–0	Shepherd 3, Rawson
	3	Crystal Palace	h	2–0	Anslow (pen), Shepherd
	4	Newcastle United	h	2–1	Anslow 2
	5	Birmingham City	h	1–4	Shepherd
1957–58	1	Brentford	h	1–0	Morrison
	2	Gillingham	h	1–1	Shepherd
	R	Gillingham	a	1–6	Summersby
1958–59	1	Hitchin Town	a	1–1	Summersby (pen)
	R	Hitchin Town	h	2–1	Heckman, Hutton
	2	Worcester City	a	2–5	Roche, Moyse
1959–60	1	Bath City	a	1–3	Wilson
1960–61	1	Reading	a	2–6	Burridge 2
1961–62	1	Northampton Town	a	0–2	
1962–63	1	Margate	h	3–1	Terry, Jones, Haverty
	2	Coventry City	h	0–0	
	R	Coventry City	a	1–2	Jones (pen)
1963–64	1	Kettering Town	a	1–1	Terry
	R	Kettering Town	h	2–3	Obeney, Fraser
1964–65	1	Kettering Town	h	2–0	Rowan 2

	2	Port Vale	h	4–0	Julians, Opp own-goal, Whitehouse 2
	3	Fulham	a	3–3	Curran, Whitehouse 2
	R	Fulham	h	2–0	Harper, Rowan
	4	Shrewsbury Town	h	1–2	John
1965–66	1	Wealdstone	h	3–1	Brown, Jacks, Rowan
	2	Hereford United	a	0–1	
1966–67	3	Tottenham Hotspur	h	0–0	
	R	Tottenham Hotspur	a	0–1	
1967–68	3	Aston Villa	a	0–3	
1968–69	3	Middlesbrough	a	1–1	Possee
	R	Middlesbrough	h	1–0	Howell
	4	Leicester City	h	0–1	
1969–70	3	Scunthorpe United	a	1–2	Bolland
1970–71	3	Stoke City	a	1–2	Possee
1971–72	3	Nottingham Forest	h	3–1	Bolland (pen), Smethurst, Possee
	4	Middlesbrough	h	2–2	Smethurst, Possee
	R	Middlesbrough	a	1–2	Burnett
1972–73	3	Newport County	h	3–0	Burnett, Smethurst, Wood
	4	Everton	a	2–0	Cripps, Wood
	5	Wolverhampton Wanderers	a	0–1	
1973–74	3	Scunthorpe United	h	1–1	Wood
	R	Scunthorpe United	a	0–1	
1974–75	3	Bury	a	2–2	Bolland (pen), Hill
	R	Bury	h	1–1	Summerill – aet score 0–0 after 90 mins
	2R	Bury	n	0–2	– at The Hawthorns, West Bromwich
1975–76	1	Yeovil Town	a	1–1	Kitchener
	R	Yeovil Town	h	2–2	Salvage, Welsh – aet
	2R	Yeovil Town	n	1–0	Hart – at the Recreation Ground, Aldershot
	3	Crystal Palace	h	1–1	Summerill
	R	Crystal Palace	a	1–2	Moore
1976–77	3	Coventry City	a	0–1	
1977–78	3	Rotherham United	a	1–1	Kitchener
	R	Rotherham United	h	2–0	Lee 2
	4	Luton Town	h	4–0	Pearson 3, Seasman
	5	Notts County	h	2–1	Chambers (pen), Walker
	6	Ipswich Town	h	1–6	Mehmet
1978–79	3	Blackburn Rovers	h	1–2	Walker – played at Blackburn due to FA ban
1979–80	1	Salisbury	a	2–1	Mitchell, Donaldson – at Southampton
	2	Croydon	a	1–1	Chatterton – played at Crystal Palace

	R	Croydon	h	3–2	Callaghan, Towner (pen), Mitchell – aet score 2–2 after 90 mins
	3	Shrewsbury Town	h	5–1	McKenna, Tagg, Lyons 3
	4	Chester	a	0–2	
1980–81	1	Kidderminster Harriers	a	1–1	Opponent own-goal
	R	Kidderminster Harriers	a	1–0	Chatterton
	2	Exeter City	h	0–1	
1981–82	1	Portsmouth	a	1–1	Chatterton (p)
	R	Portsmouth	h	3–2	Allardyce Chatterton Hayes – aet score 2–2 after 90 mins
	2	Dagenham	a	2–1	Allardyce, Chatterton
	3	Grimsby Town	h	1–6	Neal
1982–83	1	Slough Town	a	0–1	
1983–84	1	Dartford	h	2–1	Massey, Cusack
	2	Swindon Town	h	2–3	Lovell (pen), Martin
1984–85	1	Weymouth	a	3–0	Lovell, Bremner, Otulakowski
	2	Enfield	h	1–0	Neal
	3	Crystal Palace	h	1–1	Neal
	R	Crystal Palace	a	2–1	Briley, Lovell
	4	Chelsea	a	3–2	Lovell 2 (1 pen), Fashanu
	5	Leicester City	h	2–0	Fashanu, McLeary
	6	Luton Town	a	0–1	
1985–86	3	Wimbledon	h	3–1	Lovell, Fashanu, Walker
	4	Aston Villa	a	1–1	McLeary
	R	Aston Villa	h	1–0	Fashanu
	5	Southampton	a	0–0	
	R	Southampton	h	0–1	
1986–87	3	Cardiff City	h	0–0	
	R	Cardiff City	a	2–2	Leslie, Morgan – aet score 2–2 after 90 mins
	2R	Cardiff City	a	0–1	
1987–88	3	Arsenal	a	0–2	
1988–89	3	Luton Town	h	3–2	Cascarino, Sheringham, Carter
	4	Liverpool	h	0–2	
1989–90	3	Manchester City	a	0–0	
	R	Manchester City	h	1–1	Carter – aet
	2R	Manchester City	h	3–1	Goddard, Sheringham 2
	3	Cambridge United	h	1–1	Cascarino
	R	Cambridge United	a	0–1	
1990–91	3	Leicester City	h	2–1	Sheringham, Stephenson
	4	Sheffield Wednesday	h	4–4	Stephenson, Rae 2, Sheringham
	R	Sheffield Wednesday	a	0–2	
1991–92	3	Huddersfield Town	a	4–0	Thompson, Verveer, Rae 2

	4	Norwich City	a	1–2	Kerr
1992–93	3	Southend United	a	0–1	
1993–94	3	Arsenal	h	0–1	
1994–95	3	Arsenal	h	0–0	
	R	Arsenal	a	2–0	Beard, Kennedy
	4	Chelsea	h	0–0	
	R	Chelsea	a	1–1	Savage – aet Millwall won 5–4 on penalties
	5	Queen's Park Rangers	a	0–1	
1995–96	3	Oxford United	h	3–3	Rae 2, Malkin
	R	Oxford United	a	0–1	
1996–97	1	Woking	a	2–2	Savage, Crawford
	R	Woking	h	0–1	
1997–98	1	Bristol City	a	0–1	
1998–99	1	Swansea City	a	0–3	
1999–2000	1	Hartlepool United	a	0–1	
2000–01	1	Leigh R M I	a	3–0	Harris (pen), Bircham, Moody – at The Den
	2	Wycombe Wanderers	h	0–0	
	R	Wycombe Wanderers	a	1–2	Dolan
2001–02	3	Scunthorpe United	h	2–1	Sadlier 2
	4	Blackburn Rovers	h	0–1	
2002–03	3	Cambridge United	a	1–1	Claridge
	R	Cambridge United	h	3–2	Claridge (pen), Robinson, Ifill
	4	Southampton	a	1–1	Claridge
	R	Southampton	h	1–2	Reid – aet score 1–1 after 90 mins
2003–04	3	Walsall	h	2–1	Cahill, Braniff
	4	Telford United	a	2–0	Ifill, Wise
	5	Burnley	h	1–0	Dichio
	6	Tranmere Rovers	h	0–0	
	R	Tranmere Rovers	a	2–1	Cahill, Harris
	SF	Sunderland	n	1–0	Cahill – at Old Trafford, Manchester
	F	Manchester United	n	0–3	– at the Millennium Stadium, Cardiff
2004–05	3	Wolverhampton Wanderers	a	0–2	
2005–06	3	Everton	h	1–1	Williams
	R	Everton	a	0–1	
2006–07	1	Havant & Waterlooville	a	2–1	May, Dunne
	2	Bradford City	a	0–0	
	R	Bradford City	h	1–0	Opp own-goal
	3	Stoke City	a	0–2	
2007–08	1	Altrincham	a	2–1	Dunne (pen), Hoskins

	2	AFC Bournemouth	h	2–1	Brkovic, Hoskins
	3	Walsall	a	0–0	
	R	Walsall	h	2–1	May, Alexander
	4	Coventry City	a	1–2	Simpson
2008–09	1	Chester	a	3–0	Grattan, Harris, Grimes
	2	Aldershot Town	h	3–0	Alexander 2, Grimes
	3	Crewe Alexandra	h	2–2	Laird, Frampton
	R	Crewe Alexandra	a	3–2	Barron, Harris, Whitbread
	4	Hull City	a	0–2	